"A treasure of a book! Escobar includes histor [illegible]
logical information and insights that give us t [illegible]
Christology in Latin America starting with its rc [illegible]
on the Christology in the twentieth century. Th [illegible]
terweaving of the different sources and argume [illegible] I simply
could not put it down. As a practical theologian interested in matters of mission and evangelism, I had been thirsty for a resource such as this one. It is enjoyable and profoundly interesting reading."

Elizabeth Conde-Frazier, coordinator of relations with theological entities for the Association for Hispanic Theological Education

"Where do we begin the task of elaborating an Original Latin American Christology? In this well-documented account of the presence of Christ's image in Latin America, Samuel Escobar answers that question with cultural, missiological, and theological competence. I know of no other work within Protestantism that has achieved what Escobar did in this book—not another modern Christology of sorts but the path for the construction of Original Christology from the context of the American Global South, beyond normative occidentalized theological attempts."

Oscar García-Johnson, Fuller Theological Seminary, author of *Spirit Outside the Gate*

"Samuel Escobar's study of Christology in Latin America is the fruit of a lifetime of critical evangelical engagement with the challenges of Latin American society, as well as with the riches of Latin American literary culture. If you want to grasp the distinctive contours of Christianity in Latin America—whether Catholic or Protestant—read this book. If you want to understand why all Christians need an understanding of Jesus that is rooted, not simply in his death and resurrection, but also in his earthly ministry and his proclamation of the kingdom of God, read this book."

Brian Stanley, professor of world Christianity, University of Edinburgh

"One of the foremost Latin American theologians Samuel Escobar deftly weaves together the vivid colors of Latin American Christology in this clear, comprehensive, and critically engaged volume. *In Search of Christ in Latin America* is a tapestry of the dramatic portraits of Christ incarnate that emerge from the Latin American context as a gift to the *pueblo* and the global church. Escobar is a participant in the development of Latin American theology and not simply a sideline observer. As such, Don Samuel offers us a faithful as well as readable reflection on Jesus' person, presence, ministry, and significance for contemporary Christian mission."

Gene L. Green, professor of New Testament, emeritus, Wheaton College and Graduate School

"The journey of Christianity in the Americas is not complete unless an account of Jesus Christ confessed and followed in Latin America is given in its theological and religious depth. Samuel Escobar's work is a necessary map for this very task. It traces the histories of how a contextual Christology emerged from the underside of modernity and the margins of western Christianity to confront the realities of the impoverished and suffering masses. Here we find a Christian witness that announces Jesus as the liberator in history for the flourishing of all peoples. This journey takes the reader through theologies grounded in pastoral practice that seek to parse out a historical conception of God's salvific acts. From the Roman Catholic liberation theologians to the nascent Protestant evangelical theology in the 1970s, Escobar's cartography of faith is both a sacred memory and a constructive path for a Jesus lived and commended."

Jules A. Martínez-Olivieri, assistant professor of faith and culture, Trinity Evangelical Divinity School

FOREWORD BY C. RENÉ PADILLA

SAMUEL ESCOBAR

IN SEARCH OF CHRIST IN LATIN AMERICA

FROM COLONIAL IMAGE TO LIBERATING SAVIOR

IVP Academic
An imprint of InterVarsity Press
Downers Grove, Illinois

InterVarsity Press
P.O. Box 1400, Downers Grove, IL 60515-1426
ivpress.com
email@ivpress.com

Original title: En busca de Cristo en América Latina by Samuel Escobar ©2012 by Samuel Escobar, published by Ediciones Kairós, Buenos Aires, Argentina.

InterVarsity Press® is the book-publishing division of InterVarsity Christian Fellowship/USA®, a movement of students and faculty active on campus at hundreds of universities, colleges, and schools of nursing in the United States of America, and a member movement of the International Fellowship of Evangelical Students. For information about local and regional activities, visit intervarsity.org.

Cover design: David Fassett
Interior design: Daniel van Loon
Images: terracotta cross: © frankazoid / iStock / Getty Images
religious icons: © Paolo Fridman / Discovery Channel / Getty Images
red-orange wall: © bpperry / iStock / Getty Images Plus
bright yellow wall: © bpperry / iStock / Getty Images Plus

ISBN 978-0-8308-5186-7 (print)
ISBN 978-0-8308-8991-4 (digital)

Printed in the United States of America ♾

InterVarsity Press is committed to ecological stewardship and to the conservation of natural resources in all our operations. This book was printed using sustainably sourced paper.

Library of Congress Cataloging-in-Publication Data
Names: Escobar, Samuel, 1934- author.
Title: In search of Christ in Latin America : from colonial image to liberating savior / Samuel Escobar.
Other titles: En busca de Cristo en América Latina. English
Description: Downers Grove : InterVarsity Press, 2019. | Includes index.
Identifiers: LCCN 2019002864 (print) | LCCN 2019009712 (ebook) | ISBN 9780830889914 (eBook) | ISBN 9780830851867 (pbk. : alk. paper)
Subjects: LCSH: Evangelicalism--Latin America--History--20th century. | Jesus Christ--Person and offices.
Classification: LCC BR1642.L29 (ebook) | LCC BR1642.L29 E8313 2019 (print) | DDC 232.098--dc23
LC record available at https://lccn.loc.gov/2019002864

P 23 22 21 20 19 18 17 16 15 14 13 12 11 10 9 8 7 6 5 4 3 2 1
Y 38 37 36 35 34 33 32 31 30 29 28 27 26 25 24 23 22 21 20 19

To Lindy Scott,

Carlos Mondragón,

Valdir Steuernagel,

and to

Angelit Guzmán de Mesa,

Ruth Padilla de Borst,

and Lourdes de Ita,

all of them my companions

in mission and reflection,

from the new generations

CONTENTS

FOREWORD

C. René Padilla

A well-known fact about what is known as the New World that Christopher Columbus "discovered" in 1492, and which the Spanish and Portuguese conquistadors conquered and colonized at the start of the sixteenth century, is that the vast majority of countries that were eventually formed there were born under the aegis of Roman Catholicism. As a consequence, within the Catholic Church in general it was taken for granted that there was no need for a theology that addressed issues that the historical context posed in the life and mission of the church— no need for a theology that had the purpose of making disciples willing to learn to obey all that Christ taught his own disciples. As a result of this deficit, the Roman Catholic Church of the colonial period, with few exceptions, as is the case of Bartolomé de Las Casas (1484–1566), did not produce a theology rooted in biblical teaching and with the prophetic force necessary to openly oppose the oppression of the indigenous people by the conquistadors.

In contrast to Roman Catholic Christianity, Protestant Christianity did not arrive in Latin America from the Iberian Peninsula but primarily from other European countries and the United States, and with a predominant characteristic derived from the dominant culture in those countries: *individualism*. It is not surprising, therefore, that the churches resulting from the missionary movement of those countries would combine the valuable emphases of the Protestant Reformation (such as the centrality of Jesus Christ and the acknowledgement of grace as the basis and faith as the means of salvation) with a lack of appropriate recognition of the social and prophetic dimension of the biblical message.

The theological awakening of Latin America, in the Roman Catholic sector as well as in the Protestant sector, had to wait until the arrival of the twentieth century, which Escobar calls "a century of theological searching." This is the awakening that Escobar follows from a christological perspective and with great detail throughout this work. What both ecclesial sectors have in common is the Latin American context characterized by major socioeconomic, political, and cultural changes that require churches—both Protestant and Catholic—to overcome traditional concepts related to their roles in society and to seriously consider the theme of their present missionary responsibility.

In the introduction to the original edition of this book, Escobar stated that he wrote it with "the conviction that there is a well-established historical and social reality that can be described as Latin American Protestantism, and that it is possible to map the theological development within this Protestantism" (9). To draw that map, he rightly adopts a generational close-up that takes as its starting point *The Other Spanish Christ,* the classic Christological work written by the Scottish Presbyterian missionary John A. Mackay, initially published in English in 1933. He uses this classic from the erudite theologian to demonstrate the need in Latin America, both in the Catholic field and in the Protestant field, to "learn to discern the significance of Jesus as 'Christ' and of Christ as 'Jesus' in relation to life and thought in their wholeness" (62-63).

The subsequent chapters are dedicated to describing the salient lines of Latin American theological reflection in search of that discernment Mackay considered the priority for the life and mission of the church in Latin America. Concerning Protestant Christianity, he begins with the generation of the founders of Latin American evangelical thought, among whom stand out the Mexicans Gonzalo Báez-Camargo (1899–1983) and Alberto Rembao (1895–1962), the Puerto Ricans Angel M. Mergal (1909–1971) and Domingo Marreno Navarro (1909), the Argentinians Santiago Canclini (1900–1977) and Carlos T. Gattinoni (1907–1989), and the Italian-Argentinian Sante Uberto Barbieri (1902–1991). As Escobar affirms, "Several in this generation participated in important historic movements in their countries and in the task of producing culture and literature. At the same time, they understood the Protestant message deeply enough to be able to contextualize in a way appropriate for their national or continental culture." (75-76).

After the presentation of the founders of Latin American Protestant theology, Escobar dedicates some pages to briefly explore the theology of Protestant thinkers from a new generation. From among them, he highlights the Puerto Ricans Angel M. Mergal and Domingo Marrero, the Argentine José Miguez-Bonino, and the Uruguayan Eilio Castro, all representatives of the movement that our author deems "ecumenical Protestantism."

To a great extent, the Cuban revolution established by Fidel Castro in 1959 was the expression of the revolutionary climate that extended during that era to almost all of Latin America. This book demonstrates the effect that this atmosphere had on the church and on theology in the Roman Catholic as well as in the Protestant world. To that age belongs *Revolución y Encarnación* (1965), the first book from the Cuban Justo González who today is recognized as the most prolific of the Latin American theologians. And to the same period also belongs *Diálogo entre Cristo y Marx* (1967) from Samuel Escobar. The awakening of the social evangelical conscience was made evident in the memorable discourse that the same author pronounced regarding this topic in the First Latin American Conference of Evangelism (CLADE I) celebrated in Bogotá, Colombia, in November of 1969.

One of the results of CLADE I was the formation of the Latin American Theological fraternity one year later. With Samuel Escobar as the first president and with Peter Savage as the general secretary, this theological movement with a small group of representatives from various nations south of the Rio Grande was formed within the most active laboratory involved in the construction of an evangelical theology with Latin American roots. In the final chapter of his book, Escobar offers a brief synthesis of the theological contributions of this movement especially in the field of reflection regarding integral mission. Several doctoral and masters' theses make reference to these contributions not only in Latin

America but also in the United States and Europe. It is worth mentioning that the topic of integral mission reached a global dimension at the first Lausanne Conference of World Evangelization, especially through the plenary presentations presented by Samuel Escobar and René Padilla. The validity of this missiological position would be made visible with much force in the *Cape Town Commitment: A Confession of Faith and a Call to Action*, approved by Lausanne III in 2010.

In the same years in which the movement and the theology of integral mission took form in the evangelical world, liberation theology emerged from the Roman Catholic world with names as prominent as those of Gustavo Gutiérrez, Leonardo and Clodovis Boff, Juan Luis Segundo, Jon Sobrino, and Hugo Assmann. In contrast with what took place with the works of evangelical authors, the works of the Catholic authors mentioned were written and published in Spanish or Portuguese, but within a short time were translated to English and other European languages. As a consequence, the Catholic authors were read not only in the United States and Europe, but also in Asia and Africa. One of the great values of this book is that, in great detail, it objectively presents the Latin American Catholic and Protestant theological development through a Christological lens. In doing so, Escobar demonstrates his vast understanding of the subject as one of the most distinguished voices of the theological movement in Latin America.

I finish with one important fact: of the many books I have edited over the years, none required of me so much persistence and postponing of deadlines as did this book written by one of the most respected Latin American evangelical authors. The various editions of this work in Spanish and now this translation into English are for me the confirmation that such perseverance was beyond doubt worth the effort.

Buenos Aires, Argentina

ACKNOWLEDGMENTS

I want to express my sincere thanks to all those friends and colleagues who encouraged me to complete my research and write it down in this book. The constant and warm insistence of René Padilla and Pedro Arana for a couple of decades through our years of service with the International Fellowship of Evangelical Students (IFES) was especially valuable. While I ministered under Baptist International Ministries from the American Baptist Churches, José Norat Rodríguez and Stan Slade were also good companions in mission and reflection and encouraged me along the way.

During the process of writing, the libraries of Palmer Theological Seminary in Philadelphia and the Facultad Protestante de Teología of the Baptist Union in Alcobendas, Madrid, Spain, were most valuable sources of books and documents. Thanks specially to librarian and friend Melody Mazuk at Palmer. Here in Valencia, where I live in Spain, pastors and friends Eduardo Delás and Pablo Wickham also made their excellent libraries available, for which I am also thankful.

Bill Mitchell from Canada and Pauline Hoggarth from Scotland read some chapters and offered valuable suggestions. Plutarco Bonilla and Juan Stam from Costa Rica also read some chapters and their comments were helpful. My thanks to them. I am most thankful to Ruth Hicks de Olmedo and Ruth Goring for their valuable work of translation.

Here in Valencia my daughter Lilly Ester was most helpful in taking care of my wife, Lilly, who was a great companion in trips, presentations, and reflections, until Alzheimer's caught her. For them I am also deeply thankful to our Father. May he use this book for his glory.

1

FROM THE POOR CHRIST TO CHRIST OF THE POOR

Wretched Admiral! Your poor America,
your Indian virgin, beautiful and warm blooded,
the pearl of your dreams, she is hysterical
with trembling nerves and a pale forehead. . . .
Spurning the kings, we gave ourselves laws
to the sound of cannons and bugles,
and today with the sinister favor of black kings
the Judases fraternize with the Cains. . . .
Christ walks the streets, emaciated and infirm,
Barabbas has slaves and epaulets,
and the lands of Chibcha, Cusco, and Palenque
have seen the panthers all decked out.

This 1892 poem by a famous writer from Nicaragua, Rubén Darío, could be called a spiritual inventory of Latin America, taken four centuries following the Spanish conquest. The beautiful, virginal Indian had become a hysterical woman with trembling nerves and a pale forehead. Biblical references are used to describe fratricidal wars and rampant violence. Within this framework of decadence and disillusionment, the figure of Christ for Darío, as for many intellectuals and poets, was nothing more than a sickly, emaciated beggar who inspires pity: a poor

Christ. At that time in various countries, the Catholic establishment was immersed in a conflict against liberal forces that saw Catholicism as an obstacle to modernization and progress. Darío reflects this vision when he pictures a Christ who plays the social role of a helpless victim—when he is not an instrument of domination—in a world governed by corrupt and cruel military power.

Exactly one century later, when the five-hundredth anniversary of the arrival of the Spanish was marked in 1992, Gustavo Gutiérrez, a Peruvian theologian popular among progressive intellectual circles in Latin America, published a seven-hundred-page work with the eloquent title *En busca de los pobres de Jesucristo* (translated as *Las Casas: In Search of the Poor of Jesus Christ*).[1] It is a monumental study that took the author some twenty years. With a focus on the figure of Bartolomé de las Casas, Gutiérrez explores the social role of the Christianity of Latin America's conquistadors in the sixteenth century. The book reflects the profound tensions between those who converted the message of Christ into rhetoric to justify military conquest and other figures, such as de las Casas, who in the name of Christ opposed the abuses with intelligence and force. Thus, despite the passing of a century of rapid changes, a social, cultural, and political analysis of Latin America still finds Jesus Christ relevant as a point of reference. We might say that during the twentieth century, traditional, institutionalized Christianity lost political and social power, while the figure of Christ gained fresh cultural and spiritual relevance.

To examine the figure of Christ in the context of twentieth-century Latin American culture is to enter into a fascinating world of poets, priests, novelists, insurgents, social prophets, heterodox missionaries, and political agitators. It is a world of tensions between an Iberian form of Christianity inherited from colonization and an Anglo-Saxon form of Christianity that entered via liberals and Freemasons; between the relics

---

[1]Gustavo Gutiérrez, *En busca de los pobres de Jesucristo; El pensamiento de Bartolomé de las Casas* (Lima: Centro de Estudios y Publicaciones, 1992). Translated by Robert R. Barr as *Las Casas: In Search of the Poor of Jesus Christ* (Maryknoll, NY: Orbis Books, 1993).

of African and indigenous religious practices dressed up in Christian forms, and the currents of a "Protestantized" Catholicism borne on the winds of the Second Vatican Council; between the red and black flags of the Catholic fundamentalism of the Argentinian military who invoked "King Christ" in their dirty war and the "Christ-Guevara" of Cuban theologians and zealous insurgents.

"Christianity is Christ" was a favorite phrase of the evangelical Protestant message in Latin America. In contrast to a static and formal religiosity, Christ makes all things new, just as the apostle Paul says: "If anyone is in Christ, the new creation has come: The old has gone, the new is here!" (2 Cor 5:17). An encounter with Christ radically transforms both individuals and communities. *Christ* is not just a word evoking a Galilean teacher; the name of Christ has power to change human beings here and now. Christ is the model of the new humanity, but also the redemptive power that enables that new humanity to be born. Thanks to Jesus Christ, we can talk about a human history that makes sense, and his empty tomb sounds a note of hope allowing us to fully face the tragic dimension of the human condition. This idea has been expressed emphatically by Argentinian Methodist bishop and poet Federico Pagura in his well-known tango "Tenemos esperanza" (We have hope):

> Because he entered into the world and into history;
> because he broke the silence and agony;
> because he filled the earth with his glory;
> because he was light in our cold night;
> because he was born in a dark stable;
> because he lived planting love and life;
> because he broke hard hearts
> and lifted up downtrodden souls.
> This is why today we have hope;
> this is why today we persist in our fight;
> this is why today we look with confidence
> to the future.[2]

[2]Federico Pagura, "Tenemos esperanza," tango lyrics with music by Homero Perera, on *Cancionero abierto* (Buenos Aires: Escuela de Música ISEDET, 1974).

Sung in the style of Argentinian tangos, with the sounds and rhythm of an accordion accompanied by the guitar, double bass, piano, and violin, this tango exemplifies the incredible vitality of the memory of Jesus Christ, which in a continually fresh and renewed way, across an immense variety of cultures and languages, continues to inspire new generations of admirers and followers throughout all parts of the globe.

Paths of Christological Reflection

The vitality of Christian experience springs from the presence of Christ himself at the center of life. Likewise in theology, which is reflection on how our faith is lived out, vitality comes from Christ-centeredness. In this form of theological thought, Jesus Christ is the central pivot around whose person and work we strive to articulate our understanding of the content of the faith. Of course all theology called Christian should have Christ-centered aspects, in which reflection focuses specifically on the person of Christ—this dimension of theology is called Christology. However, a fully Christ-centered theology articulates all its parts and sections around the central fact of the faith: that of Jesus Christ.

In the history of Christian thought, theological reflection has approached Christ via several different paths. One of these is a Christology that concentrates on the development of dogmas after biblical times. From the first century onward, Christians sought to summarize what they believed about Christ in phrases or brief declarations known as the creeds. The Nicene and Apostles' Creeds come from the first four centuries AD and are accepted by all the major branches of Christianity. Christology developed as a commentary on the great creeds recognized by Christianity throughout the centuries.

Some of the great systematic theologians worked to explain and apply these creeds and declarations of faith in different contexts. Meanwhile Christian teachers created catechisms in accessible language in order to communicate these dogmas to the faithful. In the time of the Reformation certain important books written by the Reformers, such as Martin Luther, served as catechisms to convey Christian doctrine to illiterate believers or to children. And the great theological figure of the twentieth century, Karl Barth, framed his monumental work on dogmatics as a commentary on the Apostles' Creed. There is a brief work of Barth that follows the outline of his systematics.[3] In the work of theologians across the centuries, Christology has taken on new forms depending on the different times and on the historical and cultural context in which the church has existed.

Another path is biblical theology, which studies the form in which the message of the New Testament developed. It concerns itself not so much with commentary on the classic creeds as with a return to the original documents, considering how the Gospels, the book of Acts, the Epistles, and Revelation represent the first believers' progressive understanding of the person of Jesus, his work, and its meaning: the *fact* of Christ. This process of conscientization, or growth in understanding, began in the Jewish context, where the person and actions of Jesus of Nazareth are interpreted in the light of the Old Testament. Later it passed to the Gentile world, in which the person of Jesus began to be understood against the background of first-century Greco-Roman culture and social reality. The rich variety of christological thinking from the New Testament authors comes as pastoral and theological responses to questions raised by the missionary announcement of Jesus Christ along the routes that connected cultures and people groups in the Mediterranean world of the *pax Romana*.[4]

As we can see, the paths of dogmatic and biblical theology are mostly turned inward, toward the interior of Christian communities. We can follow a third path, however, which aims for a cultural analysis, starting from the conviction that Christian thought is the fruit of a missionary process by which the announcement of Jesus Christ crosses all types of barriers. This could be considered a missiological approach. The paths

---

[3]Karl Barth, *Esbozo de dogmática*, trans. José Pedro Tosaus Abadía (Santander: Sal Terrae, 2000); English, *Dogmatics in Outline* (New York: Harper Torchbooks, 1959).

[4]A classic interpretation of New Testament material regarding Jesus Christ is by University of the Sorbonne professor Oscar Cullmann, *The Christology of the New Testament*, rev. ed., trans. Shirley C. Guthrie and Charles A. M. Hall (Philadelphia: Westminster, 1959).

I've summarized look inward and deal with faith as it is expressed and lived out at a specific time, in dialogue with the past. A missiological theology, on the other hand, pays special attention to the process of gospel transmission. The Gospels' narration about Jesus, like the theological formulations in the Epistles and later systematic reflection, has had a powerful influence over the cultural manifestations of societies where the Christian faith found a certain degree of rootedness. At the same time, Christian perceptions of the biblical text, including reflections now considered classics of the faith, have been influenced by the different cultures in which Christianity has been rooted. Christian influence on the development of visual, musical, and literary expression in Europe, for example, not only includes the refined manifestations of the elite, such as the paintings of famous Spanish painter El Greco and Bach's music, but also can be seen in diverse expressions of popular culture, such as an array of Spanish proverbs, allegorical plays from the Middle Ages, and the Latin American use of sacred images. All of these reflect the widespread impact of the figure of Jesus Christ on Western society. On this third route, christological investigation involves analysis of the diverse cultural elements in which the footprints of Jesus Christ can be perceived.[5]

Christology in Latin America

This study aims to provide a brief exploration of spiritual life among Latin American peoples, examining diverse manifestations of the predominant culture in search of the presence of Christ's image. In the process we will consider the efforts of Christian thinkers from Latin America to articulate their own experience and vision of Christ in dialogue with Latin American realities and the Christian tradition that they have inherited. It cannot be denied that Latin American culture reflects a definite Christian presence. This tradition was brought first by the

[5]A classic work in this direction is H. Richard Niebuhr, *Christ and Culture* (New York: Harper, 1951). More recent is Jaroslav Pelikan, *Jesus Through the Centuries* (New Haven, CT: Yale University Press, 1985).

Spanish and Portuguese conquerors and missionaries in the sixteenth century, and later by Protestant immigrants and evangelical missionaries starting early in the nineteenth century.

The Christ of the Iberian Peninsula was brought to the New World as much through the presence and lifestyle of the conquistadors as through the preaching of the missionaries who came with them. It is not always easy to separate the sword from the cross in a historical examination of the period of the conquest. The religious life that developed from the introduction of this Iberian Christ took shape in a long and sad process. First was the traumatic encounter of the Spanish and Portuguese with indigenous and later African cultures, as Europeans lived for the first time with "the other" in lands separated from Europe by a great ocean. Later was the jagged process of conquest and domination, with technological superiority, military astuteness, and alliances of convenience with enemy peoples permitting the establishment of European dominance over indigenous empires at a surprising speed. Following this, church institutions were developed, Catholicism became dominant in the centuries of the Spanish and Portuguese empires, and tensions arose between civil and military powers, between sacrificial missionaries and impatient functionaries. Recent research has shown that not only did the natives of these lands suffer traumatic transformations, but likewise the conquering Europeans were transformed by their historic experience and by the native geography and culture.[6]

With the rupture of the colonial order in the first decades of the nineteenth century, the role of Christianity in society also underwent change. A nascent secularization process across the continent began to displace the Roman Catholic Church as the shaping institution of the culture, capable of applying social control by means of the Inquisition or other such mechanisms. This was the moment Protestantism made its appearance in Latin America. We should remember that the first Protestant preaching arose against the backdrop of a Christianity in decline or

[6]Solange Alberro, *Del gachupín al criollo, o de cómo los españoles de México dejaron de serlo* (Mexico City: Colegio de Mexico, 1997).

transformation and was not directed into the heart of pure paganism. Only in the case of native communities in rainforest zones can it be said that the environment in which the Protestant missionaries preached Christianity was totally foreign.

Today it is important for both Protestantism and Catholicism to thoroughly understand how the encounter between evangelical preaching and the existing religiosity played out. All of us need to ask the question, Who is Christ today in Latin America? After long and complex processes of cultural change, how have interpreters of Latin American life and culture in the twentieth century perceived Christ? This book aims to construct a partial response to these questions along theological, historical, and cultural lines. In the final analysis, this reflection will return to biblical sources and dogmas to argue for the purity and effectiveness of current testimony.

Catholic theologian Elizabeth Johnson reminds us that in 1954, in commemoration of the anniversary of the Council of Chalcedon, which fifteen centuries earlier had recognized that "Jesus Christ was truly God and truly man," theologian Karl Rahner published his seminal work "Chalcedon: End or Beginning?" Rahner recognized that Catholic thinking on Christology was paralyzed and in a lamentable state. The use of manuals purporting to explain Christ through an application of deductive logic gave the impression that what we know of Christ is complete and definite. This impeded the emergence of new perspectives. Furthermore, Johnson explains, "This manual approach tended to ignore the wealth of scripture with its narration of the events of Jesus' life, such as his baptism, prayer to God, and abandonment on the cross." A historical perspective reminds us, Johnson says, that "the Protestant reformers called for a stop to scholastic metaphysical speculation about Christ's inner constitution, and a return to a more existential, biblically based confession of Jesus Christ."[7]

During Rahner's time, specifically in the 1950s, Protestant theological debates centered on the biblical sources for understanding who Jesus

---

[7]Elizabeth A. Johnson, *Consider Jesus: Waves of Renewal in Christology* (New York: Crossroad, 1992), 10-11.

Christ is. It is striking that during the second half of the twentieth century, however, there was agreement between Catholic and Protestant theologians in Latin America: both groups sought to recover the Christ of the Gospels and Epistles.

A Starting Point

This study will focus on the development of Christology in the twentieth century. For this purpose a good starting point is the book *The Other Spanish Christ*, written by Scottish Presbyterian missionary John A. Mackay. This classic work was published for the first time in English in 1933 and in Spanish only twenty years later. It has been recognized as an accurate evangelical interpretation of the spiritual reality of Latin America, grounded in a study of the image and presence of Christ in these lands. Many Latin Americans agree with the perspective of Peruvian writer and politician Luis Alberto Sánchez, who said of it that "it is a book of fundamental importance for understanding Latin American civilization."[8] It is a christological inquiry whose methodology was historical analysis and the interpretation of diverse cultural manifestations, from a Reformed theological perspective. Mackay's intention was missional in a broad sense: he wanted to announce the true Christ, whom the English-speaking and Ibero-American contexts were equally losing from view: "A number of romantic figures, each bearing the name of Christ and incarnating the ideals of their several groups of admirers, have taken the place of the Christ. In reality a common need presses upon the Spanish and the Anglo-Saxon worlds: to 'know' Christ, to 'know' Him for life and thought, to 'know' Him in God and God in Him."[9]

Mackay's method was first to examine the character of the inhabitants found in the Iberian Peninsula and the historical process of the transplantation of Christianity to the Iberian so-called New World. This study was not limited to theology but also paid attention to the social processes of the Conquista, taking into account the currents of economy

---

[8]Luis Alberto Sánchez, *El Observador*, June 26, 1983.

[9]John A. Mackay, *The Other Spanish Christ* (repr., Eugene, OR: Wipf & Stock, 2001), xii.

and sociology that were beginning to influence historical research. It is intriguing to see how a Scottish missionary made the most of sociological analysis developed by his friend José Carlos Mariátegui, a pioneer in Latin American Marxist thought.[10] Furthermore, Mackay describes the "South American Christ" as being the result of a process of "South Americanization" of the image and vision of the Spanish Christ brought by the conquistadors. According to Mackay's interpretation, the Spanish Christ was not that of the Gospels, who was born in Bethlehem, but rather another, with roots in the north of Africa. That is, Mackay closely examines the transformations Christianity underwent during the eight centuries of Spanish and Portuguese coexistence with the Arabs who had invaded the Iberian Peninsula during the eighth century. Mackay establishes a contrast between this Christ of official religiosity and the one he calls "the other Spanish Christ," the Christ of the mystics of the golden age such as Saint Teresa of Ávila and Saint John of the Cross, and of Christian rebels of the modern age such as Miguel de Unamuno.

Nonetheless, observing the cultural reality of Latin America, Mackay signals the sterility of predominant Catholicism:

> If in the sphere of life South American Catholicism did not succeed in producing a true mystic, in the sphere of thought it failed to produce a religious literature. In the space of nearly four centuries the clergy have produced no religious work of note. As for the laity, whatever may have been the sentiments of individual men of letters among them, religion has not been considered a suitable subject for the exercise of literary talent.[11]

This statement might appear a gross exaggeration coming from a Protestant missionary. However, in the 1990s, Catholic Spanish scholar José Carro Celada took on the task of tracing the presence of Jesus in Hispano-American literature throughout the twentieth century to discover what the authors said about Jesus of Nazareth and who he was for them.

[10]Toward the end of chap. 2 in *The Other Spanish Christ*, Mackay writes: "The preceding section owes a great deal to an admirable study of religion in Peru by José Carlos Mariátegui contained in his book, *Siete Ensayos de Interpretación de la Realidad Peruana*." Mackay also quotes Mariátegui in chap. 10 of *The Other Spanish Christ*.

[11]Mackay, *Other Spanish Christ*, 199.

He found that there was a significant process of secularization, in contrast with the prominence of Christian themes during the Spanish golden age. According to Carro Celada, "in Spanish-speaking countries that retain a Catholic majority in the sociological sense, a surprising religious silence has prevailed within contemporary literature."[12]

Nevertheless, when Mackay was writing his book, he avowed, "In recent years, however, a decided change has taken place in the intellectual attitude of both clergy and laity towards religion and the religious problem. . . . In the course of the last decade writers of distinction have appeared throughout the Continent for whom religious studies have had supreme interest."[13] In his travels throughout Latin America between 1916 and 1930, Mackay was able to attract multitudes of youth to his lectures. He was convinced that there were promising signs of a rediscovery of Christ in the social, political, and cultural life of the continent. In chapter ten of his book, Mackay briefly examines the literary works of four Latin Americans: Chilean poet Gabriela Mistral, whom Mackay describes as a liberal Catholic; Uruguayan Juan Zorilla de San Martín, author of epic poems, whom Mackay describes as an orthodox Catholic; Argentinian historian and novelist Ricardo Rojas, author of the highly influential *El Cristo invisible* (*The Invisible Christ*), whom Mackay calls a literary Christian; and Argentinian Julio Navarro Monzó, characterized as a Christian member of the literati.

The most representative work in the christological search that was beginning to develop in Latin America was *El Cristo invisible*.[14] Written and published for the first time in 1927, it is structured as three long dialogues between a bishop, called Monsignor, and an intelligent and thoughtful searcher, called the Guest, who dialogue about the representation of Christ, the word of Christ, and the spirit of Christ. The Guest's observations about art, culture, sacred Scripture, and religious practices

[12]José Antonio Carro Celada, *Jesucristo en la literatura española e hispanoamericana del siglo XX* (Madrid: Biblioteca de Autores Cristianos, 1997), 18.
[13]Mackay, *Other Spanish Christ*, 199-200.
[14]Ricardo Rojas, *El Cristo invisible* (Buenos Aires: Librería La Facultad, 1927).

lay out compelling questions and gradually coalesce to mark out the difference between formal religiosity and faith in the Christ of the Gospels.

Without hiding his admiration, Mackay also presents brief portraits of young Latin American social activists such as Brazilian Eduardo Carlos Pereira and Peruvians Victor Raúl Haya de la Torre and José Carlos Mariátegui. In their search for justice and their desire to serve their neighbor, these men are for Mackay signs of great vitality in the spiritual life of the continent, indications that there is a generation searching for the true Christ. He finishes his book with a critical examination of the Protestantism that was beginning to take root in Latin American soil.

A Century of Theological Searching

When we survey the spiritual and intellectual history of the continent throughout the twentieth century, we can observe a fascinating evolution. Between the "poor Christ" of Rubén Darío and the "Christ of the poor" of Gustavo Gutiérrez, literature and theology underwent a vast journey, not always easy to follow. A few milestones can help demarcate our route. For example, in "... *Mas yo os digo*" (this title is a sentence taken from the Sermon on the Mount: "... But I say to you" [Mt 5:22, 28, 32, 39]), published for the first time in Montevideo in 1927, Mackay sums up the message he presented publicly, especially at universities, throughout Latin America between 1916 and 1930.[15] It was reissued in several other editions over subsequent years. In 1936 Peruvian journalist and diplomat Víctor Andrés Belaúnde published his controversial work *El Cristo de la fe y los Cristos literarios* (The Christ of faith and the literary Christs), an expression of the renewal of Catholic thought bolstered by Catholic theologians and Bible scholars from the French-speaking world, in addition to salutary challenges arising from the preaching of Protestant missionaries.[16] Belaúnde was a supporter of a group of young Peruvian intellectuals known as La Protervia, where he encountered Mackay. The

[15]Juan A. Mackay, "... *Mas yo os digo*" (Montevideo: Mundo Nuevo, 1927).

[16]Víctor Andrés Belaúnde, *El Cristo de la fe y los cristos literarios* (Lima: Lumen, 1936).

two men forged a firm friendship, which left its mark on the development of Belaúnde's thought.

When we turn to Latin American novels from the beginning of the century, it is clear they lack a strong Christian sentiment. On the contrary, novels from this period are marked by an indigenist orientation expressed in enraged anticlericalism. However, in 1952 Colombian Eduardo Caballero Calderón focused on Colombian political violence in his novel *Cristo de espaldas* (Christ turning his back), a strong portrait of a young priest caught in the plot of a war unto death between liberal and conservative political parties. The priest's personal Calvary on Colombian soil follows the pattern of Christ's passion. (A similar technique had been used by Spanish writer Benito Pérez Galdós in his novel *Nazarín*, and more recently was used by Nikos Kazantzakis, who in his novel *Christ Recrucified* sets his story of Jesus in a Greek village.)

As the renewing winds from the Vatican II in Europe blew through Catholicism in Latin America, particularly evident in the bishops' Medellín declaration of God's "preferential option for the poor" in 1964, *El evangelio criollo* (The criollo gospel) appeared in Argentina.[17] The décimas (ten-line stanzas) of Spanish classical romances, transformed into the Argentinian epic *Martin Fierro*, serve as a model to tell the story of Jesus in a contextualized form. The contextualizing effort following Vatican II prompted the profound theological reflection *Jesus Cristo libertador* (Jesus Christ Liberator), reflecting the themes and some of the methodology of liberation theology.[18] With this work Brazilian Franciscan theologian Leonardo Boff reached a public throughout the continent and aroused opposition at the highest levels of the Catholic hierarchy. In a preface to Boff's book, Uruguayan lawyer and journalist Héctor Borrat categorically affirms: "Here, written by a Brazilian, is the first systematic Christology that has been produced in Latin America."[19]

[17]Amado Anzi, SJ, *El Evangelio criollo* (Buenos Aires: Agape, 1964). On Medellín, see chap. 2 below under "The Post-Vatican II Catholic Analysis."

[18]Leonardo Boff, *Jesus Cristo libertador* (Petrópolis, Brazil: Vozes, 1971).

[19]Héctor Borrat, "Presentación," in Boff, *Jesus Cristo libertador*, 11.

In 1955 Catholic bishops from around the continent met together in Rio de Janeiro to evaluate the situation of their church, and they decided to found CELAM (Consejo Episcopal Latinoamericano, or the Bishops Council of Latin America). The bishops recognized two dangerous threats: the growth of Protestantism and the rising ideology of communism. Thus they sent out a call to European and North American Catholics to send missionaries to Latin America to help a church in a critical situation. In the following decades, a new generation of American, Canadian, Belgian, French, and Spanish missionaries came to Latin American countries with new ideas and a new style of doing mission. Some worked among the poorest and most at-risk sectors and were distressed to recognize that their own church was part of an oppressive and exploitive system.[20] Their calls for renewal and their choice to do mission "from below," with those who lacked social or economic power, quickly drew criticism and rejection from the more conservative sectors of the church, as well as persecution from dictatorial and military governments who had always seen the church as their ally. This new missionary practice was one context out of which liberation theologies originated.[21]

The triumph of the Cuban Revolution in 1959 began to agitate other Latin American countries, and this along with Vatican II led some Christian thinkers to rediscover the social dimension of Jesus Christ's message. They pointed out the radical nature of some of Jesus' sayings and actions, and the figure of a revolutionary Christ emerged, implying that if Christ had come in our time he would have been a guerrilla fighter. Of course, critiques of this proposed rupture with the traditional religious framework soon emerged as well. In 1973 Chilean writer and journalist Guillermo Blanco published a book that was quickly reprinted in various editions: *El evangelio de Judas* (The Gospel of Judas). In biting

[20]In the case of North American Catholic missionaries, there is a book that records the process: Gerald M. Costello, *Mission in Latin America* (Maryknoll, NY: Orbis, 1979). See also my book *Changing Tides: Latin America and World Mission Today* (Maryknoll, NY: Orbis, 2002), chap. 3.

[21]See documents that trace this process in Gustavo Gutiérrez, ed., *Signos de renovación* (Lima: Comisión Episcopal de Acción Social, 1969).

language Blanco equally criticizes the entrepreneurial vision of Christ originating in the United States and the insurgent Christ proposed by writers of the left. In 1979 Vicente Leñero, a novelist and playwright well known in his native Mexico, published *El evangelio de Lucas Gavilán* (The Gospel of Lucas Gavilán), a fresh and vigorous paraphrase of the Gospel of Luke patterned along liberation theology lines.[22]

In these ways the figure of Jesus reemerged in Latin American culture as his life and teachings became subjects of public debate, while in theological circles of diverse Christian churches the person of Jesus and the significance of faith in Jesus motivated an intense search through biblical material and the Christian tradition. The books I have mentioned are really only a limited sample, but they represent a process that I want to examine in more depth. It will be impossible to avoid controversial topics such as the decline of Catholic Christianity, the presence of Protestant missionaries and the christological focus of their message, the resulting explosive multiplication of evangelical churches, and the renewal of Catholicism. This process is related to the winds of renewal encouraged by the Second Vatican Council, the restless proposals of liberation theologies, and the massive movement of millions of poor Latin Americans into popular Protestantism.

At the end of the twentieth century in many literary, artistic, and academic circles, the figure of Christ seems to have been perceived with much greater clarity than at the beginning of the century. But more important today, as the twenty-first century is well under way, there are thousands of men and women, Catholics and Protestants alike, who are willing to take great risks to proclaim and imitate Jesus of Nazareth, to try to follow his example in the context of a new century and a new era. This process is what I want to explore and understand.

---

[22]Vicente Leñero, *El evangelio de Lucas Gavilán* (Mexico: Seix Barral, 1979).

2

THE IBERIAN CHRIST WHO CROSSED THE OCEANS

For those interested in Ibero-America's spiritual history, paying a visit to the Catholic Cathedral in the city of Cusco, Peru, is a valuable experience. This monumental baroque church has twelve small domes within its roof, one for each of the apostles. In the contrasting light of its interior, between the smoke of incense and the glow of candles lit by devoted worshipers, it would seem that we are in a church in the south of Spain or Portugal. One of the most fascinating paintings in this church is that of Jesus with his disciples at the Last Supper. The painting is modeled on works by the great European masters of the period, but if we pay attention, we can note some unusual elements. The color of Jesus' and his apostles' skin is a copper or olive shade, and the facial features of some are indigenous or mestizo. On the dinner table there is no lamb but instead a guinea pig, whose meat was highly appreciated by local indigenous people. In the fine crystal ware at one side of the table, instead of wine there seems to be *chicha*, the fermented-corn liquor of the Incas. Some of the fruits on a platter are European, brought to the New World by the Spanish, but others are species found only in the Americas. Scholars who study the communication of the Christian message call such an artistic strategy *contextualization*, the process by which a text interacts with the new context in which it is read.

The signs of a vigorous presence of Christ in Latin American culture are undeniable. There are two ways to explore this presence: through art and through popular literature. Special attention should be paid to painting and sculpture. Even though these art forms were produced by the talented elite, they gained universal acceptance in the popular mindset. Within just a few decades of the arrival of the Spanish in the Americas, schools of art such as the Cusqueña, in Cusco, Peru, and the Quiteña in Quito, Ecuador, had developed, whose expressions can still be seen in colonial churches in the Andean region. Paintings from these schools of art reveal how the received *text* has been shaped by the *context* in which it was received. These works show that artists apparently understood the story of Jesus but have translated it visually in terms of their own lives and cultures. That is, these artists took hold of biblical truths in their own way, not rendering exact copies of the missionaries' message but rather rendering the universal message in terms of the lived experience of those receiving it.

This is evidenced in the popular devotion shown to a dark-skinned image from the Cusco school called *The Lord of Earthquakes* or, even better, the phrase used by Indians to this day, *Taitacha Earthquake*. This mestizo expression captures the perception of Jesus as Lord or Father in the Quechua word *taita*. When rendered as *taitacha*, it connotes affection, respect, and an expectation of compassion and understanding. *Earthquakes* alludes to the movements of the earth common in Andean regions, interrupting daily life with unexpected moments of panic that cause people to look to God.

There is some evidence that at certain moments in the sixteenth-century missionary process the truth of Jesus Christ and the gospel took root in the popular mindset. For example, in Chile, there was what is called a "song to the divine," a musical tradition using the *décima* poetic form to render scenes from the life, passion, and death of Jesus. With respect to the work of the missionaries, Miguel Jordá says, "The people did not know how to read or write, and the only way available to them was repetition and memorization. [The missionaries] quickly realized that the *décima* could be an incredibly valuable means for transmitting the Christian message. And so in those years the catechism came to be sung and even danced."[1] Missionaries translated Bible stories into this *criollo* poetic language, and later, "on their own initiative, those who had been catechized began to versify the messages preached to them, focusing on the biblical teachings they considered most important. In these verses, orthodoxy sometimes was in jeopardy, but the singing tradition became rooted more and more deeply in the soul of the people."[2] In the late 1970s, when Jordá wrote his work, he documented some 560 popular singers throughout Chile, especially in rural areas, who sang the "song of the divine." This was a spontaneous activity, not controlled by the church, passed on from one generation to the next.

Let's consider a few examples.

"Birth"

From the trunk the branch is born
And from the branch the flower
From the flower Mary was born
And from Mary the Lord. . . .
The Merciful One was born
In the gate of Bethlehem
And because the King was from heaven
His arrival on earth was blessed.
With joy the Virgin said
This cherub has been born
And though he is so tiny
He is the Savior of the world
And with profound joy
She adored Manuelín.[3]

---

[1]Miguel Jordá, *La Biblia del pueblo: La fe de ayer y de hoy y de siempre en el Canto a lo Divino* (Santiago: Instituto Nacional de Pastoral Rural, 1978). Excerpted in Equipo Seladoc, *Cristología en América Latina* (Salamanca: Sígueme, 1984), 164.

[2]Seladoc, *Cristología en América Latina*, 165.

[3]Seladoc, *Cristología en América Latina*, 171-72. Taken from Ramón Fuentes but used by many others. *Manuelín* is a diminutive of Emmanuel.

"Jesus Christ"
He practiced humility,
The true Messiah
He stayed in a henhouse
Because there was no other place
Though he tired of walking
He converted the small, the great
He shed drops of blood
On the tree of the cross
Remembering Jesus
I feel neither fatigue nor hunger.[4]

It is undeniable that there is an Ibero-American Christ, but to understand him it is necessary to know the Christ brought by the Spanish and Portuguese during the process of conquest and evangelization. The conquistadors and colonizers, whether nobles or common people, had their own religiosity and their own way of living out and interpreting the Catholic faith, and they transplanted their customs and attitudes to the New World along with the social and economic institution of feudalism. In the colonial era the image of Christ developed in basic conformity to the medieval Iberian components, some of which have lasted to this day in popular religious expression and folklore. In some cases a process of contextualization stimulated images and expressions of devotion native to the Americas, while in other cases native religiosity was superimposed, producing a strange, syncretistic mix.

The Analysis of John A. Mackay

In our effort to understand this process, the essential lines of analysis provided by John A. Mackay in *The Other Spanish Christ* remain highly useful. However, historical and anthropological findings in recent decades can help us to finesse Mackay's judgments with regard to Latin America's religious history and to better understand the forms of Christianity that developed and have persisted until today. Mackay

[4]Seladoc, *Cristología en América Latina*, 184. Taken from Luis Inda.

sharply critiqued the Iberian missionary work of warrior monks and plantation owners (*encomenderos*). At the same time, however, he explicitly recognized that there were also "Christophers," Christ bearers whose lifestyle and missionary activity were very different: "There came from Spain and Portugal, or were born in South America itself, thousands of now forgotten names who, as priests, monks, or nuns, were 'Christophers' by profession."[5]

Significantly, Mackay's analysis doesn't fall into the trap of exaggerating or denigrating everything Spanish, a tendency known as the *leyenda negra* (Black Legend) that developed in England and France, drawing on the self-critique of Spaniards such as Bartolomé de las Casas. Mackay had become familiar with the history of the Spanish in the Americas because at the end of his theological studies in Princeton he lived in Spain for a year, staying at the famous Residencia de Estudiantes, a center of liberal thinking in Madrid. This helped him to avoid a one-sided presentation of historical realities. Protestant scholars have often resorted to the Black Legend when comparing the Iberian conquest of southern America with the Anglo-Saxon conquest in the north to explain the different ways in which religious and social life was shaped. Although Mackay avoids the Black Legend, he does acknowledge it within his comparative analysis of Catholic missions in Ibero-America versus the Protestant colonization of North America, and also in relation to the French Catholic mission in what is known today as Canada.[6]

Mention of the Black Legend plunges us immediately into an arena of conflict that has made it difficult to understand the complex and traumatic encounter between the Iberian Christ and the American soul. Much can be learned, though, from Catholic historiography that came into being to counteract the Black Legend and to praise the Spanish,[7]

---

[5]John A. Mackay, *The Other Spanish Christ* (Eugene, OR: Wipf & Stock, 2001), 103.

[6]Mackay, *Other Spanish Christ*, 72-73.

[7]See, for example, the work of Peruvian Rubén Vargas Ugarte and Argentinian Vicente D. Sierra. A useful summary may be found in José Rubia Barcia, ed., *Americo Castro and the Meaning of Spanish Civilization* (Berkeley: University of California Press, 1976).

presenting the Iberian mission in a more favorable light, and from works that avoid polemics in favor of systematic historical research.[8] Fortunately, a good part of the literature produced in celebration (or lamentation) of the five-hundredth anniversary of the arrival of Christopher Columbus had a critical but open tone.

An interesting case of positive revisionism of sixteenth-century Hispanic evangelization is that of Virgilio Elizondo, a missiologist with Hispanic roots who is well known in the United States, his home country. He asserts that there are important differences that should be taken into account in comparing the Iberian and Anglo-Saxon forms of mission. Elizondo says the Christianity that developed in Ibero-America was indigenous, rooted, and mestizo, while Christianity in North America was simply a transplant of European Christianity with no emergence of an indigenous theology and practice.[9] Elizondo has given close attention to issues of cultural fusion, and he offers his missiological reflections within this frame of reference. Consideration of processes of blending or fusion lead us to a further debated question, that of syncretism. This topic will be dealt with in some detail in the following chapter.

The Spanish Christ of the Sixteenth Century

The current general consensus regarding the way Iberian Christianity developed during the sixteenth century constitutes a complex picture of positive and negative, light and shadows, confirming some of Mackay's critical observations. More recent studies, such as those of Américo Castro and Marcel Bataillon, on religious life in Spain during the fifteenth and sixteenth centuries have provided abundant data supporting Mackay's interpretive outline. One book about Spanish Catholicism by well-known US Catholic historian Stanley Payne offers the following overall evaluation of medieval religion in the peninsula:

---

[8]Robert Ricard's work *The Spiritual Conquest of Mexico* is especially worthy of note (Mexico: Fondo de Cultura Economica, 1991). A valuable panoramic view of this process is P. E. Russell, ed., *Spain: A Companion to Spanish Studies* (London: Pitman, 1973).

[9]Virgilio Elizondo, *Christianity and Culture: An Introduction to Pastoral Theology and Ministry for the Bicultural Community* (Huntington, IN: Our Sunday Visitor, 1975), 119-28.

> Discussions by historians of religion in the Middle Ages almost invariably give the clergy low marks, which by every evidence they frequently deserved. Medieval clergy at most levels were ignorant and poorly trained. . . . Much of the clergy behaved little differently from ordinary society, indulging in popular vices and excesses. Though the Spanish clergy did not have the reputation for drunkenness enjoyed by their counterparts in some other regions, they yielded to none in concupiscence. Concubinage and bastardy were common among parish priests and hardly unknown among monks.[10]

Proof that Payne is not exaggerating in his judgment is the well-known fact that great Spanish mystics such as Saint Teresa of Ávila and Saint John of the Cross were known for the richness of their spiritual experience, of which they have left valuable literature, but also for their efforts in moral reform within the orders of which they were members. The persecution they suffered as a result of their efforts at reformation reveals the low level of spiritual and moral life that was prevalent within religious institutions.

Moreover, for eight centuries the Spanish had experienced the presence of Arabs and Jews on the Iberian Peninsula, and their interaction with these people groups marked their history and culture. Then, in the decades prior to the discovery of the Americas, the fight to expel the Moors (Muslims) took on the character of a religious crusade, with medieval Catholicism providing a warlike ideology. This crusading orientation was later reflected in the conquest of America. Following Payne's discussion of the low morals of the Spanish medieval clergy, he adds:

> Spanish frontier conditions may have made some problems worse in the peninsula than elsewhere. Clerics at all levels took part in military campaigns against Muslims, creating the famous typology of the medieval prelate "a Dios rogando y con el mazo dando" (praying to God and striking with the mace). Many of the Spanish clergy thought nothing of wearing weapons as part of their normal costume, a practice that took many generations to eliminate.[11]

---

[10]Stanley G. Payne, *Spanish Catholicism* (Madison: University of Wisconsin Press, 1984), 28-29.
[11]Payne, *Spanish Catholicism*, 29.

When we take into account this panorama of customs and conditions, we can better understand the roots of the social ills associated with colonial religion that have persisted in Latin American society. Some great nineteenth-century Latin American authors dared to describe these ills critically once the censoring power of the Inquisition disappeared.

Payne too explains and provides a thoughtful, balanced evaluation of the missionary task undertaken by Spain during the sixteenth century. His historical study offers a summary of the evolution of Spanish religion that is especially valuable for understanding its predominant Christology, developed within the spirit of the Spanish Counter-Reformation.

> It is important to point out the difficulty of separating some of the influences of the Counter-Reformation from the intensification of religion that had already begun in Spain during the late fifteenth and early sixteenth centuries. . . . One of the most pronounced new expressions was the greatly increased emphasis on Christ, the crucifix, and the Passion in general. Though this had begun perhaps a hundred years earlier, there was a major upsurge in new devotions to Christ and the Passion as the Counter-Reformation reforms advanced in the last years of the sixteenth century. This was assiduously propagated by the Franciscans, by far the most numerous monastic order in the Spanish countryside. Mariolatry remained strong, but now much more frequently stressed representations of Mary's role in the Passion of Christ. Moreover, new brotherhoods of flagellants, who scourged themselves in imitation of the sufferings of Christ, grew in number.[12]

Here we find the roots of the figure of the crucified Christ in the imagery left by the chronicles of conquest in both Spanish and mestizo colonial art. In churches and museums in the Extremadura region of Spain, especially in places such as Guadalupe, Trujillo, and Cáceres, where many of the first conquistadors came from, the images are resonant for those familiar with older Latin American churches: the contorted countenance of a suffering Jesus, his purple clothing, an abundance of blood.

---

[12]Payne, *Spanish Catholicism*, 49-50.

The Spanish Christ, Latin Americanized

What Mackay calls "the local Christ" is a replica of the Christ brought via the Iberian process of conquest and evangelization, coming to reflect life in the Latin American context as well. Although Mackay does not explore in depth the transformation of the Spanish Christ into the Ibero-American Christ, his intuitions have proved highly accurate. In the decades following Mackay, Latin American social sciences have progressed a great deal in their understanding of the processes of conquest and colonization. Those who study Catholic evangelism during the sixteenth century have accumulated research and analysis that allows us to better understand these processes.

Mackay makes two important observations regarding Latin American Christology during the early decades of the century: the popular Christ lacked characteristics of humanity, and the resurrected Christ was absent. "What first strikes us about the homegrown Christ is his lack of humanity. In all that touches his earthly life, there are almost only two dramatic roles that can be observed: a child in his mother's arms and suffering and bleeding victim."[13] The imagery as expressed in popular devotion confirms Mackay's observations. These two forms of Christ imagery indeed point us to important elements of the person and work of Christ. Critiquing Mackay, Orlando Costas, a Puerto Rican theologian, asserts that the Scottish missionary failed to grasp the significance of these two predominant images: the value and dignity of childhood, for example, and the dimension of humanity that is evoked by the figure of the Virgin.[14] However, the exclusive focus on these two christological elements produced a profound deficit: a lack of coherence and integrity in living out the Christian faith. Mackay is very clear about this:

> Why is it that the only moments in the life of Christ which have received emphasis are His childhood and death? Because the two central truths of Christianity are Incarnation and Atonement, someone answers. Yes, but

---

[13]Mackay, *Other Spanish Christ*, 107.

[14]Presentation by Costas in a christological debate in Mark Lau Branson and C. René Padilla, eds., *Conflict and Context: Hermeneutics in the Americas* (Grand Rapids: Eerdmans, 1986), 113.

> incarnation is only the prologue of a life, while atonement is its epilogue. *The reality of the former is unfolded in life and guaranteed by living; the efficacy of the latter is derived from the quality of the life that was lived.*[15]

This type of Christology offers a Christ who lends himself to being patronized or pitied. The resulting Christianity is marked by a faith that is wielded for social gain in the absence of a Christ who is a model for life. These effects are related to the other characteristic of Latin American Christology analyzed by Mackay: the absence of a vision of the risen Christ.

> His sovereign lordship over all the details of existence, a Saviour king who is deeply interested in us and to whom we can bring our joys and sorrows and perplexities, is neither visualized nor experienced. A most extraordinary thing has happened: Christ has lost prestige as a helper in the affairs of life. He lives in virtual banishment, while the Virgin and the saints are daily approached for life's necessities. The latter are considered to be much more human and accessible than He.[16]

Christ in Peruvian Stories and Poems

In early twentieth-century Latin American literature, the predominance of these christological roles highlighted by Mackay is clearly evident. Mackay, however, does not explore two writers whom I take up here because they express aspects of this popular Christology: storyteller and essayist Ventura García Calderón (1886–1959) and poet César Vallejo (1892–1938), both Peruvian.

García Calderón was one of the first Peruvian writers to incorporate indigenous and mestizo characters and perspectives into his writing. His perspective on Indians was external to the indigenous reality itself; he took the stance of an outside observer. Despite this, he captured some aspects of the popular soul very well. Three of the works in his collection *Cuentos peruanos* (1952; Peruvian stories) caught my attention because of their christological content. In the story "Fue en el Perú" (It happened . . . in Peru), Jesus' birth is told by an old coastal Afro-Peruvian woman

[15]Mackay, *Other Spanish Christ*, 110-11, italics added.
[16]Mackay, *Other Spanish Christ*, 112.

who is "chewing a stubbed-out cigarette." Jesus is born to a poor Peruvian couple: "The virgin was a young indigenous girl, and saint Joseph was mulatto." But the birth heralded by many drives fear into the hearts of the white people, and "the poor young indigenous girl had to escape on muleback, traveling a long way in the direction of Bolivia with her husband, who was a carpenter." The story then jumps without warning from Jesus' birth to his death:

> His Majesty died and afterward rose again and will one day come again here, so that the bad people see that he is the color of *capulí* [dark fruit], just like the sons of our country. And then they will be sent to kill the White people, the Negros will be the bosses, and there won't be mine or yours, nor levies [taxes], nor prefetos, and neither will the poor have to work to fatten the rich.[17]

In "The Local Holy Friday" García Calderón portrays a small-town Holy Week celebration that demonstrates how the blond image of Christ, referred to as the redhead, is manipulated, in the dramatization of the story of Calvary. The solemn, gloomy ceremony is followed by a celebration in which the people give themselves over to uninhibited intake of alcohol.

"The Rage of Christ" is another story set in Holy Week, "in a small village where each year the Passion of Christ is relived with a magnificent and bloody realism."[18] The Catholic missionaries seek the attention of the indigenous by "hanging from the cross a man of flesh and bones, a body that suffers and laments like everyone else." One day, in a tragicomic twist, one of these flesh-and-bone Christs decides to take his murderers' spear and attack them with it. The narrator reflects, "The Roman soldiers, Calvary, all this is far away. It's very confusing and of little interest, in short, for this suffering race that has chewed coca leaves while ascending all the possible Calvaries."[19]

In these three sketches, Christ appears either as a child or as a bleeding victim. Nowhere in the popular memory, folklore, or celebrations are

---

[17]Ventura García Calderón, *Cuentos peruanos* (Madrid: Aguilar, 1952), 87-92.

[18]Calderón, *Cuentos peruanos*, 245.

[19]Calderón, *Cuentos peruanos*, 245.

there any references to Jesus' life. The resurrection is mentioned in passing, with the announcement of a brief eschatological interlude.

César Vallejo's poetry is characterized by a constant search for the religious and metaphysical, often drawing on Christian metaphors and symbols common in popular religiosity: Holy Thursday, the cross, Calvary, the shroud, the nailed hands. Vallejo uses the figure of the suffering Christ as a metaphor for his own interior suffering and for human drama. In his first book, *Los heraldos negros* (The black heralds), the poem "Los dados eternos" (The eternal dice) summarizes what appears to be his unusual fight with God:

> My God, if you had been a man,
> today you would know how to be God;
> but you, who were always fine,
> feel nothing for your own creation.
> Indeed, man suffers you: God is he![20]

This poem sounds like both a petition and a protest. The protest is against a God who doesn't understand humanity because he doesn't identify with the human condition, and the petition is for an incarnate God. The background for this is a Christology lacking precisely what should be its central message: the fundamental truth of the incarnation, "the Word made flesh."

The Critical Perspective of Miguel de Unamuno

It is obvious that Mackay was deeply influenced by Spanish writer Miguel de Unamuno. In his appreciation of the Spanish Christ Mackay follows the sense of Unamuno, a Basque teacher from Salamanca who writes:

> Oh pre-Christian and post-Christian Christ,
> Christ pure matter,
> the putrid and decaying Christ
> with coagulated blood.
> The Christ of my people is this Christ,
> flesh and blood made into earth, earth, earth! . . .

[20]César Vallejo, "Los dados eternos," in *Los heraldos negros* (Lima: Souza Ferreira, 1918).

> Because the Christ of my earth is only
> earth, earth, earth, earth,
> flesh that doesn't pulse. . . .
> And you, Christ of heaven,
> redeem us from the Christ of the earth![21]

For Mackay, Unamuno's final exclamation "throws a shaft of prophetic light across the religious life and history of Spain and South America."[22] However, it should be noted that Unamuno contradicts himself in other writings—he adores paradoxes. At one point he says he would rather remain with the Christ of Spain, his land. One of his essays relates that a South American expressed repugnance toward Spanish images of a bloody Christ. "I told him that I have the soul of my people, and that I like those Christs that are bruised, emaciated, these Christs that someone has called ferocious. Lack of art? Brutality? I don't know. And I like the dismal, suffering Virgins steeped in sorrow."[23]

Unamuno concludes this essay with words that affirm a Christology that embraces Christ's earthly suffering, leaving the resurrection and its implications for the eschatological tomorrow.

> Yes, there is a triumphant Christ, heavenly, glorious, that of the transfiguration, that of the ascension, he who is at the right hand of the Father; but [that Christ] is for when we have triumphed, for when we have been transfigured, for when we have ascended. But here, in this place on earth, in this life that is nothing but tragic bullfighting, here is the other, the bruised, the bloody and deceased.[24]

Nevertheless, Unamuno's Christology of agony does not remain trapped in its love for the image of the crucified. In the extensive theological meditation offered by his poem "The Christ of Velásquez," he takes the contemplation of Christ to an ethical dimension, to a rich and renovating spirituality, to hope and joy.

---

[21]Miguel de Unamuno, "El Cristo yacente de Santa Clara (Iglesia de la Cruz) de Palencia," in *Andanzas y visiones españolas* (Barcelona: Círculo de Lectores, 1988), 314-15.

[22]Mackay, *Other Spanish Christ*, 98.

[23]Miguel de Unamuno, *Ensayos* (Madrid: Aguilar, 1951), 391.

[24]Unamuno, *Ensayos*, 395.

Mackay was not wrong to value Unamuno's work from an evangelical perspective, given that Unamuno's work scathingly criticizes many characteristics of Spanish Catholicism that any Protestant would also criticize. Unamuno's value comes from his having undertaken theological reflection within the cultural and literary arena of his time, and from his having taken the risk of expressing his faith out loud in an environment where the official religion was accepted without discussion, though rarely taken seriously. Even with his paradoxical positions, Unamuno as an expression of the Spanish ethos was trying to live out his Christianity in the context of the deep conflicts that have characterized Spanish life. The Spain represented by Unamuno was over and over again quashed by the medieval Spain, characterized by wars and inquisitions, just as the sixteenth-century mystics and many liberal spirits from the nineteenth and twentieth centuries suffered the same fate. It is this latter Spain that shaped America. Together with Mackay we could say that the North African Christ displaced the one who was born in Bethlehem.

The Chasm Between Religion and Ethics

Observing the image of Jesus in Latin American culture led Mackay to theological reflection. Within the framework of systematic theology Mackay concludes that a docetic Christology was predominant in Ibero-America. In the history of Christian doctrine, docetism affirmed the presence of God in Christ but denied Christ's humanity. Those who supported this position were know as docetists, a term originating from the Greek word meaning "appearance." For them Christ's human character was only clothing or external appearance. However, Mackay aimed not only to assign the correct theological term but also to examine the deep consequences of this theology on a practical level. Mackay observes that a Christology that focuses on the child Jesus and on his crucifixion and death produces a chasm between religious profession and ethical practice:

> The dead Christ is an expiatory victim. The details of His earthly life are of slight importance and make relatively small appeal. He is regarded as a purely supernatural being, whose humanity, being only apparent, has

> little ethical bearing upon ours. This docetic Christ died as the victim of human hate, in order to bestow immortality, that is to say, a continuation of the present earthly, fleshly existence.[25]

This Christ does not change the lives of those who follow him here and now, only guarantees a happier future life. The way this Christology operates is revealed in the popular understanding of Communion, or the sacrament of the Eucharist. Mackay says: "The sacrament increases life without transforming it. The ethical is absent, its place being taken by ritualistic magic."[26] Because of this, "Philosophically speaking, Spanish Catholicism has passed straight from aesthetics to religion, clearing ethics at a bound. The Tangerian Christ, and the religion that grew up around him, have aesthetic and religious values, but they are both unethical."[27]

Brilliant twentieth-century Spanish philosopher José Luis Aranguren, who specialized in ethics, observed the same thing in his studies of nineteenth-century Spanish morals and society. He describes a disconnect between the public religiosity necessary to keep up appearances and growing interior skepticism. Various factors "made it impossible for religion truly to speak to the whole of life." The resulting contradictions in behavior were scandalous: "great ladies, the queen at their head, extremely devout and even superstitious, whose private morality in sexual conduct bore no relation to that preached by Christianity; and similarly, gentlemen whose respectable and solemn religious appearances meshed easily with the corruption of financial and political mores."[28]

Scholars with a critical bent who investigated Spanish religiosity, such as Unamuno in the first part of the twentieth century or Aranguren in the second part, have written extensively of the contradiction between the moral and the religious life of the Iberian peninsula, a contradiction that we also see reflected in Latin America. This shows that Mackay's analysis was correct, that his judgment was not just the prejudice of a

---

[25]Mackay, *Other Spanish Christ*, 98.

[26]Mackay, *Other Spanish Christ*, 101.

[27]Mackay, *Other Spanish Christ*, 101.

[28]José Luis L. Aranguren, *Moral y sociedad: La moral española en el siglo XIX*, 3rd ed. (Madrid: Cuadernos para el diálogo, 1967), 114.

Protestant missionary from an English-speaking context. In the disconnect between religiosity and ethics lies a faulty Christology that Mackay summarizes in the following way:

> A Christ known in life as an infant and in death as a corpse, over whose helpless childhood and tragic fate the Virgin Mother presides; a Christ who became man in the interests of eschatology, whose permanent reality resides in a magic wafer bestowing immortality; a Virgin Mother who by not tasting death, became the Queen of Life, that is the Christ and the Virgin who came to America![29]

The Post–Vatican II Catholic Analysis

Some studies of popular religiosity undertaken by Catholic specialists in the movement toward reforms and self-criticism inspired by Vatican II coincide with Mackay's observations. In the period prior to and immediately following the Conference of Catholic Bishops in Medellín (1968), popular religiosity became a topic of research and evaluation out of a desire for renewal of the faith by returning to its sources, including Scripture. Segundo Galilea made an eloquent, widely applicable observation in a 1969 publication: "In summary, in regard to general characteristics of popular religiosity, we can say that this is a religion of salvation and individual security where the doctrine of the last things is valued more highly than Jesus Christ. This is equally evident in popular sermons, which are moralizing and sacramentalist, and this has created a cultural religion, tied to beliefs and traditions."[30]

Expressing pastoral concern for the content of the faith of the common people in relation to their behavior, Galilea also signals the lack of an ethical dimension in popular religiosity as well as the absence of a concept of discipleship.

> It's a matter of a religion of "having" as opposed to a religion of valuing. That is to say, rituals and doctrines are valued for what they contribute to

---

[29]Mackay, *Other Spanish Christ*, 102.

[30]Aldo Buntig, Segundo Galilea, et al., *Catolicismo popular* (Quito: Instituto Pastoral Latinoamericano, 1969), 55.

one's ego and not for what they mean in themselves, for living morally or for God's plan. . . . For this same reason it's a religion that is more hagiocentric than Christ-centered. This hagiocentrism, focused mainly on images, can descend into fetishism, where *that* image has value in and of itself, and in general the images begin to *be* the saint himself or herself.[31]

Galilea moves on from observations about ritualism and hagiocentrism to the profound christological defects of popular religiosity. His study is significant in that it is based on statistical social-scientific research as well as his personal pastoral experience.

Can it be said that popular faith in Jesus Christ contains shades of heresy? We think so. Indeed, it may be that popular Christology is quite unbalanced. . . . It is consumed by the mysteries of the Passion; Christ in glory, Christ the head of the church; Christ our source of becoming more human is not present in the popular mindset. . . . Popular Latin American Christology, without realizing it, is quite monophysitic. This attitude has complex origins; the anti-Arian attitude of the Iberian Peninsula, together with an emphasis on piety and the doctrine of Christ-God, led to an emphasis on the importance of other mediators. These had to replace the humanity of the Word, which had been darkened and absorbed in the divinity (from this comes the ardent devotion to Mary and the saints).[32]

In another essay in the same collection where Galilea's appears, Aldo Buntig pays particular attention to the ethical dimensions of ritualistic popular religiosity. Buntig applies the term *amoral* to the kind of religion driven by cosmological motives—that is, seeking the use of divine power for personal gain. His analysis repeats a number of the points that we have already seen in Mackay's writing.

The Holy Mass, far from being a liturgical action where Christ renews his paschal sacrifice and invites us to let our own lives become paschal sacrifices, is in the best of cases a ritual undertaken with the aim of winning blessings. Further, since rituals are no more than means to obtain favors with no relation to their actual meaning, the impulse [of attendees] will be to increase gestures, to make the pious practices simpler and more

---

[31]Buntig et al., *Catolicismo popular*, 56. *Hagiocentric* means "saint-centered."
[32]Buntig et al., *Catolicismo popular*, 61.

understandable, under an illusion of greater efficacy that the Lord actually condemned as a pagan way of thinking.[33]

In another section of his essay Buntig recognizes the function of rural religiosity for meeting human needs. "It is to rituals and Christian saints that the people go to seek help for the group's most pressing needs: rain, pests, plagues, sicknesses."[34] In the process certain local saints or certain prayers to the Virgin are converted into "specialized forces" that people use in service to their needs. This does not require any theological clarity; instead it is based on what Buntig calls a "denaturing" of the doctrinal values of Christianity:

> This explains why these special saints and invocations tend to occupy a much more prominent place in the process of interiorizing faith and in cultural expression than God or our Lord Jesus Christ. It is a kind of resurrection of the pagan pantheon, with local divinities enlisted to benefit local needs. Here religion does not require any true moral transformation. . . . The absence of any call to moral transformation is the reason that that . . . religious celebrations are often paired with dances and popular entertainment of dubious moral content, providing psychic release in this cultural environment.[35]

Despite legitimate critiques that might be made of Mackay's observations, then, Catholic research undertaken in the spirit of Vatican II produced various points of agreement with his observations on the predominant Christology in the Ibero-American world. Thus this evangelical contribution to understanding the spiritual dimension of Latin American culture had a pioneering value that we would do well to recognize. In the spirit of the Second Vatican Council, the 1968 Conference of Bishops in Medellín adopted some elements of the evangelical analysis of popular Latin American religion. Even liberation theologians realized what it meant to take this analysis seriously. It became necessary to change pastoral models so that Catholics could take up a Christianity in which the Christ of the Bible might be better known.

---

[33]Buntig et al., *Catolicismo popular*, 26.
[34]Buntig et al., *Catolicismo popular*, 37.
[35]Buntig et al., *Catolicismo popular*, 38.

3

THAT OTHER CHRIST OF THE INDIANS

Every time that I have written to Your Majesty I have mentioned to Your Highness the inclination that is present in some of the natives of this land to convert to our holy catholic faith. For this reason, I have sent to request our Majesty to send the provision of religious people of a good life and good example. And because until now very few have come, or almost none, and it is true that there is much fruit, I bring this again to Your Highness's memory, and I plead that you provide for this need as quickly as possible.

Letter from the conqueror of México,
Hernán Cortés, to Emperor Carlos V, October 15, 1523

The era when the Andean religion crystallized spanned the second half of the seventeenth century. It seems that the Andean population, which in a little more than 130 years had suffered the plundering of its official Incan religion and had been subjected to a largely coercive evangelization, managed in the end to undertake a religious inventory at the heart of the colonial society and adopt a worldview and religious frame of mind that "crystallized" in this period and would remain almost unchanged until very recent times. The Andean people ended up accepting the Catholic religious system, but making a series of reinterpretations of the Christian elements within an indigenous cultural framework and embedding many indigenous elements within the new religious system. But it should be underlined that this religious system is not a simple juxtaposition of the two religions . . . , but rather something new and integrated in the heart of colonial society.

Manuel Marzal, SJ,
La transformación religiosa peruana

The Spanish evangelizers would have liked to find in the Americas men and women who were like a *tabula rasa*, a virgin territory where it was possible to plant a pure Christianity, free of Protestant heresies or Jewish infiltrations. The aboriginal peoples of these lands, however, had developed civilizations and cultures with their gods and lords, their priests, rituals, and religious institutions. So it was that the Christ of Iberian medieval religiosity met with the Viracocha and the Pacha Mama of the Andean peoples, with Quetzalcoatl and Tonatiuh of the Mesoamerican peoples.

In the previous chapter I described the vision of Christ held by the Spanish and the Spanish-influenced mestizos in the context of the colonial era. There I established that Mackay's analysis is correct in signaling the clear connection between this vision of Christ and that of the Iberian popular religiosity that was brought by the conquistadors. However, we saw that in his study of the Ibero-American Christ, Mackay did not carefully explore the issue of popular religiosity as manifested in places where indigenous cultures resisted the Spanish conquest, places whose influence has endured despite centuries of oppression. The works of Segundo Galilea and Aldo Buntig reviewed in chapter two are evidence that over several decades there were a number of studies in ethnographical, anthropological, historical, and missiological research on popular religiosity. A clearer picture has continued to be revealed of how Christ was perceived by the indigenous and mestizo masses when they received the message brought by the conquistadors and the missionaries.

Catholic Affirmation and Protestant Critiques

Popular religiosity among indigenous peoples has been a matter of major dispute, and it touches on various important concerns for contemporary missiology. One of the common arguments from Catholics opposing evangelical missions was that South America was already a Christian continent, and therefore there was no reason for Protestant missionaries to come and proselytize among people who were already believers. Protestant missionary literature responded by signaling the deficiencies and vices of popular religiosity. These were particularly obvious where large indigenous populations' religious practice manifested elements of religions that existed before the introduction of Christianity. These portrayed a lack of knowledge and understanding of the basic truths of the Christian faith, a superficial and incomplete knowledge of the person of Christ, and consequently a religious experience characterized by superstition more than faith. For Protestants this was evidence that the continent was not truly Christian.

Some Protestant observations that I have already noted about the evangelization of the continent applied in a special way to indigenous religions. Missionary reports, stories of their trips, and the books promoting evangelical missions provide ample material on the subject. Given the Indians' situation of neglect and oppression, observed firsthand by Protestant missionaries, these missionaries arrived at critical conclusions regarding the absence of a transforming dynamic in the Catholicism practiced by the indigenous people and its social consequences. However, Catholics themselves recognized the difficulty of the situation. For example, in an overview of Latin American Catholicism, Panama bishop Mark McGrath summarizes the situation in the following way: "The large populations of Indians in some nations and of blacks in others, and rural communities and workers in general, have a very limited knowledge of faith. It is common that they don't know how to explain who Jesus was." A later clarification reflects the ambiguity of the Catholic perspective: "Taking everything into account, there exists among them a commitment that is sentimental, national, personal, and even, by God's grace, strongly supernatural to being Catholic. But what that commitment means is another question."[1]

In the case of Peru, evangelical missionary William Mitchell, a Bible translator and specialist in Quechua language, has made a careful study of the use of the Bible in the Christianization of Peru during the first decades of the Spanish conquest in the sixteenth century. The effort made to create appropriate catechism guides and translate them into

[1]Mark G. McGrath, "La autoridad docente de la Iglesia: Su situación en Latinoamérica," in *Religión, revolución y reforma*, ed. William V. D'Antonio and Frederick B. Pike (Barcelona: Herder, 1967), 97. English version: *Religion, Revolution, and Reform* (New York: Praeger, 1964).

Quechua was significant.[2] On the basis of both educational and pastoral needs, songs were used to transmit the Christian message, and there are songs from that period that continue to be used to this day. However, in the spirit of the Counter-Reformation of the Council of Trent, translations of the Bible into vernacular languages were put on the index of prohibited books, and initial efforts at contextual evangelization did not flourish and were discontinued.[3]

Similarly, in the case of Mexico, for example, there are studies that demonstrate how initial missionary efforts in the sixteenth century, especially by the Franciscan and Dominican orders, were intended to understand the native cultures and religious ideas of the indigenous and then adapt the communication of the Christian message to the native way of thinking. We can look at the text of the famous "Coloquios de los Doce" (Colloquies of the twelve), in which Franciscan missionaries dialogued with indigenous leaders about the Christian faith compared to the religious understanding of the natives. How was the truth about Jesus Christ expressed in this effort to communicate? Let's look at chapter five, where "Savior of Men, Jesus Christ, here on the earth He founded His precious dominion."

> He, the Only True God, Speaker, Creator of Men, and Savior of Men, Jesus Christ, here on the earth He founded His precious dominion, His honorable mat, His honorable seat, He set down, and it is this whose name is dominion of heaven, moreover, its name is Holy Catholic Church. Because of that, it is called the dominion of heaven, indeed, absolutely no one will enter heaven if he will not belong to it, the Holy Church. (A) And there, in the place of His precious speaker's abode, there are very many things, riches, prosperity. The celestial things are kept there, in His precious coffer, His precious hamper, these which belong to the Possessor of the Near, the Possessor of the Surrounding, the well encased precious things, and well guarded ones. This, the precious dominion of He by Whom All Live, which is called the Holy Catholic Church, he is the one

[2]William Mitchell, *La Biblia en la historia del Perú* (Lima: Sociedad Bíblica Peruana, 2005).

[3]A study of this process can be found in Jorge Seibold, *La Sagrada Escritura en la evangelización de América Latina*, vol. 1 (Buenos Aires: San Pablo, 1993).

> who guards it, he governs it, the great divine guardian, the Holy Father, he carries with him the instrument by which things are opened, by which it is opened. Only he alone is able to open it, not anyone else, if not by his commanding it. Furthermore, he guards it, that by which one enters heaven, [no one will be able] if he, the Holy Father, does not open it, or somebody by his honorable mandate, because, truly he is the venerable representative of He by Whom All Live, Our Lord, Our God, Jesus Christ. (B) He, the Holy Father, governs completely, he directs them all completely, the great speakers on the earth, whose name is kings, also he, the great speaker, the emperor. And now, for this reason, he sent us, so that we will cause you to see His precious dominion, and His precious riches, His precious prosperity, that of He by Whom All Live, Jesus Christ. And, thus, you will also know, indeed, that in heaven, there, is the entrance, there is that by which one enters, by which one goes there. And the instrument by which things are opened, verily, he is the one who guards it, the Holy Father, the venerable representative of God.[4]

It is worth asking what the natives who heard this presentation actually understood about Jesus. Reading the colloquies and the dialogues with the native leaders to whom the evangelizers spoke leads us to the conclusion that Christ was presented as Lord and that acceptance of his lordship essentially meant submission to the church and the conquistadors.

For both circumstantial historical and theological reasons, the Catholic missionary effort during the sixteenth century was closely tied to the subjugation of the indigenous through military conquest. This topic was closely studied during the last decade of the twentieth century to coincide with the five-hundredth anniversary of Columbus's arrival, and efforts were made to review the central tenets of the "Black Legend" that denigrated all things Iberian. Pedro Borges, from Complutense University in Madrid, has researched this topic over several decades.[5] His analysis of legislation imposed on the Indians shows that it juxtaposes civilization and mission, a process based on the assumption that first the

---

[4]Jorge Klor de Alva, trans., "Book of the Colloquies; The Aztec-Spanish Dialogues of 1524," *Alcheringa/Ethnopoetics* 4, no. 2 (1980): 96-99.

[5]Pedro Borges, *Métodos misionales en la cristianización de América. Siglo XVI* (Madrid: Consejo Superior de Investigaciones Cientificas, 1960).

Indian was to be civilized to become a "human," so that later he might become a "Christian."

> The idea that Indians first needed to become human to become Christian was voiced regularly by both religious workers and secular people; it seems to be stamped whole cloth across the sixteenth, seventeenth, and eighteenth centuries. In every occurrence it is expressed with such similar language that one is led to believe in the existence of an unknown common source.[6]

One sector of missionaries believed that to civilize, it was necessary to subjugate and that this bringing into submission had to precede evangelism. Borges quotes Capuchin missionary to Venezuela Ildefonso de Zaragoza, who said in 1692, in referring to the Indians, "It would be convenient to put them under some type of subjugation that would reduce them to being human so they can be taught how to be Christians."[7] Coercion was used as a means of civilizing, even though it was recognized that Christianization couldn't be done by force. Another Spanish Catholic historian summarizes by recalling a phrase originating in the Hispanic Middle Ages: *primero vencer, después convencer* (first win, then win over).[8] Legal instruments for the conquest were carefully constructed to justify the civilizing and military enterprise on the basis of the end goal of evangelization, thus putting theology at the service of politics. In a seminal work examining critical opposition to the Conquista by religious leaders such as Bartolomé de las Casas, Peruvian theologian Gustavo Gutiérrez studied the development of this theology. He reconstructs, for example, the writing of the Requierimiento, a document declaring the right of the king of Spain and his representatives to conquer the Indians, which was read to Indian leaders prior to attacking them militarily, if they had not already submitted. This document begins with theological statements about God and creation, the dispersion of the

[6]Pedro Borges, *Misión y civilización en América* (Madrid: Alhambra, 1987), 8.
[7]Borges, *Misión y civilización en América*, 12.
[8]Leandro Tormo, *Historia de la Iglesia en América Latina*, vol. 1, *La evangelización de la América Latina* (Bogotá: Feres-OCSHA, 1962), 150.

human race, and the responsibility of the pope to reunify the world through his representatives, the conquistadors.[9]

In justifying the conquest, ideas rooted in the medieval period were fused with ideas arising in the heat of theological debate about the rights of the Spanish to conquer for the purposes of evangelizing, and the indigenous people's lack of rights due to their paganism. On this subject, the king of Spain's advisers relied on writings of Pope Innocent IV (d. 1264) and of Enrique de Susa, cardinal of Osta, called the Ostian (d. 1271). The latter wrote, as summarized by Gutiérrez: "Since the coming of Christ the infidels have lost all authority and jurisdiction. Such authority and jurisdiction belong to the faithful alone, since they are based on faith." Gutiérrez comments, "In other words, the heathen are not the rightful rulers of their lands. They hold no legitimate authority there."[10] Arguments like these were used to justify the use of violence to obtain the evangelization of the natives.

The missionary practices deriving from this understanding continued until at least the 1960s. Peruvian novelist Mario Vargas Llosa, now a winner of the Nobel Prize in Literature, in recounting how he wrote his novel *La casa verde* (The green house), tells of a visit to a missionary outpost belonging to a Spanish Catholic mission in Santa Maria de Nieva in the Peruvian jungle in 1957: "We had the opportunity to personally meet the missionaries. . . . We could see the hard life they led. . . . We could see the enormous sacrifice that it demanded of them to remain in Santa Maria de Nieva." Later he writes of the school that the nuns had built for indigenous Aguaruna girls: "They want to teach them to read and write, to speak Spanish, to not live in nakedness, to worship the true God. There had been a problem not long after opening the school: the Aguaruna girls did not come to school because their parents did not make the effort to send them." Vargas Llosa supposes the main reason was that the Aguaruna families did not want their daughters to

---

[9]Gustavo Gutiérrez, *Las Casas: In Search of the Poor of Jesus Christ* (Eugene, OR: Wipf & Stock, 2003), 113-25.

[10]Gutiérrez, *Las Casas*, 111.

be "civilized" by the nuns. But "the problem was promptly solved. Periodically a group of nuns accompanied by a squad of policemen would collect girls from the jungle hamlets. The nuns would enter the villages, choose the school-age children, and take them to the mission in Santa Maria de Nieva, with the guards present to neutralize any resistance."[11]

Historians agree that the initial impulse toward evangelization, particularly that of certain orders such as the Franciscans and Dominicans, was displaced by the interests of the conquistadors, who wanted a rapid and widespread Christianization that would convert the indigenous into subjects of the Spanish monarchs and taxpayers contributing to the royal coffers. In this they had the support of lay clerics, whose attitude differed greatly from that of the missionary orders. However, the crisis suffered by Catholicism during the independence wars in Latin America (1810–1824) for its support of the colonial system and alignment with the Spanish weakened the church, which increasingly lost the capacity to offer pastoral care and teaching to the faithful indigenous. This was due to a lack of priests and the lack of a true inculturation of missionaries among the natives. The situation of indigenous peoples across the continent at the beginning of the twentieth century was appalling.

In an overview of the religious situation in Latin America in the middle of the twentieth century, British missionary Stanley Rycroft, who worked in Peru, sums up the observations and experience of many Protestant missionaries: "Religion has not redeemed the Indian, and neither has it brought a bettering of the living conditions or any social improvement, nor abundant life. . . . Currently the Indians are seen to be chronically impoverished or in debt because of so many [religious] festivals, or due to the many demands laid on them."[12] Rycroft bases his critical perspective on testimonies from ethnologists and anthropologists who had studied the indigenous cultures. One of the authors he cites is Weston la Barre, who studied the Aymara culture in Peru and Bolivia, and whose opinion is precisely centered in Christology:

[11]Mario Vargas Llosa, *Historia secreta de una novela* (Barcelona: Tusquets, 1971), 26-28.
[12]W. Stanley Rycroft, *Religión y fe en América Latina* (Mexico City: CUP, 1961), 121.

> Several centuries of nominal Christianity have served only to add a further alien mythology to the body of Aymara beliefs. As a people group that has been brutally oppressed and cruelly exploited, many of the Indians have accepted some of the sadomasochistic symbols of the thorn-crowned and bloody figure of Christ, and of the suffering and merciful Mother, whom some identify with their own female deity. Even when all are considered to be Christians, many of the Aymaras hate religion with the same vehemence with which they hate those who work for religion.[13]

In his penetrating study of Mexican culture, *The Labyrinth of Solitude*, writer Octavio Paz offers a rich reflection on religious celebrations, making an ironic comment about the financial burden taken on by the people to fund religious festivities. Paz says, "The life of every city and village is ruled by a patron saint whose blessing is celebrated with devout regularity," and later he shares a revealing anecdote:

> I remember asking the mayor of a village near Mitla, several years ago, "What is the income of the village government?" "About 3,000 pesos a year. We are very poor. But the Governor and the Federal Government always help us to meet our expenses." "And how are the 3,000 pesos spent?" "Mostly on fiestas, señor. We are a small village, but we have two patron saints."[14]

Some non-Protestant scholars have come to the same conclusion: a real "conversion" to the Catholic faith had not taken place. That is to say, the evangelizing process during the sixteenth century did not achieve a deep religious transformation. Writing around 1927, when anthropological and ethnological studies had not yet proliferated, nor been applied to missiology, Peruvian socialist José Carlos Mariátegui made a pointed analysis of the situation of Indians in the Andean region. He used the few studies undertaken up to that point and applied methodology based on socioeconomic analysis, nuanced with his thorough knowledge of history and sociology of religion. Mariátegui believed that "Catholicism,

---

[13]Rycroft, *Religión y fe en América Latina*, 122.
[14]Octavio Paz, *The Labyrinth of Solitude* (New York: Grove Press, 1994), 17.

due to its emotion-inducing liturgy, had a perhaps unique ability to captivate a population that couldn't immediately elevate itself to a spiritual and abstract religiosity."[15] The drama and color of the liturgy had dazzled indigenous people, but deep down there had been no conversion. Mariátegui quotes Emilio Romero, a scholar from the south of Peru, where all his life he had observed the manifestations of popular Catholicism among the Indians:

> The Indians vibrated with emotion before the solemnity of Catholic rituals. They saw the sun's image in the sparkling embroidery of the chasuble, capes and religious clothing, colors of the rainbow in the fine silk threaded on a violet background. . . . This explains the pagan frenzy of the indigenous multitude from Cusco vibrating with fright before the presence of the Lord of the Earthquakes (a popular image of the crucified), in whom they saw a tangible image of their memories and their worship. This was far from what the friars had in mind. Indigenous paganism vibrated in the religious celebrations.[16]

This type of observation led Mariágegui to conclude, "Evangelization and catechism were never able to penetrate to a deep level. . . . The aboriginal paganism lived on under the Catholic liturgy."[17]

Catholic response to Mariátegui's analysis arrived swiftly, and it is enlightening to consider the arguments presented. In a book written specifically in response to Mariátegui, Víctor Andrés Belaúnde, a Peruvian Catholic leader who later became president of the United Nations, says:

> Basically, there is undeniable evidence that the Catholic spirit did penetrate the indigenous population. I must point to the two principal types of evidence: the indigenous people's response to suffering, which today at least is not the cold, fatalistic resignation common among indigenous peoples, but rather petition and hope; and the widespread and intense nature of their Marian devotion.[18]

---

[15]José Carlos Mariátegui, *Siete ensayos de interpretación de la realidad Peruana*, 13th ed. (Lima: Amauta, 1968), 137.
[16]Mariátegui, *Siete ensayos*, 137.
[17]Mariátegui, *Siete ensayos*, 138.
[18]Víctor Andrés Belaúnde, *La realidad nacional*, 3rd ed. (Lima: Horizonte, 1964), 91.

Neither of these types of evidence that for Belaúnde constitute proof of the penetration of the Catholic spirit has to do with a core christological transformation.

FORCED ACCEPTANCE OF CHRISTENDOM

One way of interpreting the superficiality of indigenous people's acceptance of Catholicism is to argue that they were motivated by the need to survive the Conquista. Historian and ethnologist Luis Valcárcel characterizes it in this way:

> With the arrival of irreparable foreign domination, the indigenous astutely resorted to a canny use of simulation. Unable to openly and roundly reject the predominant religious values that were so decisively imposed, they pretended to accept them. They became Catholic, were baptized, practiced the faith assiduously; they participated in rituals and celebrations. However, in their hearts they remained firmly attached to their old gods.[19]

Valcárcel points out that the conquistadors' message about God and Jesus openly contradicted their behavior. Dominican friar Vicente Valverde preached to Incan Emperor Atahualpa about a merciful God who had sent his Son to redeem human beings. However, with his actions the conqueror Pizarro, whom Valverde served, contradicted the Dominican friar's preaching: "If Valverde's God was as he portrayed him, Pizarro's must be the antigod, a demon of evil, of low lusts and extreme materialism. Even more, with what surprise would [Emperor Atahualpa] have observed Pizarro worshiping the cross and receiving the sacraments from Valverde's hands?"[20]

Maybe this explains why indigenous Christology accepted the figure of Jesus that Iberian popular religiosity had, for other reasons, come to prefer in this period. The Indians saw themselves portrayed in the suffering Christ, victims, like Christ, of evil inflicted by religious and powerful people. Valcárcel says, "There is nothing more impressive than the

---

[19]Luis E. Valcárcel, *Ruta cultural del Perú,* 3rd ed. (Lima: Nuevo Mundo, 1965), 143.
[20]Valcárcel, *Ruta cultural del Perú,* 143.

Indian Christs. They are oil paintings, sculptures and wooden figures made by artists from Cusco, where the divine Redeemer is a faithful effigy of the indigenous people."[21] In his book *Tempestad en los Andes* (Storm in the Andes), Valcárcel also recognizes the transforming impact of the Protestant experience as part of the earthquake or storm that was convulsing the Andean region of Peru in the first decades of the twentieth century.

Let us return to that insightful interpreter of Mexican culture Octavio Paz, who in *The Labyrinth of Solitude* provides a complex analysis of the complex process of the transmission of Christian faith that occurred during the conquest of Mexico. He points out that the teaching of the Catholic faith had a social function in helping the indigenous reintegrate their interior world and their vision of life, which had been shaken and shattered by Hernán Cortés's defeat of the Aztecs. Paz says: "Under these conditions, the persistence of the pre-Cortesian background is not surprising. The Mexican is a religious being and his experience of the divine is completely genuine. But who is his god? The ancient earth-gods or Christ?"[22] As an example of how Catholicism was employed simply as a covering for the ancient cosmogonical beliefs, he cites the way Chamula writer Juan Pérez Jolote describes the image of Christ in a church in his village:

> This is Señor San Manuel here in the coffin; he is also called Señor San Salvador or Señor San Mateo; he watches over the people and the animals. We pray to him to watch over us at home, on the road, in the fields. This other figure on the cross is also Señor San Mateo; he is showing us how he died on the cross, to teach us respect. . . . Before San Manuel was born, the sun was as cold as the moon, and the *pukujes*, who ate people, lived on the earth. The sun began to grow warm after the birth of the Child-God, Señor San Salvador, who is the Son of the Virgin.[23]

---

[21]Valcárcel, *Ruta cultural del Perú*, 153.

[22]Paz, *Labyrinth of Solitude*, 106.

[23]Paz, *Labyrinth of Solitude*, 106. Here Paz is quoting the famous work of Ricardo Pozas, *Juan Pérez Jolote: An Autobiography of a Taotzil* (Mexico City: Fondo de Cultura Económica, 1965).

The Catholic Missiology of Vatican II

During the 1960s and 1970s a number of Catholic scholars sought to explain the complex phenomenon of indigenous religiosity within the presuppositions of traditional Catholic missiology. In their missionary practice Protestants have not been very open to adopting ideas and cultural patterns from indigenous cultures. Catholics, on the other hand, have been more open to do so, and they have been accused of syncretism.[24] Catholic Historian Enrique Dussel established a typology of the continent's inhabitants with respect to the Christian faith during the colonial era. In placing the indigenous with this typology he offers the following analysis:

> The majority of the Indians were baptized but *not fully catechized* or converted at a deep level—and much less did they have a life in Christian community (with the exception of the Indians who were organized in *villages*, *doctrines*, *missions*, or *reducciones*). Their existential attitude (on the moral or cultural plane), their faith or comprehension had not been sufficiently educated to embrace dogma and its demands. Thus drunkenness, degeneration, and concubinage could coexist with belief in the existence of *huacas* (the spirits of *places*), with certain spells and magic, and with the belief in Jesus as Redeemer.[25]

Later Dussel affirms, "The majority of Indians, who remained in their semiprimitive life, remained in the *catechumenate* state of greater or lesser consciousness of their faith with a greater or lesser level of instruments or Christian sacramental structures together with other pagan ones." However, upon arriving at his conclusion Dussel changes his tone: "On a deep, comprehensive, existential level of faith, the Indian population had not adopted Christianity superficially nor merely apparently, but *had begun to adopt it* radically, substantially, and authentically."[26]

---

[24]In chapter 6 of *Evangelical-Roman Catholic Dialogue on Mission 1977–1984*, ed. John Stott and Basil Meeking (Grand Rapids: Eerdmans, 1986), the different positions are stated and discussed.

[25]Enrique D. Dussel, *Historia de la Iglesia en América Latina*, 5th ed. (Madrid: Esquila Misional, 1983), 130, italics original. In English see the book Dussel edited, *The Church in Latin America 1492–1992* (London: Burns and Oates, 1992).

[26]Dussel, *Historia de la Iglesia en América Latina*, 130.

Another well-known Catholic scholar, Spanish Jesuit Manuel Marzal, dedicated decades of research to proving that Catholic evangelization in the sixteenth century was in reality a deep religious transformation. He wrote several books about Andean religiosity, working from primary sources in the archives of the Catholic Church. One of his books outlines his studies of syncretism in three Latin American groups: the Quechuas of Cusco, Peru; the Mayas from Chiapas, Mexico; and the African descendants from Bahía, Brazil. Marzal notes that

> the three groups were baptized in the Catholic Church during the first decades of the Spanish and Portuguese colonial process, but along with Christian rituals and practices, they have maintained a series of elements of their original religions, creating syncretistic systems to various degrees, which continue to be a theoretical concern for anthropologists and a pastoral problem for the Catholic Church.[27]

Throughout this and other books, Marzal shows a clear understanding of the deep problem that popular religiosity represents for Latin American Catholicism. However, he rejects the opinion of those who consider that it is simply a juxtaposition of two religions involving no real conversion.

A Docetist Christ in the Catechisms?

Among the large number of works published in honor of the five-hundredth anniversary celebration of Christopher Columbus's arrival in America in 1992, one was dedicated to analyzing the educational instruments used in Spanish evangelization: *Las raíces cristianas de América* (The Christian roots of America) by Luis Resines. Resines examines thirteen catechisms from different authors from the colonial era to try to understand how faith was transmitted in this initial phase. Resines recognizes the difficulties in transmission of faith to the indigenous via catechetical formulas brought from Spain. The concept of God as an eternal being or of the Trinity found no purchase in the mindset of the

[27]Manuel M. Marzal, *El sincretismo iberoamericano* (Lima: Pontificia Universidad Católica, 1985), 13.

Indians. There are not adequate primary sources to allow us to comprehend more fully what the Indians understood and how they reacted to the message they were given. In his analysis of the catechetical texts, Resines arrives self-critically at the conclusion that certain expressions used to explain the arrival of Christ communicated a docetist vision. He especially analyzes catechetical texts of Pedro de Córdova and Juan de Zumárraga, "in which the verb *vestir* [to clothe] is used when speaking of Jesus' assumption of humanity." Resines concludes, "The literal sense of the affirmations are heterodox, more concretely docetist, as [in them] Jesus is not human, but instead he clothes himself in humanity."[28] Resines was not on an inquisitional hunt for heresies; rather, he recognizes that from an educational perspective, both Córdova and Zumárraga faced a difficult task—and unfortunately the result of their efforts was negative:

> The concern of the authors seems to focus on the fact that in becoming man, no lessening of his divinity occurred: "He didn't stop being God." Yet their efforts had the opposite effect, as it is [Jesus'] humanity that is weakened, reduced to clothing, something only accidental that is put on and off. According to this, when the eternal Word of God puts on humanity, he appears to be a man, [a teaching] in line with the purest docetism.[29]

Popular Religiosity and Christology

Catholic studies of popular religiosity undertaken in the spirit of Vatican II and the Conference of Medellín in 1968 (addressed in some depth in the following chapter) describe and critically analyze the strange shapes that Spanish medieval Catholicism took in indigenous religiosity. The following authors of such works were Catholic missionaries, each for more than a decade, who lived and did pastoral and teaching work in indigenous communities. Their books combine anthropological observation with pastoral and theological reflection at a level that required an incarnational missionary immersion following the example of Jesus Christ.

---

[28]Luis Resines, *Las raíces cristianas de América* (Bogotá: CELAM, 1993), 65.

[29]Resines, *Las raíces cristianas de América*, 66.

In the specific field of Christology, some carefully descriptive works have brought to light the syncretism that is properly called Christ paganism.[30] J. E. Monast, in his expansive work titled *Los indios aimaraes* (The Aymaran Indians), studying the Aymara ethnic group in the border regions between Peru and Bolivia, demonstrates that the saints, the Christs, and the traditional local gods were all considered part of the same category by these indigenous peoples.

> We see paraded in this gallery the Christ of the Resurrection, the Christ of the Ascension, the Christ of the Exaltation, and so on. In the areas surrounding the city of Oruro, three cousins are mentioned who do not like each other: the Lord of the Lakes or of Calacala, the Lord of Quillacas, and the Lord of Calacahua. They are enemies who try to complicate life for each other as much as possible.[31]

These observations dovetail with those made by Tomás Garr, a Jesuit who studied the Quechua world in the prelature of Ayaviri in Peru, who says:

> If these campesinos' understanding of God does not correspond exactly to the orthodox concept of Christian theologians, their notion of Jesus Christ corresponds even less. In the parish of Coaza most of the people identify Jesus Christ as one of the saints of the Christian pantheon, and some describe him "as one of the three gods of the Holy Trinity." . . . Those who are familiar with the life of Christ as taught in the gospel are few.[32]

Garr shows that various cults of popular devotion to Christ, such as "the Lord of Huanca," "the Lord of the Earthquakes," or "the Lord of Miracles," do not clearly identify these objects of devotion with the person of Jesus Christ. Rather, "each cult represents a particular 'saint' with particular powers, but they do not identify his acts with the acts of Jesus Christ."[33]

---

[30]The term "Christ paganism," belonging to Protestant missiology, denotes a type of syncretism that persists where the evangelization process was deficient, leaving the local system of animist belief and practice virtually intact but mixed with some Christian elements. See Scott Moreau, ed., *Evangelical Dictionary of World Missions* (Grand Rapids: Baker, 2000), 188-89.

[31]J. E. Monast, *Los indios aimaraes ¿Evangelizados o solamente bautizados?* (Buenos Aires: Ed. Carlos Lohlé, 1972), 65.

[32]Thomas M. Garr, SJ, *Cristianismo y religión quechua en la prelatura de Ayaviri* (Cusco: Instituto de Pastoral Andina, 1972), 97.

[33]Garr, *Cristianismo y religión quechua*, 98.

Monast's and Garr's works were published in 1972, within the framework of Vatican II, whose pastoral approach called for teaching about the Christ that emphasized biblical knowledge to achieve what Monast has called "a broad corrective action." Monast also studied Protestantism among the Aymara and arrived at the conclusion that part of the transforming experience of the evangelical message was that people were freed from a religion of ignorance and fear. Monast tells how at the beginning of his ministry he met a Baptist deacon, with whom he established a friendship and who told him one day how he had converted to Protestantism: "My wife and I had been Catholics. But then we did not have Christ. We did not find him in the midst of the Virgins, or among the lords with their celebrations and parades. This is why we became Baptists. It was a pastor from this religion that helped us to discover Christ in the Holy Scriptures."[34]

Monast also gives testimony to the transforming impact for him of the love for the Bible that this Baptist deacon expressed. As I noted earlier, that historical moment of introspective realization of the deficient Christology of indigenous religiosity, and the accompanying call to return to a Christology rooted in Scripture, arose from the spirit of Vatican II and Medellín 1968, with its return to the Bible and its effort to be self-critical.

Later the arrival of the Polish Pope John Paul II launched a revisionist attitude toward Vatican II, a dedication to restore a more conservative, traditional Catholicism, and a revaluing of folk religion. Studies such as those of Garr and Monast gave way to an approach that we might call ecclesial-political. The search for a more Christocentric Christianity was replaced by an elevation of traditional Catholicism expressed in popular faith. The Conference of Bishops in Puebla (1979) followed this line, reinforced later in Santo Domingo (1992). In chapters to come I will examine some of these later calls.

---

[34]Garr, *Cristianismo y religión quechua*, 292.

The Protestant Presence and a Transformative Christology

In the nineteenth and twentieth centuries in various Latin American countries where there was an indigenous presence (in some this was a majority), significant numbers of this population were found in lamentable conditions of marginalization and exploitation that some consider even worse than conditions in the Spanish colonial era. Evangelical missionary efforts focused on these communities,[35] in some cases because the government and the Catholic Church's neglect of them allowed greater freedom to the evangelical missionary, and in other cases because mission organizations were specifically committed to working in remote areas.[36] In many cases this presence among the marginalized was dedicated from the beginning to addressing the poverty and abandonment suffered by these people. In other cases, although the initial intention was basically to evangelize, the ministry soon took on a social dimension due to the obvious needs that awoke an underlying Christian sensitivity.

An illustrative case was in the south of Peru, where in the twentieth century the Quechua- and Aymara-speaking indigenous population were among the most marginalized and exploited. Historians agree that an important shift in the national mindset took place in the first decades of the twentieth century, when intellectuals and later politicians became conscious of the condition of the indigenous, and in some cases had contact with the Protestant missionaries who worked among them.[37] Well before the beginning of literary and sociological indigenism, evangelical missionaries had begun to live among the Quechuas, to learn their languages, and to serve in various ways in the Cusco area. Historian of indigenism Luis Valcárcel notes the presence of evangelical missionaries

[35]I discuss this topic more fully in chapter 5 of my book *Changing Tides: Latin America and World Mission Today* (Maryknoll, NY: Orbis, 2002).

[36]This was the case with Regions Beyond Missionary Union at the beginning of the twentieth century in Peru and with the Bolivian Indian Mission.

[37]An excellent and well-documented study of this topic is Juan Fonseca Ariza, *Misioneros y civilizadores: Protestantismo y modernización en el Perú* (Lima: Fondo Editorial Pontificia Universidad Católica del Perú, 2002).

in 1896 and 1897 who created an experimental farm on the Urco Hacienda. Here they developed new crops, agricultural techniques, and plant processing, and offered medical services at a clinic. Meanwhile, the Adventists grew among the Aymara-speaking people, focusing on health care and education. In response to the Marxist José Carlos Mariátegui's complaint that these were "advances of imperialism," Valcárcel avers: "I want to insist, without the slightest polemical intention, that amid the desperate conditions of Cusqueño indigenous people, the gentle hand of the Adventist was the drop of cool water refreshing the thirsty lips of the abjectly poor."[38]

Another missionary movement that progressed in the south of Peru had as its protagonists American Frederick Stahl (1874–1950) and his wife, Anne, who, having paid their own fares, arrived in Bolivia in 1909. They settled close to Platería in Puno in 1911 and stayed there until 1921. Later, for health reasons, they moved to work in the Amazonian jungle in a sailboat called *Auxiliadora* (Helper), which was a floating sanatorium. The Stahls had been trained as nurses in the Adventist Sanitarium in Battle Creek, Michigan, and Anne was also a certified teacher. A book published by Stahl in 1920 reflects a clear social and spiritual sensitivity and a firsthand knowledge of the extremely bad living conditions of the region.[39] José Antonio Encinas, a Peruvian educator who was not evangelical and who later became the minister of education, wrote in 1932:

> Stahl traveled the district of Chucuito inch by inch. There are not a cabin nor a shack to which he has not carried the generosity of his spirit. He is the type of modern missionary whose behavior contrasts with the diabolical fury of the Spanish friars, who during the conquest tortured the spirit of the Indians, destroying their idols, mocking their gods, profaning the tomb of their grandfathers.[40]

---

[38]Luis E. Valcárcel, *Memorias* (Lima: Instituto de Estudios Peruanos, 1981), 71. A classic book by the same author with the title *Tempestad en los andes* (Storm in the Andes), written in 1927, gives two chapters to the evangelical presence.

[39]F. A. Stahl, *In The Land of the Incas* (Mountain View, CA: Pacific, 1920).

[40]J. A. Encinas, *Un ensayo de Escuela Nueva en el Perú* (Lima: Minerva, 1932), 148.

Encinas, a liberal thinker, continues his comparison of missionary methods, attributing the apathy and anguish of the Indians to the traditional use of the fear of hell as an instrument of religious control. He is impressed with the style of the Protestant missionary as well as his message, and contrasts it with the colonial Catholicism that he had previously critiqued:

> Before putting the Bible in the hands of an illiterate person, Stahl instilled a sense of personality, of self-confidence, of affection for life. He sought out people more as comrades than as potential converts. First of all he cared for their health. Nobody until this time had visited the miserable Indian shacks to bring them a measure of relief from their suffering.[41]

Protestant missionary literature of the time, along with letters and reports of the missionaries themselves, emphasizes the centrality of Christ in the message and the imitation of Christ in missionary style. The growth of the Adventist educative work is notable, from the first school in Platería in 1913. In 1918 there were twenty-six schools with fifteen hundred students, and by 1924 the number had risen to eighty schools with a total of 4,150 students. These schools were built at the request of the Aymara communities, and in response to their growing demand the mission developed a plan to avoid paternalism and to work toward a commitment to autonomy and self-sufficiency. When a community requested a school, it was challenged to provide a building and to guarantee a minimum of eighty students, so as to cover a teacher's wage and other basic costs.[42] All of this led Valcárcel to affirm that the presence of evangelical and Adventist missionaries during several decades had played a decisive role in the arising of a new spirit of resistance, challenging the status quo and creating alternatives: a true "storm in the Andes," precisely the title of his book.[43]

When Latin American Protestants organized the Congress on Christian Ministry in South America, in Montevideo, Uruguay

---

[41]Encinas, *Un ensayo de Escuela Nueva en el Perú*, 148.

[42]Juan B. Kessler, *Historia de la evangelización en el Perú* (Lima: Puma, 1993), 231-33.

[43]Luis E. Valcárcel, *Tempestad en los Andes*, 2nd ed. (Lima: Universo, 1972; 1st ed., 1928).

(March 29–April 8, 1925), one of the reports presented was on missionary work among the Indians. The report highlights the work of the Anglican Church in Chaco, Argentina, and that of the Adventists in the Lake Titicaca region in the south of Peru, but "it was recognized that all that is done is very little compared to what is left to be done among the millions of Indians that still live in a state of complete savagery and paganism."[44] The report is imbued with a strong sense of urgency to respond to the basic needs of the indigenous population: "Each missionary group should have evangelists, men moved by a deep love toward these poor sons of our heavenly Father." At the end the words of a veteran missionary are quoted: "The future of these unstudied tribes is in danger. Either they will be brought to Christ in great numbers, taking their place among civilized peoples, or they will be exterminated as soon as the destructive wave of commercial ventures arrives." An appendix with the conclusions from the congress includes the following recommendation.

> The Congress recommends—with the aim of understanding the problems of the Indians, winning their trust, and then sharing the Christian message—that missionaries assigned to work among the Indians:
>
> (1) Learn their native language in addition to the national language
>
> (2) Live among them as long as it is permitted by the laws
>
> (3) Remain aware that although industrial, medical, agricultural, educational, and social work among them is an urgent necessity, the fundamental problems of the Indians will not find a permanent solution if they are not led to a knowledge of Christ.[45]

---

[44] Webster E. Browning, *El Congreso sobre obra cristiana en Sudamérica* (Montevideo: Comité de Cooperación en América Latina, 1926), 73.

[45] Browning, *El Congreso sobre obra cristiana en Sudamérica*, 218.

4

CHRIST IN EARLY PROTESTANT PREACHING

On occasion the monastic peace of colonial life in Spanish America was shaken by incursions of pirates or English or Dutch raiding bands, or by uprisings led by Indians tired of the abuse inflicted by their overseers and colonial authorities. In the battles against pirates, prisoners were sometimes taken, and some of them were judged, punished, and executed by an inquisitorial tribunal. The process, which was in all senses a mockery of justice, was always presided over by an immense cross, as if the Crucified One were a powerless witness to this sinister parody, or, even worse, as if he were blessing it. Still, during the eighteenth century the rigid censoring of books and ideas did not manage to obstruct altogether the filtering in of revolutionary ideas that were shaking Europe.

The ideological ferment of the revolutionaries was often marked by an antireligious tone. As a result, the uprisings for liberty that exploded around the beginning of the nineteenth century, while not explicitly opposed to the Christian faith, were critical of the alliance between the church and colonial authorities. In the midst of tensions stirred up by the freedom movement between 1810 and 1824, the first Bibles appeared on the continent, bought and distributed by travelers such as Scotsman James (Diego) Thomson in ports such as Buenos Aires, Valparaíso, and Callao.[1] Bought by shoppers attracted to novelty or by Christians tired

[1]On Thomson, see Arnoldo Canclini, *Diego Thomso Apóstol de la enseñanza y distribución de la Biblia en América Latina* (Buenos Aires: Sociedad Bíblica Argentina, 1987).

of the contradictions of the official religion, these Bibles preceded the Protestant missionaries. Among the bold readers who risked buying and reading these prohibited books, the pages of the Gospels began to spread an image and message of a Christ different from the one predominant during three centuries of colonial life.

The Christology of Protestant Missions

The colporteurs who undertook long trips to promote the Bible throughout a significant part of the nineteenth century were followed by missionaries, some of whom came to form communities beginning with those who had received the Bible, had been reading it, and had stayed in contact with those who delivered it. These missionaries were of the working class or the emerging middle class in Great Britain and the United States. Possessed by an evangelistic enthusiasm and pietist spirituality, they were not theologians, able to articulate an understanding of faith informed by a cultural analysis of the context. Rather than being marked by a scholar's patience, they felt an urgency to make converts. However, they generally did express their faith in a Christ-centered way. Christ was the object of faith, the supreme example, and the core of their message.

As we consider the Christ who was announced in Latin America by the first generations of evangelical missionaries and preachers, I need to acknowledge the necessary limits of my research. Scholars are only in the beginning stages of wider and more careful research in primary sources since the middle of the nineteenth century, such as chronicles, stories, missionary reports, books, brochures, articles, and sermons in evangelical magazines. Historians such as German Hans Jürgen Prien, Swiss Jean Pierre Bastian, and Argentinian Pablo Deiros have opened the way with their patient and critical work in primary sources, although without specific interest in the theology of the missionaries.[2] A new

[2]Hans Jürgen Prien, *La historia del cristianismo en América Latina* (Salamanca: Sígueme, 1985); Jean Pierre Bastian, *Breve historia del Protestantismo en América Latina* (Mexico City: CUPSA, 1986), and *Protestantismos y modernidad latinoamericana* (Mexico City: Fondo de Cultura Económica, 1994); Pablo Deiros, *Historia del cristianismo en América Latina* (Buenos Aires: Fraternidad Teológica Latinoamericana, 1992).

generation of Latin American researchers such as Mexicans Rubén Ruiz Guerra and Carlos Mondragón and Peruvian Juan Fonseca Ariza are helping us better understand the historical development of theology in Latin America.[3]

For the moment this chapter is offered tentatively, as I am conscious of its selectivity and limitations. It highlights figures who seem representative, using written sources that have reached a level of thoughtful articulation, and limiting the period to the twentieth century. Three missionaries represent very different styles of preaching and literature, and their work was focused in one country but later had echoes on a continental level. In chapter five I will consider the first generation of evangelical Latin Americans. With both it is worth remembering that the missionary fervor emerged from pietist circles in central Europe, whose influence later fused with the renewal fervor of the Wesleyan movement and Great Awakening revivals in the English-speaking world. The descriptor "pietist, puritan, evangelical" indicated by historian Kenneth Scott Latourette prevailed in the missionary movement and shaped the Christology of the missionaries.[4]

The Christology of One Colporteur

Italian-Uruguayan Francisco Penzotti (1851–1925) crisscrossed the Americas, distributing the Bible and then pastorally attending to some Methodist communities that had been formed. The evangelical English-speaking press at the end of the nineteenth century and beginning of the twentieth reported on his travels with the result that he became famous, especially when, between July 1890 and March 1891, he was imprisoned in Casas Matas del Callao (Callao is Peru's chief seaport) due to accusations made by Catholic clerics in Lima. Memoirs of some of his trips

[3]Rubén Ruiz Guerra, *Hombres nuevos: Metodismo y modernización en México (1873-1930)* (Mexico City: CUPSA, 1992); Carlos Mondragón, *Leudar la masa: El pensamiento social de los protestantes en América Latina: 1920–1950* (Buenos Aires: Kairós, 2005); Juan Fonseca Ariza, *Misioneros y civilizadores: Protestantismo y modernización en el Perú (1915–1930)* (Lima: Pontificia Universidad Católica del Perú, 2002).

[4]Kenneth Scott Latourette, *Desafío a los protestantes* (Buenos Aires: La Aurora, 1956), 78.

were published as a book and offer interesting insights into the customs and living conditions of Latin American people during the final decades of the nineteenth century.[5] He also describes the pious practices specific to the evangelical spirituality of the colporteurs, makes observations about the spiritual life of the people, and includes some notes for the messages with which he accompanied his Bible distribution.

Penzotti had emigrated from Italy to Uruguay in 1864 at age thirteen, and soon his hard work and savings allowed him to be relatively successful.[6] He inherited the pious practices of a simple popular Catholicism from his maternal home, but disillusionment due to the actions of some priests had led him to reject and rebel against formal religion. One day, at a party, he received a copy of John's Gospel from a colporteur. As he read, it began to unsettle him and his wife, Josefa, and led him to a search for spiritual things. In 1875, in a church on Calle Treinta y Tres in Montevideo, he heard a message from eloquent pastor John F. Thomson, who was already famous in Argentina, and it led Penzotti to convert and decide to follow Christ. Immediately he became an enthusiastic promoter of his newfound faith, and his contact with missionaries Andrés Milne and Tomás Wood induced him to leave his employment and give himself full time to the sharing of the gospel. He took long and difficult trips to distribute the Bible and to preach in Argentina, Bolivia, Chile, Peru, and later Central America.

In a section about his travel in Bolivia and his arrival in the city of Sucre, Penzotti tells of two Indian children to whom he explained the message of personal salvation through Christ. The children became promoters of the Bible in their own way. One night, Penzotti says, he knelt to pray for the fruit of his work that day:

> I was about to finish when unexpectedly the door opened from the outside, and without ceremony a weeping woman appeared shouting, "Is there

[5]These were edited by Daniel Hall with the title *Llanos y montañas* (Buenos Aires: Imprenta Metodista, 1913). A selection appeared in Lima as *Precursores evangélicos* (Ediciones Presencia, 1984).

[6]There are brief autobiographical notes in Hall, *Llanos y montañas*, and a biography by Claudio Celada, *Un apóstol contemporáneo: La vida de Francisco G. Penzotti*, 2nd ed. (Buenos Aires: La Aurora, 1945).

> salvation for me?" It was the mother of the two Indian children. I asked her to be seated and answered, "Yes, *doña* Carmen, there is salvation for you." But she objected: "But you don't know me. I am a great sinner!" With patience and gentleness I explained that Christ came into our world precisely to "save sinners" and that those who are not saved are those who don't want to recognize their need, or those who recognize their need but look for salvation somewhere or in something other than Christ. The result was that this home, if that's what you could call the sad little hut where this Indian family of three lived, became a reason for joy among the angels. Here Christ became owner and Lord of each of these simple hearts, and as a result the light shined and the peace reigned that God gives to the consciousness of the forgiven, and the testimony that the Holy Spirit bestows on the saved soul. From then on that home was a point of light. I'm not saying that they were theologians who could teach the deep truths of the Scripture to their neighbors, but they could give testimony to Christ's power to save those who accept and to transform their lives.[7]

An Independent Missionary's Christology

John Ritchie (1878–1952) could be considered a typical representative of Protestant missionaries from independent boards.[8] He began his work in Peru under the covering of the South American and Indian Council of the Regions Beyond Missionary Union (RBMU) and later with the Evangelical Union of South America (EUSA, today Latin Link). His personal efforts in evangelism house by house, village by village, and through literature succeeded in uniting the small groups of evangelicals that already existed, resulting in the formation of the Iglesia Evangélica Peruana (Peruvian Evangelical Church), one of Peru's largest evangelical denominations to this day. Later he worked with the American Bible Society in the Andean and Pacific region and dedicated time to ecumenical activities at a continental level and to reflecting on missionary methodology. His practice and emphasis in his missionary work followed the principles he laid out in two of his books.[9] Ritchie was one of

---

[7]Penzotti, *Precursores evangélicos*, 134.

[8]Known in English as "faith missions"—that is, those not directly attached to a denomination.

[9]John Ritchie, *La iglesia autóctona en el Perú* (Lima: IEP, 2003); English original, 1932, republished as *Indigenous Church Principles in Theory and Practice* (New York: Revell, 1946).

the most articulate voices of his time, especially in the hundreds of articles and editorials he prepared for the two magazines he founded and widely distributed: *El Heraldo* and *Renacimiento*. From an examination of this flow of evangelical journalism we can gather the primary threads of his Christology.

First, we can observe a Christology that is defined in relation to salvation. The pietist and evangelical revivals drew from their Protestant heritage in emphasizing the importance of personal experience in acceptance of life-giving truth: "We believe that Jesus of Nazareth is the Christ, the Son of God, that he is the only Savior of sinners and the only mediator between God and humankind; and by his expiatory death at Calvary perfect forgiveness and eternal life are offered freely to all who trust in Christ and obey his commands."[10]

A predominant evangelical conviction found in all the missionary literature of this era is that there was a great lack of knowledge of Christ in Latin America. The first editorial in *El Heraldo*, in explaining its plan of action, says:

> We begin this work because we believe that the doctrines of Jesus Christ and his apostles are little known in the country. This is not to say that *our* doctrine is not known, neither our interpretation of Christianity. We know that there are very few people who have read even one of the Gospels that preserve Jesus' teachings. Not only this, but the Roman Church priests themselves have not studied them. That is why among the sermons that are preached in the Roman temples it is very rare to find one focused seriously on explaining the teaching of Christ.[11]

For these missionaries, the social dimension of the Christian message, incarnated in the person of Jesus, was pertinent for critiquing the socio-religious reality. In the same editorial Ritchie explains why his magazine will use the term *Romanist* and asks forgiveness in advance to those it might offend. The term *Romanist* was at that point a pejorative way of emphasizing the pagan nature of beliefs and rituals that Catholicism

---

[10]*El Heraldo* 2, no. 11 (August 1913): 82.
[11]*El Heraldo* 1, no. 1 (1912): 4.

had adopted from the religion of the Roman empire. He believed that this term was the most appropriate to describe Roman Catholicism. There is an element of irony in the reference to Christ's lifestyle in the following comment:

> Truth be told, the correct description should be "papist," since it is the papal authority that is distinctive. But for reasons only they know they do not like this name. *Christ lived as a poor person and without splendor*, but we are proud to call ourselves Christians, while the pope lives in splendor with an army, entourage, and palace, and no one wants to be called papist.[12]

Rooted in the evangelical pietism of his missionary formation, Ritchie had a conversionist understanding of the gospel as a call to repentance and personal faith in Christ, along with hope that the gospel could transform society. This hope fueled spiritual militancy and the evangelizing effort to the point of sacrifice. He expresses it this way in another editorial in the New Year 1912 issue of the magazine. Having dedicated a few lines to describe the national situation of Peru, Ritchie says:

> From our perspective, the greatest blessing that could come to this country would be a massive increase in the influence of Jesus Christ, his example and teaching, among all the social classes of the republic. . . . This is the best work that the Christian patriot could begin: bringing his compatriots to Jesus Christ. Next to this, fortune, social position, a comfortable life, and all that lies on this side of the tomb fade into insignificance.[13]

Penzotti's account and Ritchie's writings illustrate the theology of the early missionary movement that brought Protestantism to Latin America. Argentinian theologian José Míguez Bonino clearly delineates the contours of this theology. In his book *Faces of Latin American Protestantism*, Míguez Bonino describes the results of his research in the form of a thesis statement.

> My thesis is that toward 1916 Latin American missionary Protestantism was basically "evangelical" according to the model of the American evangelicalism of the "second awakening": individualistic, Christological-soteriological in

[12]*El Heraldo* 1, no. 1 (1912): 4, italics original.
[13]*El Heraldo* 1, no. 4 (1912): 4.

> a basically subjective key, with emphasis on sanctification. It had a genuine social interest, expressed in charity and mutual aid, but did not have a structural and political perspective save as it touched on the defense of its own liberty and the struggle against all discrimination. Therefore it tended politically to be liberal and democratic, but without sustaining that option in its faith, nor making it an integral part of its piety.[14]

The Christology of early Latin American Protestantism is basically defined in terms of contrast and conflict with Catholicism, but John Mackay's observation regarding the docetism of the Iberian culture takes the distinction further back, to the process of christological definition in the early centuries of Christian history. It is important to take into account that this early Christology was built basically on biblical writings and was often communicated as commentaries on texts of the Gospels and the Epistles.

Christology in Missionary Proclamation to the Elites

In contrast to Penzotti and Ritchie, who moved at ground level with the Latin American people, Mackay concentrated his attention on the elites. He founded a high school in Lima, where he hired as teachers restless young men he had met at San Marcos University, where he obtained a PhD and was later a professor. We have already discussed Mackay's valuable analysis of Latin American religiosity in *El otro Cristo Español* (*The Other Spanish Christ*). In the final pages of this book, the Scottish missionary philosopher outlines a plan for evangelizing the continent with a very clearly defined Christology: "The highest religious task that is waiting to be undertaken in Latin America is to reinterpret Jesus Christ to peoples who never considered him to be significant for thinking or for life."[15] Mackay specifies some fundamental aspects of the task that he considers urgent:

> The religious movement which has a future in South America must learn to discern the significance of Jesus as "Christ" and of Christ as "Jesus" in

[14]José Míguez Bonino, *Faces of Latin American Protestantism* (Grand Rapids: Eerdmans, 1997), 40.
[15]Juan A. Mackay, *El otro Cristo Español*, 3rd ed. (Lima: Edición Especial de Celebración, 1991), 322.

> relation to life and thought in their wholeness. It must be founded upon a myth which is more than a myth, the historic reality of God's approach to man in Jesus Christ, not only in the form of truth for the illumination of the human ideal and the meaning of the universe, but in the form of grace for the redemption and equipment of men and women to fulfil the divine plan of the ages.[16]

With these words he presents a tension within the Protestant Christology in our continent that has not yet been sufficiently resolved. On the one hand is the announcement of Jesus as a model and example of humanity, as a teacher whose teachings reveal God's love and the divine design for life. This is clear in "the form of truth to illuminate the human ideal and the meaning of the universe." In Europe and the United States this dimension of preaching about Jesus was emphasized by liberal Protestantism and was attractive to intellectually curious Latin Americans in academic contexts. However, on the other hand, as Mackay correctly shows, humans need "grace for the redemption and equipment of men and women to fulfil the divine plan." This redemptive dimension, which emphasizes the power of God available to humans in the name of Jesus Christ, is the distinctive aspect of the evangelical missionaries who proclaimed regeneration and demanded conversion.

Jesus the Teacher from Galilee

From 1926 to 1932 Mackay lived in Montevideo and then in Mexico, and from this base traveled the continent as an evangelist sponsored by the YMCA. He had begun this work three years previously when he worked in Lima as director of the well-known Anglo-Peruvian School. His missionary reports demonstrate that the openness he found among the youth and the intellectually restless convinced him of the urgent need for a deep spiritual renewal that would reach the Latin American elites. For this reason he decided to leave his educational task and focus completely on preaching and writing as he traveled. The book ". . . *Mas yo os digo*" (. . . But I say to you) summarizes the Christology of the message that the

[16]John A. Mackay, *The Other Spanish Christ* (Eugene, OR: Wipf & Stock, 2001), 274-75.

author shared with hundreds of auditoriums full of youth throughout South America.[17] The book concentrates on the personality of Jesus as Teacher, and the author says in his prologue:

> I dedicate this work to the sincere and free people who desire to join in the search for Jesus and his words, which our generation has intensified. I do not claim to present a complete portrait of the imposing figure from Galilee, nor offer a complete study of his teachings. The task I have aimed for is much simpler. I would like to illustrate the aspect of his personality where he is shown to be an excellent teacher, introducing my readers to some of the marvelous parables, where he gives some of his most beautiful and profound thoughts.[18]

The Teaching Personality of Jesus

The book's first chapter traces the educating personality of the Teacher, and in this way we come closest to the humanity of Jesus that was unknown in Latin America. As he describes the style and pedagogical methodology of Jesus, Mackay traces the traits of a real person who is presented as a model for humankind. First his *moral authority* is highlighted: "There was something in the Teacher's way of being that demanded respect and attention. . . . The sense of authority that Jesus communicated to his listeners was undoubtedly due in part to that mysterious quality, difficult to analyze, that is called personality."[19]

Here Mackay emphasizes the perfect coherence between the ideas and the person of the Teacher: "His way of being gradually influenced those who came to know him in a way that naturally resulted in their abiding by his teachings." The personality and the words of Jesus were not information to which one could respond with neutrality, but rather confronted people with themselves: "The reaction produced by an encounter is a turning point in the story of the individual, as in the light of the naked truth a neutral response is not possible."[20]

---

[17]John A. Mackay, ". . . *Mas yo os Digo*," 2nd ed. (Mexico City: CUPSA, 1964).
[18]Mackay, ". . . *Mas yo os Digo*," 10.
[19]Mackay, ". . . *Mas yo os Digo*," 12.
[20]Mackay, ". . . *Mas yo os Digo*," 15, 14.

The quality of Jesus that Mackay highlights next could be called *imaginative empathy*: "He loved things and human beings, feeling connected to each by tender bonds." Mackay says Jesus had great sympathy toward real things, toward small ones, toward the creation: "The Teacher was always reading the book of [created] things, and the Palestinian land has been immortalized in his words. He did not think in abstractions but in tangible things. He was more an artist who felt and painted reality than a philosopher analyzing it and reasoning from it."[21] Mackay continues,

> More than anyone else, it can be said about Jesus that "nothing human was alien to him." Maybe it would be more exact to say of him that "no human being was alien to him," considering that he didn't think in terms of human characteristics but of human souls. Without negating his concern for the multitudes, he was concerned especially about each individual.[22]

Jesus' sensitivity toward the poor and marginalized is very clear, but he was also sensitive to the rich and powerful, enslaved by their riches or their clinging to power.

Mackay later analyzes Jesus' pedagogical method and from this unveils his personality. The universality of Jesus' attractiveness is related to the simplicity of his teaching:

> As it was his purpose that the reach of his teaching might be as universal as the idea that inspired it, he spoke in such a way that there was no man, however humble, who did not listen appreciatively and with understanding. Because of this the Gospels have not lost their force or charm in the approximately eight hundred languages into which they have been translated.[23]

Mackay notes that Jesus did not systematize his ideas, instead "leaving them green and fresh, growing in the heart of time as nature rests in eternal youth in the heart of space, so that each generation can order them for itself with equal enthusiasm and excitement."[24] Jesus' ability to

---

[21]Mackay, ". . . *Mas yo os Digo*," 17-18, 21.
[22]Mackay, ". . . *Mas yo os Digo*," 23.
[23]Mackay, ". . . *Mas yo os Digo*," 27.
[24]Mackay, ". . . *Mas yo os Digo*," 28.

adapt his ideas to the circumstances of his listeners and to unite maximum clarity with maximum brevity is further evidence of his closeness to people of all classes and conditions, and of his sense of awareness of what was appropriate to each time and occasion.

The Central Themes of Jesus' Teaching

In concentrating his presentation of Jesus' message on the teaching of the parables, Mackay chooses central themes that he considers relevant. First is the topic of *the kingdom of God*, which for Jesus was "his concept of what constitutes the supreme reality in the life of an individual and in the history of society."[25] Here Mackay explores three series of parables. The first series highlights the existence of absolute values that confront human beings with options and decisions that set the kingdom of God in the context of their time: "It means the sovereignty of God in all spheres of human life, whether individual, at home, socially, or internationally, and concretely interpreting this sovereignty in the sense of acknowledging Christ as Lord of life and the application of his teachings to all of life's problems."[26]

The second series examines the manifestation of the kingdom throughout history, the idea of the kingdom's growth from something small and apparently insignificant, like the grain of mustard that begins to germinate. The third series takes up the idea of ferment, especially moral ferment, with its possibilities for transformation in the world:

> In this way we arrive at the conclusion that the moral fermentation at its highest effectiveness is produced by the devotion inspired by an exceptional friend. Ernesto Renán said the Christ of Saint Luke is the one who conquered the world. Luke is the writer who was able to present Jesus as the friend of publicans and sinners. Christianity has obtained great moral triumphs throughout the centuries to the degree that Christ himself has been presented as the eternal lover of souls.[27]

---

[25]Mackay, ". . . *Mas yo os Digo*," 55.
[26]Mackay, ". . . *Mas yo os Digo*," 78.
[27]Mackay, ". . . *Mas yo os Digo*," 78.

The second great theme is the *love of God*. Jesus' concept of love was "love without limits as an expression of what God is and what humankind should be."[28] This theme is also examined in a series of three parables, with a chapter dedicated to each.

> For Jesus the love of God is not reduced to general goodness; it is a quality that individualizes. God does not limit himself to loving people in the sense of the human race; he loves individual people, and this is not because of their good character but in spite of their bad character. This love is much more than a feeling. It is an active principle that is concerned, that searches, that redeems, that saves, that restores; whatever word is used to describe the supreme truth that behind the faint curtain of appearances, there is one whose loving activity is effectively felt in human experience.[29]

The third theme that Mackay considers, in another series of three parables, is the *ethical heart of Jesus' teaching*: "his concept of the principles of justice that constitute the moral economy of the universe."[30] Remember that the lack of connection between religiosity and ethics was central to the Protestant critique of Latin American Catholicism. Noteworthy in Mackay's Christology is that he doesn't broach the area of ethics without first having examined the broader field of theology in the two themes noted above, the kingdom of God and the love of God. With this a principle is set down that today's evangelical Christology should never forget: a Christian ethic cannot be expected of people who do not know the redemptive power of Jesus Christ. For this reason evangelicals do not affirm that Latin America is already a Christian continent. On this point there is an open disagreement with Roman Catholic theologians. Commenting on the parable of the good Samaritan, Mackay concludes:

> Something more is needed for the spirit of the good Samaritan to be translated into the philanthropy required in a time twenty centuries after

---

[28]Mackay, "*. . . Mas yo os Digo*," 55.
[29]Mackay, "*. . . Mas yo os Digo*," 123-24.
[30]Mackay, "*. . . Mas yo os Digo*," 55.

> Christ lived. Sporadic charity is not sufficient, nor even systematic charity, for the relief of suffering; the primary responsibility of good Samaritans today is to show their passion for humanity in working toward the disappearance of the avoidable causes of suffering. This is a much more difficult charity, more complicated and more prosaic than direct help to the needy. It will always be necessary to have oil and wine to dress the wounds, and arms to carry unfortunate travelers, but even more necessary is the charity that studies the problem caused by cruel, wounding hands and the insensitivity of those capable of witnessing human pain without feeling any responsibility.[31]

Like other evangelical missionaries, Mackay brings a pietistic perspective, attentive to personal conversion and cultivating a relationship with God in a life of disciplined devotion. But Mackay's Reformed background takes him further, to formulate the necessity for a social ethic such that the Teacher's disciples do not only serve the victims of injustice but also seek to correct unjust structures. This is the Savior and Lord that Mackay proclaimed to university youth during the third decade of the twentieth century, forty years prior to the stirrings of a movement to rediscover the Christ of Scripture and of liberation theology. Many years later, in his commentary on the epistle to the Ephesians, Mackay develops his Christology with eschatological notes from a Pauline perspective enriching an overall vision of history that discerned "the order of God and human disorder."

Thus the Christology of early Protestantism represents a current of fresh water in the middle of the desert of religious and spiritual life on the continent at the beginning of the twentieth century. All the contributions we will consider later would not have been possible without this pioneering labor of church planters such as Penzotti and Ritchie, with their simple pastoral language, or theologian-evangelists such as Mackay, who made the gospel of Jesus Christ resonate in the student world and in Ibero-American cultural circles.

---

[31]Mackay, ". . . *Mas yo os Digo*," 190-91.

The Hispanic American Evangelical Congress in Havana

An indication of evangelical progress in Ibero-America was the congress that took place in Havana (June 20-30, 1929). It was the third continental Protestant gathering, the first having taken place in Panama in 1916 and the second in Montevideo in 1925. In the sequence of these gatherings there was a progressive Latin Americanization of Protestantism. The Committee of Cooperation in Latin America was the sponsor for all three congresses. In the first meeting, in Panama, English-speaking missionary agencies took initiative, and the meetings were in English. In Montevideo the gathering was bilingual, and in Havana it was in Spanish. In Havana there were 169 delegates representing thirteen countries; eighty-six delegates were Latin Americans, forty-four were missionaries, and thirty-nine participants represented boards and specialists. In the words of Gonzalo Báez-Camargo, the chronicler of the event: "In Havana the congress was organized and led by Latin Americans. From the beginning of organizing the event, during the sessions, and even the closure, the evangelicals from the United States left the responsibility of leading on the shoulders of the Latin Americans."[32] It was a sign of the health of Latin American Protestantism, such that Alberto Rembao could say a number of years later: "There is a homegrown Protestantism, in contrast to 'exotic' Protestantism, which clusters around the missionaries, as it did fifty years ago. . . . The cultural and religious fact, palpable and tangible, is that *I know what Protestant is in Spanish*. The message now sprouts from this soil."[33]

Straightaway the congress offered a "Religious Overview of Hispano-America" that was marked by vigorous debates and interacted with the thinking of well-known intellectuals such as Argentinian Ricardo Rojas, Chilean Gabriela Mistral, and Peruvian Manuel Gonzalez Prada. In this way the generation of Protestants who participated in the congress began

[32]Quoted by Wilton M. Nelson, "En busca de un protestantismo latinoamericano. De Montevideo 1925 a La Habana 1929," in *Oaxtepec 1978: Unidad y misión en América Latina* (San José, Costa Rica: CLAI, 1980), 37.

[33]Alberto Rembao, *Discurso a la nación evangélica* (Buenos Aires: La Aurora, 1949), 15.

to reach theological maturity, able to understand the currents of renewal in their own Latin American culture. Although to the eye of a casual observer Hispano-America might have appeared deeply and completely Catholic, "delving a little deeper, a closer look discovers the complexity of the religious phenomenon." The report says, "The majority practice a strange religion that wants to be a type of traditional Catholicism, but actually it involves only vaguely Christian ideas, pagan concepts, and practices of fetishism." Meanwhile, "As for members of the upper class and the learned Catholics, they profess their religion for social convenience, as a note of status, as an indispensable element to enhance the lavishness and public drama of life's grand occasions: baptism, first Communion, marriage, and death."[34]

There are also references to the diverse festive dimensions of popular religion and the intolerance of the Catholic Church toward Protestant presence: "The Catholic multitudes constantly turn their religious enthusiasm toward practical hedonism in the festivities and the crudeness of fanaticism. To whip up their fervor, they need to appeal to subconscious sentiments of hate toward those who do not think like they do."[35] The lack of the ethical dimension in religious practice is another problem: "As for what shapes morality, we have lived and continue to live in a pagan divorce between ritual and conduct. The religion approves and is practiced as a system of external forms but does not invade the spheres of life to guide individual and social conduct."[36]

In the congress's exploration of the causes of the religious situation, there is analysis of the role played by the Roman Catholic Church in Latin American society; the church is said to be marked by "a dogmatism without space for individual thought," which has impelled curious minds into agnosticism. There is further reference to "the church's retreat from the social and spiritual needs of our people." The diagnosis

---

[34]Gonzalo Báez-Camargo, *Hacia la renovación religiosa en Hispanoamérica* (Mexico City: CUPSA, 1930), 9.

[35]Báez-Camargo, *Hacia la renovación religiosa*, 10.

[36]Báez-Camargo, *Hacia la renovación religiosa*, 11.

is direct and coincides with that made by Catholic theologians themselves decades later:

> The church interpreted the kingdom of heaven as a state of blessing in the life to come and not as a kingdom of charity, fraternity, and justice in this earthly world that we live in. And while preaching resignation and hope to the unhappy and oppressed, they forgot to preach justice and love to the pitiless owners and capitalist slave traders. They did not do anything effective to improve social conditions and to guide a wise evolution toward the liberation of the enslaved masses.[37]

The Congress and the Living Christ

In the congress there was a strong christological tone, which appears explicitly in the report in the section "The Congress and the Living Christ":

> And what place did Christ occupy in this congress? This is the touchstone to correctly evaluate the significance of a meeting like this. Individually and collectively, the lives and occasions that are most fruitful are those whose center is Jesus. So it is sufficient to examine the relative position of the Crucified One in a church, community, or representative assembly, like that in Havana, to assess its potential and to foreshadow the results.[38]

The report indicates that there had been fears that "certain corrosive currents of modern religious thought" might have influence over the development of the congress, which would have meant that "our deliberations and accords would have been presided over by a disfigured and impotent Christ." Following some discussions, however, "it was evident that all of us were committed to the living Christ of the Gospels, saying as Peter on that memorable occasion: 'Lord, to whom shall we go? Only you have the words of eternal life.'" There is also reference to an atmosphere of piety: "Daily, during the devotional hour, we did nothing more that seek the strength and inspiration for our tasks in communion with Christ." Then, at the close of each day, "during the final hour of meditation, each

---

[37]Báez-Camargo, *Hacia la renovación religiosa*, 14.
[38]Báez-Camargo, *Hacia la renovación religiosa*, 140.

one who spoke to us sought to help us feel the presence of this Eternal Christ of our faith."[39]

The report indicates that "while affirming an absolute loyalty to the essential principles of the gospel, the Congress was not willing to dogmatize these principles." This might be a reference to disquiet among some sectors of strongly pietist evangelicals who urged that the faith be articulated in dogmatic definitions. The report declares that what it advocates must be "very clear and without suspicion, with respect to the congress's position: faithfulness to the principles and the central doctrines of Christianity in terms of the person of Jesus, and at the same time, little willingness to formulate closed and rigid creeds." Among the recommendations approved by the Evangelization Commission: "Recommended priority topics are faith in Christ as Savior, repentance, and regeneration, that is, the presentation of a living Christ who regenerates the individual's heart and at the same time transforms society."[40]

---

[39]Báez-Camargo, *Hacia la renovación religiosa*, 140.
[40]Báez-Camargo, *Hacia la renovación religiosa*, 141, 142.

5

THE BEGINNINGS OF AN EVANGELICAL LATIN AMERICAN CHRISTOLOGY

In Christ a worker God is revealed. Ancient religions and philosophies conceived God as static and indifferent, or as a kind of Eastern ruler made into a god, who lay languorously in his high heavens, in sweet and eternal idleness, without more to do than receive the praises of his celestial court and take pleasure in the music of the spheres. It is as if Christ draws back in himself the curtain of heaven and shows us—I say this with total reverence!—a God in shirtsleeves, a God busy with the hard work of guiding the destiny of a world in which the sinful and rebellious will of people creates infinite problems and difficulties. Jesus once said, "To this day my Father is working, and I also work." These strong and callused hands of Christ the worker are in the first place a calling to cooperate with him.

GONZALO BÁEZ CAMARGO, *LAS MANOS DE CRISTO*

The power of encountering the Christ of the Gospels drove the first generations of Latin American evangelicals to proclamation in a rich variety of literary forms. Systematic-theological reflection came later, once the evangelical community came of age. The first expressions of Latin American evangelicalism were in journalism, hymnology, poetry, and most of all preaching. These are the manifestations that must be explored, since systematic reflection in these early generations was mostly in response to translations of evangelical classics from the English-speaking world. However, attention to these writings reveals creative uses of Scripture as well as hermeneutical and contextualizing processes that have not been appreciated for all they are worth.

In constructing Christology, we should not discount the value of these kinds of sources. If we take the example of journalism, we see an effort to reach a large public with specific aspects of the gospel referring to Jesus Christ. If we consider hymnology and poetry, we see important endeavors to form evangelical believers through liturgy and Christian education. The examples here are limited to the materials available, but I believe that they are representative.

Public reading of the Bible and singing occupied a central place in the evangelical experience, which in the early decades of the Protestant presence in Spain as well as Ibero-America contrasted with traditional services and Catholic liturgy. Both public reading of the Bible and singing were cultivated even in the most distant and rural congregations, where there often were no musical instruments. In both practices memorization played an important role. The Bible translation most commonly used by evangelicals was that of Casiodoro de Reina and Cipriano de Valera (called Reina y Valera), a jewel of literature from Spain's golden age for its beauty and clarity of expression. The small Spanish Protestant movement of the nineteenth and early twentieth centuries was persecuted and treated with intolerant hostility. Despite this it contributed a rich hymnology with high-quality lyrics to the Spanish-speaking world, sometimes original and sometimes translated from English.

During the first decades of the twentieth century, evangelicals read the Bible and sang in good Spanish. Our vocabulary was enriched with reading and learning from the Reina y Valera translation and from hymns. When I was a child in the 1930s in my birth city of Arequipa in the south of Peru, we young people of the evangelical church sang of Christ. I still remember a christological hymn that was most piercing in its refrain:

I will sing to Christ, who in humility always fulfilled the divine will
The sick he healed, the dead he raised to life,
The poor he filled with his goodness
None can equal his infinite love, for on the cross he gave his life for me
I will extol his sweet name, yes, eternal Savior, I give all praise to you!

The imagery in the words, along with the colored pictures used to tell Bible stories, worked to shape in us the image of a Christ active in service to the world, one who loved children, was effective as a teacher, and was courageous in the face of persecution and death.

Once we arrived in our teenage years, the time of decisions and professions of faith, when one's own will becomes clearer and the deep affections that begin to shape the rest of one's life are formed, our song was a prayer to Christ for direction in life:

Christ, be my pilot on the stormy sea;
Wild waves will surely cause my ship to sink,
But if you are with me soon I will arrive in port.
Guide and compass I've found in you: Christ my pilot be!
The hurricane whips everything with savage fury,
But the winds will stop at the sound of your voice;
And when you say, "Peace, be still," the sea submits.
You are Lord of the waters. Guide me, O faithful pilot!

The Founders of Latin American Evangelical Thought

In my effort to lay out the development of Latin American evangelical thought, I have assigned the descriptor "the founders" to the generation of evangelicals who began to articulately express their faith in Jesus Christ, voicing their Protestant convictions within a clear perception of their own Latin American context. Those belonging to this generation include Mexicans Gonzalo Báez-Camargo (1899–1983) and Alberto Rembao (1895–1962), Puerto Ricans Angel M. Mergal (1909–1971) and Domingo Marrero Navarro (1909–1960), and Argentinians Santiago Canclini (1900–1977) and Carlos T. Gattinoni (1907–1989). Another was Sante Uberto Barbieri (1902–1991), who was born in Italy and lived later in Brazil and Argentina, and who wrote in Spanish. Several in this generation participated in important historic movements in their countries and in the task of producing culture and literature. At the same time, they understood the Protestant message deeply enough to be able to contextualize in a way appropriate for their national or continental culture. Just as there were Latin Americans such as José Carlos Mariátegui from Peru and Pablo Neruda in Chile, who by abandoning their childhood Catholic tradition had access to a global perspective through Marxism, the generation of the evangelical founders gained access to a global Christianity when they embraced Protestantism.

Many members of this group of Latin Americans, born with the twentieth century or a little before or after, were part of a second or third generation of Latin American Protestants. They lived Protestantism from the inside and stayed within it, though with time they began to critique their history, institutions, and life. Some of them influenced the work of the previous generation of evangelical influencers, as is in the case of Báez-Camargo, whose presentation in Havana seems to have influenced the final version of Mackay's *The Other Spanish Christ*. Some members of the founders' generation were not known for their written works or theological reflection but instead for their teaching and training in theological institutions or in the churches they led. Others followed a literary vocation and left an inheritance of writings that allow us to take the pulse of thought during their time.

At this stage Christology was essentially commentary on the biblical text in the best evangelical tradition. The integrity of Scripture was not questioned, nor was how the text was formed a topic of exploration, though some considered here, such as Báez-Camargo, were biblical scholars who worked extensively in translation of the text from its original languages. In most of the works from this time there is little reference to systematic doctrinal or dogmatic development. What *is* present is creativity in reading that comes from these thinkers' immersion in the cultural and intellectual production of their time. Because of their command of the written word, they were able to communicate in challenging yet accessible ways. For example, their rediscovery of the humanity of Jesus demonstrates the richness of the biblical text and its ability to touch the heart of contemporary readers. Their writings originated in the most natural way from social criticism and the challenge of discipleship.

An example of this kind of homiletic reflection is the book *Pasa Jesús: Meditaciones sobre el evangelio* (Jesus is passing by: Meditations on the gospel) by Argentinian Santiago Canclini, one of the best preachers of his generation. Each of his ten chapters is a reflection on a passage from Luke, Mark, or John. In the introduction he refers to Teófilo Gautier's novel about an Egyptian mummy and, drawing a contrast, says:

> To discover the motive of our meditations we haven't opened a tomb, but we have opened the Living Book, finding there no dead mummy in a magnificent doctrinal sarcophagus but a powerful Savior who lives, who loves, and who works today, as yesterday and forever. May the footprints of Jesus that still pass in front of us remain indelibly stamped in our lives by the power of his Spirit![1]

Let us take the time to explore three Mexican writers representative of this generation, whose theology was expressed not so much in treatises of systematic theology as in journalism, hymnology, poetry, and preaching. These are the manifestations that we must explore, since, as previously noted, in terms of systematic reflection this generation largely depended on classic texts from European Protestantism and theological studies from the English-speaking world.

The Christology of Gonzalo Báez-Camargo

Gonzalo Báez-Camargo, primary school teacher, fighter in the Mexican Revolution, well-known journalist, member of the Academia Mexicana de la Lengua (Mexican Academy of Language), Sunday school teacher, evangelical leader in his own country, and later one of the shapers of the ecumenical movement at a global level, was a distinguished Bible scholar whose work was undertaken under the auspices of the United Bible

---

[1]Santiago Canclini, *Pasa Jesús: Meditaciones sobre el evangelio* (Buenos Aires: Junta Bautista de Publicaciones, 1944), 5.

Society and the Methodist Church.[2] But it was his work as a journalist that took his writing to the multitudes of his country, via a column in the daily newspaper *Excelsior* in Mexico. His book *Las manos de Cristo* (The hands of Christ) is a collection of these articles, published for the first time in 1950.[3] It exemplifies the Christology that was widely shared among evangelicals of his generation, communicated mostly from pulpits and by radio.

Those of us who knew Gonzalo Báez-Camargo and who had the opportunity to work him were impressed by the enthusiasm and sense of vocation with which he undertook his tasks of teaching and writing—and also by his clear sense of belonging to an evangelical community, whose fraternal language he used without dramatic gestures but also without apologies. In our conversations he called me "Brother Escobar" with simplicity and ease. Because of this, if we want to find the impulse that motivated his work, we should explore the Christology of Báez-Camargo. My interest lies less in a scholarly effort to categorize his thinking into a theological school and more in explaining the living relationship with Christ that was visible in him as a person and that formed the foundation of his published work. This approach will permit us to discern the guiding outline of his Christology.

In Báez-Camargo's poetry, works of literary criticism, and what he called "lay sermons" in the pages of the *Excelsior* newspaper, we find creative use of Scripture, a hermeneutical and contextual process that already manifested marks of an indigenous (local or autochthonous) evangelical theology. These journalistic, literary, and homiletic sources are good starting points for a christological exploration. In his journalism, for example, we observe an effort to reach a large public with specific aspects of the evangelical message centered on Jesus Christ. Selection of

---

[2]Studies of Báez-Camargo are available in *Gonzalo Báez-Camargo: Una vida al descubierto* (Mexico City: CUPSA, 1994), and Jean Pierre Bastian, *Una vida en la vida del Protestantismo mexicano: Diálogos con Gonzalo Báez-Camargo*, with prologue and notes by Carlos Mondragón (Mexico City: Centro de Estudios del Protestantismo Mexicano, 1999).

[3]Gonzalo Báez-Camargo [pseud. Pedro Gringoire], *Las manos de Cristo* (Mexico City: CUPSA, 1950; 2nd ed., 1985).

themes and passages regarding Jesus' life needed to take into account a reading audience that was respectful of the Teacher but in general ignorant about his life, and thus it also required a familiarity with the christological content of the faith and a missionary sensitivity in the forging of an appropriate writing style. In Báez-Camargo's hymnology and poetry, on the other hand, we observe important elements for the formation of evangelical Christians through liturgy and Christian education.

A Spiritual Diagnosis of Latin America

As we saw in the previous chapter, in 1929 the Hispano-American Evangelical Congress took place in Havana. Báez-Camargo was then not yet thirty years old, and he was chosen to preside over the event. Historian Wilton Nelson indicates that he performed this task brilliantly, able to "lead the congress with 'Latin American grace' and 'Anglo-Saxon efficiency.'"[4] The consensus arrived at by historians, confirmed by a review of the documents, is that this congress signaled a consciousness that Latin American Protestantism had entered adulthood. In Havana most of the participants were Latin American leaders, and of them Báez-Camargo best articulated a clearly contextualized expression of evangelical mission. The quality of his work can be appreciated in the book of proceedings from the Havana congress, *Hacia la renovación religiosa en Hispanoamérica* (Toward religious renovation in Hispano-America).[5]

As we have seen, the congress considered a sweeping panorama of Latin America's spiritual and religious situation. After describing the formal lifelessness of the continent's predominant religiosity, Báez-Camargo affirmed that not all in the Latin American panorama was dark. "Spiritual currents of various shades fight desperately to inject into this sick continent's blood faith in the highest functions of our

---

[4] Wilton M. Nelson, "En busca de un protestantismo latinoamericano: De Montevideo 1925 a La Habana 1929," in *Oaxtepec 1978: Unidad y Misión en América Latina* (San José, Costa Rica: CLAI, 1980), 38. See also William Richey Hogg, *Ecumenical Foundations* (New York: Harper, 1982), 267-68.

[5] Gonzalo Báez-Camargo, *Hacia la renovación religiosa en Hispanoamérica* (Mexico City: Casa Unida de Publicaciones, 1930).

spirit, confidence in the invisible forces that created and sustain the cosmos, and the possibility of communion with them."[6] Amid such currents—a quest for morals without dogmas, Eastern thought, social Christianity, mystical spiritualism—Báez-Camargo found another one: "But not a few people look to Jesus. They do not always see him in the fullness of his meaning. But they try to know him and interpret him."[7] He himself gave the closing message: "No to Renan's literary Christ, no to Barbusse's socialist Christ, no to the trivial Christ of the Catholic legends, beautiful half-Christs, but the unique Christ, he who is found in the Gospels, the Son of God, Redeemer of the world, eternal Spirit whose work yesterday, today, and forever is the transforming of hearts."[8]

We could say that the christological agenda that the Havana congress proposed was transformed by Báez-Camargo within his own theological and literary agenda. Let us look at some aspects of this.

The Rediscovery of Jesus' Humanity

The first noteworthy element of the Christology in Báez-Camargo's *Excelsior* articles is their attractive and robust presentation of Jesus' humanity. This presentation is 100 percent based on biblical data, but Báez-Camargo's contextualization is highly precise and relevant. One of the most eloquent essays republished in his book *Las manos de Cristo* is "The Proletarian from Nazareth." Jesus' humanity is highlighted in this account of poverty and manual labor as the lifestyle chosen by the Teacher: "Jesus was a laborer. He was what we call 'proletarian.' No other lips could have so lovingly addressed working people with the well-known word COMRADE. No other hands, strong and callused from toiling in a workshop, could have grasped with greater compassion, with greater friendship, the strong and callused hands of fellow laborers."[9]

---

[6]Báez-Camargo, *Hacia la renovación religiosa*, 19.
[7]Báez-Camargo, *Hacia la renovación religiosa*, 18.
[8]Báez-Camargo, *Hacia la renovación religiosa*, 143.
[9]Báez-Camargo, *Las manos de Cristo*, 45, capitalization original.

Báez-Camargo shows that Jesus' teaching evidences a deep sensitivity toward the poor and a style of communicating with them that flowed from his own experience of poverty: "When he entered public life, he was not equipped with the treasures of learning. His words consistently reflect his life as a poor artisan." Though Jesus' spirituality was an indisputable reality, it reflected the human circumstances of his existence: "Jesus was a working man. He had to steal hours from sleep, get up before dawn if he wanted to enjoy a few peaceful moments for prayer and meditation. Mostly he prayed and meditated while he worked in his workshop among the wood chips, accompanied by the monotonous hum of the plane."[10]

The weight of the argument in many of these pages aims to counteract two types of disfigurement of the person of Jesus present in Latin America at this time. On the one hand, the popular Marxist press described Jesus as a defender of capitalism, in opposition to laborers. On the other hand, a certain popular artisan style produced a Jesus who appears almost feminine. In other chapters in *Las manos de Cristo*, Báez-Camargo begins by reflecting on the hands of Christ, based on details of the Gospels, and later draws conclusions about a biblical view of work, surveying pages of the Old and New Testaments:

> The first thing we notice as we contemplate the hands of Christ is that they are the manly and vigorous hands of a laborer. The hands of a worker: the carpenter of Nazareth. These hands are not white and flaccid like wilting lilies, the almost feminine hands that are often shown on liturgical altarpieces and on holy cards. In these hands, hands of a laborer, we find the first and highest affirmation of the dignity of manual labor and of the proletariat.[11]

Many evangelical thinkers used Holy Week as a basis for reflection, preaching, and poetry. Its scenes and events were taken as representative of the forces at play in every drama of history, followed by moves to contextualize throughout the continent. So Báez-Camargo, who briefly

---

[10]Báez-Camargo, *Las manos de Cristo*, 49, 48.
[11]Báez-Camargo, *Las manos de Cristo*, 11-12.

describes in his essay "Nuestro Señor del Látigo" (Our Lord of the Whip) the purification of the temple scene on Monday of Holy Week:

> The temple had been made into a market where devotion was trafficked, people's remorse was exploited, and piety was turned to profit. . . . But Jesus appears, transformed by divine indignation, indignation for the exploited poor and for the profaned house. He raises a whip—virile and majestic figure of our Lord of the Whip!—that creates confusion among the sellers of the altar, while his lips hiss, like another whip vibrating into flame, the compelling and enduring phrase: "You have made my house of prayer into a robbers' den."[12]

A Personal Relationship with Jesus as the Starting Point for the Christian Life

The second important element of Báez-Camargo's evangelical Christology is his insistence on the necessity of a personal relationship with Jesus Christ. This goes much further than an intellectual decision that is assimilated or a creed that is collectively confessed. While it is true that the person of Jesus is central to the Reformed Protestant tradition, in this emphasis on a personal relationship we see the mark of pietism, rooted in the Wesleyan heritage of Methodism, together with attention to the expiatory work of Jesus on the cross. The difference is established clearly when Báez-Camargo lays out the main points of the Methodist revival:

> Possessing "a theology of experienced grace," Methodism was freed from making theology into an obsession. Searching above all for a personal experience of regeneration, it avoided dogmatism's excesses. Like Jesus with Nicodemus, it did not present human souls with a discussion of opinions but rather the great question "Have you been born again?"[13]

A few lines further along, he adds:

> For in effect intellectual dogmatism, that is, a dominant preoccupation with mere orthodoxy, usurps the gospel at a deep level. It makes salvation consist not of the redemptive work of Christ, which believers accept for

---

[12]Báez-Camargo, *Las manos de Cristo*, 65.
[13]Gonzalo Báez-Camargo, *Genio y espíritu del metodismo wesleyano* (Mexico City: CUPSA, 1962), 15.

> themselves, personally, by faith, but rather of a comprehensive and sworn consent to a system of theological formulas. For the person of the living and cherished Christ it substitutes a beautiful, compact, consistent creed *about Christ*. And thus it proclaims that what saves is not to believe in Christ but to *have orthodox beliefs about Christ*.[14]

This same conviction also guides the literary efforts of Báez-Camargo, as we can observe in one of his most interesting works of theological literary criticism. In 1949, on the occasion of the First Latin American Evangelical Conference, held in Buenos Aires, he wrote one of the preliminary studies. He sought to explore "the evangelical mark on Hispano-American poetry" along the same lines as his work for the Havana congress. Báez-Camargo defines "four key elements [that] would be required to recognize as evangelical the tone and thrust of a composition."[15] First among them is the "centrality of Christ":

> This is the essential element in evangelical religion: the God who is worshiped is the God of Christ, the God revealed in Christ and by Christ. Supreme devotion is given to Christ. Obviously this is not the Christ of legends or from manmade rituals, or the stylized Christ of stamps and icons, but the Christ, both human and divine, found in the Gospels. And what constitutes the religious life in the evangelical vision is essentially a personal relationship of the soul with this Christ, and the experience of his redeeming grace.[16]

The other three elements include "the interiority of the religious experience. This personal communion with Christ flourishes in the depths of the spirit." Then there is "the centrality of faith over works . . . giving oneself without reserve to the grace of God in Jesus Christ, placing in grace, and not in dogmatic beliefs or pious works, the hope of justification and reconciliation." Finally is "the importance of love over precept, covetousness, and fear. What is most important isn't the act but its motivation."[17]

---

[14]Báez-Camargo, *Genio y espíritu*, 16.

[15]Gonzalo Báez-Camargo, *La nota evangélica en la poesía hispanoamericana* (Mexico City: Luminar, 1960), 8-10.

[16]Báez-Camargo, *La nota evangélica*, 8.

[17]Báez-Camargo, *La nota evangélica*, 9, 10.

Appropriation of the Redeeming Death of Jesus

A third notable element of Báez-Camargo's Christology emerges in a reflection on "It is finished," the words of Jesus on the cross, in which Báez-Camargo says:

> Love is finished, consummated: "Having loved his own, he loved them to the end." . . . Consummated is the sacrifice that is offered once and for all, without need of complement or repetition. A unique sacrifice, sufficient, perfect, that achieves a perfect forgiveness. Consummated is the redemption of humankind. Our guilt has been purged; the full price of our rescue has been paid. "God was in Christ reconciling the world to himself." The cross is the way, the truth, and the life.[18]

For Báez-Camargo, "Jesus is not only a historic fact but a real presence, living, warmly loving, and close. So close that it is possible, here and now, to communicate with him, be with him, and live with him forever."[19] It is the personal step of faith that allows us to have this relationship with Jesus today:

> The truth and the power of this word of the cross, which, at the same time that it guides a person to despair of himself moves him to hope in divine grace alone, are shown in the uncountable number of souls who at the foot of the cross have let go of the cord of their efforts to be perfect and have taken the great leap into the unknown, beyond logic and all human reason, to take hold of the hand that reaches out to them from "the foolishness of the cross."[20]

Báez-Camargo's intense intellectual and literary efforts led him in 1936 to found the magazine *Luminar* (Star), which was published in Mexico until 1951. It was able to attract to its pages an array of European, North American, and Latin American thinkers, among them Russian Nicholas Berdyaev, Peruvian Luis Alberto Sánchez, Frenchman Marcel Bataillon, Argentinian Francisco Romero, German Max Planck, and dozens more Christian and non-Christian authors. As historian Carlos Mondragón

[18]Báez-Camargo, *Las manos de Cristo*, 105.
[19]Báez-Camargo, *Las manos de Cristo*, 166.
[20]Báez-Camargo, *Las manos de Cristo*, 126.

reminds us, *Luminar* became a platform for a wide-reaching and respectful dialogue and interpretation of the changing global reality of these decades: "While demonstrating an open and critical editorial stance, the editor made clear the 'Christian' character of the new publication" and specified the scope of its orientation:

> But to say LUMINAR is a Christian magazine is not at all to say it is a dogmatic or confessional magazine. LUMINAR believes that the truth is in Christ, but doesn't believe that this truth can be confined, packaged, or bottled in dogmatic declarations or formulas or definitive recipes. Christ is the way, the truth, the life. But this way is not fenced off by ecclesiastical walls.[21]

Mondragón highlights that the evangelical magazines *Luminar* and *La Nueva Democracia* (The new democracy) were forums for critiques of fascism, which during the 1930s rose to power in Spain, Italy, and Germany and then led to World War II.[22] Between 1936 and 1939 a terrible civil war raged in Spain. Many Latin American intellectuals expressed support for the republican movement that confronted the rebellion of General Francisco Franco, who with the help of Mussolini and Hitler finally gained victory and established a totalitarian regime—which the Roman Catholic Church roundly and publicly supported. Franco used the gestures, symbols, and religious motifs of traditional Spanish Catholicism. In fact he called his movement a crusade. Báez-Camargo wrote a poem in this period titled "Dejad en paz a Cristo, generales" (Leave Christ in peace, generals), in which he eloquently protests against using the Christian faith as justification for war, ideological intolerance, and the defense of militarism and capitalism:

> Leave Christ in peace, generals!
> Generals with bulging bellies,
> With sumptuous gold braids and bloody hands!
> Don't pretend to make him patron of your war,

---

[21]Quoted by Carlos Mondragón, "Báez Camargo: Una faceta de su vida cultural," in *Gonzalo Báez-Camargo: Una vida al descubierto*, 126.

[22]Carlos Mondragón, *Leudar la masa: El pensamiento social de los protestantes en América Latina* (Buenos Aires: Kairós, 2005). See especially chap. 5, "Dios y los rostros del fascismo."

Nor your henchman, nor brother in arms or accomplice
In your huge barracks and your crimes! . . .
Leave Christ in peace, generals!
Christ doesn't need gunmen
To defend him
Or swordsmen
To guard his back!
His cause and truth one day
Will flood the earth like water,
Fill the immensity of the oceans
But through the way of Love. . . .
Not by the cursed
And demonic way of war![23]

A Spirituality of Personal Relationship and Contemplation of Jesus

Few Latin Americans from the generation under consideration were able to articulate the dimensions of evangelical spirituality like Mexican poet and professor Francisco Estrello. For Estrello the Christian life is to follow Christ. Knowledge of the facts of Jesus' life is the compass that guides us on how to follow him today:

> Christ is the Way. . . . The sense of direction for the Christian is an issue that is resolved by following Christ. I would say more that the sense of direction in life of the world is resolved in the same way. But it is Christians, and especially Christian youth, who are given the task of teaching people how to follow Christ, how to set foot on Christ's terrain, how to take the routes of Jesus, how to reach the goals of Christ.[24]

Following implies contemplation, with the heart and the ear attentive to the Teacher: "Sit at the feet of the Teacher and receive his words in the silence of your heart. His words will be like a comforting balm and like rain that falls to kiss the dry and thirsty earth. . . . Don't take your eyes from his face." The book from which these quotes are taken aimed to

[23]Gonzalo Báez-Camargo, fragments of "¡Dejad en paz a Cristo, generales!," in *El artista y otros poemas*, 3rd ed. (Mexico City: CUPSA, 1987), 45.
[24]Francisco E. Estrello, *En comunión con lo eterno*, 3rd ed. (Mexico City: CUPSA, 1975), 57.

"help make the act of worship, whether in private or in a group, become deeper and more inspiring. But also it aims to make it more beautiful. The central value is in the intensity of high spirituality pulsing through each of the selections that compose it."[25] Examining its rich texts, mainly from Ibero-American authors, allows us to see that the evangelical cultivation of spirituality was profoundly Christ-centered.

In Estrello's spirituality, contemplation of Christ led to a devotion expressed in beautifully crafted poems such as this one, about the hands of Christ:

Hands of Christ
Divine hands of a carpenter. . . .
I do not imagine those hands
Forging spears, crafting swords,
Nor designing a new model of bomber;
Those hands, Christ's hands,
Were the hands of a carpenter.
Among feverish hands
That make boats and bombers,
His hands are not found!
His hands bear nail marks,
Heroic signs of sacrifice;
Those hands, bloody hands,
Strong, sinewy, hands of iron,
The sturdy hands of a carpenter
Who quietly shapes life.[26]

Another Mexican, Vicente Mendoza, wrote one of the first Latin American written hymns that was sung in churches throughout the continent. Its melody had the waltzing rhythm frequently used in Mexican songs, which allowed it to be easily memorized:

Jesus is my sovereign King, my joy is to sing his praise,
He is King and sees me as his brother, he is King and he gives me
his love.

[25]Estrello, *En comunión con lo eterno*, 103, 7.
[26]Francisco E. Estrello, *Posada junto al camino* (Mexico City: Imprenta Mexicana, 1951), 96-97.

Leaving behind his throne of glory, he came to lift me up from
life's dregs,
And I am happy, I am happy because of him.
Jesus is my yearned-for friend, and in shadows or in light he is
always there
Patient, humble by my side, and he helps and rescues me.
And so I follow him faithfully, because he is my King and my friend,
And I am happy, and I am happy because of him.

Alberto Rembao and Evangelical Culture

Alberto Rembao, a Mexican from Chihuahua and member of the Congregational Church, veteran of the Mexican Revolution and well-known educator, became known throughout Latin America and the United States mainly through his work on the magazine *La Nueva Democracia* (The new democracy), which was founded in 1920 by the Comité de Cooperación en América Latina (Committee for Cooperation in Latin America) and published until 1963. Rembao was its editor from 1931 until his death in 1962. He moved to live in New York, where he maintained correspondence with a wide group of notable Latin American intellectuals of varying tendencies. Some of his books are compilations of articles and editorials from *La Nueva Democracia*, for example *Meditaciones neoyorquinas* (New York meditations).[27] Rembao strove to make known the Protestant presence and roots in Latin America and to interpret what he called "the evangelical culture." His classic work, which had a great impact in its time, is *Discurso a la nación evangélica* (Address to the evangelical nation).[28] Possessed of a vigorous and idiosyncratic style not always easy to follow and replete with biblical and historical allusions, Rembao was an evangelical chronicler and commentator on cultural currents in the United States and Latin America. His Christology emerged from a dialogue with daily life, recent publications, visits from intellectual friends, and notable events. In a reflection dedicated to

[27] Alberto Rembao, *Meditaciones neoyorquinas* (Buenos Aires: La Aurora, 1939).

[28] Alberto Rembao, *Discurso a la nación evangélica* (Buenos Aires: La Aurora; Mexico City: CUPSA, 1949).

the topic "God is not an object of scientific study," we find this paragraph of singular theological depth:

> I do not know God; but I am willing to chance my destiny and the salvation of my soul and being to Jesus of Nazareth, the very one into whom the eternal Christ emptied himself, according to a saying of Scripture, a saying that I find most worthy of my belief. And I will anticipate your question. I do not say that Christ is like God, but rather that God is like Christ . . . from the known to the unknown.[29]

Rembao identifies as evangelical culture the way of life that evangelical communities were developing out of the commitment of their members, a collective entity that at a continental level he calls "the evangelical nation." He explains it in the following way: "A nation is valued for the sum of those who are born there, and those reborn—those who have been delivered twice, those born with him and for him. In sum, those of the contemporary spiritual aristocracy: the evangelicals of Hispano-America."[30] Commenting on Philippians 2:7, he affirms: "Within evangelical culture God is not an idea, but a divine spirit that in a historical man took earthly form, in the sacred womb of the highly favored one." Rembao considers the deity of Christ a fundamental part of the Christian perspective:

> The word *deity* is used to not fall into error or into the ambiguity of the word *divinity*. It is not proper to say that Christ is divine. Rather, we affirm that Christ is God. In any well-forged humanistic theology the divinity of Christ and the divinity of all of creation can be held simultaneously, as creation is also the work of God. In such an invention Christ is part of creation, but not the author of creation, as the Pauline interpretation states in Colossians 1:16. . . . The deity of Christ is highlighted because in it rests the uniqueness, the difference, the superiority of the evangelical culture on this topic: because this fact goes against nature and against science and against philosophy; because it is the oft-referenced stumbling block for the Jews and the unitarian humanists. . . . The central statement of the evangelical position before the world is this: Christ is God.[31]

---

[29]Rembao, *Meditaciones neoyorquinas*, 51.
[30]Rembao, "Definición del encabezado," introduction to *Discurso a la nación evangélica*, 9.
[31]Rembao, "Definición del encabezado," 21.

With Rembao we have entered into Ibero-American christological reflection with an affirmative but also challenging position.

Conclusion

The contributions of the founding generation of evangelical thinkers had a clear Christ-centered emphasis and a missionary dimension, for they were articulated with the aim that the person and message of Jesus Christ should reach the world outside the evangelical community. From their literary and journalistic pulpits, Báez-Camargo, Estrello, and Rembao proclaimed the Christ of the Gospels in ways that were faithful to the origins of the Christian faith and also relevant to the Latin American people.

The careful research of Costa Rican historian Arturo Piedra into Protestant evangelization in Latin America has paid special attention to the Evangelical Conference of Panama in 1916, which aimed to establish a foundation for greater cooperation among different organizations that worked at this time in Latin America. The Committee for Cooperation in Latin America was founded as a result. When this conference took place, colporteurs and Protestant missionaries had been preaching the gospel message for half a century in Latin America. It was organized by enthusiastic missionaries from the United States who did not accept the decision of the 1910 Edinburgh Missionary Conference to deny recognition to Protestant missionary work in countries considered Catholic or Orthodox. Among the organizers were people who had been influenced by new currents of theology in the United States at that time that put significant emphasis on the social dimensions of the Christian message and who did not accept the traditional evangelical position with regard to the person and message of Christ.[32] The noteworthy thing about the founding generation is that in their effort to contextualize faith they rediscovered the humanity of Christ and the social dimension of

[32]Arturo Piedra, *Evangelización protestante en América Latina: Análisis de las razones que justificaron y promovieron la expansión protestante*, 2nd ed. (Quito: CLAI, 2002). See especially the section "Jesús trasciende la teología" in chap. 3.

the gospel, yet they maintained the basic framework of traditional evangelical Christology. In this aspect of their understanding of faith, they maintained the orthodoxy of their predecessors.

Historian Carlos Mondragón, who has researched the social thinking of the generations we have been exploring, highlights the sociological consequences of bringing a personal relationship with Christ into the center of Christian experience. It constituted a questioning of the Roman Catholic Church's claim to be the only entity authorized to interpret Christ's teachings and offer people a relationship with Christ. Mondragón says:

> Based on their theological position, as they considered Catholicism, the Protestants asked: Why are the priestly bureaucracy and pope necessary if "only Christ saves and we can have direct access to him"? Why are the mediation of the saints and penances necessary? This perspective justified their life independent of the authority of Rome, along with their proselytizing activity in a Latin America that for them was Christian in name only.[33]

[33]Carlos Mondragón, *Leudar la masa: El pensamiento social de los protestantes en América Latina: 1920–1950* (Buenos Aires: Kairos, 2005), 86.

6

CHRIST IN ECUMENICAL PROTESTANT THOUGHT

Barth helps to center all our theological thought truly and effectively on the person of Christ. And it will be without a doubt a help with significant practical outworkings. In the face of the fanaticism and superstition of the environment, we are reminded that while the task of Christian preaching is to destroy false gods, this task is a secondary, a posteriori, consequence of the first task of preaching the true God. It is from the gospel that all natural theology is destroyed. It is from the gospel that humanity can be convinced of sin. It is from the gospel that all the denials of Christ that have arisen in America can be destroyed from their roots.

Emilio Castro, 1956

As noted in chapter one, Catholic theologian Elizabeth Johnson reminds us that 1951 was the year in which it can be said that the European Catholic world began its renewed christological search. We remember also that theologian John Mackay pointed out the lack of a vigorous presence of Christ and the Christian in Latin American literature. Regarding this lack, Spanish Catholic scholar José Antonio Carro Celada writes:

> The better-known narrators only employ the Christian theme, when they do so at all, as a contextual resource that produces good results, either artificial or real. Such background allusions to the Christian life are not

> integral to the story or have very little significance; they remain mere anecdotes or are decorative, exemplifying the customs of popular religiosity, more as a cultural phenomenon than as an expression of faith.[1]

For this reason, it is noteworthy that in literature from the 1950s we see new references to Christ in both prose and poetry.

Caballero Calderón and Christ with His Back Turned

A Colombian novel published in Buenos Aires in 1952 led to notable repercussions in Colombia and throughout the American continent: *El Cristo de espaldas* (Christ with his back turned) by Eduardo Caballero Calderón. The novel bears as its epigraph Matthew 10:16-22, where Jesus speaks about the presence of his disciples as sheep among wolves and about the violence that will arise against them. The central character is a priest recently graduated from seminary and sent to serve in a small Colombian village that, like many others in that country, is shaken by the devastating political violence that continues to be felt today. The dark world of political corruption, the clash of social classes, and fratricide that was destroying Colombia is reflected in the novel as the priest, similar to Christ, lives out a painful Calvary between Thursday and Sunday. With surprise and pain he discovers a tangled web of vested interests, disloyalties, and abuses that he dares to identify and denounce amid a tragedy in the village. He wants to be Christ among the country people, and in the end he is met with violence from the faithful of his parish and a lack of understanding from his religious superiors. The bishop who admonishes him to return to seminary accuses him of letting himself be dominated by pride and concludes by saying to him, "My son, it is as if Christ has turned his back on you. But be assured that you will find him again among the children, in the seminary." The priest imagines replying but does not dare to do so: "Christ has not turned his back, Your Excellence, for I feel him alive and burning in my heart, and my heart is not mistaken.

[1]José Antonio Carro Celada, *Jesucristo en la literatura española e hispanoamericana del siglo XX* (Madrid: Biblioteca de Autores Cristianos, 1997), 18.

You will see, Your Excellence: what has happened is that men have turned *their* backs on Christ."[2]

Caballero Calderón's work is similar to the novel *Nazarín* by Spanish author Benito Peréz Galdós, where the presence of a priest who desires to be like Christ in a setting of misery and contradictions offers a way to explore social ills and the Christian's presence in the world. *Nazarín* was adapted for film by director Luis Buñuel in 1958 but in the film is set in Mexico at the beginning of the twentieth century. It is considered one of the hundred best movies made in Mexico. The characters created by Caballero Calderón and Pérez Galdós are able to plausibly incarnate the knot of contradictions generated in a community by an unexpected appearance of goodness and innocence. Both are marked, however, by impotence before the power of evil. These literary works, in which a protagonist evokes the figure of Christ among human beings, set a precedent for Mexican novelist Vicente Leñero's novel *El evangelio de Lucas Gavilán* (The Gospel of Lucas Gavilán), a paraphrase of the Gospel of Luke set in a poverty-stricken neighborhood in the Mexican capital.

Christological Notes in Latin American Poetry

The First National Prize for Poetry of 1944 in Argentina was won by Francisco Luis Bernárdez (1900–1978), who is widely recognized for his literary oeuvre and for the quality of his poetry. Remarkably, many of his poems express his Christian faith without inhibitions and with eloquent, well-crafted lyricism. Some of his poems touch on stories from the life of Jesus, such as these excerpts from poems about the nativity and the cross.

> He knocked with a tired hand
> at the door of the inn,
> but there was no place
> for God to be born.
> He made his way all through Bethlehem
> without finding a heart

[2]Eduardo Caballero Calderón, *El Cristo de espaldas* (Bogotá: Editorial Victor Hugo, 1952), 165.

that would make a small space
out of love for this birth.
Lord, a stable will be best.

Bird that has settled
on the shoulder of Jesus:
sing out your whole song
while the light goes out,
for in the silent world,
none is able like you
to comfort with a song
the Lord who is on the cross.
Man, flower, star, bird:
This cross is your cross.[3]

In certain moments his poems achieve particular theological acuity. For example, in his "Soneto de la encarnación" (Incarnation sonnet), published in 1937 in the collection *Cielo de tierra* (Heaven of earth), the figures of speech expressing all that the coming of Christ means for the human experience give evidence of a rich Christology:

So the soul may live in harmony
with the matter of day to day,
and, paying the original debt,
the human night is turned to day;
so that your poverty and mine are changed
by extraordinary riches
and so that the necessary death
becomes an everlasting freshness,
what has no beginning begins,
what is beyond space shrinks down,
the day transforms into dark night,
immense wealth changes into poverty,
the model of all imitates us,
the Creator becomes a creature.[4]

---

[3]Francisco Luis Bernárdez, "El establo" and "La cruz," in *Antología poética* (Madrid: Espasa Calpe, Colección Austral, 1972), 131, 144.
[4]Bernárdez, "Soneto de la encarnación," in *Antología poética*, 51.

Christological themes take a different turn in a famous poem by Peruvian Alejandro Romualdo Valle, who uses vocabulary and imagery from the Gospels to highlight the heroic sacrifice of Tupac Amaru, an indigenous revolutionary leader who was brutally dismembered by the Spanish in Cusco in May 1781. The poem "Canto coral a Tupac Amaru que es la libertad" (Choral song to Tupac Amaru, who is liberty) was first published in the collection *Edición especial* (Special edition; Lima, 1958). It describes the barbarous torture inflicted on the indigenous hero and repeats a litany that includes the line "¡Y no podrán matarlo!" (And they will not be able to kill him!). The poem seems to contain a type of warning regarding popular revolutions in general:

> They will want to carve him up, to crush him,
> to stain him, trample him, take away his soul.
> They will want to blow him up and will not be able to blow him up.
> They will want to break him and will not be able to break him.
> They will want to kill him and will not be able to kill him.
> On the third day of his sufferings,
> when it is thought that all is finished,
> shouting "Liberty!" over the earth,
> he will return.
> And they will not be able to kill him.[5]

The allusion to the third day, among other christological motifs in the work of this poet, brings us to a current that emerged in the following decades from some forms of liberation theology: the identification of messianic motifs in Scripture and the Christian tradition with popular uprisings of the past and the present.

The Beginnings of Protestant Theological Thought

During the 1950s a Protestant theology began to take shape that moved from proclamation of Christ in the ways we have already explored to a systematic reflection on the Christian message. I have called the generation that introduces this era "ecumenical Protestantism," because it was born

---

[5]In Alberto Escobar, ed., *Antología de la poesía peruana* (Lima: Peisa, 1973), 1:147.

within the Protestant denominations that were attracted to the ecumenical movement, which culminated in the formation of the World Council of Churches in 1948. The ecumenical movement had greatest impact where for historic reasons a missionary Protestantism with English and Scottish roots had developed, such as among the Methodists and Presbyterians. This was joined with the Protestantism brought about through migration or transplantation, such as the Anglicans who formed part of the British migration, the German Lutherans, and the Waldensians from Italy and Switzerland, into countries such as Argentina, Uruguay, Brazil, Mexico, and Chile. Some of the oldest theological seminaries in Latin America, which would become centers of theological reflection and production, were connected to these churches and to the ecumenical movement.

These older denominations are usually called "historic" to distinguish them from the newer interdenominational or independent mission organizations that arrived post–World War II, particularly from the United States. Missiologist Kenneth Strachan coined the term "nonhistoric groups" to refer to these missions, although that term may be misleading since as far back as the late nineteenth century there were mission organizations and national churches that did not share the ecumenical vision of the older denominations. Tending toward theological conservatism, many of these groups were suspicious of the ecumenical movement and began to form their own theological institutions. The 1950s saw the beginning of a divergence in Latin American Protestantism between the ecumenical groups and the more conservative ones, who adopted for themselves the adjective *evangelical*.[6] José Miguel Bonino must be credited with the most precise description or typology of the different "faces" of Latin American Protestantism.[7]

In 1950 the ecumenical journal *Cuadernos Teológicos* (Theological notebooks) was founded in Buenos Aires, sponsored by four interdenominational seminaries and faculties of theology in Buenos Aires,

[6]I have devoted more space to this topic in chap. 3 of my book *La fe evangélica y las teologías de la liberación* (El Paso: CBP, 1987). See also Daniel Salinas, *Latin American Evangelical Theology in the 1970s* (Leiden: Brill, 2009), especially chap. 1.

[7]José Míguez Bonino, *Faces of Latin American Protestantism* (Grand Rapids: Eerdmans, 1996).

Argentina; Matanzas, Cuba; Mexico City; and Río Piedras, Puerto Rico. Analysis of the journal's content reveals that these seminaries were centers of reflection nurtured not only by reflection on the work of European and North American authors but also by a contextualized Latin American theological articulation. Its editors were Bowman Foster Stockwell, a Methodist missionary settled in Argentina, and Baptist thinker Angel M. Mergal, from Puerto Rico. There is a christological focus in the intention of the directors, eloquently expressed by Mergal: "These *Theological Notebooks* are sent out into the extensive fields of intellectual life of Latin America with a purpose: to unravel, to illuminate, and to enrich these crucial ideas that are for us the unique and marvelous Word that comes to us from the very heart of God, and that which the sacred Scriptures call the Word made flesh."[8]

Stockwell, the other editor, had been a Methodist missionary in Argentina since 1927 and stood out as an educator and writer. His 1936 book *¿Qué podemos creer?* (What can we believe?) was an effort to articulate the basics of the Christian faith for thinking Christians. Stockwell had been educated in Germany and was familiar with the theological debates of the first decades of the twentieth century. The chapter in his book focused on Jesus Christ offers a clear summary of the christological issues in the European and North American academic context at that time, though with a pastoral focus rather than an academic one. Beginning with an exposition of the origin of the names *Jesus* and *Christ*, he explains:

> In modern times sometimes a distinction has been drawn between "the historical Jesus" and "the Christ of faith." But this distinction, although helpful in certain discussions, is not very precise. Both of these two names represent abstractions of the reality of global history and the Christian experience. This global reality is best expressed by saying "Jesus Christ" instead of using "Jesus" or "Christ."[9]

---

[8]Angel M. Mergal, editorial, *Cuadernos Teológicos*, no. 1 (1950): 4.

[9]B. Foster Stockwell, *¿Qué podemos creer? / ¿Qué es el protestantismo?* (Buenos Aires: La Aurora, 1987), 182. This is a combined edition of the two early Stockwell books that has been reedited for the series Obras clásicas del Protestantismo.

Further, he says that though many find it difficult to accept the divinity of Christ, "perhaps you will be surprised to learn that during the early centuries of Christianity one of the greatest problems was not the divinity of Christ but his humanity." Later he explains docetism and makes a statement that surprised many: "The church had to fight against this wave of thought. Truth be told, it has been said that the four Gospels would never have been given so much importance in the church if it hadn't been for the urgent need to uphold the true humanity of Christ."[10]

In his book *¿Qué es el protestantismo?* (What is Protestantism?), written in 1954 for general readers, Stockwell affirms Christ-centeredness as central to Protestant faith and experience: "The sixteenth-century Reformation was not born out of doubts regarding the traditional dogmas of the church, but rather from a new experience of the grace of God in Jesus Christ and a new understanding of the Christian faith as a personal way of life." A few lines down he adds: "The Protestant Reformation meant an affirmation of the supremacy of Jesus Christ, of the living and spiritual Christ in the life of the believer and of the church; and Protestantism in all its forms has been characterized by this essential characteristic."[11]

The article that opens the first issue of *Cuadernos Teológicos* is a clear and passionate reflection from John Mackay on "the restoration of theology." Mackay, who was at that time rector of Princeton Theological Seminary and very active in the ecumenical movement, strives to explain the need for theology, recognizing that within evangelical churches there are people who suspect that theology is an unnecessary and unfruitful exercise. He also affirms the need for theology for the church in a world in which totalitarian ideologies have gained the absolute loyalty of whole societies, giving rise to the Second World War. Only five years had passed since the end of that war, and the cultural atmosphere in Europe and North America was marked by disillusionment with the impotence of established Christianity to prevent that catastrophe. The vision of Christ that Mackay had been developing from the time that he adopted his

[10]Stockwell, *¿Qué podemos creer? / ¿Qué es el protestantismo?*, 183.
[11]Stockwell, *¿Qué podemos creer? / ¿Qué es el protestantismo?*, 59, 60.

christological agenda in *El otro Cristo español* led him to formulate the theological task with a christological principle:

> The Church needs to remember that God has spoken by word and deed on the plane of history. His everlasting "Nay" has sounded against all ultimate loyalty to whatever is not God. Be it Baal or Caesar that disputes his sovereignty, be it his rival the Mammon of materialism or the self of Idealism, God alone must be God in the life of men and nations. His everlasting "Yea" has also sounded in Jesus Christ, the God-Man. This must the Church also remember for her life and effective service. The God-Man is the starting point and soul of Christian theology, the center of history and the clue to its meaning, the mirror in which man comes to know himself and God, the Redeemer through faith in whom he is enabled to become what God intended him to be.[12]

In his book *A Preface to Christian Theology* (1946) Mackay had coined a metaphor that had circulated in the Latin American cultural environment. It is the difference between two contrasting human attitudes that he describes as "the balcony" and "the road," referring to the perspective from which humans search for truth. "The balcony," a small wooden or stone platform that juts out from a wall next to the high windows of the Spanish and Hispano-American houses "is the classical standpoint, and so the symbol, of the perfect spectator." On the other hand, the road is "the place where life is tensely lived, where thought had its birth in conflict and concern, where choices are made and decisions are carried out."[13] One does not come to know Christ observing the procession from the distance and comfort of the balcony, as a purely aesthetic experience that moves us to say "poor Christ." To know Christ one must walk the path and follow him to know whether what he says is the truth, and one must be willing to accept the consequences. With this same idea Mackay completes his reflection in 1950:

> Our role as teachers or students of Christian theology will be worthily fulfilled; we shall succeed in erasing the stigma attaching to theological

---

[12]John A. Mackay, "The Restoration of Theology," *Princeton Seminary Bulletin* 31, no. 1 (1937): 13.
[13]John A. Mackay, *A Preface to Christian Theology* (New York: Macmillan, 1946), 29-30.

> learning and escape the perils inherent in such learning in the measure, and only in the measure, in which faith in the Crucified commits us to the way of the Cross. Then as teachers and students we shall share the fellowship of His sufferings and follow our Master in loving, humble obedience in the tasks He assigns us in the life of today.[14]

Evangelical Thinkers in Puerto Rico

Another center for reflection was the Evangelical Seminary of Puerto Rico. In the case of this country we have a study about key Protestant theologians thanks to Puerto Rican theologian Luis Rivera Pagán.[15] Two of them are worth mentioning, and some of their works were published during the decade under consideration: Angel M. Mergal and Domingo Marrero. Mergal was a passionate scholar of the Reformation in Spain during the sixteenth century, as is shown in his book *Christian Reform and the Spanish Soul*, in which he suggests that the Reformation had a greater impact in Spain than scholars of that time wished to acknowledge.[16] Mergal in all his works aims to recuperate the elements of Hispanic culture that can connect with his exposition of an evangelical faith. We find clear christological emphasis in his book *The Christian Art of Preaching*, a work on homiletics that uses resources that were new in his time, such as anthropological, linguistic, grammatical, and rhetorical studies.[17]

In the first part of his book Mergal offers a theological introduction to the art of preaching. Within it is a lengthy meditation about the Christian experience of the preacher, from which sermons are birthed:

> We have seen that the qualities of a sermon can only be achieved when one has a global perspective of the truth, that which is the immediate and long-term goal of our preaching. The Christian minister is the adminis-

---

[14]Mackay, "Restoration of Theology," 17-18.

[15]Luis Rivera Pagán, *Senderos teológicos: El pensamiento evangélico puertorriqueño* (Río Piedras, Puerto Rico: La Reforma, 1989).

[16]Angel M. Mergal, *Reformismo cristiano y alma española* (Buenos Aires: La Aurora, 1949).

[17]Angel M. Mergal, *Arte cristiano de la predicación* (Puerto Rico: Comité de Literatura de la Asociación de Iglesias Evangélicas, 1951).

trator of the Word of God. He is the clay pot. He is not preaching about himself. Paul says, "It is my goal to know nothing among you, except Jesus Christ and his crucifixion, Jesus Christ and the meaning of his cross" (1 Cor 2:1). These two phrases are those with the fullest meaning and the most practical for the Christian preacher.[18]

The christological aspect of Mergal's reflection always appears within the trinitarian framework. Making reference to the internal witness of the Holy Spirit, according to Calvin's teaching, Mergal says: "The understanding of all God's truth, as it has been supremely and finally expressed and incarnated in Jesus of Nazareth, is known in the measure that the Holy Spirit illuminates our experience throughout our life." He finishes this section of his work with the following affirmation:

> All other truths will find their full meaning only within this framework. This is the content of Christian preaching. This is the treasure of God's revelation in his son Jesus Christ by his Holy Spirit. The preacher is the clay vessel; in his weakness the power of God is manifested (1 Corinthians 12:8) for the salvation of all who believe (Romans 1:19). This is the glory of the ministry of preaching and the weight of its yoke.[19]

The poet in Mergal allows him to discover the reality of the human existence and the meaning of an encounter with Christ:

> From dust of the earth came man,
> Maker of fantasies,
> And in breaking the illusion of his anguish
> It disappears as a shooting star.
> If in walking the way of the grave
> In Jesus the door is found
> toward the mystery where God dwells,
> he is born again for eternal life;
> through the Word of God he enters life,
> redeemed from the dust of the earth.[20]

---

[18]Mergal, *Arte cristiano de la predicación*, 81.
[19]Mergal, *Arte cristiano de la predicación*, 94.
[20]Mergal, "The angel of life," in *Arte cristiano de la predicación*, 71.

Two Evangelical Thinkers from Rio de la Plata

A review of the magazine *Cuadernos Teológicos* allows us to see the way in which early Protestant thinkers, specifically those from Argentina and Uruguay, entered into dialogue with European theology and began to process the thought of well-known Protestant theologians of that time, such as Karl Barth, Rudolf Bultmann, Emil Brunner, and Dietrich Bonhoeffer. The two theologians we will consider here studied first in Buenos Aires and then enhanced their education in Europe. In the 1950s José Míguez Bonino was a Methodist pastor but also devoted time to study. He traveled to Europe, where he studied the theology of Oscar Cullmann and Rudolf Bultmann. In 1958 he received a scholarship to study at Union Seminary in New York and wrote his thesis on the relationship between Scripture and tradition in contemporary theology, both Catholic and Protestant. In 1955 Míguez Bonino published *El mundo nuevo de Dios* (God's new world), a brief study guide on the Sermon on the Mount that was a result of his teaching role in youth and student groups belonging to ecumenical churches.[21]

Two works published in the magazine in 1956 allow us to examine the christological reflection that was developing. Míguez Bonino wrote a careful and critical response to Rudolf Bultmann's *Theology of the New Testament*, published in Germany in two volumes (1951 and 1955). He identifies the methodology followed by Bultmann in his reading of the New Testament through existential hermeneutics, which recognizes a "preunderstanding" of the text expressed in categories specific to existential philosophy.

Historical and textual criticism had developed during the final part of the nineteenth century and the beginning of the twentieth, altering the way many scholars approached the witness to Christ in the Gospels and the Epistles. Bultmann, with his proposal to demythologize the text, had become an influential figure in the area of biblical studies, which also affected theological works dedicated to Christology. Míguez Bonino

[21]José Míguez Bonino, *El mundo nuevo de Dios: Estudios bíblicos sobre el Sermón del Monte* (Buenos Aires: Consejo Metodista de Educación Cristiana, 1955).

presents Bultmann's hermeneutical project with precision and respect, recognizing the significant contribution of the German theologian. However, he also critiques his methodology, taking into account the work of other respected authors of that time such as Cullmann, T. W. Manson, and J. W. Bowman, whose works participated in questioning the skeptical position Bultmann held regarding the historicity of what the New Testament says about Jesus, particularly regarding the resurrection. Míguez Bonino argues that Jesus is the central pivot of the New Testament. To try to read the New Testament bringing to it questions from the field of existential philosophy, as Bultmann did, is an unacceptable approach to hermeneutics:

> All the New Testament gives testimony to Jesus Christ. Therefore it twists the meaning of the New Testament to introduce a question that is not one that is about Jesus Christ. . . . The only common space between the author and the exegete is to whom the text gives witness. He is the only valid hermeneutical "principle" for interpreting the Bible, because very simply the intention is not to speak to us of this or that understanding of existence, but of Jesus Christ.[22]

Uruguayan Emilio Castro first studied in Buenos Aires and then at the University of Basel, where he was the first Latin American student of theologian Karl Barth, later returning to ministerial activity in his country as pastor of Central Methodist Church in Montevideo. In the above mentioned issue of *Cuadernos Teológicos*, which was dedicated to Karl Barth on the occasion of his seventieth birthday, Castro writes about the theological situation of Latin America and of Karl Barth's theology. Having originally written for European readers, Castro makes clear that now he is referring to the Latin American theological situation in the evangelical or Protestant environment. "The topic of the Catholic reality of these peoples is not commented on—it not being the background against which the evangelical theology works—as sadly it [the Catholic Church] has shown itself as

[22]José Míguez Bonino, "La teología del Nuevo Testamento de Bultmann," *Cuadernos Teológicos*, nos. 18-19 (1956): 56.

being completely impenetrable to all theological influence outside its own church."[23]

Castro indicates that conflict with Catholicism was one of the initial expressions of Latin American evangelical thought and explains the reasons:

> The presence of Roman Catholicism is a form of church authoritarianism, with elaborate rituals without connection to a moral life, with emphasis on the veneration, almost worship, of Mary, who in general has overshadowed Christ in the life of believers, and with an intellectual and religious darkening almost impossible to conceive of outside the Hispanic peoples.[24]

Castro understands that Latin American Protestantism must respond to an urgent question: What message must be shared? How should it be preached? How should it be announced? He describes the context within which it should be preached: "Living in the middle of a culture that believes itself to know Christianity has as a result removed it as a possible source of the truth . . . and facing the problem of fanaticism and superstition of the Catholic masses converted to nominal Christianity."[25] In this situation the tendency is to adopt an apologetic message destined in the first place to criticize the errors as a way of opening the way for the truth. But Castro finds in Barth the force of a theology that above all and before any apologetic intent is centered on announcing Jesus Christ.

> Barth helps to center all our theological thought truly and effectively on the person of Christ. And it will be without a doubt a help with significant practical outworkings. In the face of the fanaticism and superstition of the environment, we are reminded that while the task of Christian preaching is to destroy false gods, this task is a secondary, a posteriori, consequence of the first task of preaching the true God. It is from the gospel that all natural theology is destroyed. It is from the gospel that humanity can be convinced of sin. It is from the gospel that all the denials of Christ that have arisen in America can be destroyed from their roots.[26]

---

[23]Emilio E. Castro, "La situación teológica de Latinoamérica y la teología de Karl Barth," *Cuadernos Teológicos*, nos. 18-19 (1956): 5.

[24]Castro, "La situación teológica de Latinoamérica," 7.

[25]Castro, "La situación teológica de Latinoamérica," 14.

[26]Castro, "La situación teológica de Latinoamérica," 15-16.

This Christ-centeredness that has revelation as its source, which is typical in the thought of Míguez Bonino, Castro, and other ecumenical thinkers, played a crucial role in the theological controversies in the following decade. We could say that in this way a young Protestantism in the process of growth entered into dialogue with European postwar Protestantism, which was marked by a certain negativity and lacking a clear sense of mission.

The Magazine *Pensamiento Cristiano* (Christian Thought)

Although this chapter is focused specially on ecumenical theologians, it is worth observing at this point the appearance of a vehicle of expression for the evangelical population. In 1953 a group of laypeople and evangelical pastors from historic denominations in Argentina such as the Brethren, Baptists, and Methodists founded the quarterly magazine *Pensamiento Cristiano* (Christian thought), directed by Alejandro Clifford, a university professor in Cordoba. He explains its purpose in this way: "As its name indicates, it will present a panorama of current Christian thought, understanding Christian thought to be that which is based on the sacred Scriptures. Its position will be that of those who believe in the complete inspiration of the Bible and in the expiatory work of the Lord on the cross."[27] These two doctrinal points were at the center of controversy in the English-speaking evangelical context, in which a new generation of thinkers was looking to express and defend the evangelical theological heritage without falling into the extremes of fundamentalism. Outstanding among them were biblical scholars such as F. F. Bruce, Geoffrey Bromiley, and Donald Wiseman from Britain, and theologians such as Bernard Ramm from the United States.

One of the first books of F. F. Bruce, who was then dean of the Department of History and Biblical Literature at the University of Sheffield, explored the proved veracity and authenticity of the Gospels and Epistles.

[27] Alejandro Clifford, *Pensamiento Cristiano*, no. 1 (1953).

Originally published in English, it first appeared in Spanish during 1956 in the form of articles in *Pensamiento Cristiano* and then was published as a book: *¿Son fidedignos los documentos del Nuevo Testamento?*[28] With the magazine being distributed to the public at a continental level, Latin American writers were united as a new generation from a great variety of Protestant churches. Writers included Plutarco Bonilla, Juan Stam, and Miguel Ángel Zandrino, in addition to Spanish authors such as José Grau and Ernesto Trenchard. Later René Padilla and Samuel Escobar would also be contributors. The bibliographical section of this magazine was for many years the most complete register of evangelical and ecumenical works published in Spanish, and of Catholic books that might be of interest to the evangelical reader.

Christ the Hope for Latin America

The ecumenical reflection of this decade culminated in the beginning of the following decade, where we find the same theologians from Rio de la Plata already mentioned affirming their Christ-centeredness in messages given to the second Latin American Evangelical Conference, which met in Lima in 1961 with the theme "Christ the hope for Latin America." Two of the three plenary talks were "Our message," given by José Míguez Bonino, and "Our unfinished task," given by Emilio Castro. Míguez Bonino began by affirming: "Our proclamation is not that of a Jesus Christ invented by ourselves, whom only we believe, we imagine, or even whom we experience. It is the Jesus Christ of the Scriptures. On the other hand, Christians do not proclaim only a book but a person who is presented by the book and who is placed as the object of our faith: Christ-Scripture."[29]

Míguez Bonino creatively elaborates on the significance of what is involved in presenting Christ of the Scriptures, which includes giving first place to the fullness of Jesus Christ. He identifies three predominant

---

[28]F. F. Bruce, *¿Son fidedignos los documentos del Nuevo Testamento?* (San José, Costa Rica: Caribe, 1957).

[29]CELA II, *Cristo, la esperanza para América Latina: Ponencias, informes, comentarios de la II Conferencia Evangélica Latinoamericana* (Buenos Aires, 1962), 70-71.

Christologies in the evangelical Latin American context. Making clear the limitations of titles, he affirms that "conservative" Protestantism has exclusively emphasized Jesus Christ the expiatory victim whose blood cleanses all our sin. "Liberal" Protestantism has shown Jesus as the Teacher whose teaching about God the Father, love, and the kingdom of heaven according to the Sermon on the Mount is central. The third presentation of Jesus, by some evangelical groups, has been of the Judge who will return at the end of time to consummate his work. In evaluating these options Míguez Bonino affirms:

> Without a doubt, these three aspects of biblical Christology are essential and irreplaceable; without them the gospel message is a mere caricature. But it is important to insist that these three characteristics should be kept in constant relation, and in this we have sometimes sinned. The insistence on Jesus the teacher has produced an impotent moralism. The exclusive focus on the second coming produces a passive otherworldliness, a kind of fanaticism. The separation of the sacrifice of Christ from his life and teachings produces a figure of Christ who is passive and whose true humanity lacks meaning. It is necessary to maintain the three aspects together: Jesus Christ who sacrificed for us, Jesus Christ our teacher, Jesus Christ the Judge and King who will come in glory.[30]

Later Míguez Bonino connects the Christian message with the characteristics of the Latin American context in which churches are working to fulfill their mission. First, the message is proclaimed in a world that is ever changing and hungry for a total transformation. Here Míguez Bonino affirms truths that were explained, discussed, and deepened in the following decades:

> The Christ we proclaim responds to the anxiety for the transformation of our people. He is the one who truly makes all things new. He is never distant from those who suffer, from those who search for him, or from those who desire him. His coming was announced as the act with which God "demolished the powerful from their thrones, sent away the rich empty, and filled the poor with good things."[31]

---

[30]CELA II, *Cristo, la esperanza para América Latina*, 72-73.

[31]CELA II, *Cristo, la esperanza para América Latina*, 84. The reference is to Luke 1:52-53.

Second, in a disoriented world the meaning of being human is proclaimed. Third, in a world where the Roman Catholic Church is dominant, it should be confronted with the judgment of Jesus Christ. Fourth, in the heart of evangelical churches pride, arrogance, and self-sufficiency must be avoided.

Míguez Bonino adds that there are two aspects of the fullness of Christ that have been given little attention in Latin America: "The first of these is the incarnation: Christ is God in the flesh. He is God made truly man for our salvation. I think that in Latin America a recognition of the practical consequences of the incarnation has been missing." As a consequence he raises the question: "In evangelical work, has the sense of identification with the Latin American person that corresponds to the incarnation, a sense of solidarity with the lost, with sinners, with those who have lost their way, been missing?" The second aspect is "the real and present sovereignty of Jesus Christ over the entire universe." In relation to this he raises the question: "Doesn't it seem that evangelicals work from the position that Christ has only the right to sovereignty in the church but not over the world? Hasn't Satan been given rights to sovereignty over the world that are not his but that have been usurped and so should not be recognized?"[32] The consequence is that we operate with a double standard: in the world Satan is obeyed, and only in the church is Jesus Christ Lord. We work as if Jesus Christ were only interested in the things that take place within the church.

In relation to the search for human significance, Míguez Bonino outlines an anthropology with Christian roots, in this way announcing the need for a deeper exploration during the following decades. He signals that the human being in Latin America is faced with various images of what is human, the alternatives being "the man from Europe, tired, disillusioned, or pessimistic; the angry man from Africa; the sacrificed man

[32] CELA II, *Cristo, la esperanza para América Latina*, 73, 74, 75.

from the Eastern world; or the ambitious and reality-making man of North America."[33] Later he suggests that Pilate's phrase about Jesus, *ecce homo*, here is the man, points toward the real man:

> He is the joyful, free, spontaneous, and deep man. He is the model of man, the true human existence. He is the Son of God existing in the flesh. He is the man, made by God and for God, the man whose will has been subordinated joyfully and willingly to the divine will, and he is the man for all other men, whose love has anointed him to serve his neighbor. This is the authentic human existence, the image of true humanity that Latin American people vainly search for. But not only this. Jesus is not only the model of true humanity but also the source of true humanity. . . . God offers new life. We become part of this true humanity by the grace of his Spirit. Christ is the hope of the Latin American man, anxious to find the true dimension of human existence.[34]

The lecture given by Emilio Castro concerning "Our unfinished task" is taken from the Great Commission of Jesus Christ in Matthew and from the classic christological passage in Philippians 2 about the incarnation. With a clearly pastoral perspective, Castro analyzes the situation of Latin American churches, rejoicing in the gains made but at the same time offering critical analysis to allow for self-evaluation in the future. A crucial point on the agenda suggests exploring the topic of the incarnation, which in the following years would be a focus of reflection, debate, and christological elaboration: "The task that our generation must take up and that it will only now be able to is the incarnation of the gospel at all levels of our community and our society. The Great Commission, the proclamation of the gospel, should be understood in terms of community."[35] Important sections of the lectures given by Míguez Bonino and Castro were incorporated into the reports of the commissions that worked with each lecture, and the reports can be viewed as the conference's message to the church throughout the continent.

---

[33]CELA II, *Cristo, la esperanza para América Latina*, 85-86.

[34]CELA II, *Cristo, la esperanza para América Latina*, 86.

[35]Emilio Castro, "Nuestra tarea inconclusa," in CELA II, *Cristo la esperanza*, 97.

Christology from the Evangelical Pulpit: Cecilio Arrastía

In addition to developing from systematic-theological reflection in the ecumenical theological institutions, evangelical Christology in Latin America also developed from preaching. For this we refer to an ecumenical theologian and preacher who was widely accepted among Protestants and whose Christology was shared in innumerable pulpits throughout the Americas: Cuban Cecilio Arrastía (1922–1995), described by Plutarco Bonilla as "the most eloquent and sacred evangelical orator from Latin America of the twentieth century."[36] Arrastía's homiletics contained deep theology and reached a level of literary brilliance comparable to that of the journalism of Báez-Carmargo. Arrastía was a Christian theologian because he was always, as Plutarco Bonilla said, "in a theological frame of mind," which is to say having an attitude of observing the world and speaking of it from the position of faith in Jesus Christ.

There is no book in which Arrastía systematized his theology. He could have written one, without a doubt, and it would have been a beautiful book in terms of content and form, the former because it would have contained the homiletic structure peculiar to his style of thinking and preaching that made him so effective in the pulpit, and the latter because it would have been composed in his majestic prose, polished, precise, and elegant, in which all that he left us is written. However, all the books he published and in particular his *Theory and Practice of Preaching* in the series Hispanoamerican Bible Commentary are authentically theological books.[37] His sermons with christological content have been brought together in three books. The first was *JesuCristo Señor del pánico* (Jesus Christ, Lord of panic), which opens with a meditation on the word *Emmanuel* and later makes theological comments on twelve passages and characters from the Gospels.[38] Later came *Diálogo desde una cruz*

[36]In Justo L. González, ed., *Diccionario ilustrado de intérpretes de la fe* (Terrasa, Spain: CLIE, 2004), 44.
[37]Cecilio Arrastía, *Theory and Practice of Preaching*, Hispanoamerican Bible Commentary (Miami: Caribe, 1996).
[38]Cecilio Arrastía, *JesuCristo Señor del pánico* (Mexico City: CUPSA, 1964).

(Dialogue from a cross), and the cycle was completed with *Itinerario de la pasión* (Itinerary of the Passion), a series of meditations for Holy Week.[39] What characterizes these homiletic works is movement from reading and contextualizing of the text to theological reflection, or from theological formulation to a contextual exposition of the biblical text.

Listening to or reading Arrastía's works, one is confronted at each step with phrases or paragraphs that are gems that could be joined in a valuable anthology to create a theological work of art. Plutarco Bonilla began the work of presenting Arrastía's biography and systematizing his contributions in a study preceding a collection of Arrastía's essays titled *La predicación, el predicador y la Iglesia* (Preaching, the preacher, and the church). Taking some notes from Bonilla's work and giving my own brief summary, I think we can sketch some guidelines of Arrastía's Christology, always expressed in the context of the homiletic vocation from which he spoke and wrote. He says:

> The Christian preacher proclaims from a double platform. On the one hand is his own religious experience, his encounter with Christ, about whom he will share; on the other is the interpretation of this encounter. Behind both elements we always find God's initiative. If, at the end of the day, we think that theology is the interpretation of what God does for humankind, it can be concluded that the Christian pulpit and a certain level of theology are inseparable.[40]

A brief definition of theology summarizes Arrastía's theological vision well: "Theology is the interpretation of what God does for humanity." The Reformed antecedents of his posture are clear here: God's initiative and preeminence. Before the preacher, before the church, before theology, is God and his great action in favor of humanity. Theology is the humble task of listening to the Word of this God who has spoken and trying to interpret it, remembering that the action of God is always for the benefit of human beings.

---

[39] Cecilio Arrastía, *Diálogo desde una cruz* (Mexico City: CUPSA, 1965); Arrastía, *Itinerario de la pasión* (El Paso, TX: Casa Bautista de Publicaciones, 1978).

[40] Cecilio Arrastía, "Teología para predicadores," in *La predicación, el predicador y la Iglesia* (San José, Costa Rica: CELEP, 1983), 47.

In his birth country, Cuba, as well as in Puerto Rico, his country of residence, and later in the United States, where he lived in forced exile as a result of political circumstances, Arrastía was a social activist. When, with much vigor, he planted a Hispanic church in the heart of "El Barrio" in New York, he simultaneously undertook a pastoral and community role. His social activism was rooted in the life of the church because Arrastía's theology highlighted God as he who acts in history, who promises and fulfills his promises. He says, "The Christian preacher preaches . . . from a promise, with the conviction that his promise is fulfilled in Christ."[41] And though this leads us to take history seriously, on the other hand Christ and God point toward the future and are in the future. With great vigor he affirmed this in the following way:

> God is God of history and in history. He cannot be isolated away in a concentration camp, restricted to the past, because the history that occurs today comes from what happened yesterday. The Hebrew form of understanding history is a line projected toward the future. It has direction and meaning. God is drawing the line and moves ahead of the line. He does not push history from behind. He pulls it from the front. It is the God of hope of Moltmann; the God who is not only above us; or the subjective God who lives inside us. It is correct to think of the God who goes before us, he who guided the people of Canaan after he rescued them from Egypt. To live looking at the past is a comfortable way of escaping the present. And those who escape the present cannot discern the hand of God.[42]

One of the essential theological themes defined by Arrastía for my generation was that of the relation of faith to culture. When I heard of it for the first time, I was a university student from an evangelical church in which a rejection of "the worldly" had given rise a veiled or open attitude of anti-intellectualism. This experience was shared by many colleagues of my generation. For this reason it was refreshing to hear from Arrastía a reading from the Bible that begins with God the Creator, showing the Christian obligation to participate in the creation of culture

---

[41] Arrastía, "Teología para predicadores," 28.
[42] Arrastía, *Itinerario de la pasión*, 44-45.

and to fulfill the cultural mandate for which God has placed us in the world. In this sense his theology also reflects a Reformed perspective that clearly moves in the direction of mission, because surrounding the Christian people is a society in need of the gospel. He maintained that a reform was needed that returned theology to the pulpit:

> This reform does not aim for external changes, but rather essential changes in the communication of the gospel and in the doctrinal focus. This does not mean inventing new doctrines, but it does mean interpreting the only redemptive reality—Christ himself—in such a way that a true connection is made between the gospel and the Christian church with secular society, pregnant with fatal emptiness.[43]

As in the case of my experience in Peru, in various other Latin American countries Arrastía was invited to give lectures in universities precisely because he was an expert in the art of making a real connection with secular society for the hundreds of university students who went to hear him. In his lectures he outlined the grand narrative of the biblical message in a creative dialogue with the Latin American novelists of his time, or with the predominant philosophical trends expressed in art and film. University students found in the ideas articulated by Arrastía not only the satisfaction of following the logical strand of a clear argument but also reflection that connected Genesis to the Gospel of John with the challenges of today. We also found in this theology an inspiration that has sustained us in vocational ministry, as university professors, and in the political arena. It is not theology from a handbook but theology forged in dialogue with daily life.

Christology is central to Arrastía's theology. His sermons contain masterful passages of description and narrative. His rich expression sets scenes that bring the pages of the Gospels to life with renewed strength, describing Jesus' actions or demonstrating the intense presence of his teaching. In this sense we can place Arrastía in the continuity of Latin American evangelical thinkers. He follows the agenda of his predecessor

---

[43] Arrastía, *Itinerario de la pasión*, 47.

John Mackay and of cornerstone Gonzalo Báez-Camargo, announcing the humanity of the unknown Jesus in our culture. Arrastía also knew how to express with clarity and vigor the deepest theological meaning of Jesus' crucifixion, God's incarnate Word: "We let go of speculations regarding the double nature of the Lord and say directly that the first thing that this Word tells us is that there he is dying, not the gnostic God but the Christian God, not an apparition but God-Man, very much flesh, very much bone."[44]

As a good Latin American evangelical, Arrastía's Christology also had a missionary focus. His sermons invited people to contemplate Christ and were able to open our eyes to the rich humanity, the beauty, and the strength of the Jesus of the Gospel writers. However, it was not a Christology that remained in contemplation or in ecstatic delight. It was always an invitation to action, to discipleship, and to follow-up. This is because he who died on the cross and rose again has a transformational agenda here and today: "No one who draws near to Christ remains apathetic or indifferent. Sooner or later a change occurs and life begins again. The man has passed from a biological level that ends in the tomb to a moral level that remains in history, and finally enters into the spiritual level that has conquered the grave and has transcended history."[45]

It is significant that both evangelical and ecumenical thinkers in the historical moment under consideration had as the raw product of their christological reflection the Christ of the Gospels and the Epistles. The European theologians with whom these works began to engage also connect their Christology fundamentally to the biblical witness, and like Barth, Bultmann, or Cullman, they do their exegesis, though beginning from different theological angles. Almost two decades later these same theologians, among others, influenced an awakening of reflection among Latin American Catholic theologians regarding the person of Christ. Catholic theologian Elizabeth Johnson offers a perspective of this situation:

---

[44] Arrastía, *Diálogo desde una cruz*, 33.

[45] Arrastía, *Jesucristo, Señor del pánico*, 90.

In the middle of the twentieth century, when the renovation of Christology in Catholic circles had begun, Catholic thought, in distinction to Protestant, was stuck in focusing on knowing Jesus Christ through dogma and was almost not affected by the turbulent debates regarding biblical issues that had a marked influence in Protestant Christology.[46]

[46]Elizabeth A. Johnson, *La cristología, hoy: Olas de renovación en el acceso a Jesús* (Santander: Sal Terrae, 2003), 11-12.

7

CHRISTOLOGY IN TIMES OF REVOLUTION

The truth is that Christ is respected and admired by the inhabitants of the great cities of our Ibero-American world. But it is also true that Christ is unknown, and romantic admiration of an idealized figure that can be accommodated to each person's ideology could transform into open rejection if Christ were studied more deeply. Christ when admired from a distance is inoffensive. An unknown Christ constructed as a useful symbol does not bother anyone; rather, he can be a tool. But a Christ whose categorical words and absolute demands make concessions to no human idealism becomes intolerable and requires people to choose sides: with him or against him.

SAMUEL ESCOBAR, *¿QUIÉN ES CRISTO HOY?*

Of the many attacks rationalism has launched against Christianity, the most serious have undoubtedly been those bent on undermining the historicity of Jesus. Their seriousness resides in that they attack an aspect of the Christian message without which that message would completely lose its validity. For some religions history does not play an essential part in the faith of its followers: the object of their interest is not historic events but rather ideas or truths that transcend time. Christianity, however, rests on the affirmation that God revealed himself through a series of actions in history that culminated in the life of Jesus. For this reason, to deny the historic reality of Jesus is to deny the central fact of Christianity.

RENÉ PADILLA, *¿QUIÉN ES CRISTO HOY?*

The 1960s were a time of changes and new hope, during which Latin America seemed to be a continent caught up in a revolution. Justo González, a Cuban historian and theological educator who taught at the Seminario Evangélico de Puerto Rico, wrote these lines in 1965 in the introduction of his book *Revolución y encarnación* (Revolution and incarnation): "If we are to treat the relationship between Christianity and the revolutionary movements of today's world—particularly communism—with justice and care, we should begin with a clear concept of the nature of Christianity. In my judgment, this concept can and should be rooted in the fact of the incarnation."[1]

Meanwhile, in Peru in 1967, I published the book *Diálogo entre Cristo y Marx*. In the first chapter, which gives the book its title, I suggest the possibility of a dialogue between Christ and Marx and respond to those who think that this would be impossible. After all, in the Gospels Jesus dialogues with all type of people:

> We are often presented with a distorted Christ who appears to fear dialogue, loves the comfort of monologue, and has no concern for the ideas and concerns of the souls of people. In the Gospel stories we find that various dialogues Jesus had with the people of his time ended in violent scenes. More than once, Jesus' life was in danger because his words stirred up strong feelings. Christ was not afraid of dialogue, yet he never compromised the truth.[2]

Thus theological work that had Christ as its point of reference during this decade could not avoid responding to the challenge of revolution and of communism.

A Revolutionary Atmosphere

The triumph of Fidel Castro's Cuban revolution in 1959 began a new era of agitation, protest, and search for social change in Latin America. The challenge of Marxism and the nationalist left in general had stopped being only ideological and political and entered into the realm of armed

[1]Justo L. González, *Revolución y encarnación* (Río Piedras, Puerto Rico: La Reforma, 1965), 12.
[2]Samuel Escobar, *Diálogo entre Cristo y Marx* (Lima: AGEUP, 1967), 15.

conflict. Armed guerilla forces, representing the possibility of gaining power and transforming the world, suddenly became a highly attractive idea and practice, especially in universities. All the ensuing questions regarding violence and subversiveness touched in one way or another the area of theology and biblical teaching. During the course of this decade the figures of the Argentinian doctor Ernesto "Che" Guevara and the Colombian priest Camilo Torres, who joined a guerilla group, became for many youth objects of a curious mixture of sometimes fanatical hero worship and a kind of religious vocation.

The social awareness that exploded during this revolutionary era in Latin America stretched into the following decades, becoming the frame of reference for the life of churches and for theological reflection. As the theme of the revolution came to dominate the cultural life of the continent, significant sectors of youth in various Latin American societies abandoned their normal life and embraced various revolutionary causes. The revolutionary movements presented a challenge to evangelicals' concept of the Christian life, one to which evangelical pastors and theologians had to respond. My own *Diálogo entre Cristo y Marx* was a compilation of public lectures I had presented in universities of Brazil, Peru, Argentina, Bolivia, and Mexico from 1963 onwards. It focuses on themes such as a Christian response to Marxism, an analysis of the Christian versus Marxist vision of history, the Christian concept of work, and the meaning of liberty. It was used as an instrument for communication of the gospel in the universities of Peru during a year of special missionary focus known as "In-Depth Evangelism" (Evangelismo a Fondo [EVAF]), in 1967. For its part, González's *Revolución y encarnación* carried weight because he was recognized as an historian of Christian thought, and it was the first contextual approach to Christology written from an evangelical perspective by a Latin American. As we will see further on, during the following decades González continued with his christological reflections along the lines first laid out in this book.

In the 1960s Cuba represented an open challenge to the hegemony of the United States in the Americas and to the big neighbor in the north's influence over the political and cultural life of Latin American countries.

Big US companies dominated the economy, while the mass media spread North American music, movies, literature, and news about US social movements. Globally, colonialism was being rejected, and new countries were being formed in Africa and Asia. In Latin America a cultural resurgence began to occur, with a strong emphasis on and affirmation of Latin cultural values, both those of Spanish/Portuguese heritage and those of the cultures native to the land prior to the Spanish arrival. The historic expectation awakened by the Cuban revolution and the revolutionary militancy among Latin American intellectuals began to be reflected, for example, in folk music, which underwent a great resurgence in Argentina, Mexico, and Brazil. This music was an expression "of the people," in contrast to that coming from Europe and North America. These three countries, which had always wielded a strong cultural influence throughout Latin America through literature, film, and music, were now sources of a cultural revolution.

This created the urgent need to face a problem for Protestantism in general: the Anglo-Saxon origins of a high percentage of Latin American missionary work, and the institutional relationships that existed between Latin America churches and North American Protestantism. By the end of the decade, churches with an ecumenical tendency were openly questioning this relationship. For example, a consultation sponsored by the recently formed ecumenical organization UNELAM and the National Council of Churches of the United States and Canada was titled "Why Should There Be North American Missionaries in Latin America?"[3] Further, in 1969, during the first Latin American Evangelization Congress (CLADE 1) in Bogotá, we said: "For the historic reasons already mentioned, the churches in South America have frequently lived within an Anglo-Saxon subculture. There is only too often in our leaders and pastors a total ignorance of the literature, folklore, and history of Latin America."[4]

---

[3]UNELAM, *Misioneros norteamericanos en América Latina ¿Para qué?* (Montevideo, 1971).

[4]Samuel Escobar, "The Social Impact of the Gospel," in *Is Revolution Change?*, ed. Brian Griffiths (London: Inter-Varsity Press, 1972), 90; "Responsabilidad social de la iglesia," in *Acción en Cristo para un continente en crisis* (San José, Costa Rica: Caribe, 1970), 34.

However, such examples do not indicate a closed, regionalist position. Protestant theological exploration in Latin America took place within the framework of relationships with global Protestantism. There was a growing Latin American participation in ecumenical events organized by the World Council of Churches with its different agencies and organisms, in which the mission of the church was revisioned in the light of European and North American theology that was also concerned with interpreting what was called "rapid social change." For example, at the beginning of the decade two Latin Americans participated in the World Conference of the Student Christian Movement (SCM) in Strasbourg, France. José Míguez Bonino presented a lecture called "El movimiento cristiano en un continente descristianizado" (Christian witness in a dechristianized continent), in which he examined the spiritual condition of Latin America. Explaining his use of the term *dechristianized*, Míguez Bonino clarified that of course a witness to Christ had not been absent from Latin America: "Roman Catholicism has worked here for four centuries." Later he averred: "But I believe it is fair to say that Latin America has not experienced *evangelization* in the sense of a genuine penetration of Christian character and thinking in the interior life of its people." Drawing on Catholic sources, he described how many people active in political and intellectual life were abandoning the Catholic Church: "The rebellion against Christ in Latin America is the rebellion of a world that does not want to be tied to a religion. In our history, in one way or another, religion has always opposed all that was in movement; and movement is the essence of our life." Míguez Bonino proposes: "The Christian church in Latin America must learn the way of incarnation. How can it intercede for a people whose problems it ignores and of whose hopes it has not the slightest notion?"[5]

At the same conference Uruguayan Valdo Galland, in the role of general secretary of SCM, presented SCM's mission and highlighted

[5]José Míguez Bonino, "El testimonio cristiano en un continente descristianizado," *Testimonium* 9, no. 1 (1961): 32, 38.

the spirit of service needed to fulfill the mission. He did so using a christological reference:

> Modern exegetes of the New Testament have shown the important role that the Old Testament's concept of the servant, especially in the book of the prophet Isaiah, had in Jesus' thinking about his own mission. As he demonstrated in washing his disciples' feet during his last supper with them, he wanted to be a servant to the very least of humanity. We can draw conclusions from this act for the church that the New Testament calls the body of Christ. She also is a servant to human beings and not only a servant of God.[6]

Interpreting Actions of Revolution

During this decade theological gatherings and publications were dedicated to the topic of revolution as a framework for Christian activity, but also as a challenge toward a new understanding of Christianity and the mission of the church. Within ecumenical Protestantism there was an attitude of openness toward revolutionary action and an effort to interpret it from a prophetic perspective. Let's consider two examples of what was taking place in the heart of mainline denominations. In 1963 the Committee of Cooperation of the Presbyterian Church of Latin America (CCPAL) organized a gathering about the nature of the church and its mission in Latin America. Here careful attention was given to the revolutionary nature of the social situation within which the churches were called to carry out their mission. Colombian pastor Gonzalo Castillo Cárdenas said: "The primary reality of 'the times' in which we live in Latin America is revolution, or rapid change. This fact is obvious to all. The institutions that represented our people are broken down and do not satisfy."[7] Brazilian theologian Joaquim Beato said:

> We have confidence that the church is, through Jesus Christ, the legitimate heir of a prophetic mission for the contemporary world. And so we must make the effort to discover the way in which the church must undertake

---

[6]Valdo Galland, "La misión de la Federación," *Testimonium* 9, no. 1 (1961): 53.

[7]In CCPAL, *La naturaleza de la iglesia y su misión en América Latina* (Bogotá: IQUEIMA,1963), 40.

> this mission, which has become urgent and vital in the decisive and revolutionary situation in which we are living in all the world, especially the underdeveloped areas of Asia, Africa, and Latin America.[8]

In 1966 the Methodist Church organized the Consultation on Continental Evangelization in Cochabamba, Bolivia, with the theme "Evangelization and Revolution in Latin America." A book that compiles documents prepared before, during, and after the consultation, edited by Uruguayan Methodist theologian Mortimer Arias, allows us to observe how one sector of Latin American Protestantism interpreted the revolutionary situation of the continent. The book opens with this statement: "It is by now a common assertion, yet still a compelling fact, that we live amid revolution." Later it goes on to affirm:

> In general terms, the revolutionary impulse of our times is a movement that assigns radical value to the human condition, that destroys structures and traditions that have maintained inequality, dominion, and privilege. The new thing appearing on the horizon is the possibility to be more human in a more human society, calling into question every perspective or human structure that isolates man from his neighbor.[9]

The book enumerates a diversity of revolutions: the past American and English revolutions, socialist revolutions, uprisings of people of color against white dominance, and the existentialist revolt in Europe against objectification of human beings. It concludes that "in all these four movements Christianity properly sees the hand of God, humanizing, liberating, judging, redeeming. Evangelization in this context is the proclamation of the presence of God in these secular movements."[10] Further, the book affirms that "evangelization is also a revolution, considering that it aims for a total revolution of humankind by the action of the Spirit of God."

> This is an explosive dimension of the gospel, revolutionary and dynamic. If evangelical preaching is to fulfill its mission, it will have to be a force

---

[8]CCPAL, *La naturaleza de la iglesia*, 19.

[9]Iglesia Metodista en América Latina, *Evangelización y revolución en América Latina* (Montevideo, 1969), 18.

[10]Iglesia Metodista en América Latina, *Evangelización y revolución*, 18.

> that disrupts, disorients, unsettles, maybe even leads to disturbances, because the people who are touched by this force cannot go on being as they were. This explosive and revolutionary character of the gospel is vividly demonstrated in the ministry of Jesus.[11]

CHURCH AND SOCIETY IN LATIN AMERICA (ISAL)

Ecumenical Protestantism also produced Iglesia y Sociedad en América Latina, or ISAL (Church and Society in Latin America), beginning with meetings sponsored by the World Council of Churches in 1957 as part of a study of churches in the midst of rapid social change. Its first Latin American consultation took place in Huampani, Peru, in July 1961, and the specific agenda was to deepen the theme of social responsibility among Christians. ISAL began trying to articulate the biblical bases for responsible social action by Christians. Those of us from evangelical churches who had the same concerns became aware that at the time ISAL's gatherings and publications were the only forums in which urgent questions such as these were being disclosed and discussed. Pedro Arana Quiroz wrote in his book *Providencia y revolución*: "We must give the members of ISAL credit for having thought and worked in this important aspect of Christian witness, while many of us who pride ourselves on being evangelical have forgotten our responsibility toward society."[12]

Evaluating the first decade of this movement, its first general secretary, Uruguayan theologian Julio de Santa Ana, indicates two distinct eras in its development, "the first being a period in which the thinking of ISAL was elaborated in close dependency on Barthian theology (1962–1964)." De Santa Ana gives negative marks to this initial period, in which language and reflection were rooted in so-called revelational theology: "This developed closely bound to the Bible (understood as the foundational book), which made the resulting deliberations little suited or

[11]Iglesia Metodista en América Latina, *Evangelización y revolución*, 21.

[12]Pedro Arana Quiroz, *Providencia y revolución*, 2nd ed. (Grand Rapids: Subcomisión de Literatura Cristiana, 1986), 15.

useful in circumstances like those of Latin America at present."[13] This judgment left ISAL without reference points in biblical revelation, and over time it distanced the movement from both the ecumenical churches and the rest of Protestantism.

ISAL's second period, beginning in 1965, was for de Santa Ana "a theological project that became increasingly original" and consisted of "inquiring into the being of God in Jesus Christ, by the action of his Spirit, and in the form of the church, for the meaning of Christian witness in revolutionary situations, such as are those now experienced in the various countries of Latin America." The thought of Brazilian Rubem Alves and American Richard Shaull, at that point living in Brazil, began to have significant influence in this era of ISAL. One key question taken up was how God acts in history today, and in exploring this theme ISAL arrived at the necessity of ideology. Thus, where ideology was earlier seen in a negative light, it came to be seen as having a positive role in social change. De Santa Ana says: "The type of social transformation proposed by certain Latin American ideological streams coincided with the central movement toward new forms of humanization that we Christians discerned throughout history." Later he recognizes the positioning of ISAL within the social and political panorama of Latin America, though he sees the conceptualization of this lining up as an unfinished task: "Unfortunately, although there are elements that indicate a certain leftist current, with a Marxist inspiration, within ISAL, up to now this has not been faced with total honesty."[14]

The new position led to questioning the role of churches in the world. According to de Santa Ana, Shaull had proposed a "dispersion" of Christians in the world so that they could participate in the revolutionary movements. "It was then that Rubem Alves distinguished the believing community because of its eschatological nature, given that it is 'midwife

---

[13]Julio de Santa Ana, "ISAL, un movimiento en marcha," *Cuadernos de Marcha*, no. 29 (September 1969): 50. Although, as we will see later, there are careful studies and critics of ISAL, here I depend on this panoramic article by its first general secretary.

[14]De Santa Ana, "ISAL, un movimiento en marcha," 52.

of a new morning.' This morning belongs not only to believers but to all people, to whom a future of liberty has been promised." This perspective led de Santa Ana to "erase every distinction between the ecclesiastical and the secular. The people of God and the human race meet in shared participation in a community that lives toward a new future." With this also came a new concept of ecumenism. From its beginnings ISAL had fostered cooperation between Catholics and Protestants, but now there was a new element: "Therefore it will be ecumenism of believers with nonbelievers, of Christians and Marxists, reconciliation through the action of God in Christ that opens the way so that people will come together and fight together for their liberation."[15]

As de Santa Ana recognizes in this honest effort to evaluate ISAL at the end of the first decade, though its publications such as the magazine *Cristianismo y Sociedad* (Christianity and society) and its books were widely distributed, in reality it was a movement that mobilized few people. The rejection of revelational theology and of the biblical source of the theological task began to create distance from churches and from Protestant centers for theological reflection. A further consequence was that ISAL made no specific contribution to the development of Christology in Latin America.

Revolution and Evangelization

Meanwhile, among the new denominations and independent missions described by missiologist Kenneth Strachan as "nonhistoric groups," ones that did not participate in the ecumenical movement, the 1950s had been a period of intensive evangelization through the so-called crusades, mass outreach that involved available communications media such as radio. Some of these US-based missionary organizations were reacting to the experience of missionaries in China, where the triumph of Mao Tse Tung's communism in 1948 had led to the expulsion of all foreign missionaries. They fell into the cold war mentality wherein all

[15]De Santa Ana, "ISAL, un movimiento en marcha," 55.

communism was seen as a global threat and which found all references to Christian social responsibility suspect, as if it originated in liberal theology or in communism. However, at the beginning of the 1960s a movement emerged that critically reflected on the search for more effective evangelization practices to unite dispersed efforts and respond to the specific needs of the Latin American situation. Accompanying this self-critiquing reflection were efforts to forge a theology that could speak anew into to the urgency of the revolutionary situation.

One of the focal points of this reflection was in Costa Rica, where the Latin America Mission (LAM) had its headquarters. LAM director Kenneth Strachan, an Argentinian, worked with a multinational team to launch Evangelismo a Fondo (EVAF; Evangelism in depth), a campaign to mobilize the greatest number possible of churches and church members in a given country to communicate the gospel in all areas of society in the course of one year. In explaining the idea, Strachan gives his own reading of the Latin American situation:

> Our evangelistic concern becomes more agonizing every day because of the apocalyptic nature of the time in which we live. All of our Christian institutions are in crisis. Today's social, political, scientific, and technological revolution is challenging the very existence of the church of Christ and calling into question the validity of all its traditional models for life and witness. This means that everything must be reconsidered in terms of our reason for existing. The essential mission of the church and of each individual Christian should therefore be redefined and reaffirmed.[16]

The EVAF initiative's proponents came to consider it revolutionary, and those who wrote about the movement shared a conviction that it was not only a revolution in evangelization methods but indeed a theological revolution. Costa Rican theologian Juan Stam said, "EVAF is a different kind of theological revolution. Its aim is to make all theology revolutionary, placing doctrine within its original context of evangelism."[17] Reflection on

---

[16]Kenneth Strachan, "Llamado al testimonio," *Cuadernos Teológicos*, nos. 54-55 (April-September 1965): 68.

[17]Juan Stam, "Evangelismo a Fondo como revolución teológica," *En Marcha Internacional* 17 (July-December 1970): 4-6.

EVAF was carried out particularly at the Latin American Biblical Seminary (SBL) in San José, Costa Rica. Stam and various other professors at this seminary wrote regularly in EVAF publications.

Strachan had studied at Wheaton College and later at Dallas Theological Seminary, two centers of conservative Protestantism in the United States. But following a few years of missionary experience, he went on to study at Princeton Theological Seminary, where he took a class taught by John Mackay, and his theological and missionary vision was broadened. Then his experience in Puerto Rico and his deep study of the biblical material about the church had led Strachan to abandon the exclusivism and separatism found among fundamentalist missionary organizations that cooperated only with fellow fundamentalist organizations in evangelization and mission. In 1957 Strachan had been invited to a consultation of the International Missionary Council, an ecumenical agency affiliated with the World Council of Churches. The contacts he made there permitted him to garner broad support among all kinds of evangelical churches in a Billy Graham crusade that he helped to organize.[18]

By the middle of the 1960s, EVAF had produced a notable impact not only in Latin America but also in other parts of the world. In 1964 theologian Lesslie Newbigin, editor of the prestigious *International Review of Mission*, invited Strachan to write about his experience and vision for EVAF. Victor Hayward, director of the Division of Studies of the World Council of Churches, was asked to respond to Strachan's work, and Strachan was then able to respond to Hayward. The resulting debate became famous among scholars of Christian mission; it appeared in Spanish in the magazine *Cuadernos Teológicos* alongside writings from other European theologians and from Uruguayan Emilio Castro.

The debate focused on the scope of the work of Christ in the world and the way the church should understand its missionary task, hot topics

[18]I have written at some length about Strachan and the Latin America Mission in "The Two Party System and the Missionary Enterprise," chap. 18 in *Re-Forming the Center: American Protestantism 1900 to the Present*, ed. Douglas Jacobsen and William Vance Trollinger (Grand Rapids: Eerdmans, 1998), 349-60.

in missiological reflection at this time. Among EVAF core principles, Strachan said, was that "every Christian, without exception, is called to be Christ's witness, according to one's giftings and situation. The energy of a church's witness and its growth are directly affected by the level of participation of its members."[19] He emphasized that "this individual and communal activity should be related constructively with the whole testimony of the whole body of Christ. The result should be that in a practical way, without compromising or tarnishing the truth, a tangible witness is given to the unity of the body of Christ."[20] EVAF's program aimed to train all members of every church so they could give personal and collective witness.

Without questioning these principles, Hayward raised a set of questions regarding the nature of the gospel message:

> Is Christ the Savior of the world or the Savior only of the church? Is he Savior only of "those who believe," Lord only of the church? Or is he Savior of all people, though especially of "those who believe," and Lord of the world as well as the church? Do we proclaim his coming as a secular or religious event? Is his salvation the means by which people's souls escape from this evil world, or do we dare to announce "the redemption of the world through our Lord Jesus Christ"?[21]

Strachan recognizes that these questions imply a critique of those who conceive of evangelization simply as a means to increase membership in their own church, but he also critiques Hayward's challenge as a false dichotomy and asks: "Shouldn't we recognize that despite the failures in its attitudes and behavior, the church of our time is present *in* the world and the gospel has been trusted *to* the church *for* the world?"[22]

In the end what this debate brought to the surface was the difference between people from churches that, while not denying the importance

[19]Strachan, "Llamado al testimonio," 72.
[20]Strachan, "Llamado al testimonio," 72.
[21]Victor E. Hayward, "Llamado al testimonio—¿Pero qué clase de testimonio?," *Cuadernos Teológicos*, nos. 54-55 (April-September 1965): 80.
[22]Kenneth Strachan, "Un comentario más," *Cuadernos Teológicos*, no. 54-55 (April-September 1965): 88.

of evangelization, did not see it as an essential component of their mission, and on the other hand people from churches that had made evangelization their central task, around which all church activities revolved. In an editorial in *International Review of Mission* in the year following the debate, Newbigin summarized these two positions, affirming that "to deny that mission is the same as the extension of the church is not to deny that mission aims at conversion. This is one of the topics that should be clarified in the current debate around missions." He concludes by saying that in the ecumenical world the second position needed to receive increased attention.[23]

Approaching Biblical Christology

In Costa Rica's Seminario Bíblico Latinoamericano and its environs, scholars were researching the biblical basis for a theology of evangelization. A valuable example of this is the undergraduate thesis written by Plutarco Bonilla at the University of Costa Rica, which he defended in 1961: "El concepto paulino de Logos" (The Pauline concept of Logos). Bonilla probes Paul's thought with regard to Jesus Christ in the Greek text.[24] Placing the texts within their original cultural context, Bonilla shows that Paul did not use the Greek term *logos* in the same sense that John the Evangelist did, yet he demonstrates that Pauline and Johannine Christology are in clear agreement. His work's presuppositions regarding the veracity of the biblical text rested on recent studies that had gone beyond liberal theology's skepticism with regard to biblical documents about Jesus Christ. Bonilla emphasizes that the Christ on whom Paul constructs his Christology is the historic Christ, the person of Christ whom the Gospels affirm:

> Indisputably Paul the apostle to the Gentiles is the predominant figure in Christianity during the first century, second only to the figure of Jesus Christ, the founder and animating center of Christianity. For this reason

---

[23]Lesslie Newbigin, "From the Editor," *International Review of Mission* 54 (April 1965): 148-49.
[24]Plutarco Bonilla Acosta, *El concepto paulino de Logos* (San José: Publicaciones de la Universidad de Costa Rica, 1965).

> Paul has been appropriately called "the interpreter of Christ," as in reality the theological foundation, the "exegesis" of the person and work of the historic Jesus, the carpenter of Nazareth, is owed to the immortal figure of the quintessential apostle.[25]

For Bonilla, Paul presents Christ as the message, the Christian *kerygma*: "That is to say, Christ not only defines the meaning and the theological value of the proclamation but *is* also himself the message, as in the end what is important is not the external nature of the shifting, unstable human presentation." Here Christology connects with what we can call holistic anthropology: "It is Jesus Christ, the historic Christ theologically interpreted, from the point of view of what biblical scholars have called *the history of salvation*, the salvation of man through the fully human Man, the complete man, of flesh and bone, as Unamuno put it."[26]

Bonilla also points to the centrality of the cross in Paul's message:

> Pauline theology rests completely on the fact of the crucifixion, established and confirmed in its meaning by the other key fact: the resurrection. In relation to *kerygma*, Paul does not pretend to speak of Christ as the creator of the universe or of the radiance of God's glory. He is presented exclusively as Savior of the Greeks and of the Jews, as the one who 'died for our sins and rose again for our justification' (Romans 4:25). His meaning is not philosophical; rather, it is theological.[27]

Bonilla's use of his academic study on a pastoral level can be seen in the article "El cristiano de hoy frente a la cruz" (Today's Christian before the cross), published in the EVAF bulletin *En Marcha* and reprinted in the magazine *Pensamiento Cristiano* (Christian thought). He begins by stating that at this moment in Latin America there is a growing difficulty in believing in God as well as an institutionalization of violence as the means to resolving critical socioeconomic-political problems. "This set of conditions forces us to ask ourselves what does Christ mean today, what is the message of the cross (there is no Christ without the

---

[25]Bonilla Acosta, *El concepto paulino de Logos*, 14.
[26]Bonilla Acosta, *El concepto paulino de Logos*, 31.
[27]Bonilla Acosta, *El concepto paulino de Logos*, 31.

cross, nor a valid cross that is not Christ's), what it says to the man of our times."[28] Bonilla summarizes the proclamation of the cross in three statements: the cross proclaims the final victory of love, the cross proclaims the possibility of restoration, and the cross proclaims the reality of a new tomorrow.

EVANGELIZATION IN THE UNIVERSITY WORLD

Another center of theological reflection related to evangelization developed in relation to evangelical witness in the university context. A generation united around the magazine *Certeza* (Certainty), founded in 1959, and the Comunidad Internacional de Estudiantes Evangélicos (International Fellowship of Evangelical Students, or IFES). It was natural that during the turbulent decade of the 1960s theological reflection be guided by the christological agenda proposed by Mackay. In the case of Peru, I and Pedro Arana Quiroz had been representatives in student unions in the University of San Marcos in Lima and were familiar not only with the theory of Marxism but also with the Marxist political strategy within student politics, which was an extension of national politics.[29]

In Latin American universities it was necessary to proclaim the basics of the life and teachings of Jesus to generations that had rejected traditional religion without having been confronted with the heart of the faith. In addition to the kerygmatic, apologetics with regard to the historicity of Jesus were often required, due to ongoing debate with Marxist spokespeople who sometimes limited themselves to repeat what they had read about Jesus in the *Enciclopedia Soviética* (*Great Soviet Encyclopedia*). *Certeza* published a series of articles by René Padilla, me, and Edwin Yamauchi under the theme "Who is Christ today?" These writings emerged from public lectures in universities and at the end of the decade

[28]Plutarco Bonilla, "El cristiano de hoy frente a la cruz," *Pensamiento Cristiano* 16, no. 62 (June 1969): 85.
[29]Samuel Escobar, "Heredero de la reforma radical," in *Hacia una teología evangélica latinoamericana* (San José, Costa Rica: Caribe, 1984), 59-60.

were collected in a book, whose two editions were widely distributed in educational institutions across the continent.[30]

Another important pastoral challenge for witness in the student environment was practicing an academic profession amid the tensions of a continent in revolution. The central themes of what it means to be disciples of Christ had to be understood afresh in light of the demanding social context. A kerygmatic framework for proclamation of the gospel began to develop, a discipleship and social responsibility rooted in Christology. As we worked on this, René Padilla and I found a great affinity with the theological work of British theologian John Stott, who had contributed to a change in christological perspective of Christian mission. In the Berlin Evangelization Congress (1966) Stott noted the importance of the Great Commission of Jesus as the basis for a theology of evangelization. His proposal was that John's version of the Great Commission (Jn 20:21) contains a christological richness better suited to the current context than Matthew's version (Mt 28:18), which had been used traditionally by evangelicals. The text from John offers not only the imperative "I am sending you" but also an indicative, a model: "as the Father sent me"—that is to say, the incarnation as a model for our missionary presence.

A summary of the material developed at a Latin American and global level was presented in my lecture "Responsabilidad social de la Iglesia" (The social responsibility of the church) during the First Latin American Evangelization Congress (CLADE 1, Bogotá, 1969), to which I will make further reference later on.[31] The lecture took the incarnation of Jesus, his crucifixion, and his resurrection as key to articulating the presence of the church in the world, which should precede any attempt at proclamation.

This agenda of challenges, in the spreading of the gospel and in the pastoral care of university students, guided the advanced theological

[30] Samuel Escobar, René Padilla, and Edwin Yamauchi, *¿Quién es Cristo hoy?* (Buenos Aires: Certeza, 1970).

[31] This text is available in Samuel Escobar, *Evangelio y realidad social* (El Paso, TX: Casa Bautista de Publicaciones, 1988).

study of René Padilla and Pedro Arana Quiroz in Europe during this decade. Padilla did a PhD in biblical science (1963–1965) under the guidance of F. F. Bruce at the University of Manchester in England. He has written of how the questions that emerged during his student days, those raised by his Marxist professors and those arising from his experience doing evangelism in the Latin American university context, led him to the topic of his dissertation, which was titled "Iglesia y mundo: Un estudio de la relación entre iglesia y mundo en el pensamiento del Apóstol Pablo" (The church and the world: A study of the relationship between the church and the world in the thought of the apostle Paul).[32] Arana Quiroz, who was a chemical engineer, went to study theology at New College, Edinburgh, Scotland (1967–1969); he wrote his master's thesis, "Providence and Revolution," to contextualize his understanding of the Calvinist inheritance within the Latin American revolutionary era.[33] Also during his time studying in Scotland, Arana Quiroz gathered lectures that he had given on college campuses into a brief book that was published in the following decade.[34]

The Christ of Jorge Luis Borges

At the end of the 1960s many Latin Americans who admired Argentinian poet and fiction writer Jorge Luis Borges were surprised that his eagerly awaited book *Elogio de la sombra* (first translated as *In Praise of Darkness* by Norman Thomas di Giovanni) opens with a poem about Jesus, with a Bible verse from the introduction of John's Gospel: "And the Word became flesh and made his dwelling among us. We have seen his glory, the glory of the one and only Son, who came from the Father, full of grace and truth" (Jn 1:14). Professor Alejandro Clifford commented that the book's title was moving, as it makes reference to the progressive blindness of the poet and also indicates that Borges had a

[32]René Padilla, "Siervo de la palabra," in *Hacia una teología evangélica latinoamericana*, 115-16.

[33]Pedro Arana, "De la ingeniería al ministerio pastoral," *Boletín Teológico*, nos. 23, 24, 25 (1986–1987); Arana, *Providencia y revolución*, 2nd ed. (Grand Rapids: Subcomisión de Literatura Cristiana, 1986).

[34]Pedro Arana, *Progreso técnica y hombre*, 2nd ed. (Barcelona: Ediciones Evangélicas Europeas, 1973).

deep knowledge of the Bible and of its influence on world literature, particularly English literature.[35] The poem has a poignant tone; it imagines Jesus sharing a memory:

> I who am the Was, the Is, and the Is to Come
> again condescend to the written word
> which is time in succession and no more than an emblem. . . .
> I knew things smooth and gritty, uneven and rough,
> the taste of honey and apple,
> water in the throat of thirst,
> the weight of metal in the hand,
> the human voice, the sound of footsteps on the grass,
> the smell of rain in Galilee,
> the cry of birds on high. . . .
> Sometimes homesick, I think back
> on the smell of that carpenter's shop.

José Juan Garcia is poetically correct in his affirmation that "the Christ that Borges presents here is the image of a God who is nostalgic for human experience."[36]

Although Borges demonstrates familiarity with the Gospel accounts about Jesus, he did not consider himself a Christian, and his antipathy to systematizing meant that he never tried to establish a connecting thread among his numerous and varying references to Christ. In a dialogue about Christ with María Esther Vásquez, she asks him about how he sees Christ and says: "Jesus Christ was just." Borges responds:

> And furthermore he must have been an extraordinary man. At the same time, if a person believes that he is the Son of God, if he confesses such extraordinary opinions as this, I don't know to what point we can evaluate him. Undoubtedly he is one of the most unusual and most admirable people to have lived in this world. But I do not know if Christians bear any resemblance to Christ.[37]

[35]Alejandro Clifford, "Libros en ratos de ocio," *Pensamiento Cristiano*, no. 66 (June 1970): 103.
[36]José Juan García, "El Cristo de Borges," *Criterio*, no. 2170 (March 14, 1996): 49.
[37]María Esther Vásquez, *Borges, sus días y su tiempo*, 2nd ed. (Madrid: Suma de Letras, 2001), 117.

From Christology to Social Ethics

To understand the impact and the significance of the theological work begun by Justo L. González with his book *Revolution and Incarnation*, recall what I said in chapter two regarding the great chasm between religion and ethics, particularly in Ibero-American cultures. The critical opinions offered by Protestants such as Mackay and Rycroft during the forties were rejected by official Catholicism as exaggerations by proselytizing missionaries wanting to justify their intrusion into a world that was already Christian and devout. However, twenty years later, within the currents of Vatican II, a spirit of self-criticism within Catholicism began to appear, and the same critical observations made by Protestants took a new form in the writings of lay Catholics such as Chilean Alejandro Magnet and priests such as Uruguayan Juan Luis Segundo. This will be discussed in the next chapter.

Revolution and Incarnation is a historic study of the development of the doctrine of the incarnation during the early centuries of Christianity, and of the christological controversies in response surrounding the heresies that began to appear.[38] González gives attention to the apostle John's texts, especially the first epistle. For the first time in the Latin American evangelical context, christological themes were being approached from a systematic perspective to respond to pastoral needs. In his introduction González takes distance from liberal theology, which he characterizes as an era that is past in the history of Christian thought. He also distances himself from Marxism, remarking that since the time of Karl Marx, the Christian church had gone back to her original sources and had advanced toward a deeper and more authentic understanding of the character of Christianity. As an historian he offers a very clear focus: "Taking into account that our study is about two historic realities, that is to say, on the one hand revolution and on the other hand Christianity, it should be understood that from the beginning we are not discussing the veracity of the incarnation. What interests us is that Christianity is based on the doctrine of the incarnation."[39]

---

[38]Justo L. González, *Revolución y encarnación* (Río Piedras, Puerto Rico: La Reforma, 1965).
[39]González, *Revolución y encarnación*, 13.

As noted earlier, Mackay had affirmed that the Christ that predominated in Ibero-American religiosity was in reality a docetist Christ. Without referring to Mackay, González deepens this initial observation and offers a history of the doctrine of the incarnation of Jesus Christ and of the ways the doctrine has been wrongly approached, such as docetism and its contemporary equivalents:

> All too often we Christians, despite rejecting all insinuations of docetism in reference to the person of Christ, fall into docetism at a practical level through an implicit negation of the incarnation of God in Christ. This docetism is characterized by a spiritualized interpretation of Christianity, as if Christianity had to do only with certain spiritual and superheavenly realities. According to this hyperspirituality, all that is material is far away from Christianity.[40]

On the other hand he indicates the danger of falling into the opposite error, Ebionism. For example:

> The error of the "social gospel" was in the theological interpretation of the meaning of history—the kingdom of God would come about on the horizontal level in which we live as the culmination of our own efforts in social reorganization—and it is not simply a coincidence that its Christology was clearly Ebionite: Jesus was simply the maximum expression of the possibility of human morality.[41]

Next González examines the relationship between the incarnation and the sacramental life of the church, and he suggests that the church's service should be sacramental. He goes on to examine the church's vocation of service in relation to revolution. His interpretation of revolution and its challenges is rooted in the truth of the incarnation, which forces Christians to be interested in the meaning of revolution as among the material realities within which God is revealed.

> The doctrine of the incarnation is based on that fact that "God so loved the world that he gave his only Son." That is to say, the doctrine of the incarnation implies a relationship between God and the world that is

[40]González, *Revolución y encarnación*, 22.
[41]González, *Revolución y encarnación*, 37.

> different from the one that is usually imagined. The world, and not the church, is the primary focus of God's love. This is because our God is not a God who intends to yank us out of the world he himself created, because our God is not a God who is made known in "the spiritual" as opposed to the material, because our God is Emmanuel, God with us, God in the world.[42]

González also explains the Christian vision of history and its eschatological roots in contrast to a purely teleological vision such as that of Marxism. Finally he discusses the meaning of the incarnation in relation to the Christian position in the current revolutionary world and the options open to them. González's work makes clear that the central doctrine of the incarnation of Jesus Christ is intimately united to the vision of how God acts in the world and in history, and to the Christian vision of history in contrast with teleologies such as that of Marxism. González calls evangelicals to become aware that they have fallen into a docetic Christology that impedes the development of a social ethic appropriate to the needs of the time. His book was a constructive step toward building foundations for social ethics within a christological paradigm. As we will see, González's later theological work continued to deepen into this initial proposal.

Conclusion

The decade of the 1960s closed with two Latin American continental gatherings in which the theological work that had been developed was the object of debate and reflection in both the ecumenical and conservative evangelical contexts. In July 1969 the ecumenical world celebrated the Third Latin American Evangelical Conference, CELA III, in Buenos Aires. Puerto Rican theologian Orlando Costas sees this conference as the appearance of "a new Protestant conscience." Later he characterized the initiatives emerging from CELA III as an incarnational missiology, a diaconal ecclesiology, an indigenous Christology, and a liberating anthropology. During the conference there were two commissions focused

---

[42]González, *Revolución y encarnación*, 22.

on the topic of Christology. Their conclusions were not in complete agreement, but Costas affirms:

> Both sets of findings denounced Latin American Protestants not only for falling into christological heresy but also for distorting the evangelizing mission of the church. With this an interesting theological insight was brought to light: a distorted mission can be, and often is, rooted in distorted theology. Even more important, both reports detected a contradiction between the Christ preached by Protestants and the biblical Christ they claimed to follow.[43]

Meanwhile, among conservative evangelical Protestants the First Latin American Congress for Evangelization (CLADE 1) was celebrated in Bogotá, Colombia, in November 1969, which aimed to bring together the widest spectrum of Latin American Protestantism. As an initiative related to the previously mentioned Berlin Evangelization Congress in 1966, the program and the selection of participants were the responsibility of an ad hoc committee with a strong US presence. However, the development of the congress demonstrated that the revolutions shaking the continent were motivating a search for theology that was truly Latin American. The final ten-point declaration summarized material presented in papers and reports. There are two points worthy of special note. The third point, regarding theology and evangelism, is as follows:

> Our theology of evangelism determines our evangelizing action or its absence. The simplicity of the gospel is not at odds with its theological dimension. Its nature is the self-revelation of God in Christ Jesus. We reaffirm the historicity of Jesus Christ as is given witness in the Scriptures: his incarnation, his crucifixion, and his resurrection. We reaffirm the unique character of his mediating work, thanks to which the sinner finds forgiveness of sins and justification by faith without repetition of the sacrifice.

On the other hand, the sixth point makes an explicit reference to the Latin American context at that time:

---

[43]Orlando E. Costas, "Una nueva conciencia protestante: La III CELA," in *Oaxtepec 1978, Unidad y misión en América Latina* (San José, Costa Rica: CLAI, 1980), 88.

The process of evangelization takes place in concrete human contexts. The structures of society influence the church and the receivers of the gospel. If this reality is ignored, the gospel is disfigured and the Christian life impoverished. The time has come for evangelicals to become conscious of our social responsibilities. To fulfill them, the biblical foundation is evangelical doctrine and the example of Jesus Christ taken to their ultimate consequences. That example must be incarnated in the critical Latin American reality of underdevelopment, injustice, hunger, violence, and desperation. People cannot build the kingdom of God on earth, but evangelical social action will contribute to creating a better world as a foretaste of the one for whose coming they pray daily.[44]

[44]All the presentations, studies, and reports of the congress, and the final declaration, were published in CLADE I, *Acción en Cristo para un continente en crisis* (Miami: Caribe, 1970).

8

A CHRISTOLOGICAL RENEWAL IN CATHOLICISM

> *If in Latin America Christianity can survive social change only in the measure that it becomes in each person a life that is personal, heroic, and internally formed, pastoral leadership must take on a task that is formally new. New in relation to this Constantinian era that we have lived in until now; but on the other hand the oldest and most traditional, the task of* evangelizing. . . . *What does it mean to evangelize? According to what we have already said, it is to present Christianity to each man in such a way that by its own content, its intrinsic value, it produces in the person a personal, heroic, and internally formed commitment.*
>
> JUAN LUIS SEGUNDO, *DE LA SOCIEDAD A LA TEOLOGÍA*

Those of us who closely observed religious and cultural development in Latin America witnessed immense changes during the 1960s. One of these was the widespread attention given to the effort of some Catholics to make the expression of their faith more contemporary. In Argentina in 1964 *El evangelio criollo* (The homegrown gospel) was published by Jesuit Amado Anzi, a paraphrase of material from the four Gospels in the gaucho verse style of *Martin Fierro*, the national Argentinian poem, representing deeply rooted national traditions.[1] The first printing of

[1]Amado Anzi, SJ, *El evangelio criollo* (Buenos Aires: Agape, 1964). This first edition was followed by various others, and the work has continued to be published by another company.

twenty thousand copies quickly ran out as readers started to become acquainted with the story of Jesus, which had previously been little known. Corresponding to a resurgence in national culture, in contrast to Europeanizing and North American tendencies imposed by mass media, multitudes reread biblical material as never before.

The contextualization of the biblical text within an Argentinian countryside setting allowed many to see for the first time the richness of the Evangelists' story and its meaning for the present. Through this work many youth understood for the first time the life of Jesus incarnated as "one of us." The christological search that Mackay had called for decades earlier was becoming a reality in Catholic thought. The prologue to the first section of *El evangelio criollo* is a theological summary of what is to come in the narration:

So man could be God
The same God became man,
and to raise with renown
our being to heaven,
he came down to the world to have
our flesh and our name.
For that time of God,
seeing man so untamed,
the celestial Master
sent Jesus, our Lord,
to be tied with this rope
to the wooden fence of his love. . . .
The Lord simply continued
teaching the poor;
he took his rest in small ranches
and explained throughout the land
that God was here in person
to save sinful man
"Everyone do penance!"
he called out.
His fame spread quickly
as he healed with a word,

while at the same time bringing
the gospel of God.[2]

This proclamation of Christ's reality and the meaning of his life and death, directed intentionally to a mass readership, was part of a liturgical and formational renovation that had begun to occur in some progressive circles of European and Latin American Catholicism even prior to Vatican II. Then, for Catholicism at a global level and especially for Latin America, the 1960s was a time of turmoil and change, a response to the revolutionary process that was shaking the continent. It is helpful to understand the conscientization process that had begun prior to the renewal movement.

Pastoral Concerns That Led to Vatican Council II

Vatican Council II (1962–1965) was a notable effort to bring the Catholic Church up to date (*aggiornamento*) so it might face the new historic situations in the world. Given that by the 1960s more than a quarter of the world's Catholics lived in Latin America, the problems of Latin American Catholicism had to be acknowledged in the agenda of the council, and its decrees were in part a response to the region's problems. During the previous decades some theologians and pastors in Catholicism expressed concern over dechristianization in some places where Christianity had been important in society. In 1943 two French priests, Henri Godin and Yvan Daniel, published their celebrated book *La France, pays de mission?*, analyzing religious practices of the French and their adherence to the Catholic Church to show levels similar to those of mission countries in Africa or Asia, where those who practiced Christianity were only a small minority of the population.[3] From this concern grew new mission practices after the Second World War—for example, "worker priests" who sought to incarnate a Christian presence among working people to call them back to faith in Christ. Dechristianization was being acknowledged as a reality.

[2]Amado Anzi, *El evangelio criollo* (repr., Buenos Aires: Patria Grande, 1994), 6, 18, 19.

[3]Published in English as Henri Godin and Yvan Daniel, "France: A Missionary Land?," in *France Pagan? The Mission of Abbé Godin*, ed. Maisie Ward (London: Sheed and Ward, 1949), 65-191.

Belgian Carmelite Ireneo Rosier studied the same phenomenon in different European countries and later came to study it in Latin America, which allowed him to undertake a comparative analysis. His description of the process affirms: "The specific element of dechristianization is a religious indifference in which no excitement for Christ or his gospel is found, or for his message of truth and happiness."[4] Explaining further, Rosier says, "The concept of dechristianization as such indicates a dynamic reality, that is to say, a gradual loosening, from a state in which Christ has a central and normative place in the thoughts and actions of people, in the direction of an attitude toward life that does not take Christ into account."[5] In his book *Ovejas sin pastor* (Sheep without a shepherd) he summarizes his research over a number of years, particularly in Chile.

The surprise for Rosier was that in Chile, though the Catholic masses were dechristianized, there was a vigorous and growing Protestantism that was Christ-centered. For Rosier, "Protestantism has opened the way directly to Christ, while in Catholicism it is as if the authentic face of Christ were veiled by civilization and by the complications of many centuries."[6] In contrast to other Catholic books from this era that referred to Protestantism in a wholly hostile manner, as if it were an anomaly unworthy of existence, Rosier's book, while maintaining a critical stance toward Protestantism, was a call to alertness rooted in the conviction that Catholicism had to make fundamental pastoral changes: "Because if Catholic pastoral care is inadequate to the demands of our times and thus leads the people toward Protestantism, it means that over time the lack of vital pastoral care will be responsible for a rebirth of paganism."[7]

An ecumenical Protestant gathering organized in 1965 by the Centro de Estudios Cristianos del Río de la Plata (Argentina) deliberated topics related to Protestant presence in a Catholic continent. Participants spoke

---

[4]Ireneo Rosier, *Ovejas sin pastor* (Buenos Aires: Carlos Lohlé, 1960), 19.
[5]Rosier, *Ovejas sin pastor*, 20.
[6]Rosier, *Ovejas sin pastor*, 104.
[7]Rosier, *Ovejas sin pastor*, 108.

of dechristianization, but they treated the process as the end of Christendom, part of the disappearance of "sacred" societies and the coming of "secular" ones, with these terms used in their sociological and not theological senses. However, positive interpretations of the phenomenon by theologians such as Anglican Dennis Munby were highlighted. Munby said, "Such a society is framed more nearly in accordance with the Will of God as we can see it in Scripture, in the Incarnation, and in the way God actually treats men, than those societies which have attempted to impose on the mass of men what a small Christian group have believed to be in accordance with God's Will."[8] Personalist Catholic philosopher Emmanuel Mounier, who likewise values the end of Christendom and the appearing of a pluralist society as an opportunity, was quoted:

> It would seem that, having for many centuries flirted, as it were, with the Jewish temptation, of trying directly to establish the Kingdom of God upon the plane of terrestrial power, Christianity is slowly returning to its first position; renouncing government upon earth and the outward appearances of sacralization in order to give shape to the unique work of the Church, the community of Christians in the Christ, mingled among all men in the secular work,—neither theocracy nor liberalism, but a return to the double rigours of transcendence and incarnation.[9]

The Threefold "Return to Pristine Origins" of the Conciliar Movement

In a certain way Vatican II was not a beginning point but rather a point of arrival, the official acceptance of a renewing ferment that had been taking place for a while, especially in French, Belgian, and Dutch Catholicism. Canon Gustavo Thils summarized this theological ferment in the heart of Catholicism through 1959 with an eloquent term: *repristinación* in Spanish (in French *ressourcement*), that is to say, a "return to the sources." For Thils it was a process with three dimensions: a

---

[8]D. L. Munby, *The Idea of a Secular Society and Its Significance for Christians* (Oxford: Oxford University Press, 1923), 34.

[9]Emmanuel Mounier, *Personalism* (1949; repr., New York: Boughton, 2007), 122.

return to biblical sources, to the patristic sources, and to liturgical sources.[10] This process connected with the primary intention of the council, summarized in the words of the pope who called it together: "It is clearly evident that a Council is concerned primarily with the Catholic Church. Its purpose is to show the Church's vigor and to emphasize its spiritual mission. It also aims to adapt its methods so that the Gospel teaching may be worthily lived and more readily heeded by the people."[11]

Here are some aspects of this process. From the beginning of the twentieth century, with the foundation of the Bible School of Jerusalem (1892) and the Papal Bible Institute (1909), Catholics had been increasingly emphasizing biblical study. In 1943 the encyclical *Divino Afflante Spiritu* by Pope Pius XII encouraged intensive Bible study as part of the life of the church. Observable effects of this return to the Scriptures did not come immediately, but by the middle of the century they could be observed even in Latin America. Beginning in 1938, a German missionary in Argentina, Monseñor Juan Straubinger, had begun a biblical apostolate that produced an excellent translation to Spanish of the Bible from the original Greek and Hebrew. The old Catholic opposition to the diffusion of the Bible was beginning to give way to new efforts to emulate Protestant zeal for the Bible.

The return to patristic sources meant a rediscovering of the church fathers from the first three to four centuries of the Christian era, prior to the time when theology was hardened into scholastic categories originating in the study of Aristotle. Patristic theology was more kerygmatic than casuistic—that is to say, it had in view preaching for the people of God, rather than debates between prominent theologians. In this sense it is closer to the biblical exposition and preaching that later characterized the ministry of Luther and Calvin.

---

[10]Gustavo Thils, *Orientaciones actuales de la teología* (Buenos Aires: Troquel, 1959).

[11]John XXIII, "Address to Extraordinary Diplomatic Missions Representing Their Governments at the Solemn Opening of the II Vatican Ecumenical Council (October 12, 1962)," Vatican website, https://w2.vatican.va/content/john-xxiii/en/speeches/1962/documents/hf_j-xxiii_spe_19621012_missioni-straordinarie.html.

The return to the sources of primitive liturgy involved efforts to discover what worship services and communication of the truth were like in the primitive church. It meant returning to the sources and styles that preceded the Latin sources and forms that had become sacred during the Middle Ages. All this ferment found expression in the reforms and proposals for renewal that flowed from Vatican II. It was impossible to deny that winds of change were blowing all over the world.

In Latin America, it can be said that the presence and growth of Protestantism were and continue to be an incentive and an undoubtable stimulus that forced Catholics to seek self-critique and renewal. The triple process of returning to the sources produced *De Divina Revelatione*, a council decree that was particularly appreciated by Protestants due to its novel treatment of the relationship between Scripture and tradition. Although traditional Catholic doctrine remained unchanged, the approach encouraged by the council involved a greater appreciation for the Bible and its presence in the life of the church. It was especially important for Catholic theological work, which began an intensive use of the Bible. This was an outstanding mark of the liberation theologies.

Self-Critique Within Latin American Catholicism

In a similar spirit to that of Vatican Council II, beginning in the middle of the twentieth century a series of self-critiquing efforts were initiated by Latin American Roman Catholics. An important step in the renewing force was the Third Inter-American Catholic Action Week in the port of Chimbote, Peru, in 1953. One of its conclusions was that "the vast majority [of Latin American Catholics] are Catholic only in name, that is to say nominal."[12] In February 1960 priest Carlos Ranken, CSC, said in an interview in the North American magazine *Maryknoll*, "What is needed in Latin America is to revivify a dead body. This may sound too strong, but the Church is a shell whose vitality and religious dynamism have

[12]US Catholic missionary William J. Coleman presented a valuable translation and interpretation of the conclusions from Chimbote: *Latin American Catholicism: A Self-Evaluation* (Maryknoll, NY: Maryknoll Publications, 1958).

been absorbed and defeated. It no longer has influence over the life of the people. . . . Faith is implicitly understood as an inheritance or social tradition. It is too bound to Hispanic culture."[13]

The Catholic pastoral leadership came to admit that the process of evangelization of the continent had been deficient. Writing about Peru, Cesar Arróspide, a lay Catholic leader, said: "In Peru, though it has been four centuries since the arrival of Christianity and the establishment of the church hierarchy, there are vast areas of mission in the strict sense, that is, where the gospel has not been preached among the pagans."[14] The Catholic Church began to realize that even in Latin America, Christ was not present as Savior and Lord in the daily lives of Latin Americans. Catholicism began to admit the validity of what Protestant missionary pioneers such as Mackay and other diverse analysts had already pointed out. The critical mission situation of the continent was being recognized.

At Rome's request, a gathering of bishops from throughout Latin America was held in Rio de Janeiro in 1955, and the Latin American Episcopal Council (CELAM) was founded. Later historians of CELAM recognized that the growth of Protestantism was a determining impetus for the formation of a continental council of bishops.[15] One of the council's first actions was to issue a call for Catholic missionaries from other regions to come and help a church that felt threatened by the growth of Marxism and Protestantism among the masses.[16] How did the Catholic hierarchy explain the need for missionaries in this continent that had previously been presented as Christian? The proposed Catholic missionary effort to Latin America from North America and Europe was presented as a necessary investment that would allow for the mobilization of a Latin American missionary force to other parts of the world later. This was the reasoning of Pope Pius XII when he wrote in 1955:

[13]Cited by W. Stanley Rycroft, *A Factual Study of Latin America* (New York: UPCUSA, 1963), 211.

[14]Cesar Arróspide, quoted in Ricardo Pattee, *El catolicismo contemporáneo en Hispanoamérica* (Buenos Aires: Editorial Fides, 1951), 388-89.

[15]Hernán Parada, *Crónica de Medellín* (Bogotá: Indo American Press Service, 1975), 25; Alberto Methol Ferré, "De Río de Janeiro al Vaticano II," in *Elementos para su historia 1955–1980* (Bogotá, 1982).

[16]See Samuel Escobar, "Mission and Renewal in Latin American Catholicism," *Missiology* 15, no. 2 (1987): 33-46.

> We have the firm hope that the means undertaken now will be multiplied greatly in the future. And these fruits will surely bring Latin America back to the Church of Christ when, as we can expect, many precious energies have been activated that now seem to await only the priest's action to contribute intensely to growth in the kingdom of Christ.[17]

Five years later, in this same spirit, Monsignor Casaroli, special envoy of Pope John XXIII, gave a celebrated speech before the superiors of the main religious orders in the United States. He asked that each religious province in North America send 10 percent of its lay workers, priests, and nuns as missionaries to Latin America. It should be remembered that China, where various North American orders had planted missions, had been closed to Christian missionaries since the arrival of Mao Tse Tung's communism into power some years before this. Monsignor Casaroli's call was taken up with an enthusiastic response, and a famous North American mission promoter arrived to ask that forty thousand missionaries be sent. The goal proposed by the pope was never met, but much enthusiasm was generated, and many men and women from the United States and Canada went as missionaries to Latin America. Waves of French, Belgian, Irish, and Swiss arrived as well and joined the Spanish and Italians who had already been serving among Latin American Catholics.

These Catholic missionaries from Europe and North America had great influence in subsequent critical analysis of the situation of Latin American Catholicism and the awakening of the Catholic social conscience, which later resulted in the theologies of liberation. Immersion in the world of poverty and marginalization transformed the missionaries themselves. This is dramatically expressed by a missionary who worked in Nicaragua for thirty years:

> Unless a person wants to "put on the mind of Christ," he'd be better not to enter Latin American work. . . . Christ came as one of the oppressed with a message of life for the oppressors. We, the church today, tend to come

[17]I Conferencia General del Episcopado Latinoamericano, *Documento de Río* (Lima: Vida y Espiritualidad, 1991), 10.

> as the oppressors to the oppressed, telling them *we* have a message of life—and they say to us, "Oh, really? Show us!"[18]

The next CELAM meetings, in Medellín, Colombia (1968), and Puebla, Mexico (1979), registered the impact of this influence, although the effects of the labor of Catholic missionaries from Europe and North America during this time have not been fully studied.[19] Research on missions in Latin America has itself been heavily influenced by foreign missionaries settled in Latin American countries, such as North American Juan Gorski, Spanish Manuel M. Marzal, SJ, Belgian Franz Damen, and Swiss Roger Aubry.

A New Pastoral Proposal

Two theologians who became famous for their work in liberation theology allow us to appreciate how the spirit of the Vatican Council was interpreted at the level of emerging theological reflection in Latin America during this decade. Early works of Peruvian Gustavo Gutiérrez and Uruguayan Juan Luis Segundo powerfully described critically the pastoral situations that the Latin American Catholic Church faced. There were serious crises in Peru, a mestizo country with indigenous minorities and scandalous social inequality, and Uruguay, the most secularized country of Latin America. The ideas of these authors had influence in the CELAM conference in Medellín, in which Gutiérrez participated as one of the seventeen specialists advising the bishops.

Here we consider texts these two theologians wrote in the 1960s, prior to the formal appearance of liberation theologies. Generally, liberation theologies are connected to political praxis, but it is important to understand that the initial impulse of Gutiérrez's and Segundo's theological work was of a pastoral nature, and one of their concerns was the necessity of taking seriously the task of evangelization. Thus they were both rooted

---

[18]Gerald M. Costello, *Mission to Latin America* (Maryknoll, NY: Orbis, 1979), 41.

[19]Regarding Catholic missionaries from the United States, two important works are Costello, *Mission to Latin America*, and Mary M. McGlone, *Sharing Faith Across the Hemisphere* (Maryknoll, NY: Orbis, 1997).

deeply in their church, although taking a critical position that did not always coincide with that of the church hierarchy.

Gustavo Gutiérrez, Prophetic Pastoral Analysis

Gutiérrez analyzes the pastoral situation in Latin America on the basis of formal study but also from his practical experience as a staff worker for the National Union of Catholic Students (UNEC) of Peru and his teaching at the Catholic University of Lima. In his book *Líneas pastorales de la Iglesia en América Latina* (Pastoral trends in the church in Latin America) he includes works presented in conferences in 1964 and 1967. He first offers a panoramic history and then describes four types of pastoral leadership present in the Catholic Church throughout the continent at that time: the ministry of Christendom, which covers the most extensive and enduring type of work; the ministry of new Christendom; the ministry of maturity in the faith; and prophetic pastoral ministry, which is the direction in which Gutiérrez leans. He describes each of these kinds of ministry carefully, exploring their underlying theology. This theological exploration concentrates on ecclesiology, but Gutiérrez sustains that in Vatican II "we face a transition from ecclesiocentrism to Christocentrism. Christianity over time had led the church to be focused on itself, with the tendency to occupy the place of Christ in history. The council has renewed the church's faith in the centrality of its Lord, in whom all was created and in whom all things subsist."[20]

It could be said that the critical work of Gutiérrez arises from a christological position. He maintains that the evangelization of Latin America took place in the midst of the era of Christendom, and that Spain and Portugal did not pass through the crisis of Christianity that affected other European countries due to the Protestant Reformation. This, he says, is the reason "Christianity did not take root deeply in Latin America."[21] He also maintains that Vatican II sought to leave behind Christendom-style pastoral leadership but that it remains in force in Latin America. He characterizes this pastoral style thus:

[20]Gustavo Gutiérrez, *Líneas pastorales de la Iglesia en América Latina* (Lima: CEP, 1970), 87.
[21]Gutiérrez, *Líneas pastorales de la Iglesia*, 16.

> With regard to access to the faith, this pastoral option assumes an equivalence between conversion (the conversion of the heart, an interior change) and belonging to the visible church, which is accomplished through baptism. The baptized one is considered a believer, although in practice he might not be. . . . Evangelization is neglected in favor of immediate sacramentalization.[22]

When sacramental practice is used to measure people's faith, "it can go to the extreme of treating the sacrament as insurance guaranteeing salvation, with no concern for the person's subsequent behavior."[23]

Applying a methodology that was later adopted by liberation theologies, Gutiérrez applies social analysis to the situation of the church in Latin America:

> Moreover, the church appears strongly tied to the traditional forms of society, to certain social classes, presenting a image that repels many men. . . . Pastoral leadership of Christendom seeks to appeal to a sector of Latin American men, the proletarian and subproletarian masses; but curiously it appeals also to members of the conservative oligarchy who appreciate this traditional Christianity and recognize it as their own. . . . The church with this leadership receives economic support from the oligarchy to build churches, schools, seminaries, etc.[24]

In contrast to the Christendom style, which assumes that "outside the church there is no salvation," Gutiérrez's preferred pastoral emphasis presupposes a new concept of salvation. Given the new situation emerging with Christendom's disappearance,

> The theology of prophetic pastoral leadership is marked by concern for the religious status of non-Christians, that is to say, their position before Christ. . . . The perspective from which the notion of salvation is worked out within a dialogic pastoral approach is fundamentally christological, focusing on texts of Saint Paul telling us that in Christ all has been created, all has its being, all men have been saved.[25]

---

[22]Gutiérrez, *Líneas pastorales de la Iglesia*, 16-17.
[23]Gutiérrez, *Líneas pastorales de la Iglesia*, 17.
[24]Gutiérrez, *Líneas pastorales de la Iglesia*, 20-21.
[25]Gutiérrez, *Líneas pastorales de la Iglesia*, 63-64.

Gutiérrez calls for a theology of salvation "that takes the logical consequences of the affirmation that all men have in principle been saved by Christ."[26] In outlining this theology, Gutiérrez draws on the thought of Catholic theologians such as German Karl Rahner and Dutch Edward Schillebeeckx, known for their universalist vision that includes "the notion of the implicit or anonymous Christian, one who exemplifies charity without realizing it, without explicitly confessing faith."[27] But there is a distinctive element in Gutiérrez's proposal: "Prophetic pastoral leadership affirms that the condition for salvation is love; salvation is the fruit of love; those who love are saved, that is to say, those who enter into communion with men enter into communion with God."[28] At this juncture in Gutiérrez's theological work there is no reference to the mediating work of Jesus Christ, nor the expiatory nature of his death.

Juan Luis Segundo: Evangelization and Socialism

The work of Juan Luis Segundo includes his firsthand pastoral observations, exploration of biblical texts, and exegesis of Vatican Council II texts. In 1964 he published an article titled "Pastoral latinoamericana: Hora de decisión" (Latin American pastoral leadership: A time for decisions) in Chilean Jesuit magazine *Mensaje* (Message), in which he invites a revision of traditional attitudes, given the new facts of this time: "The major reality of the modern world that presents a radical question to our Christian pastoral leadership is the destruction of closed environments."[29] He is pointing out that the church can no longer control the lives of the people like it did in the era of Christendom, when the church was like an immense Christian-making machine that transmitted ideas, values, symbols, and habits from one generation to another. "Now this machine no longer functions," says Segundo. "There is no longer a machine to make Christians, and it is futile to try to gather its

[26]Gutiérrez, *Líneas pastorales de la Iglesia*, 64.
[27]Gutiérrez, *Líneas pastorales de la Iglesia*, 69.
[28]Gutiérrez, *Líneas pastorales de la Iglesia*, 64-65.
[29]The *Mensaje* article is reprinted in Juan Luis Segundo, *De la sociedad a la teología* (Buenos Aires: Carlos Lohlé, 1970), 32.

scattered pieces and make them work again." Today, unable to apply force, relying only on whatever inherent attractiveness it possesses, the church will have to appeal to what is deep within each human being, the need for authenticity:

> If in Latin America Christianity can survive social change only in the measure that it becomes in each person a life that is personal, heroic, and internally formed, pastoral leadership must take on a task that is *formally new*. New in relation to this Constantinian era that we have lived in until now; but on the other hand the oldest and most traditional, the task of *evangelizing*. . . . What does it mean to evangelize? According to what we have already said, it is to present Christianity to each man in such a way that by its own content, its intrinsic value, it produces in the person a personal, heroic, and internally formed commitment.[30]

For Segundo it is clear that the task of evangelization requires evangelizers to travel to the origins of their faith, to grasp the central truth of the gospel. Referring to Acts 8, in which the deacon Philip shares the gospel with the Ethiopian official, Segundo notes the simplicity of Philip's explanation and how soon thereafter the official requests baptism and Philip baptizes him: "The man departs a Christian, continuing on the desert road toward a country where no catechists await him, no priests or theological manuals, nor Catholic universities."[31] The essentials of the faith have been communicated to a man who had been reading the book of the prophet Isaiah. Segundo comments: "To evangelize presupposes, in effect, these two inseparable and complementary elements: first, that we ourselves know how to discover and communicate the essentials of the good news, and second, that we know to stop there and accept the rhythm of the maturing of the Word of God."[32]

In 1968, Segundo published an article about social justice and revolution in the magazine *America*, a Jesuit publication in the United States. It was an effort to communicate to the North American public the reasons for the intensified social activism of Latin American Catholics

---

[30]Segundo, *De la sociedad a la teología*, 37.
[31]Segundo, *De la sociedad a la teología*, 38.
[32]Segundo, *De la sociedad a la teología*, 39.

and their understanding of the social doctrine of the church. In Vatican II documents and the Final Document of Medellín alike, there are open critiques of capitalism that doubtless surprised North American Catholics. Segundo describes the dramatic situation of Latin America:

> Paradoxically, at the same time that Latin American guerrilla movements suffer with the death of Ernesto "Che" Guevara, condemnation of the capitalist system is increasingly emphasized by the Latin American [church] hierarchy. It seems that a latent desperation is present and growing in Latin America day by day regarding the possible victory of the last apparent means to bring down legally enshrined injustice and human exploitation: the violence of the victims.[33]

Next he offers a historic overview of the development of Christian thinking regarding poverty and wealth, to help readers understand why recent papal and conciliar documents make reference to socialism as an economic alternative to the harshness of pure capitalism:

> The Gospels, or better, the New Testament, do not present a theory of society or special procedures to change it. Christ said, "Woe to the rich," in different ways and on different occasions. And he explained why. But it is not possible to deduce from this a political or economic system. Rather, it is a human orientation that rejects profit as the center of a man's activity and interpersonal relationships.[34]

He provides a schematic view of the evolution of Christian thought regarding wealth and poverty and concludes with an eloquent observation that bears a touch of irony:

> In other words, if we read with seriousness and courage, in the context of Latin American development, these repeated orientations, we again meet forms of socialism that international politics, particularly that of the United States, will interpret and castigate as communist and hostile to North American interests, twisting them practically and fatally into Soviet communism. Nevertheless, in themselves, they constitute Christian thought.[35]

---

[33]Segundo, *De la sociedad a la teología*, 127.
[34]Segundo, *De la sociedad a la teología*, 130.
[35]Segundo, *De la sociedad a la teología*, 139.

◆ ◆ ◆

In such ways the Catholic theological reflection leading up to the Medellín conference expresses urgency regarding social issues in Latin America, on the one hand, and on the other hand displays a self-critical awareness that the church itself needs to return to basic tasks such as evangelization. Chilean pastoral theologian Segundo Galilea, one of the most prolific scholars on this topic, refuses to call the Latin American continent a "mission field," yet even so, he recognizes that there are vast sectors in need of primary evangelization: "Today there are groups of Latin Americans who need to be evangelized in an even stricter sense of the word. They may include nonbelievers, Amazonian indigenous, student groups, intellectuals, polemicists, those who have taken an aggressive stance. Many times baptized people have abandoned religion and the church. Some are 'post-Christian.'"[36]

The Medellín Statement

In 1968 the second CELAM assembly, held in Medellín, presented a clear contrast with that of Rio de Janeiro in 1955. Now the Catholic Church was not on the defensive toward Protestants and communists; rather, it was a church experiencing transformations that an outside observer would recognize as signs of vitality. Writing with the wisdom of a longtime observer, Methodist bishop Mortimer Arias summarizes correctly the significance of Medellín:

> It seemed as if the old Catholic Church of the Counter-Reformation suddenly was trying to undertake a reformation that had been put off for four hundred years, and at the same time become involved in the revolution of the twentieth century. The new era of the Church was visibly dramatized by the presence of Pope Paul VI, and, for the first time in history, representatives of non-Catholic churches were present. . . . The official representatives of the Roman Catholic Church were seeing Latin America as "a world that has not been evangelized, a new continent still needing to be Christianized."[37]

[36]Segundo Galilea, *Evangelización en América Latina* (Quito: CELAM-IPLA, 1969); see also his work *La responsabilidad misionera de América Latina* (Bogotá: Paulinas, 1981).

[37]Esther Arias and Mortimer Arias, *El clamor de mi pueblo* (New York: Friendship, 1981), 116.

However, for Arias, in addition to this new missionary consciousness, "the essential and revolutionary meaning from Medellín was the church's discovery of the poor, and with this the recovery of the full biblical gospel. . . . Never before on this continent had the church taken human and social conditions so seriously."[38]

The Medellín Final Statement, its document of conclusions as we know it now, was originally drafted by a group of experts and circulated among the bishops months prior to the gathering. The different national conferences of bishops made their comments and contributions, and the final content was worked out in commissions during the gathering. As a result, it has a consensual character, reflecting the thinking that was in process throughout Latin America. The document is divided in three parts: human advancement, evangelization and growth of faith, and the visible church and its structures. In its introduction it recognizes that the episcopal Conference "centered its attention on the men of this continent, who are living a decisive moment in a historic process." The bishops chose to take a christological perspective on human struggle: "The church has tried to understand this historic moment of the Latin American people in the light of the Word, which is Christ, in whom the mystery of man was manifested." The fifth point of the introduction says:

> The fact that the transformation that helps our continent reaches the totality of man is a sign and a demand. As Christians, we must not close off our awareness of the presence of God, who wants to save the whole man, soul and body. In the definitive day of salvation, God will resurrect our bodies, for whose redemption we groan now, in having received the Spirit's initial presence. God has resurrected Christ and as a result all who believe in him. Christ, actively present in our history, anticipates his eschatological action not only in the impatient desire of man for his total redemption, but also in those victories, as forward-pointing signs, gained by man through an activity undertaken in love.

Another key point of the section regarding human advancement is the one addressing peace. Awareness of life in a conflictive society and

[38]Arias and Arias, *El clamor de mi pueblo*, 116.

interpretation of the conflict, before which the church must not remain indifferent, was a passionately discussed theme. Here the pronouncement is clear:

> In the end, peace is the fruit of love, the expression of a real fellowship among men: fellowship given by Christ, the Prince of Peace, in reconciling all men to the Father. Human solidarity can not truly occur except in Christ, who gives peace that the world cannot give. Love is the soul of justice. The Christian who works for social justice should always cultivate peace and love in his heart. (Peace, 9c)

In the light of this theological declaration, a pastoral warning was issued: "The peace of God is the ultimate foundation of interior peace and social peace. In the same way, where social peace does not exist, where social, political, economical and cultural inequality exists, there is a rejection of the Lord's gift of peace; even more, a rejection of the Lord himself" (Peace, 9c).

Probably one of the most fruitful concepts in the document from Medellín is what came to be known as "the preferential option for the poor." The section "Poverty of the Church" seeks a biblical understanding of poverty. There are references to poverty as being a lack of material possessions and a spiritual poverty as an attitude before God. But there is also another type of poverty:

> Poverty as a commitment that takes on voluntarily and out of love the condition of the needy of this world to give witness to the evil present in the world, and spiritual liberty in response to possessions, follows Christ's example, who took on himself the consequences of the sinful condition of men and "being rich, became poor" to save us.

Writing in 1988 with the perspective of two decades, Gustavo Gutiérrez explains that this is a key idea for liberation theologies:

> This is the context of a theme that is central to this theology and that today is widely accepted in the universal church: *the preferential option for the poor*. Medellín spoke of "giving preference to the poorest and needy sectors and to those segregated for whatever reason" (Poverty, No. 9). The

> very term preference rejects all exclusivity and underlines who should be first—but not the only ones—to receive our solidarity[39]

For an evangelical observer it is important to remember that, amid the social conflicts of the decades following Medellín, the fact that some priests, nuns, and bishops openly expressed their preferential option for the poor put them under the critical view of the dominant oligarchies and of the totalitarian regimes that multiplied following General Pinochet's 1973 coup in Chile, overthrowing the elected president, Salvador Allende. In Latin America at the time, for an evangelical pastor to place himself on the side of the poor did not have the impact or provoke the shock that occurred when a Catholic bishop did so. It was a radical, even scandalous, shift.

Priorities in Catechetical Renewal

If biblical and theological renewal found expression in the statement's affirmations regarding justice, peace, and poverty, the self-critiquing pastoral reflection that had been occurring throughout this decade, encouraged by missionaries and pastors, was expressed in the document's agenda for the future of the church, calling for new forms of catechism, evangelization, and Christian education.

> In accordance with this revelation theology, the current catechism should take on all the anguishes and hopes of today's man, with the aim of offering him the possibility of complete liberty, the riches of a complete salvation in Christ, the Lord. For this, the transmission of the biblical message must be faithful, not only in its intelectual content, but also in its vital reality incarnated in the life action of today's man. (Catechesis, 6)

The influence of the ideas of education for liberation can be observed in the catechetical agenda. These ideas had been developed by Brazilian educator Paulo Freire, whose first experiences in literacy and popular

[39]Gustavo Gutiérrez, "Mirar lejos," introduction to the new edition of *Teología de la liberación: Perspectivas* (Lima: CEP, 1988), 24.

education had occurred in Catholic circles in northeastern Brazil.[40] The text must be read within the community's context:

> The historic situations and the authentically human aspirations form an indispensable part of the content of the catechism; they should be seriously interpreted, within their actual context, in the light of the lived experiences of the people of Israel, of Christ, and of the church community, in which the Spirit of the risen Christ continually lives and works.

The evangelizing emphasis originated in acknowledgment of the precariousness of the faith of those baptized within the church, for historic reasons but also because of developments such as immigration and social mobility. A great variety of regional and national situations were recognized, but a shared commitment to evangelizing was said to be essential:

> Despite this plurality of situations, our catechism has a common point in all life's spaces: it must be eminently evangelizing, without presupposing a reality of faith, but following suitable verification. The fact of being baptized as small children, trusting in the family's faith, makes an evangelization of the baptized necessary as a stage in the education of faith. And this need is urgent, taking into account the disintegration that families have suffered in many areas, the religious ignorance of the adults and the scarcity of Christian base communities.

Juan Luis Segundo had made a comparative historic reference in relation to evangelization: although the task of primitive Christianity was to baptize the evangelized, in the current Latin American context the task was evangelizing the baptized. The document says:

> This evangelization of the baptized has a specific aim: lead them to a personal commitment to Christ and a concious surrender in obedience to faith. From here comes the importance of revising the the pastoral processes for confirmation, in the same way as the new forms of the catechetical process for adults, insisting on preparation for the sacraments. We should also review all in our lives or our insitutions that might be an

[40]On Freire, see my book *Paulo Freire: Una pedagogía latinoamericana* (Mexico City: Kyrios-CUPSA, 1983).

> obstacle for the reevangelization of adults, in this way purifying the face of the church before the world.

In the light of this agenda, contextualizing works such as *El evangelio criollo*, mentioned at the beginning of this chapter, can be better understood. Also in Argentina in the same year, 1964, distribution of the *Misa criolla* had reached across the country. This was a musical work for soloists, choir, and orchestra created by popular Argentinian musician Ariel Ramírez. The liturgical texts were translated and adapted by priests Antonio Osvaldo Catena, Alejandro Mayol, and Jesús Gabriel Segade. Its different parts move from minor tones in the style of an Andean lament to the tropical joy of the songs of northeast Argentina. In 1965 the work was launched publicly as an album, sung by Los Fronterizos, one of the most famous musical groups in Argentina, with singers of the Basílica del Socorro in Buenos Aires. Similar experiments soon followed in countries such as Mexico, Peru, Chile, and Nicaragua, adopting the rhythms and literary style popular in each country. Popular Protestantism had done this since the 1950s, demonstrating the value of the people's participation in the reading of the Word, songs, and prayer in their own style and language. Now Catholicism took up the same task. Many Catholics heard the texts of the Gospels for the first time in the words of the Creole Mass in Spanish, with the rhythm of folk music, and in this way discovered the christological center of liturgy.

The Medellín Statement said:

> The language with which the church clothes itself is of particular importance. It involves the ways in which simple teaching takes place—catechism, homily—in local communities, as well as the more universal ways of the magisterium. It involves a permanent effort so the message of salvation contained in the Scripture, liturgy, magisterium, and the testimony will be today Word of life. It is not enough to repeat or explain the message, but rather repeatedly express in new ways, the gospel in relation to the form of human existence, taking into account the human, ethnic and cultural environment, and *always protecting the faithfulness of the revealed Word.* (Medellín 8.15)

A Protestant Reading of Vatican II and Medellín

The two large Protestant gatherings that concluded this decade registered the changes that were occurring in Latin American Catholicism. The ecumenical conclave CELA III gathered under the theme "Indebted to the World," based on the affirmation of the apostle Paul in Romans 1:14. One of the main presentations was that of José Míguez Bonino. It should be remembered that Míguez Bonino was the only Latin American evangelical observer at the Second Vatican Council; his account and evaluation of the event can be read in his book *Concilio abierto* (Open council), the text of the Strachan Lecture he presented at the Latin American Biblical Seminary of Costa Rica.[41] His presentation at CELA III was titled "Deuda evangélica para con la comunidad católica romana" (The evangelical debt to the Roman Catholic community). Míguez Bonino summarizes the crisis in Roman Catholicism in Latin America due to the many changes that were taking place, some of which Pope Paul VI had come to describe as "practically seismic change" or "centrifugal tendencies." Reviewing the positive changes advocated in various Catholic sectors, Míguez Bonino returns to the traditionally conflictive attitude of Protestants toward Catholicism. The Catholic crisis also puts Protestants in crisis, he said: "A Catholicism with Bible in hand, free of images, and with a reduced number of clerics but ethically purified and consecrated to the gospel—this Catholicism leaves us perplexed. Our traditional controversy 'strikes only the air.' What should we do?"[42]

Míguez asserts, "What we owe is the gospel. We have nothing else of value, and nothing else is comparably necessary for the Roman Catholic community, for ours, or for any other." Our debt, he says, can be summarized in three points: we owe an evangelical attitude that flows from the love that the Holy Spirit pours out in each believer, we owe them the service of correcting and rebuking in love, and we owe them the proclamation of the gospel to all creatures. He concludes by saying: "Jesus Christ is greater than our traditions. The gospel is greater than our doctrines.

---

[41]José Míguez Bonino, *Concilio abierto* (Buenos Aires: La Aurora, 1967).

[42]José Míguez Bonino, "Deuda evangélica para con la comunidad católica romana," *Pensamiento Cristiano* 17, no. 66 (June 1970): 125.

The power of the Spirit transcends our church boundaries. The mission of God on a continent thirsty for justice and thirsty for Christ is greater than all our churches. It is this debt that should govern our relationships with the Roman Catholic community or any other group or person."[43]

In the evangelical conclave CLADE I in Bogotá, which concentrated on the task of evangelism, Salvadoran theologian Emilio Antonio Núñez gave a talk titled "Posición de la iglesia frente al *aggiornamento*" (The position of the church in the face of *aggiornamento*; this term, which means "updating," had been used since Vatican II to speak of the Catholic Church's process of reform and renewal). His presentation was divided into three parts: the reality of *aggiornamento*, its risks, and responsibility toward it. Núñez recognizes the liturgical renewal and biblical rebirth:

> It is undeniable that the Roman Catholic Church is making an unprecedented effort regarding translation, distribution, and use of the Bible. . . . Of all the postconciliar changes in Catholicism, there is no other more promising of better things in the life of thousands of Catholics than that related to the new attitude of the Roman Church toward the sacred Scriptures. We should trust in the redeeming power of the written revelation.[44]

He also points out the limitations of the theological revolution and that "the conciliar documents reflect opinions sustained by progressive theologians, but at the same time they leave the positions of traditional Catholicism intact." He sustains that there is a sense of ambivalence in the council and a pendulum movement under pressure from the more influential conservative element in the Vatican, but he does not lose hope: "It is the hope of many that the seed planted in the council declarations will germinate vigorously and put down roots capable of opening deep cracks in the monolithic structure of the Roman Church."[45]

For Núñez, the new attitude toward evangelical Christians is what has had the greatest resonance among Latin Americans: "The turning of the Roman Church toward ecumenism seems almost unbelievable to many

---

[43]Míguez Bonino, "Deuda evangélica," 129.
[44]CLADE I, *Acción en Cristo para un continente en crisis* (Miami: Editorial Caribe, 1970), 40.
[45]CLADE I, *Acción en Cristo*, 40.

evangelicals who have not had time to ponder the attitude which with they should accept the hand of ecumenical fellowship that has been extended by Catholics."[46] The answer should be a dual one: edifying the body of Christ and evangelizing the multitudes who do not know Christ. The conciliar documents should be objects of study among evangelicals, but Núñez does not see it as urgent to launch institutional dialogue to seek unity among the churches: "There is a great difference between ecumenical dialogue that is entered to foster the unity of all the churches, and the evangelistic dialogue that we participate in with the goal of presenting Christ as the only answer to the spiritual problems of contemporary man."[47]

[46]CLADE I, *Acción en Cristo*, 41.
[47]CLADE I, *Acción en Cristo*, 43.

9

JESUS CHRIST AND THE REVOLUTIONARIES

Traditional theological language seems to lean too heavily on the hidden world of eternity. In language that only grudgingly allowed, or outright negated, a relationship with the world, history, and life . . . that vernacular theology that Catholics and Protestants are doing tries to connect the same sources of biblical faith with the social and political categories that are at play in the Latin American context (conscientization, imperialism, monopolies, social classes, developmentalism). That theology "on the making" sees the church as the "institutionalized memory of the dangerous liberty of Christ," as a "phenomenon that is critical of society."

Mauricio López, "La liberación de América Latina y el cristianismo evangélico"

On February 15, 1966, Colombian priest Camilo Torres died in a confrontation between the Colombian military and a group of guerillas connected to the group Frente Unido (United Front), led by Torres, and the National Liberation Army. Torres was a sociologist and priest and had studied theology at the University of Louvain in Belgium together with Gustavo Gutiérrez. On his return to Colombia, his social activism in favor of the poor had created difficulties with the religious authorities, and in June 1965 he requested that his status be reduced to that of a layperson. His political stance became more radical, to the point of advocating taking up arms as the only way to achieve social change.[1]

Less than two years later, on October 9, 1967, Argentinian doctor Ernesto Guevara de la Serna, known as "Che," died by extrajudicial execution in La Higuera, a remote village in Bolivia. He had participated in Fidel Castro's guerrilla force that took power in Cuba in 1959 and had become the minister of the economy, representing Cuba in various international forums. However, from 1965 he dedicated himself to being a guerrilla in the Congo and then in Bolivia, where his project to light a revolutionary fire that would spread throughout Latin America failed.

Jesus, Camilo, and Che

The 1970s opened with the growing impact of these two figures, Camilo Torres and Che Guevara, over a sector of the Latin American population. In various countries iconography was created with images of these two men similar to some traditional images of Jesus Christ. In 1968 magazine and newspaper stands throughout the continent sold an image of a reclining Che amid clouds and with a shining cross in the background. On Argentinian buses we saw stickers with this reclining figure and a line of text: "Mi vida di por ti" (I gave my life for you). This drive to draw visual parallels between the heroes of the leftist revolution and Jesus says much about the respect and admiration that the average Latin American felt for Jesus—a respect that was confirmed repeatedly to me in dialogue with university students throughout the continent during more than fifteen years. One cannot be sure whether it was merely a deliberately chosen revolutionary propaganda strategy or a spontaneous expression of impatience with a socially and politically oppressive and unjust status quo.

In the first chapter of his introduction to liberation theology, José Míguez Bonino makes reference to this phenomenon, what he calls the "christologizing" of the figure of Che. Míguez says:

[1]Hernán Parada, *Crónica de Medellín* (Bogotá: Indoamerican Press Service, 1975), 124-31.

> It should not surprise us, then, that the figure of Christ takes on the face of a person—real or imagined—that in a historic moment seems to best embody what the Christian religion or that wider humanity represents. . . . What is new and somewhat scandalous is that a group of Christians would choose for this role a guerrilla fighter, and particularly someone who—with full lucidity and awareness—did not consider himself a Christian but rather a Marxist revolutionary.[2]

Of course, it was not just a question of iconography. There was an effort in certain circles to demonstrate that if Jesus had come to Latin America he would have become a guerrilla fighter like Che and Camilo Torres—and even more, that this was the only authentic way of being a Christian. Observe the fusion of theological and political categories in this speech of Fidel Castro from October 1967:

> Che has become a model man, not only for our people, but for all people in Latin America. . . . His blood was shed on this earth when he was wounded in various battles, . . . his blood for the redemption of the exploited and oppressed ones. . . . For this reason let us lift our thinking, and with optimism for the future, with absolute expectation of the definitive victory of the people, we say to Che, and to the heroes who fought and fell together with him: . . . Toward victory always! Homeland or death! We will win![3]

In 1971 Catholic Peronist magazine *Cristianismo y Revolución* published a statement issuing from a meeting in Cuba in homage to Camilo Torres. The document contains very telling paragraphs. At its heart is a sentence by the deceased Colombian priest: "Revolution is a Christian imperative." Among other things, the document affirms:

> We want to climb the mountains of Our America in the genuinely Christian way of Camilo and never unite ourselves to those who blessed his assassins. We believe that we should proclaim our admiration for those who by "giving their life for their brothers, give proof that no one

[2]José Míguez Bonino, *La fe en busca de eficacia* (Salamanca: Sígueme, 1977), 23-24; English, *Doing Theology in a Revolutionary Situation* (Philadelphia: Fortress, 1975).

[3]Fidel Castro, "Fidel habla del Che," text of speech given in Havana, October 1967, in *Cristianismo y Revolución*, nos. 6-7 (1968): 35.

> has greater love than this." Camilo Torres and Ernesto Che Guevara are in our opinion the highest examples in Latin America today of a legitimately Christian attitude and of a true realization of the new man in Our America.[4]

This identification of guerrillas and revolution with Jesus should be examined with care. Note that not any revolution mirrored the teaching of Jesus. Not just any change was desirable. The document specifically refers to a revolution that emerges from Marxism. Revolutions from totally different angles, for other political reasons, occurring at that moment, were of no use. Only a Marxist revolution would do. The statement expresses this clearly:

> We condemn every attempt to drastically and dogmatically contrast that which is revolutionary and what is Christian, what is Marxism and what is the gospel, what is communism and what is the church. We believe that in today's revolutionary world, all that is antirevolutionary for the true revolutionary is antigospel for the true Christian.[5]

A clearer definition could not be requested. At the dawn of the 1970s, theological work and especially christological understandings were surrounded by controversies unleashed by declarations such as this one. It was in this environment that evangelical theological reflection developed, and in particular developed around the Latin American Theological Fraternity (FTL), which would play a leading role in the task of producing Protestant theology.

Revelation and Revolution

Facing the culture of revolution that characterized this time, Bible scholar René Padilla suggested that Christians could not remain indifferent, recognizing that revolutionary ferment is found in the biblical message and that Jesus Christ presented his own mission with clear dimensions for social transformation. At the same time Padilla warned against the risk

---

[4]"Cuba: Los cristianos en la sociedad socialista," *Cristianismo y Revolución*, no. 28 (April 1971): 29.
[5]"Cuba: Los cristianos en la sociedad socialista," 29.

of the revolution itself being converted into a source of theological truth. I have just illustrated this with the christologizing of revolutionary figures, which acquired a mythical dimension. At the beginning of the 1970s Padilla published an article in the student magazine *Certeza* that provided a biblical framework for understanding the revolutionary phenomenon. After quoting Amos 5:7-13, which vigorously condemns exploiters of the poor, Padilla summarizes: "The same courageous accusation of abuses by the powerful is found in the other prophets of Israel: Isaiah, Micah, Jeremiah, Ezekiel. One of the greatest glories of the Jewish people was that among them emerged the first champions of social justice. This prophetic note also erupts in the world of the first century through the preaching of John the Baptist."[6]

He goes on to consider the clear challenge to the social status quo that is present in the work and message of Jesus Christ, quoting the famous "manifesto" of Nazareth recorded in Luke 4:18-19, and highlighting significative elements of Jesus' missionary style:

> His whole ministry is marked by a constant identification with the destitute—an identificaction that won him the title "Friend of tax collectors and sinners." The crowds move him to compassion because they are "like sheep witout a shepherd." He chooses his disciples from among the common people, the *am-ha-arets*, scorned for their ignorance of the law. He teaches that no one can serve God and wealth, He cautions against the deceitfulness of riches, He warns the rich that their comfort in this world will be limited to their material possessions, and He accuses those who in the name of religion exploit widows. In the actions and words of Jesus there is a revolutionary ferment that apparently at least corroborates the Jewish leaders' accusations against him before the Roman authorities.[7]

As a Bible scholar, Padilla considers it important to clarify that the thesis that Jesus was a Zealot is not supported by biblical evidence. Still, "it must be recognized that there is grain of truth in it—that Jesus shares

---

[6]René Padilla, "Mensaje bíblico y revolución," *Certeza* 10, no. 39 (January–March 1970): 197.
[7]René Padilla, "Revolution and Revelation," in *Is Revolution Change?*, ed. Brian Griffiths (London: Inter-Varsity Press, 1972), 73.

with the Zealots their dissatisfaction with the established powers and their hope for the coming of the kingdom of God."[8]

He dedicates one section of his work to an in-depth examination of the topic of revolution and human nature, demonstrating historically that if a revolution is limited to changing social structures without changing people at a deep level in their relationship with God, the new order that is born will soon show the same defects that led to drastic sociopolitical change. In the third section he critically considers what he calls "the gospel of the revolution." He questions the thesis sustained by some contemporary theologians such as Harvey Cox, Richard Shaull, and Paul Lehman: "To them revolutions are nothing less than the means through which God is carrying out his purpose in history."[9] Although Padilla does not specifically mention the movement Iglesia y Sociedad en América Latina (ISAL), it should be remembered that these theologians were very influential in that movement. Padilla does point specifically to the Church and Society Conference held in Geneva in 1966, which became a platform for the ISAL-style theology of revolution. Padilla summarizes the theology of revolution in the following way:

> All its errors stem from the fact that it takes as its starting point the revolutionary situation and interprets Scripture on the basis of presuppositions derived from leftist ideologies. Instead of showing the relevance of revelation to revolution, it makes revolution its source of revelation. The result is a secular gospel whose dominant emphases parallel those of Marxism.

An important aspect of the article is the eschatological note that is a key piece in Padilla's Christology and that in the future became part of the theological agenda pursued by Padilla and the FTL: "Every revolution sets before the Christian faith the question of the relation between the kingdom of God and the kingdoms of men, between eschatology and history. In the final analysis, every revolution is a human attempt to create here and now the perfect society that God has promised to create at the end of the present age."[9]

[8]Padilla, "Revolution and Revelation," 78.
[9]Padilla, "Revolution and Revelation," 77.

The Search for an Evangelical and Contextual Theology

I noted at the end of chapter seven that the 1960s concluded with two Protestant events of continental impact, the Third Latin American Evangelical Conference (CELA III) and the First Latin American Congress of Evangelization (CLADE I). The first was organized by the ecumenical sector within Protestantism, as a continuation of the previous Latin American evangelical conferences: CELA I in Buenos Aires (1949) and CELA II in Lima (1961). Meanwhile CLADE I marked the emergence of a cooperative effort of new evangelical denominations, conservative in their theology, together with older churches that had stayed outside the ecumenical movement.[10] Under the initiative of the Latin America Mission in Costa Rica, these gatherings took place for cooperation at a continental level with literature (LEAL) communication, mass media (DIA), and evangelism (CLASE). CLADE I aimed to include the widest possible spectrum of Latin American Protestants. It achieved this because among the over nine hundred participants in Bogotá were not only those who represented denominations outside the ecumenical movement but also members of ecumenical churches who were interested in evangelization and professors from ecumenical seminaries.

The enthusiastic response of CLADE I participants to a presentation about the social responsibility of the church, which had a clear christological structure, showed that the theological conservatism of a generation was beginning to open up, faced with the need to respond to the social convulsions of Latin America. The slogan of the congress was "Action in Christ for a Continent in Crisis," and the final declaration, produced during the congress, stated in its introduction:

> This declaration also aims to reflect the awakening of conscience that in these days the Lord Jesus Christ has wanted to give us, making us feel the sharpness of the multiple crises that our people are passing through and

[10]Regarding the context and development of these events see Dafne Sabanes Plou, *Caminos de unidad* (Quito: CLAI, 1994), chap. 3. A well-balanced multiauthor summary of developments in Protestantism can be found in Guillermo Cook, ed., *New Face of the Church in Latin America* (Maryknoll, NY: Orbis, 1994).

> the imperative nature of the mandate to evangelize. Together we have recognized the need to live the gospel fully, proclaiming it in its totality to Latin American people in the context of their multiple needs.[11]

One process of conscientization crystallized into action and movement concerning the theological task. From this emerged the Latin American Theological Fraternity (FTL). Although its principal intention was theological, the emergence of the FTL brought to light realities such as missional dependence, externally provoked polarizations, the identity crisis of new generations of evangelicals, and the absence of contextualized reflection.[12]

During the course of the congress, a diverse group of pastors, evangelists, missionaries, and seminary professors met to establish a fraternity dedicated to study and reflection. The desire to create a common platform for development of theological work had begun to germinate. Those who conceived it did not feel represented by theology elaborated in North America and imposed by means of conservative evangelical seminaries and Bible institutes, whose programs and literature were repetitive and servile translations shaped in a context totally foreign to ours. Neither did we feel represented by the ecumenical Protestants, whom we perceived as elitist, generally exact replicas of European molds, and often disconnected from the evangelizing spirit and the core convictions of the majority of evangelical churches of the continent.[13] The organizing genius and untiring work of missionary Pedro Savage must be credited with ensuring that the dream of Bogotá became reality.[14]

---

[11]The text of the "Declaración de Bogotá" is in *Acción en Cristo para un continente en crisis* (San José, Costa Rica: Caribe, 1970), 134.

[12]With respect to the history of the FTL see *Boletín Teológico,* nos. 59-60 (July–December 1995), a special edition celebrating the first twenty-five years. There are historical references in Plou, *Caminos de unidad*, chap. 3. Sadly, Swiss historian Jean Pierre Bastian offers a reference full of errors due to the ideological interpretive outline he uses in his *History of Protestantism in Latin America* (Mexico City: CUPSA, 1990).

[13]For both René Padilla and me, these convictions had been strengthened through our experience as observers in the Tercera Conferencia Evangélica Latinoamericana (CELA III), which took place in Buenos Aires in July 1969.

[14]Pedro Savage was born in Peru to missionary parents and had the unique and favorable status of being bicultural and bilingual, plus he had unflagging energy. He convinced his mission to let him dedicate himself full time to this task.

One year later, in December 1970, the founding assembly for the FTL was held in Cochabamba, Bolivia. The organizing committee suggested that this assembly would set the foundations of the evangelical theological task that would be developed. The talks that provoked much dialogue in this first consultation were given by four thinkers, all of whom had both a theological and a university education. Pedro Arana Quiroz, a Peruvian Presbyterian, focused on the revelation of God and theology in Latin America; Ismael E. Amaya, an Argentinian from the Nazarene church, the inspiration of the Bible in Latin American theology; René Padilla, an Ecuadorian Baptist, the authority of the Bible in Latin American theology; and J. Andrew Kirk, a British Anglican who taught in Argentina, hermeneutics and the Bible in relation to Protestant theology in Latin America. Each participant received the printed version of the main talks, in some cases weeks prior to the consultation, and one whole day was dedicated to discussing each of them. The published text of the talks includes in many cases clarifications and additions that were the fruit of this communal work.[15]

Theology Under the Authority of the Bible

In his presentation on the authority of the Bible, Padilla argued with a christological tone, highlighting the necessity of understanding Christ within the framework of the entire Bible, which should be read as testimony to the history of salvation:

> The substance of the special revelation is the redemptive action of God in the heart of history—the history of salvation. This is the emphasis throughout all the Bible: God is not a faraway being who sends a letter from a distance; rather, he is a God who inserts himself into human history, a God who undertakes great achievements and through them

[15]Pedro Savage, ed., *El debate contemporáneo sobre la Biblia* (Barcelona: Ediciones Evangélicas Europeas, 1972). This methodology of circulating work, writing in advance and asking for responses from those who would participate in the event, allowed for a thorough reflection prior to the event and led to a richly fruitful process. In 1973 I suggested this method to the program commission preparing for the 1974 Lausanne Congress, and the suggestion was adopted based on the experience of the FTL.

progressively implements his purpose of redemption. That is, the redemption accomplished by God is not gnostic; rather, it is historic: it does not occur through doctrinal formulas but through historical events.[16]

On the basis of this affirmation, Padilla critiques fundamentalist theology that tends to isolate the Bible from the history of salvation, treating it as an autonomous source of revelation that occupies the place that belongs to God. On the other hand, responding to the theological positions that would separate the historic Jesus of the Bible from the apostolic interpretation given in the biblical revelation itself, Padilla tries to establish with complete clarity:

The acts of God in the history of salvation are not isolated events: they are interpreted events and are inseparable from their interpretation. . . . The word of interpretation is as much part of the history of salvation as the events themselves. Event and interpretation are part of an inextricable whole. Normally the act precedes the Word, but it is the Word that discovers the meaning of the act and complements it.[17]

Applying this principle to the christological task means a recognition that "in the New Testament, the fact of Christ is inseparable from the apostolic doctrine. The apostles hold a unique place within the history of salvation as mediators of the final revelation of God in Jesus Christ."[18] A consequence of this is that if the authority of the Bible is recognized, for the construction of Christology one must take seriously the apostolic witness regarding the fact of Christ and also the apostolic interpretation of this fact: "The only historic Jesus is the Jesus of the New Testament, and if the validity of the apostolic function is accepted for the transmission of the historic fact, the doctrinal interpretation should also be accepted. The possibilities are an apostolic Christianity or a mystical Christianity with an imaginary Christ who is incapable of redeeming."[19]

[16]René Padilla, "La autoridad de la Biblia en la teología latinoamericana," in *El debate contemporáneo sobre la Biblia*, 126.
[17]Padilla, "La autoridad de la Biblia," 130-31.
[18]Padilla, "La autoridad de la Biblia," 132.
[19]Padilla, "La autoridad de la Biblia," 134.

Another key point for the theological task that Padilla stresses is that the apostolic message is aimed at making possible an encounter of human beings with God through Jesus Christ: "The purpose of the authorized biblical "information" is the encounter, the personal experience of God's judgment and grace."[20] As a consequence:

> An encounter with Jesus Christ is rooted in the doctrine of the apostles. It is not an encounter with an imaginary Christ but rather with Christ mediated by the apostolic tradition; it is not an indescribable encounter but rather an encounter that can be expressed in a confession of faith. If this is denied, all possibility of forming theology is removed, as theology presupposes to "be in the truth" and to "know the truth," the encounter *and* the doctrine, the existential *and* the conceptual.[21]

These convictions guided the christological work of Padilla and the other members of the FTL in the following decades.

The Context of Reflection

Laying out the context of the reflection in Cochabamba was my own responsibility, and my talks suggested that the evangelical theological task should proceed in two directions. On the one hand, we needed to process the theological inheritance received from missionaries in order to distinguish between biblical content and Anglo-Saxon baggage, which would require an initiative of self-critique within Latin American Protestantism. On the other hand, it was necessary to offer a response to the revolutionary movements that affected the life of Latin Americans and of the churches.

For the first task, it was necessary to better understand Ibero-American reality and the cultures of our peoples, and in that light review what, within our theological inheritance, belonged to the Anglo-Saxon world. We had to review, for example, the anti-Hispanic controversy, the fundamentalist-modernist controversy, the ascetic inclinations inherited from pietist missionaries: "The reflection must be ours, born from our

---

[20]Padilla, "La autoridad de la Biblia," 137.
[21]Padilla, "La autoridad de la Biblia," 137.

situation, emerging from the urgency of the problems that the church faces here. It is as men rooted *here* that we reflect on and shape theology, we rediscover the emphases that are lacking today, and we criticize the heresies that we ourselves have fallen into."[22] In practice this implied, among other things, revaluing what is Hispanic in order to rediscover and value the Reformation in a fresh way, to create an atmosphere of maturity and liberty; fighting against the blockage and labeling that condemns brothers and sisters without knowing or listening to them; and giving a pastoral dimension to theological work: "The theologian under the impact of God's Word can help the church be able to distinguish between simple ecclesiastical traffic and the mission of the church."[23]

With respect to the Bible and social revolution, my presentation sought to define the use of the term *revolution* and went on to examine the transforming impact of the biblical message in Western history and the experience of Latin American Protestantism. It later addressed the transforming ferment of the biblical message, the social nature of biblical anthropology, and the example of Christ as the basis for Christian ethics. Finally, it proposed three theological themes that needed urgent attention: Marxist anthropology and biblical anthropology, Christian eschatology and Marxist hope, and a critique of religion and ideology.[24]

The Dual Agenda of Evangelical Theology

The presentations given by Arana Quiroz about revelation and by Kirk about hermeneutics accomplished a double purpose: they constructively articulated a contextual and evangelical position on the theme, and they critically evaluated the alternative theologies that had emerged during the previous decade. This way of approaching the theological task characterized much of the work undertaken by members of the FTL in the

---

[22]Samuel Escobar, "El contenido bíblico y el ropaje anglosajón en la teología latinoamericana," in *El debate contemporáneo sobre la Biblia*, 23.

[23]Escobar, "El contenido bíblico," 35.

[24]My presentation was not published in the book that resulted from the founding assembly of the FTL. A summary appeared in the magazine *Certeza* (vol. 11, no. 43), and the complete text was published for the first time in *Evangelio y realidad social* (El Paso, TX: Casa Bautista de Publicaciones, 1988), 43-76.

future. Both Kirk and Arana Quiroz criticized the subjectivity of fundamentalism's conceptions of biblical revelation and interpretation. They also critically evaluated ISAL's theology (referred to in chapter seven here). Both recognized the novelty and originality of ISAL's efforts to create a Latin American theology, and they carefully considered the evolution of the movement as described by its own general secretary. Kirk dedicated twenty pages of his paper to summarizing the hermeneutic process used by ISAL theologians such as Julio de Santa Ana and Rubem Alves, who had eventually abandoned the idea of a revelational theology. Kirk said: "The problem for ISAL in becoming detached from the concept of revelation as verbal communication is how to avoid simply ending up in a history that is silent."[25] Here Kirk coincides with what Padilla said with respect to the biblical witness about Jesus Christ: "If the validity of the apostolic function is accepted for the transmission of the historic event, then what is concerned with doctrinal interpretation should also be accepted."

Arana Quiroz also revisits the evolution of ISAL thought and offers his own summary of the most recent process:

> A basic synthesis of the findings they have reached could be presented in the following way: God is revealed in history in the humanization of man. Humanization is a process of liberating man from the structures that oppress and exploit them. The way to achieve this liberation is through revolution. This revolutionary fight is about the transformation of the currently unjust society into a just society. Later, God is revealed to us in the movements and in the people who fight for the humanization of man. Thus God is revealed in the revolutions and through the revolutionaries.[26]

The critical conclusion Arana Quiroz came to might have seemed exaggerated at the time, but it was based on a careful examining of textual evidence: "In ISAL ideology God is translated as revolution, the people of God as revolutionary troops, the purpose of God as humanization,

---

[25]Andrés [J. Andrew] Kirk, "La Biblia y su hermenéutica en relación con la teología protestante en América Latina," in *El debate contemporáneo sobre la Biblia*, 186.

[26]Pedro Arana Quiroz, "La revelación de Dios y la teología en Latinoamérica," in *El debate contemporáneo sobre la Biblia*, 77.

and the Word of God as revolutionary writings. It escapes no one that all this is Marxist humanism."[27]

A Theology of Evangelization

Another axis for theological reflection in the evangelical world became the Seminario Bíblico Latinoamericano (SBL) in Costa Rica, whose teaching staff had been working on the questions evangelization presents to theology. A seminar was organized for the second quarter of the academic year in 1970 to explore the theology of evangelization, sponsored by the Secretariat of Theological Studies of EVAF and the Department of Christian Ministry. Both professors and students participated. Theologian Orlando Costas edited the three-hundred-page volume that resulted from this gathering. Considering the framework of that time, the result is a work noteworthy for its variety and quality of theological reflection.[28] The first part of the book, which explores the biblical foundations, is titled "Evangelization in the history of salvation," and the various authors consider the call of Israel, the message of the prophets, Jesus' ministry, Pauline motifs, and eschatology. Later comes "Evangelization in theological perspective," which explores God as the starting point; revelation, grace and creation; the centrality of Jesus Christ in evangelization; and the church as an evangelizing agent. The third section is "Evangelization in unfolding history," and the fourth and final is "Evangelization in the contemporary world," where themes of secularization and revolution are explored, with the search for relevance as the context for the task of evangelization.

Costas centers his reflection on Christology in dedicating one chapter to certain aspects of Jesus' ministry and their implications for evangelization. In another he looks at the centrality of Jesus Christ in evangelization. He places Jesus' preaching in the framework of the history of salvation and of biblical eschatology, and shows the distinctive nature of Jesus' call to his disciples:

---

[27]Quiroz, "La revelación de Dios," 78.

[28]Orlando Costas, ed., *Hacia una teología de la evangelización* (Buenos Aires: La Aurora, 1973).

> Jesus' call to discipleship was not an invitation to become part of a traditional rabbinic school with discussions of the Torah. Rather, it was a call that emanated from the proclamation of the gospel of the kingdom. It was an invitation "to accept the sovereign reign of God, to enter into a new and intimate relation with God, to be. . . . a recipient of his salvific power" and follow with obedience. Above all it was a call to participate in the life and death of Jesus.[29]

Costas also emphasizes the importance of the cross and the resurrection, which he considers the most relevant aspect of Jesus' ministry for evangelization. Writing about Luke 24:44-48, he affirms:

> Note that for Jesus, the cross and the resurrection were a necessity. Not for the mere fact that it was written [by the prophets], nor because he did not have another alternative, but because of the sin of all the nations, of all humanity. That is to say, the reconciliation of the nations, the restoration of the unity of all humanity and repair of broken communion, depended on a solution to the problem of sin. It was thus through the affliction of the Lord's servant that forgiveness was made possible, because Jesus took upon himself the hostility and the anger of men.[30]

For Costas this is the main motivation that will invigorate and provide the foundation for the evangelizing activity of the church, rather than love for the lost or the church's need to see growth in membership: "the death and the resurrection of Christ. If [evangelization] is not founded on this reality, then it has no basis or meaning; it is anything but Christian mission."[31]

Venezuelan professor José M. Abreu focuses on Christian mission in Johannine thought. After locating John's teaching as a response to the cultural and religious context of the community that received this Gospel, Abreu affirms the importance of the incarnation: "It is not just another theme of the Gospel, and neither is it the only central theme; it is the total perspective in which all the theological reflections in

[29]Costas, *Hacia una teología de la evangelización*, 39.
[30]Costas, *Hacia una teología de la evangelización*, 42.
[31]Costas, *Hacia una teología de la evangelización*, 42.

John are made."[32] He also points out the centrality of the theme of mission in John:

> In no other Gospel is Jesus' missionary status affirmed more categorically. Jesus the incarnated one, who is at once the glorified Christ, calls himself "the sent one." The reason of all his work, his teaching, all his ministry as the Son of God incarnate, is the mission the Father has given him. The Father and the Son are one in the mission, and this theological affirmation involves God as the first one who sends in the soteriological sense. Men are divided between those who receive the sent one and those who do not receive him. To reject the sent one is to reject the Father who sent him, as his words and teachings come from the Father (John 7:16; 12:49; 14:24).[33]

For Abreu the consequence of the centrality of the incarnation for understanding the mission of Jesus and the nature of this mission itself is that the church today, in fulfilling its mission and in evangelizing, should be incarnated in Latin American reality: "The church must be a reality that is actualized in the world and for the world. The Word, the communicating principle of God with the world, in becoming incarnate established the standard for missionary work. Without incarnation there is no true communication, and without communication there is no authentic mission."[34]

The richness of the bibliographic notes by the different authors of this volume, just as in the works of the founders of the recently formed FTL, show that in the previous decade Catholic and Protestant publishing houses had released an abundant basic set of biblical materials that was essential for the theological task. Together with christologically focused classics published by La Aurora in Buenos Aires, such as *God Was in Christ* by Donald M. Baillie and *The Christology of the New Testament* by Oscar Cullmann, Spanish Catholic publishers such as Sígueme, Fax, Marova, and Herder had begun to publish the work of both Bible scholars and Catholic and Protestant theologians. This was a valuable contribution

[32]Costas, *Hacia una teología de la evangelización*, 58.

[33]Costas is quoting Abreu's unpublished thesis, "Un enfoque político del Evangelio de Juan" (A political approach to John's Gospel) (Seminario Bíblico Latinoamericano, 1972).

[34]Costas, *Hacia una teología de la evangelización*, 64.

to the rise and development of theological reflection in Latin America, and it continues to be.

The reflection of René Padilla regarding the topic of revolution in 1970 alongside those of the recently founded FTL and the Seminario Bíblico Latinoamericano in that same year basically constituted an inter-Protestant dialogue in which a "theology of revolution" had emerged. It had its origins in the pioneers, the founders, and the evangelical theologians who had developed a christological agenda. Up to this point the theologies of liberation had not been articulated. So Latin American evangelical theology did not emerge as a response to liberation theologies but had taken its own course, connected to the life of evangelical churches with their strong evangelizing impulse and sense of mission.[35] When the theologies of liberation did appear, evangelical theology incorporated into its agenda the challenges arising from this new Latin American Catholic theology.

Toward an Evangelical Social Ethic

From its beginnings, the FTL aimed to be a wide platform for theological reflection, and in its consultations we find contributions of ecumenical theologians from the historic churches and evangelical theologians connected to younger, theologically conservative churches. But always FTL reflection placed itself within the framework of acceptance of the authority of the Bible for the theological task. The agenda considered in the founding assembly began to be developed with two consultations that took place in 1972 in Lima, one in June about social ethics and the other in December about the kingdom of God.

The consultation on social ethics took place in three stages. First, I guided the process of becoming conscious of the Latin American situation, while the situation of evangelical churches was described by Orlando Costas and Fred Denton. Second, the two prevailing theological

[35]Alan P. Neely, who was a Baptist missionary in Colombia and later professor at Princeton Theological Seminary, wrote his doctoral thesis about the Protestant precursors to liberation theology: "Protestant Antecedents of the Latin American Theology of Liberation" (PhD diss., American University, 1977).

alternatives were considered: Church and Society in Latin America (ISAL) was analyzed by René Padilla, and the new Catholicism by José Míguez Bonino.

Padilla presented a frontal critique of ISAL's theology for its concepts of the action of God in history and of humanization, as they were derived from an uncritical adoption of revolutionary ideology that did no justice to revelation but rather reduced it radically. He concludes that "in this route the theological task results in an ideology whose only kinship with the Bible is found in the use of certain terms that have been emptied of their original content and put in service of a cause foreign to their intention in the biblical context."[36]

Míguez Bonino, for his part, offered a rich descriptive analysis of post-conciliar Catholicism in Latin America, comparing different attitudes, concepts, and behavior that are expressed especially in the sections "Justice" and "Peace" of the Medellín Statement. His description of Catholicism places theology within a framework of sociological analysis of the Catholic ecclesial reality, an analytical tendency that grew visibly during the 1970s. He dedicates twenty-two pages to the topic of the search for a theology that is committed to history and offers a thorough analysis of four theologians who represent the origins of the different streams that were developing in liberation theology: Uruguayan Juan Luis Segundo, Argentinian Lucio Gera, and Peruvian Gustavo Gutiérrez, whom he puts alongside Brazilian Hugo Assmann.[37] This rigorous analysis of the beginnings of liberation theology was the first to appear from a Protestant source. Three years later Míguez Bonino dedicated a whole book to this subject.[38]

Third, a possible route toward an evangelical social ethic was suggested in talks about incarnation and history by Justo L. González, the orders of creation and Christian responsibility were discussed by Pedro

[36]Published as René Padilla, "Iglesia y sociedad en América Latina," in *Fe cristiana y Latinoamérica hoy*, compiled by René Padilla (Buenos Aires: Ediciones Certeza, 1974), 126.

[37]René Padilla, "Iglesia y sociedad en América Latina," 83-118.

[38]José Míguez Bonino, *Doing Theology in a Revolutionary Situation* (Philadelphia: Fortress, 1975), still in my opinion the best introduction to liberation theologies.

Arana Quiroz, and a Pentecostal perspective on the church and society was given by Argentinian preacher Juan Carlos Ortiz.

Incarnation and history. The book *Revolución y encarnación* (Revolution and incarnation) by González, written in 1962 and published in 1965, had been received with great interest in various evangelical circles. In the consultation on social ethics, Gonzalez affirmed that in the basics his position continued to be the same; he summarized it in this way: "All, or almost all of us, are in agreement in rejecting the docetism of those who see the task as only saving souls for a future life. Almost all of us also agree that we reject the Ebionism of those who imagine that their action within the history of society will establish the kingdom of heaven."[39]

In relation to the social responsibility of Christians, docetism would negate all relevance of the believer's relationship with the physical world: "Implicitly, docetists are the Christians who profess to serve God only in their church, with their hymns, prayers, and meditations."[40] Contrastingly, Ebionism would lead to the belief that people's establishment of justice in the world is equivalent to the action of God. "Implicitly Ebionites are the Christians who follow Marxist or humanist guidelines, as if God were asking that we please help him to establish his kingdom because he cannot do it(!)."[41]

However, González sought to correct his presentation from the previous decade in two directions. First, he refined the typology so as to include intermediate alternatives between the positions that he had designated "docetism" and "Ebionism." Second, he nuanced the distinction that he had made between eschatology and teleology. While the distinction was valid, he said, "It runs the risk of leaving Christians without criteria for their action in history, and so if this is not clarified, it could lead to a new form of docetism."[42]

[39]Justo L. González, "Encarnación e historia," in *Fe cristiana y Latinoamérica hoy*, 166.
[40]González, "Encarnación e historia," 156.
[41]González, "Encarnación e historia," 156. Exclamation point is González's own.
[42]González, "Encarnación e historia," 152.

Though we accept that in Christ both divinity and humanity are present, the question remains how they are unified in him. González characterizes two extreme positions: Nestorianism and monophysitism. For the Nestorians there was a constant and clear division between the human and the divine: "If Christ did miracles, it was his divinity that did it; if he ate or cried, that was his humanity. This position, while extremely rational, has the enormous difficulty that in the end it dissolves the incarnation into two realities that can never be joined."[43] Over time, this position prompts a perception of a sharp distinction between the church and the state, and the difficulty of suggesting how these two realities should relate or be unified. In Catholicism, emerging from this is the classic struggle between the papacy and the empire. With the Reformation this type of Nestorian division was used to defend the separation between the church and the state.

On the other hand, monophysitism followed the opposing line: "It is true that Jesus Christ is God and man. But in him the two are joined in such a way that the distinction does not exist, and given the extreme incommensurability between God and man, humanity is lost in the immensity of the divine."[44] Political monophysitism thus leads to theocracy. This can be "ecclesial, such as the case of Münzer's 'revolutionary saints,' or civil, such as in Byzantine caesaropapism."[45] González says, "Between the extreme Nestorian distinction and the monophysite confusion—let's say between an independent politics of faith and theocracy—the church (or the majority of it) adopted the Definition of Faith from Chalcedon."[46]

Gonzalez clarifies that many critiques can be made of the Chalcedonian definition, such as the adoption of Greek terminology and categories such as "nature" or the tendency to refer to Jesus Christ in static terms such as *essence* instead of *relationship*. "But in spite of all this, and given the circumstance and the vocabulary of the era, Chalcedon was

[43]González, "Encarnación e historia," 157.
[44]González, "Encarnación e historia," 157.
[45]González, "Encarnación e historia," 158.
[46]González, "Encarnación e historia," 156.

correct in its way of understanding the incarnation."[47] "Human wisdom," which the apostle Paul criticizes in 1 Corinthians, conceives God in terms of absolute universality, incapable of being particularized, or as eternity, beyond the boundaries of temporality, incapable of participating in time:

> What Chalcedon affirmed, then, albeit indirectly, was that the God who was incarnated in Jesus Christ is neither the impassive idol of philosophers nor the capricious idol of pagan cults. Neither the universality of "First Cause" nor the particularity of Baal, but rather the particularity of the universal meaning of Jesus of Nazareth. . . . The Christian God is such that his eternity is given to us in a moment of history, and his universality bumps against us in the particular event that is narrated in the New Testament.[48]

In addressing ways to see history, González argues that the christological typology is defining: "Docetism leads us to deny all meaning to history—except perhaps as an obstacle that separates us from eternity—while Ebionism gives history a teleological meaning." For González, teleology begins with the presupposition that history has meaning in itself and of itself, while eschatology affirms that history receives its meaning externally. Applying Nestorian and monophysite typology, he argues that the Nestorian distinction between divinity and humanity in Jesus Christ leads some theologians to distinguish between secular history (*Weltgeschichte*) and the history of salvation (*Heilsgeschichte*). This kind of distinction led many German Christians to accept the horrors of Nazism and Hitler's totalitarian government, until (or for some, despite) the emergence of the Confessing Church.

On the other hand, the monophysite position is reflected in theocratic tendencies inside Latin American Protestantism itself. Sometimes charismatic figures set up sectarian theocratic communities that separate members from society and require strict obedience. In the same way, there are systems and states that hope to act in perfect synchrony with the final aim of history. Without attributing it, González quotes a famous aphorism from Fidel Castro: "He who adopts this position can say

---

[47]González, "Encarnación e historia," 159.

[48]González, "Encarnación e historia," 160.

'history will absolve me' with the same religious certainty with which the apostle could say 'it is necessary to obey God rather than men,' because for him, history is God."[49] González says that in such a perspective it is not that God was incarnated but rather that humanity has been deified. But the Chalcedonian position, which does not free us from these tensions and ambiguities, leads to the conviction that "we cannot sacrifice our responsibility toward our neighbor for the sake of the future, nor think that our obedience does not demand a responsible attitude toward the entire process of human history."[50]

As an important complement to his book *Revolución y encarnación*, in 1971 González published *Jesucristo es el Señor* (Jesus Christ is Lord), in which he clearly outlines the development and meaning of the basic confession of the Christian faith, the lordship of Jesus Christ.[51] Together these two works of González are contextualized readings of Christology as the paradigm for the mission of the church. The pastoral intention of both books is evident in their lucidity, brevity, and direct style, but they had as a foundation the systematic research displayed by the author in works that are now classics both in English and in Spanish.[52]

A social ethics and the orders of creation. In his presentation for the consultation, Pedro Arana Quiroz did not go directly to biblical material but took up Calvinist teaching regarding the orders of creation. His topic was the order of creation and Christian responsibility, and he followed the path of systematic theology. He formulated a notion of justice using the perspectives of Karl Barth and Emil Brunner. Arana Quiroz's pastoral sensitivity was expressed in his concern over the fact that although there were significant and ongoing efforts in evangelization in Latin America, these efforts had begun to leave behind the biblical content: "It seems that the convert is not preparing himself to live his 'new life' as a transformative element in a sick society, but rather to accommodate himself

---

[49]González, "Encarnación e historia," 164.

[50]González, "Encarnación e historia," 166.

[51]Justo L. González, *Jesucristo es el Señor* (Miami: Caribe, 1970).

[52]Justo L. González, *History of Christian Thought*, rev ed. (Nashville: Abingdon, 1987); González, *Mañana: Christian Theology from a Hispanic Perspective* (Nashville: Abingdon, 1990).

to it." Neglecting the development of an adequate teaching ministry prolongs the weaknesses of faulty evangelism. Arana Quiroz argues, "The evangelical church is called to teach the full counsel of God, taking into account that the transformation of society will not automatically result from individual conversions."[53]

Arana Quiroz arrives at the theme of justice and the political task of the Christian, suggesting it as an aspect of responsibility derived from the recognition that God has established orders of creation that frame the actions of obedient disciples. Beginning with this teaching, he describes the concept of a just society, toward which a Christian should work. God, the Creator of human nature, has established in this its forms of expression: the orders are a result of the physical, psychological, sociological, and spiritual characteristics of human beings. God has introduced them in the human constitution, and therefore they are reflected in human nature. In other words, these spheres of social relationships are God's orders in two ways: they have their origin in God, and through them the Creator has given the human race certain responsibilities with the aim of helping it to relate and unite. Arana Quiroz points out the following orders: (1) sex, marriage, procreation, and family; (2) work and culture; (3) Saturday as a day of rest. He does not include either the state or the church, as these were instituted following the fall and not in the act of creation.

The first task for evangelicals, then, was to rediscover and proclaim biblical teaching about this theme; second, the evangelical church, recognizing and obeying God's mandate, should teach that the action of Christians in the spheres of family, work, culture, and rest is the path of obedience to their Creator and Redeemer. In relation to this teaching function, critique of the values that have guided our society and that have conditioned the life of believers in Latin America was lacking. The third task was to carry out a holistic ministry that includes worship, preaching, teaching, and service, sacrificial and prophetic service with

[53]Pedro Arana Quiroz, "Órdenes de la creación y responsabilidad cristiana," in *Fe cristiana y Latinoamérica hoy*, 172.

the tone of hope. The fourth task for Arana Quiroz was justice: the evangelical church in Latin America must proclaim and live justice. If justice belongs to the very character of God as revealed in Jesus Christ, the only role for Christians in this world is that of messengers, signals, and signs of God's justice, at both personal and social levels; this task particularly involves participation in politics. Some missionaries had taught that Christians should not participate in the political sphere. Arana Quiroz critiqued this attitude and demonstrated its lack of coherence, later pointing out a fifth task that involves the search for a social ethic and an ethic for the new person. The change must begin in the church itself, and it will bring new forms of action in the areas of money, power, and social distinctions. Here Arana Quiroz expressed his agreement with the emphasis found in Anabaptist theology, specifically the work of John Howard Yoder, that the Christian community itself, in its quality of life and practice of the justice of God's kingdom, is the major transforming factor in a society.[54]

In 1978, when an eleven-year military regime ended in Peru, that country's return to democracy was preceded by the elaboration of a new political constitution. Pedro Arana Quiroz was a representative to the Constituent Assembly, having been elected with one of the highest numbers of votes. His conduct in the assembly and his contributions to the wording of the new constitution reflected the convictions he had expressed in 1972 in the consultation on social ethics.[55]

A Pentecostal Contribution

A contribution from a Pentecostal perspective was entrusted to Juan Carlos Ortiz, one of the leaders of the charismatic renewal movement that had emerged in Argentina. His participation was a vigorous self-critique and a radical proposal: "In the fundamentalist evangelical church of which I am part, we have been governed by all the verses that talk about the past glories of the apostolic era and the marvelous future

---

[54]John Howard Yoder, *The Politics of Jesus* (Grand Rapids: Eerdmans, 1972). See especially chap. 12.
[55]See Pedro Arana, *Testimonio político* (Lima: Ediciones Presencia, 1987).

in heaven. But we have avoided the responsibility of giving a solution to the problems here and now. We have offered very little in the present."[56] For Ortiz, besides the four Gospels in the New Testament, there was another, the "Gospel According to Saint Evangelical." Created out of a self-interested picking and choosing of certain aspects of Jesus' message, the false Gospel "in a systematic way has grouped together passages from the Gospels that talk about what God offers, and has hidden and often ignored in a smooth and simple way the demands of Jesus Christ, especially those related to our neighbor."[57]

In Ortiz's perspective evangelical churches can dare to lift a prophetic voice in society only if they first correct the injustice that is present in internal church life. Ortiz highlights in the biblical testimony an undeniable social dimension: "If we do a sincere study of the New Testament regarding the destiny of all the offerings and collections, we are surprised that in no cases were they used for what they are used for today. They were not for the temple, for the organ, for the carpets, and so on, but almost always for the needs of the community."[58] A change in structures, values, and behavior inside the church can only come from a deep spiritual renewal: "For a horizontalism that is safe, a clear and evident verticality is required. This is perfection: the cross. The horizontalism of loving one's neighbor and a social commitment, accompanied by faith in God, the charisms of the Holy Spirit, fervent worship, ongoing devotion, the lordship of Jesus Christ and continuous coming to God in prayer."[59]

◆ ◆ ◆

In this way, the christological reflection developed in the FTL contributed an important element to the Lausanne movement in its effort to develop a missiology with both the sense of urgency for evangelization particular to the evangelical tradition and the christological modeling that would give it integrity. Today it is recognized that evangelical

---

[56]Juan Carlos Ortiz, "Iglesia y sociedad," in *Fe cristiana y Latinoamérica hoy*, 186.
[57]Ortiz, "Iglesia y sociedad," 187.
[58]Ortiz, "Iglesia y sociedad," 188.
[59]Ortiz, "Iglesia y sociedad," 193.

theology at this global level arrived at new readings of the biblical text that respond to the urgent questions of the context in which the church lives and ministers. This chapter's overview points to the Latin American evangelical contribution to this dialogue.

10

THE KINGDOM OF GOD

All these explicit or implicit understandings of the kingdom, throughout Christian history, have focused on some aspects of the kingdom at the cost of others, by putting emphasis on its present or future reality, on its historical or eternal nature, its social or personal dimension. Each interpretation has understood a part as being the whole, thus contributing to a distortion, an eclipse, a reduction of the biblical message of the kingdom. It is time to risk recovering the totality of the kingdom gospel, to appreciate its multidimensionality and to take on our commitment to the challenge that the kingdom presents to us here and now. This requires a sincere biblical exploration.

MORTIMER ARIAS, *VENGA TU REINO*

In 1971, while Chile was governed by socialist doctor Salvador Allende, who had been recently elected by popular vote, the evangelical organization World Vision organized a retreat for Protestant pastors in the port of Valparaíso. I had been asked to give a series of expositions on the topic of church and state, and the teaching responsibilities were shared with African evangelist Festo Kivengere and North American Presbyterian pastor Richard Halverson, chaplain to Congress in his home country. The majority of the pastors participating were Pentecostals, and in long conversations in the hallways they told me that they and their churches had voted for Allende because "we are the people and he is one of us." At some point in my expositions I touched on the theme of the kingdom of God, and during the dialogue that followed, one of the pastors said to me: "This idea of the kingdom of God is antiquated. We should be talking about the republic of God." This made me think further about contextualization.

Only three years later, in 1974, one of those pastors I had met in Valparaíso participated in the World Evangelization Congress in the Swiss city of Lausanne. He bore an official letter of greeting from the Chilean Congress signed by General Augusto Pinochet, who in a bloody coup in September 1973 had removed President Allende and unleashed a brutal repression against those who had been part of the Allende government. In this pastor's church, a large group of evangelicals had celebrated an "evangelical Te Deum" supporting the dictator Pinochet.

The organizers of the Lausanne Congress did not permit the public reading of Pinochet's greeting and had to face the protests of part of the Chilean delegation. Seeing this sudden change of unconditional loyalties, I realized with sadness that my teaching to those pastors about the kingdom of God in 1971 had fallen on deaf ears despite my efforts to contextualize.

The Kingdom of God and Latin America

When I was still a teenage university student in Lima, a copy of the book *¿Es realidad el reino de Dios?* (Is the kingdom of God real?) by missionary, evangelist, and Methodist theologian E. Stanley Jones fell into my hands. In a clear, pastoral, and very challenging way, Jones wrote of the kingdom of God, reminding readers that this was the central theme of Jesus' teaching. Becoming aware that I was enthusiastically reading this book, a missionary friend believed it opportune to warn me that the kingdom of God was the concern mostly of liberal proponents of the social gospel such as Walter Rauschenbusch, on the one hand, and on the other Jehovah's Witnesses, who called their meeting places "Kingdom Halls."

It was paradoxical that despite evangelicals' emphasis on proclaiming and knowing Jesus, they had forgotten the theme of the kingdom of God, as if it were a topic for heretics. However, it is important to remember that back in the 1920s in Latin America John Mackay had focused on the kingdom of God when he presented Jesus' teachings. As we saw in chapter four, Mackay said that for Jesus, the kingdom of God was "his concept of the principles of justice that constitute the moral economy of the universe."[1] The parables highlight the presence of absolute values that confront human beings with options and decisions. The kingdom of God "means the sovereignty of God in all spheres of human life, whether individual, at home, socially, or internationally, and concretely interpreting this sovereignty in the sense of acknowledging Christ as Lord of life and the application of his teachings to all of life's problems."[2] In the theological situation of the evangelical world of 1960, we could say that the kingdom of God had been eclipsed.

Having experienced this insufficiency, in 1966 new generations of evangelical university students listened to expositions by René Padilla on the eschatological dimension of Jesus' message and ministry with marked warmth. Recently returned from his doctoral studies in New Testament, in training seminars organized by the International Fellowship of Evangelical Students (IFES) Padilla dug into the theme "What is the gospel?" and demonstrated the centrality of Jesus' teaching about the kingdom of God.[3] His emphasis on New Testament eschatology provided the foundation of a Christian vision of history, needed as never before in this transitional period in Latin America, to understand the dynamic hope that sustains the activity of Christ's disciples in the world.

The kingdom of God was the topic of the second consultation held by the Fraternidad Teológica Latinoamericana (FTL) in December 1972. The first had established the foundations for the group's theological work. In the second, there were twenty-seven participants originating from

---

[1]John A. Mackay, "*. . . Mas yo os Digo*," 2nd ed. (Mexico City: CUPSA, 1964), 55.

[2]Mackay, "*. . . Mas yo os Digo*," 78.

[3]A summary of these presentations appeared as a chapter in René Padilla's book *El evangelio hoy* (Buenos Aires: Certeza, 1975), 17-42; English, "What Is the Gospel?," in C. René Padilla, *Mission Between the Times: Essays on the Kingdom* (Grand Rapids: Eerdmans, 1985; 2nd ed., Carlisle, UK: Langham Monographs, 2010).

twelve different countries and from a wide diversity of denominations. There were five core presentations. Emilio Antonio Núñez from the Iglesia Centroamericana in Guatemala was asked to present the dispensationalist perspective on the nature of the kingdom of God, while Baptist pastor René Padilla presented "The Kingdom of God and the Church." José Míguez Bonino, a Methodist from Argentina, presented "The Kingdom of God and History," and North American Mennonite John Howard Yoder spoke on "The Messianic Expectation of the Kingdom and Its Central Character for Developing an Appropriate Contemporary Hermeneutics." I, another Baptist pastor, closed the presentations with the topic of "The Kingdom of God, Eschatology, and Political and Social Ethics in Latin America."[4]

The Nature of the Kingdom of God

Emilio Antonio Núñez and René Padilla approached the theme from different angles but were unified by the common conviction that the life of a Christian and of the church in the world can be understood only within the wider framework of the kingdom of God for human history. Núñez worked directly with biblical texts, offering extensive references to the kingdom of God in the Old Testament, both the universal reign and the promise of messianic reign in the message of various prophets: "The Messiah will govern the world with a rod of iron and will institute his justice. The economic and social changes will be radical. There will be justice for all, and peace will reign." He also described the natural and geological changes announced by the prophets but highlighted that "the greatest blessings will be spiritual. The demonic powers will be imprisoned, human beings will have a new heart; the knowledge of God will be universal; the Holy Spirit will be poured out over all flesh, and there will be joy and peace for humanity."[5]

---

[4]The presentations, responses, and summaries of the discussion were edited by René Padilla and published as *El reino de Dios y América Latina* (El Paso, TX: Casa Bautista de Publicaciones, 1975).

[5]Emilio Antonio Núñez, "La naturaleza del reino de Dios," in Padilla, *El reino de Dios y América Latina*, 23.

Núñez described the sense of messianic expectation in the society in which Jesus undertook his ministry and how the Lord rejected the popular impulse to make him king. "Before Pilate, he said that he had been born to be king but that his kingdom was not of this world. He would be king but not in the way of men. . . . He did not come as the triumphant Messiah but as the suffering Messiah. Expiation precedes exaltation. The cross comes before the crown." While it is true that Jesus did not establish the Davidic kingdom as some expected, after his ascension he introduced into the fulfillment of the divine purpose a reality that had no precedent in the history of Israel or in the world. The Christian church was born in response to Christ's prophetic statement "I will build my church."[6]

Núñez highlighted that the weight of New Testament teaching shows that the church is not the kingdom, and he spoke of the current consensus among Protestant and Catholic theologians on this point.[7] After receiving the Holy Spirit at Pentecost, he said, the disciples were first and foremost interested in developing the evangelization program that Jesus had assigned to them, and in this task they were motivated by the eschatological hope of Jesus' final return.

> They yearned for the coming of the messianic kingdom but were conscious that this could not be established in the absence of the Teacher, and they would not attempt to establish it themselves on the basis of purely human effort. They waited for the kingdom as a cosmic intervention of God that will permanently defeat the powers of evil and enact good for all men.[8]

Núñez affirms emphatically: "No matter the method of critical study applied to the New Testament: it will always be impossible to show that those first Christians attempted to found a type of political kingdom in opposition to the Roman Empire."[9]

---

[6]Núñez, "La naturaleza del reino de Dios," 25, 26.
[7]Núñez, "La naturaleza del reino de Dios," 26.
[8]Núñez, "La naturaleza del reino de Dios," 26.
[9]Núñez, "La naturaleza del reino de Dios," 28.

Finally, he offers a summary of the concept of kingdom in the history of theology, remembering that in the fourth century the church went from being persecuted by the Roman Empire to being protected by it. Later Augustine identified the triumphant church of the empire with the kingdom. In this way "the visible church became the goal of history on earth," and outside it there was no salvation. (Let me add that as this was the predominant theology during the Iberian conquest of America. It justified the use of considerable force for evangelization, similar to the use of the Inquisition to fight religious and social heresies.) Núñez says: "The Augustinian doctrine of the kingdom is the one that has traditionally prevailed in Latin American Catholicism. However, following Vatican II there has been a change in the emphasis of this teaching. The kingdom that has not yet come but is coming is given more attention, as is a pilgrim church that has not arrived but is on the road."[10]

In a self-critical way, and making reference to a majority of the independent missionaries who came to Latin America at the end of the nineteenth century and the beginning of the twentieth, Núñez says that "they were definitely futurists and separatists and were not able to integrate their teaching on the kingdom with the cultural reality of our continent, something that we ourselves, the evangelicals of more recent generations, have likewise failed to do." In part for this reason, "the vast majority of Latin American evangelicals are found, at least in theory but also in practice, within end-times apocalypticism. And the concept of the kingdom present among us is very weak."[11]

The Kingdom of God and the Church

The emphasis of the presentation given by René Padilla on the kingdom of God and the church was to correct the excesses of a futurist eschatology that tended to ignore that with the coming of Christ into the world, the kingdom of God has come, although not yet in its fullness. The structure of Padilla's work is simple and direct: (1) eschatology in the

[10]Núñez, "La naturaleza del reino de Dios," 30.
[11]Núñez, "La naturaleza del reino de Dios," 32.

New Testament, (2) the church and the "already" of the kingdom of God, and (3) the church and the "not yet" of the kingdom of God. He begins with a reference to the concept of two ages in Jewish eschatology, expressed in the rabbinic formula "this age and the age to come." However, at the moment of Jesus Christ's arrival, the Jewish vision had taken a predominantly futurist direction, losing the sense of divine action in the historic present that had characterized the message of the prophets, in which the present and the future were maintained in eschatological tension. The arrival of Jesus Christ marked a difference:

> Throughout the New Testament the doctrine of the two ages is present, but it is interpreted in light of the death and resurrection of Jesus Christ. It is impossible to exaggerate the importance of the fact of Christ for the eschatology of the primitive church. The life and work of Jesus Christ means that God has acted definitively with the aim of fulfilling his redemptive purpose. It is now not possible to restrict his intervention to a cataclysm at the end of "this age." The main actor has appeared, and the eschatological drama of Jewish hope has begun! Eschatology has invaded history, and its impact has produced what has been appropriately described as "the new division of time."[12]

For Padilla, an understanding of eschatology in the New Testament and the tension present in it is necessary if we are to understand the relationship between the kingdom of God and the church: "The church reflects the tension between the 'already' and the 'not yet' of the kingdom of God, and apart from its very existence is unconceivable. The church is the simultaneous affirmation of the kingdom of God as a present reality and as a future reality." Thus it is at the same time an eschatological reality and a historical reality. Separated from its connection with the kingdom of God, the church would be no more than a human institution "whose study relates more to sociology than to

---

[12]René Padilla, "El reino de Dios y la iglesia," in Padilla, *El reino de Dios y América Latina*, 44. Padilla recognizes here the significance of the work of Oscar Cullmann with respect to the importance of the presence and message of Jesus in forging the concept of time in the New Testament and the expression of the "already" and "not yet" of the kingdom. A more recent expression of Padilla's view appears in his book *Mission Between the Times*, 200-201.

theology."[13] This warning was especially important during the period under consideration, because the church in its current historic form and the primitive church were indeed being studied from a sociological perspective, so that many times the theological reality was not being taken into account and a reductionist vision of the ecclesial realities began to be offered.[14]

Padilla pays attention to the soteriological aspect of the church's existence with the eschatological tension between the "already and not yet" of the kingdom. Christ has been enthroned, and from this position he commissions his disciples. Here a question is presented that we have seen appear among both Protestant and Catholic theologians: "This relationship between the affirmation of the Lord's cosmic dominion and the mission delegated to his church is useful to make clear the question regarding the kingdom of God and the church: In what way is the church related to the kingdom, and in what way is it related to this world?"[15] Here Padilla expresses disagreement with the universalism of Cullmann, who maintains that all human beings are members of Christ's kingdom and even unconsciously are fulfilling their vocation within it. Cullmann writes: "The fundamental distinction, then, between all the members of the lordship of Christ and the members of the Church is that the former do not know that they belong to this lordship, whereas the latter do know it."[16] Padilla makes his position clear:

> "Between the times" of Jesus Christ, between the fulfillment and the fullness, Jesus Christ reigns as Lord. But the kingdom of God in the cases when it is considered to be an order does not automatically include all men. It is an eschatological order into which one must *enter*. It is a soteriological order to which believers in Christ have been *transferred*, having been liberated from the cosmic powers ("the powers of darkness").[17]

---

[13]Padilla, "El reino de Dios y la iglesia," 46.

[14]Along these lines, Swiss sociologist Lalive D'Epinay published a study of Chilean Pentecostalism titled *El refugio de las masas: Estudio sociologico del protestantismo chileno* (Santiago: Editorial del Pacifico, 1968).

[15]Padilla, "El reino de Dios y la iglesia," 53.

[16]Oscar Cullmann, *The Christology of the New Testament*, rev. ed., trans. Shirley C. Guthrie and Charles A. M. Hall (Philadelphia: Westminster, 1959), 231.

[17]Padilla, "El reino de Dios y la iglesia," 54.

In a footnote to this point, Padilla offers numerous texts from the Gospels on this theme and emphasizes that "according to Jesus' teaching this entering is impossible without the fulfillment of certain conditions stipulated in his *kerygma*." This affects the nature of the proclamation of the kingdom undertaken by the church: "Consecutively, the proclamation of the kingdom of God is not only the proclamation of an objective fact with respect to which men need to be informed: it is simultaneously the proclamation of an objective fact and a call to faith."[18]

Padilla's careful review of New Testament teaching leads to a response to his previous question—this affirmation: "The church has a cosmic meaning because it is the affirmation of the universal authority of Jesus Christ. *In* it and *through it* the powers of the new age, set at liberty by the Messiah, are present in the midst of humankind. The correlate of the kingdom of God is the world, but the world that is redeemed in the church and through the church."[19]

The current vision of the church in light of the kingdom of God helps Latin American Protestant Christians in fulfilling their responsibilities as citizens of this world: it allows the social isolation caused in part by their condition of religious minority in an environment of Catholic Christianity to be broken. The consequence is decisive for the way in which the church sees its own role in the world and its relationship with the world. Padilla insists that "the church still shares with the world the marks of 'this age,' which yet remains under the power of the evil one. It lives in the midst of the tension between the 'already' and the 'not yet,' and this tension conditions all aspects of its existence in history."[20] A very important consequence that applies later in the reflection regarding political power is derived from this premise: the church cannot make its own structures or those of society absolute:

> [The church] awaits the coming of the kingdom, and therefore it limits its loyalty to the powers that govern the kingdoms of men. Beyond the structures

[18]Padilla, "El reino de Dios y la iglesia," 65n72, 54.
[19]Padilla, "El reino de Dios y la iglesia," 55, emphasis original.
[20]Padilla, "El reino de Dios y la iglesia," 60.

> created by these powers, the hope of the church is placed in the new heaven and the new earth, where "justice dwells." It sees itself as a sign of God's new creation, in the face of which all human intent to build a perfect society carries within itself the seed of destruction. When the church stops understanding itself in these terms, it limits itself to either the status quo or, on the other extreme, to some ideology that promises change but, like that status quo, dehumanizes man and makes him a screw in the social machine.[21]

The Kingdom of God and History

The specific contribution of José Míguez Bonino to this reflection was the question of mediations, that is to say, the step from biblical theology to consideration of the ethical options available in the reality of this time. Although Míguez Bonino could not be present at the consultation for health reasons, he sent his presentation, which was read and thoroughly discussed. As with all the presentations, except that of Núñez, Míguez Bonino revised his manuscript for publication in light of the consultation discussions. Taking into account the biblical work undertaken in the other presentations, Míguez Bonino presented his own work as "a brief systematic-ethical thesis." He expressed the conviction that the problem was not an abstract one to be resolved in an academic discussion, "but rather a very pressing and concrete question, to discover *how we can understand the active presence of the kingdom of God in our witness and action, particularly at this specific time in Latin America in which we have been called to profess our faith and serve our Lord.*"[22]

Míguez Bonino accepts the biblical work of the other presentations and expresses his agreement with Cullman's interpretation of how the eschatological question has a dialectic relationship between the "already" of the present kingdom and the "not yet" of the hoped-for fulfillment. He offers his own understanding of the kingdom "in the wider theological sense and heartbeat of God's active sovereignty over the world (natural

[21]Padilla, "El reino de Dios y la iglesia," 61.

[22]José Míguez Bonino, "El reino de Dios y la historia," in Padilla, *El reino de Dios y América Latina*, 75, emphasis original.

and historic in its unity and totality), specially and representatively exercised and given testimony to in Israel, made perfect in Jesus Christ and promised in complete manifestation in the parousia of the Lord."[23] The path of his reflection leads him first to establish the relationship between the history of salvation and secular history, then to examine the urgent issue of monism and dualism in the interpretation of history. He goes on to consider discernment of the kingdom in obedience and concludes by explaining his own proposal concerning the kingdom in relation to the Latin American sociopolitical-economic dilemma.

Míguez Bonino explores the vision of God's action in history presented in the Old Testament, noting that the sovereignty of God occurring in history is controversial. It seems necessary to say this in another way: "the sovereignty of God is an effective work that historicizes and makes history, calling together and rejecting men and peoples in relation with the divine purpose." Commenting on the distinction some make between "mere historic facts" and "prophetic interpretation," Míguez Bonino sustains that "such a distinction does not hold for the Old Testament: the prophetic message is in itself both act and efficacy, and is not primarily destined to 'explain' but rather to call, invite, or condemn." Also in the Old Testament, God's conflict with his people has a political nature, "with 'political' understood both in the wider sense meaning all areas of life of the collective entities that are peoples, and in the narrower sense relating to power."[24]

Arriving at the New Testament, he calls attention to a change, especially in the Pauline and Johannine literature. Míguez Bonino critically examines some of the explanations given with respect to this change and makes the following suggestion:

> In the New Testament, the history of salvation takes on a certain consistency on its own, a certain "distance" from the totality of human history. To make this clear: it is not about a separate history; it is always the history of Herod, of Pilate, of Nero, or of the Ephesian businessmen. But in the

[23]Míguez Bonino, "El reino de Dios y la historia," 76.
[24]Míguez Bonino, "El reino de Dios y la historia," 76, 77.

> emerging of a mission that is indissolubly tied to a particular historical nucleus (the history of Israel and of Jesus Christ), the faith of converted pagans is subject to a double historical reference: to its own and to this other, which now becomes constitutive for their faith.[25]

Míguez Bonino moves on to focus on dualist and monist positions in the interpretation of the relationship between the history of salvation and world history. Observing the theological scene at that time in Latin America, he says that Christians do not know how to integrate these two historical dimensions. He summarizes what he calls the dualist position, which could hark back, with certain reservations, to Saint Augustine's *City of God*: "Essentially it consists in fastening the kingdom to one of the histories, that of faith, which is transformed in this way into a univocal line, sacred and distinct, and reducing the other history to a mere general framework, in episodes, without eschatological meaning: a backdrop." But an honest reading of the Bible itself makes it impossible to continue affirming that general history is a mere episode, and Míguez Bonino continues: "For this reason it is not surprising that diverse solutions have emerged that I would call monist."[26]

This vision appears in ancient theologians such as Irenaeus and Origen, but what catches Míguez Bonino's attention is its appearance in the emergent liberation theologies. He considers the monist form taken by Gustavo Gutiérrez's idea regarding "one sole history" in his book *Teología de la liberación*. However, despite Míguez Bonino's sympathy for this theology, he observes serious risks in the monistic formulation: "To give concrete meaning to a history, it is necessary to find a transcription of the gospel that can be seen operating significantly at the level of 'general' history. To say this in another way, it is necessary to 'name the kingdom' in the current historical language of men."[27]

It is in such a "transcription" that Míguez Bonino sees the risk of taking words such as *love*, *new man*, and *liberation* and uprooting them,

---

[25]Míguez Bonino, "El reino de Dios y la historia," 78.
[26]Míguez Bonino, "El reino de Dios y la historia," 79, 80.
[27]Míguez Bonino, "El reino de Dios y la historia," 82.

separating them from the history of faith to the point where they lose their content: "Which God are we talking about then? And what kingdom? If this is taken to the extreme, we end up deifying history or man, and it would be better, as some say, to call things by their names and confess a full immanentism."[28] This is the same risk Pedro Arana Quiroz pointed out as a failing of ISAL, as we saw in chapter nine above.

The Kingdom and the Historic Options

Míguez Bonino firmly maintains that discernment of the kingdom can be done only in acts of obedience:

> It seems to me that the main question is not "Where is the kingdom present or visible in our present history?" but rather "How can I participate (not just as an individual, but as a community of faith and those inserted into history) in the world to come, in the promised kingdom?" . . . The kingdom is not an object to understand but a calling, a convocation, a force that creates movement.[29]

He maintains that as we cannot skip from the biblical text to present reality, we need to take into account a series of historic mediations that allow us, on the one hand, to understand Scripture with hermeneutical theological tools and, on the other hand, to understand the historical context. "Regarding this last aspect, alike in individual and collective actions, political or economic, or 'face-to-face' relationships, in all an understanding of reality is synthesized, of man, of the future—in summary, an ideology."[30]

As an illustration, in the fourth part of his work Míguez Bonino explains with great clarity why the search for justice in Latin America had led him and other Christians to a defined political option. First, they confronted Latin America reality with biblical teaching about what a life of justice, solidarity, and liberty should be. Second, they analyzed the Latin American situation by applying social and political theories that

---

[28]Míguez Bonino, "El reino de Dios y la historia," 82-83.
[29]Míguez Bonino, "El reino de Dios y la historia," 84.
[30]Míguez Bonino, "El reino de Dios y la historia," 86.

they considered scientific and that served as indispensable tools. The conclusion is clear:

> It is this double process that has convinced me—and a number of Christians on this continent and in others—that liberal capitalism, framed in the current international monopolistic system, is not a viable structure to generate in history the quality of life that has a future in the kingdom. On the contrary, its way of defining the conditions and human relationships constitutes (at least in his historic reality, which is the only one that we can judge and participate in) a negation of the quality of life. It is an anti-liberation: in kingdom terms, it is oppression and slavery. For this reason the term *liberation* connects me historically—ambiguous as the relationship may be—with those who fight for the elimination of this slavery.[31]

In addition to rejecting the capitalist order, Míguez Bonino explains that he has opted for socialism as a concrete option that creates better conditions in which to live the life of the kingdom of God. He understands the term *socialism* in its wider sense as including "diverse possibilities of instrumentation and structuring, within a common global understanding of the appropriation of material goods and the consequent way of organizing society and human life." Without going into detail or being more precise regarding the type of socialism he refers to, Míguez Bonino says: "Socialism as a social structure is for me today in Latin America the means of active correlation with the presence of the kingdom for its effects on the structure for a human society. This is, in this sphere, my obedience in faith."[32]

The Counterculture of the Kingdom of God

Mennonite theologian John Howard Yoder had been teaching for a year in Montevideo and Buenos Aires during one of the most volatile and politically violent times. The author of a book in English about Jesus titled *The Original Revolution*, Yoder had the opportunity to present Anabaptist theology with its emphasis on radical pacifism and living out

[31] Míguez Bonino, "El reino de Dios y la historia," 88.
[32] Míguez Bonino, "El reino de Dios y la historia," 89.

the values of the kingdom of God as the task of the church, as a minority who aim to follow the example of Jesus in their relationships within and outside the ecclesial community.[33] His presentation to a large audience of university students in Córdoba, Argentina, was published in the magazine *Certeza* in 1970 and was widely distributed. His exposition centered on the political options available in Jesus' time—those of the Pharisees, Sadducees, and Zealots—and argued that Jesus followed his own path, his own option, which had a political dimension and its own radicality.[34] In the Lima consultation he had been asked to speak on the kingdom of God as an interpretive key to all of Scripture.

Yoder introduced his reflection by discussing the difficulty of the hermeneutical task, especially when the terms forged in one culture are read in a totally different cultural context. However, "the thesis can be sustained that the concept of 'kingdom' is a key concept, more determining than many others. All theologies speak of 'sin' or of 'love' in relatively parallel terms, but when 'kingdom' is mentioned, the ways part. . . . It is possible to argue that the touchstone of today's theology could be what is done with the key concept of kingdom."[35]

Yoder goes on to outline the implications of the centrality of kingdom. First, those who speak of "kingdom" speak of a king: "In an honest hermeneutics, the person of Jesus Christ cannot be made into an abstraction. He was a person of his time, of his people. He cannot be translated into a particular equivalent." Second, those who speak of "kingdom" speak of history, and "this point must be emphasized due to the impact the Neo-Platonic and Augustinian dualist inheritance has had, especially in forms of mysticism and pietism within Christianity."[36] Third, those who say "kingdom" say "community," and this goes against the strong individualist mark in our culture: "A religious message that promises

---

[33]John H. Yoder, *The Original Revolution* (Scottdale, PA: Herald Press, 1971).

[34]In that same year, 1972, Yoder published *The Politics of Jesus,* which was widely hailed for its powerful Anabaptist reading of the New Testament. It was published in Spanish in 1985.

[35]John Howard Yoder, "La expectativa mesiánica del reino y su carácter central para una adecuada hermenéutica contemporánea," in Padilla, *El reino de Dios y América Latina*, 104.

[36]Yoder, "La expectativa mesiánica del reino," 104.

illumination or nobility, heroism or secret initiation, joy or ecstasy, could well be directed toward an individual isolated from his neighbors. A message that proclaims a kingdom cannot genuinely be heard without a people's being formed." Yoder observes that in the so-called Third World "evangelicals have experienced the reality of a visible community: especially in situations of persecution, cultural isolation, or economic disadvantage, the evangelical community has always been conscious of its social nature." The problem is that preaching and evangelical hermeneutics were individualistic: "So then . . . Latin American evangelicals have experienced the reality of being community without having had the corresponding doctrinal consciousness."[37]

Fourth, those who say "kingdom" say "obedience." "We must reject the tendency to separate ethics from theology and obedience from faith. The announcement of the kingdom in Matthew 4:17 and 23 leads directly to a new moral model in Matthew 5."[38] Fifth, those who say "kingdom" say "politics": "It is not sufficient to say 'history' and 'community.' We must add that it is about power, structures, interests and task." Yoder observes that a variety of factors have influenced the apolitical stance of Latin American evangelicals:

> Among them are the individualism originating in modern humanism, dualism derived from ancient Hellenism, the modesty of the missionary who is a guest at the mercy of the government of the country in which he works, the political conservatism of the missionary who comes from a powerful country, the relative naiveté of religious workers regarding economic and political knowledge that is understood in the light of their particular and limited education.[39]

The Political Relevance of Jesus

For Yoder the apolitical stance of evangelicals originates from a hermeneutical error because it closes its eyes to the political relevance of Jesus.

---

[37]Yoder, "La expectativa mesiánica," 105, 107.
[38]Yoder, "La expectativa mesiánica," 107.
[39]Yoder, "La expectativa mesiánica," 108.

The word *politics* can be understood in various ways: "in the wider sense, political is all that has to do with life between men in the polis." In a more limited sense, "'politics' means the battle between parties to gain or maintain control of a government." The political character of the person and work of Jesus is perceived between these two ways of understanding the political: "He did not try to destroy Herod or Pilate to govern in their place. However, his presence and his message threatened Herod's peace and gave reason to denounce him before Pilate as an enemy of Caesar."[40]

The consequences of these formal implications, which Yoder groups as "substantial implications," have a critical impact for the follower of Jesus Christ. First, in speaking of kingdom, one must distinguish this kingdom from other kingdoms: "If Jesus is Lord, others are not: neither demons, nor kings of the nations. If we obey him, we will not submit—at least not in the same absolute sense—to other leaders, structures, or loyalties." Second, in speaking of the kingdom that comes from outside our experience, we are obliged to consider an epistemology that "does not conform to the world." Jesus presents a completely different way of understanding what the king is in his kingdom. We associate the term *king* with a throne, territory, soldiers, and a sword. He presents a radical change. With a certain irony Yoder says, "Seen from this perspective, the Jesus of certain evangelicals says: 'I am not King yet, except in a spiritualized sense. Later, however, I will come back, and then I will fulfill the previous definition: with a throne, sword, territory, soldiers, and everything.'"[41]

Third, knowledge of the concept of king brings with it a reversal of values: "When Jesus says to his listeners: 'Yes, I am King, but not like other kings,' the new content given to the concept of kingdom is 'service.' It is a *Servant Lord*." Fourth, the Servant King does not impose his will by force. While the Lord calls with persistence, proclaims with authority, and promises exacting judgment, he leaves each listener free to follow him or not. Drawing on long Anabaptist experience, which during the

[40]Yoder, "La expectativa mesiánica," 109.
[41]Yoder, "La expectativa mesiánica," 110.

sixteenth century offered the first critical theology of Christendom in Europe, Yoder says: "In this, which is the simple consequence of what we have previously demonstrated, the kingdom of God is distinct from other kingdoms. It is offered in love but favors the liberty of men. Its voluntary character leads as a natural consequence to its minority status."[42]

Fifth, to proclaim the kingdom means keeping the problem of power in its central place. Yoder reminds us that according to the Gospel testimony, it was the temptation of power, more that the other temptations, that Jesus had to confront. He takes from here two conclusions that are very pertinent to the Latin American situation.

> As a result, the church (normally a minority and often persecuted) must always look with certain suspicion at the pretensions of those who exercise the authority that Jesus did not accept. The church can speak of government as if it were directly under Satan's disposition [Mt 4:8ff; Rev 13] or as if it were under the highest control of God [Rom 13:1-7; 1 Tim 2:1-4, 1 Pet 2:13-16]. In either case it doesn't put up obstacles for the pretensions of any government.[43]

This suspicion of the church toward the pretensions of those who already exercise power in society also should extend to the ideological constructions of those who try to gain power. Yoder says: "Because of our suspicion with regard to the kings of this world, neither can we put faith in global solutions—capitalism, socialism, revolution, national renovation—that want to impose themselves from the top down." Better to be a church with a watchful attitude, attentive to social and political developments: "It is better to observe, criticize abuses, create alternatives, promote movements, than to imagine and hope for solutions that would be more satisfactory but are actually unfeasible."[44]

Finally, Yoder expounds the substantial implications of the centrality of kingdom. First, "those who say kingdom push toward change." The role of the church is

---

[42]Yoder, "La expectativa mesiánica," 111.

[43]Yoder, "La expectativa mesiánica," 112. The bracketed Scripture citations here were included in Yoder's footnotes.

[44]Yoder, "La expectativa mesiánica," 113.

> to act as a bearer of hope . . . by its preaching of divine justice; by its promise of the renewing and creative force of love, forgiveness, and service; by its invention of models of service; by its experience of the voluntary community of the companions of Jesus; workers, for the physical presence of the believing people whose nonconformity within the world, acting as salt, as light, as a city that, like a mountain, cannot be hidden.[45]

Second, if we proclaim the kingdom we affirm that its ethical content can serve as discerning criteria for that which "God is doing to make man's life more humane." For Yoder, the Sermon on the Mount offers an outline of the basic elements of the original ethic of the kingdom. Third, beyond the relevance of the message of the kingdom, we should confess the relevance of the presence of the people of the kingdom as a paradigm or sign of the gospel.

Yoder also challenged us to understand the identity of Latin American Protestants, taking as a paradigm the Anabaptist vision of the Christian community as the one that first practices justice internally. Only from there are the conditions prepared to transform society and to announce a different reality. Yoder suggested this path to the FTL itself. He reminded us that this vocation begins with a doubly critical attitude: rejection of an exaggerated identification of the missionary movement with Anglo-Saxon culture and North American power, but also rejection of the opposite attitude, a simplistic identification between the work of God and the revolution. Yoder asks how it is possible to oppose these identifications without having another support point and what tools are available for the task. He himself answers:

> I propose as a thesis that the "support point," the starting point, the ground on which it is possible to build, is the kingdom. It has its laws and customs, its slogans and songs. The kingdom as culture offers friends and advice. It calls me to abandon and follow. In this way the kingdom is made real in each situation: as a base for resistance and a model of nonconformity. In the United States, the hippie phenomenon has proved the cultural power that a minority counterculture can have. This is a weak

[45]Yoder, "La expectativa mesiánica," 114.

> analogy to what the children of the kingdom should be. They should embody in their message and in their experience of community a distinct lifestyle, not because it is imported but because it is redeemed.[46]

Social and Political Ethics and the Kingdom of God

This perspective that is central to Anabaptist theology was useful also to me in the final presentation of the consultation, to understand the place of Latin American Protestantism and suggest an outline for a social and political ethic. The thesis was that, to be located as a religious minority within a context of Christendom in Latin America, the earlier Protestants of the first decades of the twentieth century had seen themselves as agents of change, not through political alliances but out of faithfulness to their basic vocation as the people of God with a distinct lifestyle. Although the protagonists of early Protestantism were from different denominational backgrounds, in their attitude and their self-image, their way of seeing their social project and minority status, they very much resembled Anabaptists:

> In the heart of a Christendom nurtured in the political more than the spiritual, evangelicals affirmed the spiritual nature of the kingdom of God. In the heart of a Constantinian Christianity of "the official church," evangelicals affirmed an absolute separation between the throne and the altar (or the pulpit). Their presence in the heart of a nominal Christianity was fruit of their emphasis in the transforming experience of *personal and conscious conversion* rather than *traditional baptism*. The way to explain this presence was guided by force in highlighting the historic fall of the Roman Church. That is to say, we have a series of theological elements that point to an Anabaptist tradition.[47]

However, in examining the eschatology of evangelical circles during the 1970s, strongly influenced by Anglo-Saxon evangelicalism with its dispensationalist and premillennial emphasis, it was obvious that the capacity for social critique had been lost and that "the North American way

---

[46]Yoder, "La expectativa mesiánica," 112.

[47]Samuel Escobar, "El reino de Dios, la escatología y la ética social y política en América Latina," in *El reino de Dios y América Latina*, 132.

of life, capitalism, the so-called free market, and liberal democracy, had come to be for evangelicals something like the social and political manifestation of the kingdom of God on earth." This type of eschatology "was conditioned more by the social and historic situation in the interests of its preservation than by what is taught by the Word of God, which had lost all its dynamism. As we see it today in Latin America, it cannot resist or respond to the challenge of Marxist eschatology."[48]

It was important to highlight the key function that Marxist eschatology fulfilled in various political projects that were advocated at this time as the only alternative for Latin America, and to contrast them with the Christian hope growing from a renewed understanding of the kingdom of God.

> The eschatological dimension of Marxism is given in the vision of a new order that will come with the revolution. Any effort to reform the capitalist society (from which Marxism has emerged) is utopian when it does not take seriously the source of social evil. The only way to take evil seriously [in Marxism] is to recognize the presence of class struggle that progressively arrives at a revolutionary phase, when the proletariat takes power. The efforts to help the needy and poor are scorned as "palliatives." The great evil itself must be cured and not only the symptoms. Today many evangelicals who embark on diverse forms of social service are criticized because in offering "palliatives" they are only helping to postpone the coming of the revolution.[49]

Ironically, this Marxist eschatology had a similar effect to dispensationalism, in which "doing good to a neighbor" is postponed in theory and in practice because the preaching of the gospel is considered more urgent. When the gospel message is extended further, according to dispensational thinking, the second coming of Jesus Christ and the establishment of his millennial reign are accelerated. In this way Marxism and apocalyptic futurism coincide to theoretically devalue a kind, compassionate action to help a neighbor with an immediate need.[50]

---

[48]Escobar, "El reino de Dios," 137, 140.
[49]Escobar, "El reino de Dios," 142.
[50]Escobar, "El reino de Dios," 143.

The presentation concluded by examining the dimensions of the kingdom in our life: an ethical, critical, apologetic dimension, one full of hope. With respect to ethics and the critiques, I pointed out that to be a citizen of the kingdom of God is more than to obtain a letter of citizenship by which one can prove that "I've taken the crucial step" that brought me into the kingdom: "It is not just being convinced of certain things about Jesus Christ and singing and praying about them. It is a way to live among men, having discovered again the meaning of being human/man in God's design . . . (because) anytime we consider the type of society that is desirable, we are really asking about the purpose of the Creator for his creatures."[51]

With the theme of peace as an example, I said that the messianic hope for peace and the arrival of the "Prince of Peace" has begun to be fulfilled with the coming of Christ, and in the present "the disciple of Christ should be an attentive guardian of peace, not only in the midst of the Christian community but indeed in his relationships with all men; he is, in summary, a peacemaker, one who brings calm, an instrument of the Prince of Peace among men." And given that in Latin America social peace is threatened by injustice over centuries in the established order and the consequent revolution, "The Christian cannot be content with desiring 'social peace at any cost.' Closing their eyes to the injustice that feeds social war, many Christians have limited themselves to praising the dictatorships that have brought 'peace'—peace in the cemetery—without realizing that under a peace imposed by terror, revolutionary violence was germinating."[52]

In Latin America it is necessary to rescue the histories of those who have lived out kingdom values and in so doing have contributed to social and political change. It should be remembered, however, that these attainments have no value in the eyes of the apocalypticists of Marxism and of the gospel. For some,

[51]Escobar, "El reino de Dios," 145.
[52]Escobar, "El reino de Dios," 146, 147.

> there are more human values in Spartacus than in Henri Dunant [founder of the Red Cross] and in Che Guevara than in the British, North American, and Latin American doctors who have submerged themselves in working among the indigenous communities in Latin American countries. For others, the "fiery" preachers who gather multitudes and produce "results," statistics are worth more than those teachers whose vision of kingdom includes giving a good education to the poor children of Latin America.

The hope of the kingdom must be lived with realism and clarity: "When passive conformity, disguised or spiritualized as realism, says that there is no value in trying to change the world, we can respond that just by being faithful to Christ we are already changing the world, when we live our social and political action in the light of the hope of the kingdom."[53]

Conclusion

The theological work that preceded the consultation in Lima regarding the kingdom of God, and what followed in later years as a number of the participants continued their reflection, had a global projection especially in the Lausanne movement. I will consider this in the following chapter. In Lausanne, Padilla and Yoder were key members of a group of more than three hundred people that met spontaneously to express their sense that the Lausanne Covenant should have been more explicit on some points. Their "Response to Lausanne" opened with an affirmation that clearly reflected truths that had been articulated two years previously in Lima:

> The *evangel* is God's good news in Jesus Christ; it is Good News of the reign he proclaimed and embodies; of God's mission of love to restore the world to wholeness through the cross of Christ and him alone; of his victory over the demonic powers of destruction and death; of his lordship over the entire universe. It is good news of a new creation, a new humanity, a new birth through him by his life-giving Spirit, of the gifts of his messianic reign contained in Jesus and mediated through him by his Spirit; of the charismatic community empowered to embody his reign of

[53]Escobar, "El reino de Dios," 153.

shalom here and now, before the whole creation, and makes his Good News seen and known. It is Good News of liberation, of restoration, of wholeness, and of salvation that is personal, social, global, and cosmic. Jesus is Lord! Alleluia! Let the earth hear his voice![54]

[54]J. D. Douglas, ed., *Let the Earth Hear His Voice: International Congress on World Evangelization Lausanne, Switzerland. Official Reference Volume: Papers and Responses* (Minneapolis: World Wide Publications, 1975), 1294.

11

LATIN AMERICA ENTERS THE THEOLOGICAL SCENE

> In the face of the current evolution of monetary imperialism, we should say to our faithful ones and to ourselves the warning given by the seer of Patmos to the Christians in Rome when facing the imminent fall of this great city prostituted in luxury, thanks to the oppression of the peoples and to slave trafficking: "Come out of her, my people, so that you will not share in her sins, so that you will not receive any of her plagues" (Rev 18:4).
>
> Jesus took upon himself all of humanity to guide them to eternal life, whose earthly preparation is social justice, the first expression of fraternal love. When Christ through his resurrection frees humanity from death, he guides all human liberations to their eternal plenitude.

These eloquent paragraphs are part of "Message from Bishops of the Third World," signed by eighteen Catholic bishops from Asia, Africa, and Latin America in August 1967.[1] This initiative was born in northeastern Brazil, encouraged by Bishop Hélder Câmara in response to "the anguished call" of Pope Paul VI in the encyclical *Populorum Progressio.* The bishops' message articulated a position in response to the power of money and issued an exhortation to fight against injustice and toward a more just social order, based on theological reflection.

[1]The text of this message appeared in *Signos de renovación: Recopilación de documentos post-conciliares de la Iglesia en América Latina*, a collection of thirty-nine documents, speeches, and conferences by Latin American Catholics, published in Lima by the Comisión Episcopal de Acción Social in 1969, with an introduction by the theologian Gustavo Gutiérrez. In it he outlines his liberation theology.

In this way, in the 1970s Latin America entered into the global theological scene as a protagonist. Until this moment scholars had recognized that despite the numerical weight of the Catholic presence and the notable numeric growth of Protestants, in this part of the world there was no indigenous theological production. This changed visibly during this decade. In the Catholic context the books of liberation theologians such as Gustavo Gutiérrez, Leonardo Boff and Clodovis Boff, Juan Luis Segundo, Jon Sobrino, and Hugo Assmann were translated into English and other European languages soon after appearing in their original Spanish or Portuguese, and they were well received.

Quickly across the world, many social groups that had developed a consciousness of oppression found in liberation theologies language and thought categories with which they identified. Ethnic minorities such as Hispanics and African Americans in the United States, women in feminist movements, and emerging Christian thinkers in Asia and Africa began to use the vocabulary and liberation themes to express themselves. The fact that a number of these new Catholic theologians were making use of the Bible was a novelty in Latin America; it opened doors to a new and wider dialogue with ecumenical Protestantism and also had repercussions in evangelical Protestantism.

Meanwhile, as we have seen in previous chapters, Latin American Protestant theologians had begun to actively participate in global theological reflection, and their voices contributed to a dialogue that in this stage definitely became global. Proof of this is the book by Mortimer Arias *Salvación es liberación* (Salvation is liberation), exploring the meaning of the conference Salvation Today organized by the Evangelism and World Mission Commission of the World Council of Churches in Bangkok in December 1972. Arias, then bishop in the Methodist Church of Bolivia, writes of the global missionary situation and declares, "The themes that are presented and discussed in this book are vital for the future of the Latin American Christian community."[2]

---

[2]Mortimer Arias, *Salvación es liberación* (Buenos Aires: La Aurora, 1973), 5.

In the evangelical context the most notable case that had repercussions beyond theological circles was René Padilla's presentation "Evangelism and the World" at the International Congress for World Evangelization, which took place in Lausanne, Switzerland, in July 1974. Organized by a wide spectrum of evangelical institutions and convened by evangelist Billy Graham, the congress represented the crème de la crème of evangelical missionary activism that at this time was flowering in the world. Following the mechanism adopted by the congress to obtain wide participation, Padilla's presentation had been circulated in Spanish, English, French, German, and Indonesian months prior to the event. In his oral presentation Padilla responded to hundreds of critiques and comments that he had received from all over the world. Sharp debate had arisen because in establishing the nature of the gospel with a biblical foundation, he criticized versions of the gospel made popular by evangelistic and missionary activism. In many cases these were actually a "culture Christianity" that, consciously or unconsciously, identified the Christian message with the North American lifestyle. Padilla affirmed his evangelistic passion but trenchantly called out these false versions of the gospel. Key parts of the text from his presentation came to be incorporated in the Lausanne Covenant, a document that in the following decades had decisive influence among theologians and evangelical scholars in Christian mission, and among missionaries open to change who were seeking direction in the new global situation. In both ecumenical and evangelical contexts, then, the Christology forged in Latin America came to occupy an important place in theological debates.

Liberation Theologies

As we have seen in previous chapters, the language of "liberation" had begun to be used in reflection on Christian social and political responsibility. In Africa and Asia, the movements that had adopted the term *liberation* referred to the fight against European colonialism and its consequences. In Latin America the term had a socioeconomic and cultural meaning, sometimes applied to a distinctive and opposite political and social alternative and other times indicating the "development" model following the US pattern. Facing the revolutionary upheavals that the triumph of the Cuban Revolution brought from 1959 onwards, John F. Kennedy, the first Catholic president of the United States, had reoriented his country's Latin American policy with a series of structural reforms in the framework known as the Alliance for Progress. However, a group of social scientists who sought to diagnose the Latin American situation arrived at the conviction that progress and development were not possible if the dependence and social order imposed by capitalist powers were not first broken. This diagnosis utilized a Marxist social analysis, particularly its theory of imperialism. Thus "dependence theory" emerged, its proponents affirming its scientific character. Gustavo Gutiérrez wrote:

> Underdevelopment as a global fact appears increasingly clearly and primarily to be the consequence of an economic, political, and cultural dependence on centers of power outside Latin America. The dynamics of capitalist economics lead simultaneously to the creation of greater wealth for a few and greater poverty for more. Acting complicitly with those centers of power, the national oligarchies maintain for their benefit and through diverse mechanisms a situation of internal domination in each country.[3]

Gutiérrez goes on to argue that "characterizing the Latin American reality as dependent and dominated leads logically to speaking of liberation and to participating in the process it requires. It is a term that expresses a new posture of man in Latin America." Going beyond social analysis, he proposes a notion of liberation:

> It is, on a deep level, to see the rise of humanity in a certain perspective of philosophy and theology of history, as the process of emancipation of men oriented toward a society in which man is free of all slavery, in which he is not an object but an agent of his own destiny. A process that leads not only to a radical change of structure, a social revolution, but goes further: to the permanent creation of a new way of being man.[4]

---

[3]Gustavo Gutiérrez, introduction to *Signos de renovación*.
[4]Gutiérrez, introduction.

Thus Gutiérrez went from social analysis to an eschatological exaltation that promised a new anthropology. The themes outlined in this introduction in 1969 were later developed extensively in his book *Teología de la liberación: Perspectivas* (Liberation theology: Perspectives, published originally in 1971 and then later appearing in English, as *A Theology of Liberation*, and German in 1973). In this work Gutiérrez suggests a new way of doing theology: "The theology of liberation offers us not so much a new theme for reflection as a new way to do theology. Theology as critical reflection on historical praxis is a liberating theology, a theology of the liberating transformation of the history of humankind and also therefore that part of humankind—gathered into ecclesia—which openly confesses Christ."[5]

This definition helps us begin to grasp what is new in the proposal. For Gutiérrez, throughout the history of the church, theology has fulfilled different functions, though "by changing modalities, the essential effort for an intelligent faith is maintained." For example, theology as *wisdom* in the patristic era was a help in living a spiritual life in the world, and theology as *rational knowledge* in scholasticism had developed as an intellectual systematization that made use of Greek philosophy.

Having adopted a certain form of action, a *praxis* based on social analysis in response to the political and social demands particular to Latin America, Christians were critically reflecting on their praxis—and now *this* was theology, following and issuing from action. Gutiérrez attributes this emphasis on practice to the discovery of charity as the center of Christian life; a new lay spirituality resident in the world and not only in the contemplative life; the importance of theology and reading the "signs of the times," following John XXIII and the Second Vatican Council; and the philosophy of action proposed by lay Catholic philosopher Maurice Blondel. Later he says, "To these factors should be added the influence of *Marxist thought*, focusing on praxis and geared to the

---

[5]Gustavo Gutiérrez, *A Theology of Liberation* (Maryknoll, NY: Orbis, 1988), 12. I will cite from the 1988 edition of this book; in it the author made corrections and clarifications requested by Vatican censorship.

transformation of the world. The Marxist influence began to be felt in the middle of the nineteenth century, but in recent times its cultural impact has been greater."[6] Finally he notes:

> The rediscovery of the *eschatological dimension* in theology has also led us to consider the central role of historical praxis. Indeed, if human history is above all else an opening to the future, then it is a task, a political occupation, through which we orient and open ourselves to the gift which gives history its transcendent meaning: the full and definitive encounter with the Lord and with other humans.[7]

As the proposed praxis was identification with and service to the poor, this theology put great emphasis on the perspective of the poor. Gutiérrez, writing in 1979, said:

> From the beginning, the theology of liberation had two fundamental insights. Not only did they come first chronologically, but they have continued to form the very backbone of this theology. I am referring to its theological method and its perspective of the poor. From the beginning, the theology of liberation posited that the first act is involvement in the liberation process, and that theology comes afterward, as a second act.[8]

As I have explained elsewhere, starting from these concepts and their theological method, Latin American liberation theologians began a triple rereading that affected their proposal of Christian practice and theological reflection.[9] First was a critical rereading of the history of their church, relating ecclesiastical actions with the social role undertaken by the church in its conflictive history in Latin America. Second was a rereading of the Bible in its totality, highlighting the perspective of the poor and of themes related to liberation and social justice. In this way, for example, Exodus as a narrative of liberation of enslaved Hebrews in Egypt becomes key for understanding God's action in history. Third was a rereading of what Christian praxis should be, oriented toward the

---

[6]Gutiérrez, *Theology of Liberation*, 8, emphasis original.
[7]Gutiérrez, *Theology of Liberation*, 8, emphasis original.
[8]Gustavo Gutiérrez, *The Power of the Poor in History* (Eugene, OR: Wipf & Stock, 2004), 200.
[9]Samuel Escobar, *La fe evangélica y las teologías de la liberación* (El Paso, TX: Casa Bautista de Publicaciones, 1987), esp. chaps. 5-9.

transformation of social structures more than simply practicing charity or helping the needy. In the following decades these theologians produced a notable heritage of works on church history, on the Bible, and on Christian ethics, all from a liberationist perspective.[10]

Jesus Christ as Liberator

The first person to systematically formulate a Christology in the Latin American Catholic context was Brazilian Franciscan Leonardo Boff, who had completed his doctorate in Germany under Karl Rahner. Ordained as a priest in 1964, he soon became known in Brazil for his intense activity as an editor, writer, and professor. In 1974 his book *Jesucristo el liberador* (*Jesus Christ Liberator*) first appeared in Spanish; its original, *Jesus Cristo libertador*, had been published in Portuguese in 1971, and thus it reached an audience throughout the continent.[11] In the prologue to the Spanish version of the book, the Uruguayan lawyer and journalist Héctor Borrat categorically affirms: "Here, written by a Brazilian, is the first systematic Christology produced in Latin America."[12] Borrát also recognized that even in Europe Catholics had been left behind in their Christology and had not produced works like those of Protestants Wolfhart Pannenberg, Günther Bornkamm, and Rudolf Bultmann. He enthusiastically affirms that Boff's work is up to the standard of those studies: "The works of the Brazilian Franciscan reaches this level in a language and from a country habitually absent in modern Christology."[13]

Argentinian biblical scholar Monsignor Jorge Mejía, who wrote a careful critique of Boff's work, nevertheless recognizes the qualities of this work:

---

[10]In my judgment, the best global presentation of this stage of the movement is that of José Míguez Bonino, *Doing Theology in a Revolutionary Situation* (Philadelphia: Fortress, 1975). A careful historical chronicle is that of Robert Oliveros Maqueo, SJ, *Liberación y teología: Génesis y crecimiento de una reflexión 1966–1977* (Lima: Centro de Estudios y Publicaciones, 1977).

[11]Leonardo Boff, *Jesucristo el liberador* (Buenos Aires: Latinoamérica Libros, 1974).

[12]Héctor Borrat, foreword to Boff, *Jesucristo el liberador*, 11.

[13]Borrat, foreword, 11.

> It is a pleasure to affirm that the author and his work are inspired by a refreshing love and reverence for the Jesus of history and of the faith that moves people to draw near to him, not as an archaeological object nor as a mere critical problem whose code must be deciphered, but as the God-with-us who must be received with the attitude of a believer and in worship.[14]

Both critics and enthusiasts of his work recognize Boff's notable effort, which summarizes the state of the christological theme in Europe, especially in works by German authors, and sets forth his own path. In the summary of the christological search offered in his first chapter, he pays special attention to Bultmann, to continue with the search for the historical Jesus. He examines diverse current christological positions of that time, with brief references to the cosmic-evolutionist interpretation of Jesus Christ presented by Teilhard de Chardin, the interpretation of Jesus using the depth-psychology categories of Jung, the secular and sociocritical interpretation, and the emergence of a renewed interest in Jesus Christ among youth around the world. In the second chapter, examining hermeneutical questions, Boff makes reference to the specific questions that emerge from the Latin American reality and the way they should be presented: "In attempting to delineate our position with regard to Jesus in a Latin American context, we insert all our peculiarities, our life and preoccupations into this task. In so doing, we would wish that he prolong his incarnation within our history and reveal a new face especially known and loved by us."[15]

Boff explains the historical-critical hermenuetics that he will adopt, making reference to European erudition that he will depend on, but he clarifies that "it is with preoccupations that are ours alone, taken from our Latin American context, that we will reread not only the old texts of the New Testament but also the most recent commentaries written in Europe."[16] He outlines the keys to his Christology: (1) the primacy of the

[14]Jorge Mejía, "'Jesucristo el Libertador' de Leonardo Boff," *Criterio* (1976): 458.
[15]Leonardo Boff, *Jesus Christ Liberator* (Maryknoll, NY: Orbis, 1980), 32.
[16]Boff, *Jesus Christ Liberator*, 43.

anthropological element over eschatology, (2) the primacy of the utopian element rather that the facts, (3) the primacy of the critical element over the dogmatic, (4) the primacy of the social over the personal, and (5) the primacy of orthopraxis over orthodoxy.

In chapters three through seven he examines the figure of Jesus as he appears in the Gospels, exploring significant, creative, suggestive aspects of the personality and behavior of Jesus and his teaching in the Gospels. For Boff,

> Initially, Jesus preached neither himself nor the church, but the kingdom of God. The kingdom of God is a realization of a fundamental utopia of the human heart, the total transfiguration of this world, free from all that alienates human beings, free from pain, sin, divisions, and death. He came and announced: "The time has come, the kingdom of God is close at hand!" He not only promised this new reality but already began to realize it, showing that it is possible in the world.[17]

Boff holds that "before giving divine titles to Jesus, the Gospels allow us to speak of him in a very human way. With him, as the New Testament tells us, 'appeared the goodness and humanitarian love of God.'"[18] In chapter five of his book, with particularly rich literary expression, he suggests that Jesus was a man of extraordinary good sense, originality, and creative fantasy. He dedicates a chapter to the meaning of Jesus' death. With exhaustive use of texts from the Gospels, he describes the bewilderment and crisis provoked among the Jewish leaders by the popularity of Jesus, and their concerted action to kill Jesus, condemning him as a blasphemer and terrorist. Boff eventually turns to historical form criticism. For example, he comments on Jesus' trial before Caiaphas and the question in Mark 14:61-62, "Are you the Messiah, the Son of the Blessed One?" and Jesus' answer, which is "I am; and 'you will see the Son of Man, seated at the right hand of the Power,' and 'coming with the clouds of heaven'" (NRSV). Boff says: "Catholic and Protestant exegetes ask many questions: Is this a historical account or a profession of faith of

[17]Boff, *Jesus Christ Liberator*, 49.
[18]Boff, *Jesus Christ Liberator*, 20.

the primitive community, which in the light of the resurrection interpreted the figure of Jesus as being the Messiah-Christ and the Son of man in Daniel 7? It is difficult to decide this question by exegetical methods."[19]

His take on the meaning of Christ's death leads to key points for all christological interpretation, and in this he reflects Dietrich Bonhoeffer's thought. He summarizes Christ's life by saying:

> The whole life of Christ was a giving, a being-for-others, an attempt to overcome all conflicts in his own existence, and a realization of this goal. Jesus lived the human archetype just as God wanted, when he made him to his own image and likeness; Jesus always judged and spoke with God as his reference and starting point. Jesus thereby revealed a life of extraordinary authenticity and originality.[20]

In referring to Jesus' death, Boff highlights the sense of abandonment by God that is prominent in the Gospel texts, particularly in Mark's Gospel: "By his preaching of the kingdom of God he lived his being-for-others to the end, experiencing the depths of despair of the death (absence) of God on the cross. In spite of the total disaster and debacle he did not despair." Later he reflects on the meaning of Christ's death: "The universal meaning of the life and death of Christ, therefore, is that he sustained the fundamental conflict of human existence to the end: He wanted to realize the absolute meaning of this world before God, in spite of hate, incomprehension, betrayal, and condemnation to death."[21]

Boff dedicates another chapter to the resurrection, about which he affirms: "In this lies the central nucleus of Christian faith. Because of the fact of resurrection we know that life and meaningless death now have meaning."[22] The chapters that follow are a theological elaboration in dialogue with the teaching of the church and with classic Christologies. The three final chapters explore ecclesial and pastoral issues in light of the theological conclusions that he has come to.

---

[19]Boff, *Jesus Christ Liberator*, 107.
[20]Boff, *Jesus Christ Liberator*, 118.
[21]Boff, *Jesus Christ Liberator*, 118, 119.
[22]Boff, *Jesus Christ Liberator*, 121.

In other christological essays, Boff specifically explains his adoption of liberation-theology methodology and describes the nature of his christological reflection. Here is one example:

> When we talk about Jesus Christ the liberator, we are presupposing certain preliminaries that must be noted. Liberation is the opposite correlate of domination. To worship and proclaim Jesus Christ as the liberator is to ponder and live out our christological faith within a sociohistorical context marked by domination and oppression. This faith seeks to grasp the relevance of themes that will entail structural changes in a given sociohistorical situation. It explores this relevance analytically and produces a Christology centered on the theme of Jesus Christ the liberator. Such a Christology entails a specific sociopolitical commitment to break with the situation of oppression.[23]

The commitment that Boff makes reference to has specific characteristics; it is not about serving the needs of the poor, or efforts to change legislation or correct injustices in the predominant socioeconomic system. Rather, "it presupposes an option for the dialectical approach to social analysis and for the revolutionary 'project' of the dominated. To say 'liberation' is to express a well defined option that is neither reformist nor simply progressivist. It is truly liberative because it implies a break with the status quo."[24] The restrictive terms *reformist* and *progressivist* belonged to the strategic political language of Marxism and reflected the status of science that Marxism claimed and some theologians conceded, which led to the rejection of ways of seeing reality that did not employ Marxist categories.

Boff affirms that this theology is Latin America's great contribution to the universal christological task and contrasts his position with those of some European theologians or those from affluent countries, whom he calls "theologians at the other pole." Furthermore, he warns:

> There are theologians who are very enlightened, critical-minded, secularized, and progressive. Yet all too often it turns out that this is a cover for political positions that are highly conservative and that serve to

[23]Leonardo Boff, "Jesucristo liberador: Una visión cristológica desde Latinoamérica oprimida," in *Cristología en América Latina*, ed. Equipo Seladoc (Salamanca: Sígueme, 1984), 17.
[24]Boff, *Jesus Christ Liberator*, 274.

> reinforce the status quo. Others wish to adopt a liberation approach, but for want of more critical analysis of the existing system their practices are structurally supportive of it.[25]

Jon Sobrino: The Cross and Following Jesus

The second notable christological work of this decade is *Cristología desde América Latina* (Christology from Latin America) by Jon Sobrino, a Spanish Jesuit settled in El Salvador. Due to its identification with the poor and the left in El Salvador, the Jesuit order was persecuted violently by the military government. Sobrino's thought is both vigorous and rigorous. He develops his argument with clarity and lucidity, first summarizing his main thesis and then developing its various elements. His work, similar to that of Boff, insists on placing on the table of Catholic theology that which Protestantism had been suggesting from the beginning of its reflection: knowledge and proclamation of the Christ of the Gospels and the Epistles. Like Boff, Sobrino uses critical methods that had been developed in the European academic environment in his study of biblical texts. He affirms: "Liberation theology has given value to the figure of the historic Jesus within theology. It thus aims to overcome an overly abstract and for this reason easily manipulated idea of Christ, and to positively root Christian experience in following this historic Jesus."[26] The method that should be followed is explained in contrast to what had been the Catholic tradition up to that time:

> Dogmatic affirmations guard in clearly defined and doxological statements the truth about Christ; but true knowledge of Christ, while formulated in dogmas, is not possible or authentic without thinking about Christ from our own situation and praxis. . . . This Christology aims to be a historic Christology, not just in the explicative sense that it is rooted in current history, but in the very process of reflecting on Christ and analyzing the contents of Christology. If the end objective of Christology is to confess Jesus as the Christ, the beginning point is to affirm that this Christ is the Jesus of history.[27]

---

[25]Boff, *Jesus Christ Liberator*, 294.
[26]Jon Sobrino, *Cristología desde América Latina* (Mexico City: CRT, 1977), 59.
[27]Sobrino, *Cristología desde América Latina*, xvii.

One of the dominant elements of Sobrino's Christology is that he pays particular attention to the fact and the meaning of the cross in understanding and following Jesus, but also for understanding God and the relationship between the Father and Son. He highlights in particular the historic circumstances of the crucifixion and the political motives behind the accusations that took Jesus to Calvary. He argues that from early times in Christian thought, even from the New Testament documents themselves, there was a tendency to sweeten the cross and to interpret it in a way that ended up devaluing the fact that Jesus actually died the death of a subversive criminal, stripping the cross of its deep significance.

> In the very description of Jesus' death in the New Testament a movement to theologically soften the death can be observed. In Mark's version, the most original and primitive, Jesus' death is described with solemnity and tragedy: "Then Jesus gave a loud cry and breathed his last" (Mark 15:37). On the cross Jesus recites Psalm 22:1: "My God, my God, why have you forsaken me?" It is possible that it was Mark who put this psalm into Jesus' mouth, but he would not have dared to do so without a strong historical basis, because for Jesus to voice this psalm would have been scandalous. Furthermore, this form of death is consistent with other details of the Gospel, such as the agony in the garden (Mark 14:34-42), and with all the theological context of Jesus' life.[28]

Sobrino believes that in the Gospels of Luke and John, a movement can be observed to soften the edge of the scandal of Jesus' death and his sense of being abandoned by God. "In Luke, Psalm 22 is replaced by Psalm 31, a psalm of trust in God: 'Father, into your hands I commend my spirit.' . . . Psalm 22 is not mentioned in John either; there Jesus dies more majestically, as someone who is in charge of the situation until the very end."[29] In this way, Sobrino is critical of the idea that "Jesus the man in his earthly life knew that he was Son of God in the strict and metaphysical sense of the term"; even more, he argues that quotations such as those in John 10:30, 36, 38 and Matthew 11:27 do not authentically belong to Jesus.

[28]Jon Sobrino, "La muerte de Jesús y la liberación en la historia," in Seladoc, *Cristología en América Latina*, 47. This text by Sobrino is dated 1975 and placed in San Salvador.
[29]Sobrino, "La muerte de Jesús," 48.

Sobrino also critiques arguments pointing to the titles of Jesus to prove he was conscious that he was the Messiah.[30]

In this effort to soften the cross, which would have been a later development by a church already under the influence of Greek thought, Sobrino sees a connection with the Greek notion of the impassibility of God, so that Jesus' death must be aligned with the attitude of the immutable God, who cannot suffer nor experience the anguish of the cross. Sobrino states,

> In Latin America, however, the impression spontaneously emerges, which [Dietrich] Bonhoeffer expressed intuitively and poetically, that "only a God who suffers can save us." The paradoxical nature of this phrase must not let it be relegated to the sphere of piety or to paradoxical rhetoric, but should be analyzed, because what is in play here is the essence of the Christian God.[31]

Sobrino's reflection interacts here with modern European theology of his time, especially with Bonhoeffer's later works and with Jürgen Moltmann's *The Crucified God*.[32]

From the point of view of the Jewish authorities, Jesus was condemned for blasphemy, for questioning by his behavior and his teaching the "official" concept of God they espoused. Sobrino shows how Jesus questioned the God of the dominant official religiosity and presented a different God, specifically a God who drew near to tax collectors, prostitutes, and lepers, and in doing so brought into sharp relief the injustice in the social order that marginalized these people. For Jesus, God could be found precisely in the encounter of taking in and serving these people and their needs.

While true that Jesus' death resulted from the Jewish leaders' charge of blasphemy, those representing the Roman government treated him as a Zealot, a revolutionary, and that should remind us of the political dimension of Jesus' teaching and ministry. With his Roman judge just

---

[30]Sobrino, *Cristología desde América Latina*, 60.

[31]Sobrino, "La muerte de Jesús," 57.

[32]Jürgen Moltmann, *The Crucified God* (London: SCM Press, 1973).

as with his Jewish judges, there was an exercise of power that was questioned by Jesus' person, as he had done earlier through his teaching. It could be said that Jesus performed a demythologizing of power, bringing to light the mechanism of power and confronting not only the powerful as individuals but the institutions that they represented collectively. For Sobrino there is some Zealotism in Jesus' attitude, although his path is clearly different from that of the Zealots. Sobrino summarizes the option Jesus chooses in categories from liberation theology: "[Jesus'] love for the oppressed is demonstrated by his being with them, giving that which returns their dignity, that could humanize them. His love for the oppressor is demonstrated by his being against them, seeking to take away that which dehumanizes them." He rounds out his reflection with a key theme for liberation theologians: "The systematic importance of this consideration for historic liberation theology is that the privileged mediation of God continues to be the real cross: the oppressed. . . . Where the oppressed are served, there 'one remains with God in the passion.'"[33]

In a thoughtful study of Sobrino's Christology, René Padilla reminds us that Sobrino highlights the concept of two stages of Jesus' ministry and that what is called the "Galilee crisis" "marks a harsh break in Jesus' consciousness." The first stage was the proclamation of the kingdom as an eschatological reality, and the second was characterized by conflicts and suffering.[34] Sobrino emphasizes Jesus' humanity and sees in the passion of Jesus a process of discovery, a slow conscientization in which he "discovers" little by little the meaning of his mission. This contrasts with the traditional vision in which Jesus fulfills step by step a plan that he already knew and in which there were no surprises. This is the difference between a Christology that comes from above and one that comes from below. In this sense Sobrino has serious questions with regard to Chalcedon.

---

[33]Sobrino, *Cristología desde América Latina*, 181, 189.

[34]René Padilla, "Cristología y misión en los dos terceros mundos," *Boletín Teológico*, no. 8 (October–December 1982): 41ff.

Christology for Evangelization

It is not a coincidence that in Latin American evangelical Protestantism, Christology has been forged as part of a theology of evangelization. Protestants in Latin America have always had as part of their identity the sense of mission in a continent that does not know Christ as Savior and Redeemer, and the certainty that an encounter with this Christ leads to a conversion that has transforming consequences at individual and social levels. As has already been shown, this was the case equally in early historical Protestantism, whose first thinkers became involved in ecumenism, and in conservative evangelical Protestantism when, having begun with an imported theology, it began to find a path of its own that was both evangelical and contextual. The theological renovation of Catholicism began from a pastoral concern: while it was supposed that people who had received the sacrament of baptism were already Christians, as seen in chapter eight, theologians such as Gutiérrez and Segundo questioned the reality and quality of this Christianity. But Protestants, based on missionary concern and a strong emphasis on evangelization, wondered whether nominal Catholics were Christians at all.

Protestant theology is intentionally mission focused. Regarding the relationship between theology and evangelization, Orlando Costas eloquently declares:

> Theology and evangelization are two interrelated aspects of the life and mission of the Christian faith. Theology studies the faith; evangelization is the process by which it is communicated. Theology plumbs the depths of the Christian faith; evangelization enables the church to extend it to the ends of the earth and the depth of human life. Theology reflects critically on the church's practice of the faith; evangelization keeps the faith from becoming the practice of an exclusive social group. Theology enables evangelization to transmit the faith with integrity by clarifying and organizing its content, analyzing its context, and critically evaluating its communication. Evangelization enables theology to be an effective servant of the faith by relating its message to the deepest spiritual needs of humankind.[35]

[35]Orlando E. Costas, *Liberating News: A Theology of Contextual Evangelization* (Grand Rapids: Eerdmans, 1989), 1.

This is evident, for example, in the work of René Padilla, whose Christology is explained in core essays such as "What Is the Gospel?" (Lima 1966–1967, Austria 1975) and "Evangelism and the World" (Lausanne 1974). The first was part of formation courses offered by IFES in Latin America for student leaders doing evangelization in their universities, and the second was a theological presentation for the International Congress of World Evangelization in Lausanne. Explaining the importance of asking "What is the gospel?" Padilla warns that evangelical activism requires deep corrections. In a series of regional evangelization congresses that had begun to take place following the congress in Berlin in 1966, there was a growing consciousness of the need to evaluate the evangelism of missions and churches in the light of biblical teaching. In this theological process the conviction developed that it was not just about modernizing strategies and methodologies to fulfill Jesus' missionary mandate, as some thought. Taking seriously the context in which evangelism takes place requires a deep understanding of the gospel of Jesus Christ, which will lead to missionary practices in Jesus' style.[36]

The theological work of Padilla, which expressed the evangelical reflection that had been developing in Latin America, can be said to have played a key role in the development of a fresh mission consciousness. Padilla applied the same theological method he had suggested to the FTL and to which I made reference in chapter nine. The question regarding the gospel was important because summaries of the gospel that were easy to memorize and were said to ensure a "fast and efficient" evangelism were being imposed from the United States. Padilla knew it could not be taken for granted that all evangelicals knew what the gospel was. There were three reasons the question "What is the gospel?" needed to be asked. First, the most basic requirement for effective evangelization is certainty regarding the content of the gospel. Second, the only answer that biblical evangelization has the right to expect is a response to the gospel. Third, the distinguishing nature of Christian experience is an

[36]I focus on this process of conscientization in *The New Global Mission* (Downers Grove, IL: InterVarsity Press, 2003), 23-29.

experience of the gospel. In exploring the historical background of the Greek term *euangelion*, Padilla demonstrated that the New Testament gospel was rooted in the prophetic hope of Israel, as was the context of its first announcement.[37]

Four points can be highlighted in Padilla's characterization of the gospel. First, it is an eschatological message:

> It is quite clear that for the primitive church the Christian evangel derived all its meaning from the fact that in the story of Jesus Christ (including his life, death, resurrection and exaltation) the Old Testamjent prophecies had been fulfilled. . . . They saw the story of Jesus as the culmination of an age-old redemptive process that went back to Abraham, the father of Israel.[38]

In Padilla's theological methodology, the New Testament is taken in its totality based on the conviction that there is a basic unity despite the particularities of diverse authors. For Padilla, "this view of the unity of the gospel, as news regarding a new eschatological reality made manifest in Jesus Christ, is confirmed by the testimony of the whole of the New Testament." Second, the gospel is a christological message: Christ himself, his person and work, is the gospel, and he is the topic of apostolic preaching. "The key to understanding Jesus' evangel is in the dynamic meaning of the term 'kingdom' (*basileia*). The kingdom that Jesus proclaims is the power of God active among people in his own person and ministry. Before the end of the age God has irrupted into history to accomplish his redemptive purpose, and he has done so in Jesus Christ."[39]

Padilla enumerates the various expressions used in the New Testament to refer to the gospel: for example, word of life, word of God, word of truth, gospel of grace, gospel of salvation, and many more. This variety of descriptions shows the multiform character of the gospel, but it must be taken into account that behind all these descriptions, and giving them unity, is the figure of Jesus as Messiah come from God as

---

37 René Padilla, *Mission Between the Times* (Carlisle, UK: Langham Monographs, 2010), 91-94.
38 Padilla, *Mission Between the Times*, 86.
39 Padilla, *Mission Between the Times*, 91.

the climax of the history of salvation, with the goal of fulfilling the Old Testament promises. The central events through which God fulfills his purpose are the death and resurrection of Jesus Christ. "The emphasis that the New Testament places on them can be explained only on the basis of Jesus' own understanding that his messiahship was being fulfilled in terms of the servant of the Lord (*ebed Yahweh*)." Padilla concludes the section this way: "At the heart of the gospel is Jesus Christ, who, as the exalted Lord, remains a crucified Messiah (*Cristos estauromenōs*) and as such the 'power of God and wisdom of God' (1 Cor 1:23-24, cf. 2:2)."[40]

Third, the gospel incarnated and preached by Jesus is a soteriological message. "His gospel is good news in relation to a new soteriological order, an order that has interrupted history in the person and ministry of Jesus." This order includes a new relationship with God and also a new relationship between oneself and one's neighbor: "For this reason the apostolic task involves a concern for the total restoration of man according to God's image. From a New Testament perspective, the salvation (*sōteria*) brought by the gospel is liberation from all that interferes with the fulfillment of God's purpose for mankind."[41] That is, salvation is liberation from the consequences of sin and liberation from the power of sin, which involves belonging to the people of God, moral transformation, and the gift of the Holy Spirit.

Fourth, the gospel contains a call to repentance and faith. This theme is present throughout the New Testament, and so if our evangelization is to be faithful to the gospel, it must include this theme. Beginning with John the Baptist, the gospel involves repentance, which is "the total reorientation of life: breaking with sin and adopting a new lifestyle; in other words, repentance evidenced by specific works (*erga*)."[42] That the gospel always includes a call to repentance and faith leads Padilla to an important clarification:

---

[40]Padilla, *Mission Between the Times*, 94.
[41]Padilla, *El evangelio hoy*, 33, 34.
[42]Padilla, *El evangelio hoy*, 40.

> Clearly the salvation of God in Christ Jesus has a universal reach. But the universality of the gospel must not be confused with the universalism of contemporary theologians who affirm that in virtue of Christ's work, all men have received eternal life, irrespective of their position before Christ. . . . To proclaim the gospel is not only to proclaim something that is completed, but to proclaim a completed action and simultaneously give a call to faith.[43]

A Self-Critique of Evangelical Evangelization

From this vision of the nature of the gospel, with its rich christological structure, Padilla began in Lausanne in 1974 the crucial task of evaluating evangelism among evangelicals. His starting point was the conviction that "the work of God in Christ Jesus is directly related to the world in its totality, not merely with the individual. Therefore, a soteriology that does not take into account the relationship between the gospel and the world does no justice to biblical teaching." Padilla sees a triple meaning in the New Testament use of the word *world*. First is the world as the sum of all creation, the universe that was created by God in the beginning and that will be re-created at the end. Second is a more limited sense of *world* as the present order of human existence, the spatio-corporal context of the life of a human being. Third is the sense all of humanity, reclaimed by the gospel but hostile to God and enslaved by the powers of darkness. However, "the most categorical affirmation of God's will to save the world is given in the person and work of his Son Jesus Christ."[44] This is the foundation of the work of Christ and of its continuation through his followers.

The concept of evangelization proposed by Padilla emphasizes the lordship of Jesus Christ: "To evangelize is to proclaim Jesus Christ as Lord and Savior, by whose work mankind is liberated both from guilt and from the power of sin and integrated into the purpose of God to place all things under the rule of Christ." This proclamation is possible

---

[43]Padilla, *El evangelio hoy*, 100.

[44]Padilla, *El evangelio hoy*, 96-97, 99.

because the work of Christ has a cosmic reach: "The kingdom of God has become present in the person of Jesus Christ. Eschatology has invaded history. God has expressed in a definitive way his purpose of placing all things under Christ's rule. The powers of darkness have been defeated. Here and now in union with Jesus Christ men have the blessings of this new age within their reach."[45]

The preaching of the gospel enters into conflict with the organized lies of a humanity that makes themselves god: "The great lie that men believe trying to be God without God: that their lives consist of the material goods they own; that they live for themselves and are captains of their own destiny." Padilla sees the emerging of a "secular Christianity" as a concession to this great lie in reducing salvation to an economic, social, and political liberation: "Eschatology is absorbed by the utopia, and Christian hope is confused with in-this-world hope proclaimed by Marxism."[46]

At the other extreme lies the conception of salvation as only spiritual salvation or future salvation of the soul, in which this life has meaning only as "preparation for the world beyond world." In this case, "History is assimilated by a futurist eschatology, and religion is converted into a means of escape from present reality. The result is a total misunderstanding of society's problems in the name of 'being separated from the world.' This is a distortion of the gospel that has led to Marxist criticism of Christian eschatology as 'the opiate of the people.'"[47]

Padilla saw much evangelism of evangelicals as propagating this reductionist vision of the gospel. And given the strong presence of organizations and ideas originating in the United States, it could be said that what was spread was the North American lifestyle more that the gospel of Jesus Christ. It was another way of imposing a "Christianity culture" such as occurred in the sixteenth century with the Catholic missionary work that came with the Iberian conquest of the American peoples. In his Lausanne presentation, Padilla made reference to evangelical voices

[45]Padilla, *El evangelio hoy*, 107, 117.
[46]Padilla, *El evangelio hoy*, 117, 121.
[47]Padilla, *El evangelio hoy*, 121.

within North America who pointed out the danger of identifying the "American way of life" with the gospel.

While it's true that these self-critiquing admonitions from Padilla occasioned much debate in the months prior to and during the Lausanne Congress, it was evident that by 1974 many evangelicals in different parts of the world had become conscious of the concerns presented by Padilla in the light of a rigorous evangelical theology. This collective process of becoming conscious is expressed in the Lausanne Covenant, signed by twenty-five hundred participants at the end of the event, which in time brought a renewal of missionary concepts and practices in the direction of holistic mission in line with Jesus' way of being. Here are some of the paragraphs from the covenant that express this new vision:

> 4. The Nature of Evangelism
>
> To evangelize is to spread the good news that Jesus Christ died for our sins and was raised from the dead according to the Scriptures, and that, as the reigning Lord, he now offers the forgiveness of sins and the liberating gifts of the Spirit to all who repent and believe. Our Christian presence in the world is indispensable to evangelism, and so is that kind of dialogue whose purpose is to listen sensitively in order to understand. But evangelism itself is the proclamation of the historical, biblical Christ as Saviour and Lord, with a view to persuading people to come to him personally and so be reconciled to God. In issuing the gospel invitation we have no liberty to conceal the cost of discipleship. Jesus still calls all who would follow him to deny themselves, take up their cross, and identify themselves with his new community. The results of evangelism include obedience to Christ, incorporation into his Church and responsible service in the world.
>
> 5. Christian Social Responsibility
>
> We affirm that God is both the Creator and the Judge of all men. We therefore should share his concern for justice and reconciliation throughout human society and for the liberation of men and women from every kind of oppression. Because men and women are made in the image of God, every person, regardless of race, religion, colour, culture, class, sex or age, has an intrinsic dignity because of which he or she

should be respected and served, not exploited. Here too we express penitence both for our neglect and for having sometimes regarded evangelism and social concern as mutually exclusive. Although reconciliation with other people is not reconciliation with God, nor is social action evangelism, nor is political liberation salvation, nevertheless we affirm that evangelism and socio-political involvement are both part of our Christian duty. For both are necessary expressions of our doctrines of God and Man, our love for our neighbour and our obedience to Jesus Christ. The message of salvation implies also a message of judgment upon every form of alienation, oppression and discrimination, and we should not be afraid to denounce evil and injustice wherever they exist. When people receive Christ they are born again into his kingdom and must seek not only to exhibit but also to spread its righteousness in the midst of an unrighteous world. The salvation we claim should be transforming us in the totality of our personal and social responsibilities. Faith without works is dead.

10. Evangelism and Culture

The development of strategies for world evangelization calls for imaginative pioneering methods. Under God, the result will be the rise of churches deeply rooted in Christ and closely related to their culture. Culture must always be tested and judged by Scripture. Because men and women are God's creatures, some of their culture is rich in beauty and goodness. Because they are fallen, all of it is tainted with sin and some of it is demonic. The gospel does not presuppose the superiority of any culture to another, but evaluates all cultures according to its own criteria of truth and righteousness, and insists on moral absolutes in every culture. Missions have, all too frequently, exported with the gospel an alien culture, and churches have sometimes been in bondage to culture rather than to Scripture. Christ's evangelists must humbly seek to empty themselves of all but their personal authenticity in order to become the servants of others, and churches must seek to transform and enrich culture, all for the glory of God.

◆ ◆ ◆

With theologians such as Boff, Sobrino, and Padilla, the global theological conversation about following Christ came to include some Latin American voices whose thought had been forged in the effort to be faithful to Jesus Christ. They did so in a continent that was turbulent and agitated due to the extremes of the poverty of the masses and the wealth of insensitive elites, as well as due to institutionalized injustice. These voices proposed a return to biblical sources, with a renewed vision of the historic Jesus.

12

CHRIST IN LATIN AMERICAN CULTURE ONCE AGAIN

Returning to the area where he had lived during his childhood, to the villages where he has worked as a laborer, Jesucristo Gómez heard of John the Baptist's death.

It all began when they came to don Horacio Mijares with the story that the John the Baptist Common Front had been reorganized and his men were nervously pacing the territory. John the Baptist commands them from prison, they told don Horacio Mijares. They are from the Common Front, those who robbed the rural bank, those who kidnapped Commander Perales's son, those who blew up the electricity towers. Any act of terrorism or crime committed in this area got blamed on the extinct movement of John the Baptist. Of course Mijares doubted the veracity of this information, but as he did not want to have problems with the people, he washed his hands and said, Do what you want.

First they beat him up badly in his own cell, and later, with the pretext of moving him to the state capital for who knows what procedure, they applied the desertion law without mercy.

Mijares thought the problem was dealt with, but he was not cured of his nightmares—night after night he dreamed of the dead man—and then he received news of another troublemaker, more irritating than John the Baptist.

We need to immediately get rid of this bandit right now, before he begins to give us serious problems, was the advice they gave don Horacio.

Really—it's that bad?

> It's really that bad, boss.
> And who is this man? he asked.
> His name is Jesucristo Gómez, they responded.[1]

This passage from the book *El Evangelio de Lucas Gavilán* (The Gospel of Lucas Gavilán) gives us an idea of the effort made by a well-known Mexican journalist, dramaturgist, and novelist to contextualize Luke's version of the Gospel of Jesus. Vicente Leñero first published it in 1979, and numerous reprintings followed. Leñero adapted it as a theatrical work in 1986. The work reflects well the intense christological debate that during this decade not only caused ferment in the theological world but also penetrated a wide sector of Latin American culture. Leñero places Jesus in a contemporary Mexican context, among scavengers and garbage pickers—that is to say, among the poor—speaking and relating to others as they would, and facing the realities they faced. Carefully following Luke's Gospel, Leñero seeks to update the stories using colloquial language particular to the environment in which the characters are placed. Jesucristo Gómez is the son of carpenter José Gómez and of Maria David. Herod is don Horacio Mijares, a petty tyrant. John the Baptist, son of the sacristan Zacharias and founder of the Common Front, has organized the poor into cell groups and is not afraid to say what he thinks.

In the book's prologue, the author, who signs off as Lucas Gavilán and who writes to "dear Theopholus," confesses that "just the idea of writing a new literary work about the theme in these times feels just a little less than intolerable," and lists some of the many literary works that exist about Jesus. And he continues: "Despite this and despite the insurmountable obstacles that battered me, I decided to attempt my own narrative version motivated by the current trends in Latin American theology." He mentions the stimulating effect of works by Jon Sobrino, Leonardo Boff, and Gustavo Gutiérrez,

> but above all, the practical work undertaken by numerous Christians against the grain of institutional Catholicism encouraged me to write this

[1]Vicente Leñero, *El Evangelio de Lucas Gavilán* (Mexico City: Seix Barral, 1979), 128-29.

> paraphrase of the Gospel according to Saint Luke, searching the most precise possible translation of each teaching, of each miracle, and of each passage into the contemporary context of Mexico today, from a rational viewpoint and with the purpose of demythologizing.[2]

Although Leñero's literary-theological effort might appear at times arbitrary or exaggerated, we must confess that the story catches our attention and, even more, faces us with an intellectual and theological challenge to take seriously the fact of the incarnation and to explore all the implications of this truth. In becoming man—and truly man—the Word of God was put into human hands: in the hands of Mary and Joseph, in the hands of his disciples, in the hands of Herod and Pilate, in the hands of theologians, and in the hands of many who throughout centuries have tried to understand the mystery of this story told by the Gospels with gravity but also with surprising and clarifying details. In the 1970s once again Jesus came to be a celebrated personality in Latin American and world culture. There even emerged youth movements that described themselves as the Jesus Revolution.

A Jesus for the Counterculture

If in Latin America during the '70s the term "Jesus revolution" brought to mind a leftist political and theological movement, the same term in the United States and Canada made reference to a trend called "the counterculture." In 1971 a cover article in the newsweekly *Time* arrested the attention of its millions of readers throughout the world, describing an explosion of religiosity among certain sectors of North American youth.[3] Where it was least expected, in the heart of countercultural youth, a religious awakening had caught fire. It was characterized by hundreds of thousands of youth, a simple faith expressed in biblical phrases without theological elaboration, spontaneous piety that might erupt in songs or prayers in the middle of a football game or the middle of the street. Other

---

[2]Leñero, *El Evangelio de Lucas Gavilán*, 11.

[3]"The New Rebel Cry: Jesus Is Coming," *Time*, June 21, 1971, 28-37. Various Latin American newspapers translated this article, among them the Argentinian *La Opinión*, June 22, 1971.

characteristics included an evangelistic zeal that led participants to use unexpected means to spread their faith, a community spirit that motivated them to live together and work through small groups in an intense communal life, a total lack of concern for the old denominational barriers of established churches, and a dynamically youthful spirit. The movement was not promoted by any of the established denominations; it emerged with vitality, spontaneity, and the impatience and the spirit of protest of a new generation.

To understand the movement it is necessary to take into account the ground from which this revolution grew. In the latter half of the 1960s, a diverse variety of hippie movements in the United States, along with student unrest and other expressions of youthful restlessness, together formed a phenomenon that historian Theodore Roszak appropriately dubbed "the counter culture."[4] It was indeed a new culture involving the creation of a lifestyle, gestures, habits, literature, art, music, film, theater, and a shifting moral code that contrasted with what had been the characteristic lifestyle of the average North American. In a culture that imposed mass uniformity, now originality was to be cultivated; in a society that worshiped work and material progress, it praised free time and scorned savings; in a society that appreciated cleanliness, it cultivated and flaunted earthiness; in a society that idealized the clean-cut "good guy" with short hair and tie, it fostered long hair and an image of untidiness. The sense of profound protest motivating this counterculture cast wide social, political, and even religious ripples. Roszak and various other scholars analyzed it.

The related religious awakening known as "the Jesus revolution" emerged in the fertile soil of protest and maintained an openly rebellious focus. Thousands of young people's conversion to Christ did not mean that they left behind the symbols of the counterculture and its lifestyle. In fact, images of a smiling, bearded Jesus with long hair and flowing robes, reminiscent of traditional Euro-American Christian representations but

[4]Theodore Roszak, *The Making of a Counter Culture: Reflections on the Technocratic Society and Its Youthful Opposition* (New York: Doubleday, 1969).

incorporating spontaneous and informal elements, became wildly popular. Participants in the movement did adopt a morality different from that of the wider counterculture, rejecting alcohol, drugs, and sexual promiscuity. Even more, they adopted a certain asceticism in the Franciscan style, valuing simplicity and frugality. *Time* recognized that "the Jesus revolution rejects not only the material values of conventional America but the prevailing wisdom of American theology." In addition to spurning material success as a measure of all things, participants also scorned a secular and decadent theology expressed in the sensationalist verbal fireworks of the "death of God" theology.[5]

Maybe this explains the open, charismatic emphasis of the majority of these Jesus revolutionaries in noisy and expressive worship, in glossolalia (speaking in unknown tongues) and in actions such as praying for the sick with a belief in God's healing. Such practices had been forgotten, if not rejected, by the typical denominations of the numerous North American middle class. These practices were signs of nonconformity, as were the music and art used in their services and evangelization: for example, rock bands, pop images of Jesus, and sermons illustrated with folk dance.

During those years I observed that some of the characteristics of this North American Jesus counterculture also began to attract Latin American youth. My experience suggests that this movement grew particularly in the countries more permeable to US influence, such as Brazil and Mexico. I noted in my diary what occurred in July 1973 in classrooms of the Universidad Nacional Autónoma de México (Mexico City), where COMPA, the International Fellowship of Evangelical Students movement in Mexico, had invited me to give a public lecture on the topic "Jesus and the meaning of history." I was prepared for dialogue with Marxist students, who always asked clarifying questions. But the first students on their feet almost shouted their questions: "We are not interested in changing the world; what we want to know is if Christ has the

[5]Roszak, "New Rebel Cry," 28.

answer to learning self-control techniques, to control our mental forces and the development of our personality." Later students mentioned yoga, Carlos Castañeda, a North American guru who lived in the desert close to the border, and their personal battles against the temptation of sex and drugs.[6] The student revolt of 1968, the killings at Tlatelolco, and the sociopolitical rhetoric that had sought to make Jesus a paradigm for twentieth-century Zealots now lay behind us. Together with renewed interest in novelist Herman Hesse and books by Carlos Castañeda came the search for a Jesus who was more than a religion professor.

In Search of a Guru

For thousands of youth around the world, a desire emerged to have a guru: a life teacher who would reveal the secret of existence, perhaps in the solitude of a desert, amid the practice of a disciplined life, rather than in a classroom or within the four walls of a church building. It was as if a generation that had rejected the father figure, in a society sick with badly assimilated Freudianism, wandered in search of a substitute authority, one who would not only assign lessons to memorize but also teach ascetic techniques and make demands. During this time many messianic personalities emerged. Some of them reached newspaper headlines, shrouded in grotesque halos of tragedy, as in the case of Charles Manson, an assassin who assembled a clan of passionate disciples willing to obey his orders blindly, even to the point of killing actress Sharon Tate.

Gurus employing the name of Jesus appeared all over. An entrepreneurial spirit and political connections allowed some to win thousands of followers and make huge sums of money from them. A famous one was South Korean Sun Myung Moon, who eventually had a private bodyguard, CIA protection, a jet, two yachts, and a fortune estimated at eleven million dollars that was constantly multiplying.[7] He affirmed himself

---

[6]I gave an account of my reflections in "El hombre Jesús ¿guru o payaso?," *Certeza*, no. 64 (October–December 1976): 240-44.

[7]Numerous magazines published research on Moon. One well-documented article in Spanish appeared in the Catholic magazine *Vida Nueva*, February 21, 1976, 23-30.

to be the new incarnation of the Messiah. Another was Mo Berg, a fifty-year-old North American who from his European refuge commanded one of the most militant youth sects ever to exist, the Children of God.[8] Common factors among these messiahs/gurus were the rigidity of the rules imposed, the unconditional devotion of their followers, the open conflict stirred up systematically in the heart of the families of followers, and dogma that included a few ideas carefully selected from the Christian message, mixed with openly anti-Christian ideas. Another famous example was Prem Pal Singh Rawat, who was surrounded by an exotic aura and called himself Guru Maharaj Ji, a young Indian American who accumulated a fabulous fortune over a few years but whom no one took seriously in India except those responsible for collecting taxes from those in possession of a fortune worth millions.

In Argentina and Chile at the beginning of the '70s a sect with messianic leaning led by an Argentinian named Silo became well known. Silo was the name taken on by Mario Luis Rodríguez Cobo, who in 1969, at age thirty-one, founded the Humanist Movement, whose message rejected discrimination and praised pacifism, a form of spirituality, and solidarity. Centered near the city of Mendoza, the movement began with some five hundred followers but grew and extended to other countries. During the '80s it left an impact in Argentinian political life. Silo was a charismatic personality who proclaimed spiritual values and considered himself a life teacher. This Latin American version of the global guru phenomenon became famous because of the references to Silo in the novel *Palomita blanca* (White dove), published in 1971 by Chilean author Enrique Lafourcade.[9] When I visited Chile in 1972 it seemed that all youth had read it. It became the bestselling novel ever in Chilean literature, with four editions and more than a million copies published. In

[8]See "Religion: Children of 'Moses,'" *Newsweek*, October 28, 1974, 70. Also see the French *L'Express*, April 1970.

[9]Enrique Lafourcade, *Palomita blanca* (Santiago: Zig-Zag, 1971). Upon the death of Silo in September 2010, an email was circulated by his followers: "We ask for his well-being there where we are in his transit to the light. Peace in the heart, light in understanding" (Diario *Clarín* [Buenos Aires], September 18, 2010).

this novel written in the first person, María, a Chilean girl, describes the life of a generation that explored the world of drugs, sexuality, and religious experiences.

It was hunger for a life teacher that led thousands of youth in this search for a guru. It is worth noting that the messianic personalities mentioned all emerged among a public that had a high level of Christian tradition. These figures amassed their followers and made their profits in Europe, in North America, and to a lesser degree in large Latin American cities. They caused an impact in a Western world where a blurry image of the Christ of the Gospels remained. Perhaps more should be said. The roots of this search can be found in the weakening of institutionalized official Christianity and the failure of pastoral alertness in churches. Seeming to anticipate these times, Bob Dylan, musical interpreter of so many spiritual questions, had written in 1964:

> You say you're lookin' for someone
> Who's never weak but always strong
> To protect you and defend you . . .
> But it ain't me babe[10]

Observing this social phenomenon in Brazil and globally led Leonardo Boff to ask, Why do these youth not join the church? Why is their Jesus not the Jesus of church preaching, or of its dogmas, but of the Gospels? His theological-pastoral diagnosis leads us from Christology to ecclesiology:

> Jesus Christ does not exhaust his unserchable wealth in ecclesiastical formulas that may be venerable. That is valid for the councils of Calcedonia or Constantinople, but also for the several Christologies that are developed in the New Testament. Jesus Christ knows a *parousia* in each generation. In other words each generation has to be confronted with the ministry of Jesus and in its attempt to define Jesus it will define itself. . . . Who is Jesus is not a question that may be answered in an academic way or in conciliar rooms. It is by following Jesus, trying to live that for which

[10]Bob Dylan, "It Ain't Me Babe," *Another Side of Bob Dylan* (Columbia Records, 1964). The song was made popular by Joan Baez and other singers as well as Dylan himself.

he lived, fought, and was rejected, that we start to understand his true and deep ministry. Only at the end of history we will know who is he, in fact.[11]

Ecumenical Christological Exploration

Latin American theology was ready to respond to this new presence of the image of Christ in diverse sections of Latin American society, contributing to the interpretation of Christ's image in the light of the Bible and Christian thought. In 1972, pastor Emilio Castro, who was at that time secretary of UNELAM, the Latin American organism of ecumenical cooperation related to the World Council of Churches in Geneva, suggested the urgency and relevancy of the question "Who is Jesus Christ today in Latin America?" as a topic for ecumenical study. Two theological consultations were sponsored: a national one in Brazil organized by the Association of Evangelical Seminaries (ASTE), in November 1973, and a continental one in Lima in 1974.[12] Both consultations were ecumenical in the wider sense of the word in that they included participants who were Catholic, ecumenical Protestants, and evangelical Protestants. The resulting books from these two consultations communicate the breadth and richness of the reflection that took place in these gatherings. They reflect the varying intensity of Christ's presence in the most diverse spheres of cultural life for Latin Americans—and theological reflection accompanied by a variety of practices.

The book *Quem é Jesus Cristo no Brasil?* (Who is Jesus Christ in Brazil?) appeared in 1974, edited by Episcopal pastor J. C. Maraschin, general secretary of ASTE, with the participation of theologians and sociologists.[13] The authors offer studies about images of Christ in different spheres of Brazilian society. Franciscan Leonardo Boff explores the image of Christ in what he calls liberal Christianity, Dominican Hubert

---

[11]Leonardo Boff, "As imagens de Cristo presentes no Cristianismo liberal no Brasil," in *Quem é Jesus Cristo no Brasil?* (Sao Paulo: ASTE, 1974), 17.

[12]In her historical outline of ecumenism in Latin America, Dafne Sabanes Plou argues that for the analysts of UNELAM, this christological study was their more ambitious project: *Caminos de Unidad* (Quito: CLAI, 1994), 115.

[13]J. C. Maraschin, ed., *Quem é Jesus Cristo no Brasil* (Saõ Paulo: ASTE, 1974).

Lepargneur in popular culture, sociologist Beatriz Muniz de Sousa in Pentecostalism, Presbyterian pastor João Dias de Araújo in village culture, Lutheran scholar Klaus Van der Grijp in conservative Protestantism, J. C. Maraschin in popular Brazilian music, scholar Myriam Ribeiro S. Tavares in Brazilian colonial art, and Baptist Walter Willik in Afro-Brazilian cults. The result is a valuable, multicolored mosaic that allows the reader to see the penetration of the Jesus figure at all social levels, and at the same time the great variety and often contrasting images and attitudes of people toward him.

The richest and most illustrative work of this book is that of Lepargneur, who aims to describe the diversity of ways in which popular Catholicism understands and gives honor to Christ. The summary paragraph with which he opens is eloquent:

> In the country with the most Catholics in the world, the figure of Christ is surprisingly blurry. The conclusion of our research is that between a God who is distant and rather vague, and the saints, lively and omnipresent in popular devotion, the figure of Christ does not find its appropriate place and as a result is harmed, an indication that this Christianity was not nourished by an ongoing or immediate reading of the New Testament.[14]

However, the more than forty pages in this chapter demonstrate the richness of the expressions of popular devotion to "Bom Jesus" (Good Jesus) as well as the importance of Holy Week and the suffering of Christ. A considerable part of the Brazilian people celebrate Bom Jesus. "Although perhaps the people cannot explain it clearly, the mortal suffering of 'Bom Jesus' has a meaning and importance for popular piety that the death or martyrdom of any other saint does not possess." Lepargneur adds: "The realism with which they imagine his human suffering disproves any suspicion of docetism or a lack of historical incarnation in the coming of God in Christ, in the eyes of the people."[15] In his conclusion, the author affirms:

[14]Hubert Lepargneur, "Imagens de Cristo no catolicismo popular brasileiro," in Maraschin, *Quem é Jesus Cristo no Brasil*, 57.

[15]Lepargneur, "Imagens de Cristo," 76-77.

> To understand the Christ of the people and to do justice to him, we should take sufficient distance to see how beyond the words, the gestures, and the representations, this figure brings together the Christ-God, the Christ-saint, and the Christ-people (who suffer). Taken in isolation, each of these perspectives is easily criticized, and in fact too quickly criticized. However, in combination they represent the authentic mystery of a divine person who was incarnated, suffered among us, and is now alive and intercedes for us.[16]

Jesus: Neither Defeated nor a Celestial Monarch

As a result of the continental gathering in Lima in 1977, *Jesús: Ni vencido ni monarca celestial* (Jesus: Neither defeated nor a celestial monarch) appeared, another collection edited by José Míguez Bonino.[17] The work contains twelve articles grouped in four sections. The first section is titled "The Christs of Latin America" and contains the works of Maraschin, Boff, and Dias de Araújo in the preceding volume, now translated into Spanish, and a work by Juan Stam and Saúl Trinidad, "El Cristo de la predicación evangélica en América Latina" (The Christ of evangelical preaching in Latin America). The second section is interpretive: "What Do These Latin American Christs Mean?" It features contributions from Saúl Trinidad, Pedro Negre Rigol, and Georges Casalis. The third section, "Christ and Politics," contains works by Ignacio Ellacuría, Segundo Galilea, and Severino Croatto. Fourth, "Theological and Pastoral Reflection" offers works by Hugo Assmann, Raúl Vidales, and Lamberto Schuurman.

The brief introduction by Míguez Bonino carefully describes the christological agendas that the different authors have taken up. He suggests that the question of who Jesus Christ is today in Latin America can be answered with different approaches. One approach is the normative dogmatic: How should Jesus be correctly understood? Another approach is descriptive and analytical: How is Jesus in fact understood today in Latin America? A third approach is theological-confessional: How can

---

[16] Lepargneur, "Imagens de Cristo," 82. The author actually uses full caps for the various Christs.

[17] José Míguez Bonino et al., *Jesús: Ni vencido ni monarca celestial* (Buenos Aires: Tierra Nueva, 1977).

the power of Jesus Christ be made present and active today in Latin America? As this collection of works demonstrates, it is impossible to ask these questions without paying attention to both the current Latin American context and the context in which Jesus lived—and the way he situated himself within his context: "A new awareness of the historic situation acts as a hermeneutic key that permits recovery of themes and resonance within the biblical message that had remained hidden or forgotten. It is as if current awareness and the commitment produce a fresh receptivity and increase our capacity to 'hear the Word.'"[18]

Míguez Bonino cautions that "it is not about trying to find a new path toward an old irrelevant speculation"; in other words, the task is to reformulate texts, doctrines, and concepts to find out who Jesus Christ is today in Latin America. "In terms of faith, it surely must be said that only *he himself* can reveal his presence. 'I am who I am' . . . is also true in Christology. And this self-manifestation occurs in the context of an active obedience, as highlighted by the Johannine writings in the New Testament."[19]

The title "Jesus: Neither defeated nor a celestial monarch" heads the work of French theologian George Casalis, who in his chapter in this book reminds us that during the Spanish conquista these two images of Christ functioned as symbols of the experience of the two sides. For the defeated indigenous people, the suffering Christ came to be the representation of their tragedy and defeat, while the Spanish used the figure of Christ as a celestial monarch to legitimate their conquest:

> With the cult of the celestial Christ, the political, pedagogical, religious power . . . is consolidated and insulated from any attack, is sacralized forever and is fastened tightly to [Christ's] throne, his royal furnishings, his columns. . . . Thus just as Christ of the Passion was converted into a symbol of the secular defeat of the peoples, the glorified Christ is degraded, lowered to the level of minister of propaganda for authoritarian and torture-wielding governments.[20]

---

[18]Míguez Bonino et al., *Jesús: Ni vencido ni monarca celestial*, 12.

[19]Míguez Bonino et al., *Jesús: Ni vencido ni monarca celestial*, 16.

[20]George Casalis, "Jesús: Ni vencido ni un monarca celestial," in Míguez Bonino et al., *Jesús: Ni vencido*, 122.

Along similar lines, in his chapter "Cristología—conquista—colonización" Peruvian scholar Saúl Trinidad summarizes the work of various historians and social scientists seeking to highlight social conditioning surrounding the Christ images brought by Spanish missionaries and the key role they fulfilled in the colonizing process. For Trinidad the christological projection of the American indigenous followed three paths. First, a Christology of *resignation* played the role of "sacralizing the conquest/oppression system and making suffering virtuous."[21] Second, in the Christology of *domination* Trinidad sees the Spanish and the defeated indigenous people conceiving of Christ's sovereignty in a parallel way: the dichotomy of Christ "defeated" on the one hand and "celestial monarch" on the other. Third, Trinidad writes of a Christology of *marginalization* that treats Jesus as a "forgotten child," perhaps because in the popular imagination his mother is more important than he is, or because in religious manifestations that have social connotations the "child" is a pretext for a self-interested practice of benevolence ("assistentialism"), whose advocates focus more on their personal agenda than on service to the needy.

Chilean theologian Segundo Galilea's pastoral sensibility and ability to synthesize is evident in his chapter, "La actitud de Jesús hacia la política" (Jesus' attitude toward politics). His reading of biblical material is similar on many points to readings that were beginning to develop in the evangelical sphere. He offers several points as a working hypothesis—a synthesis seeking to correct what he calls incomplete interpretations. On the one hand, he says, there is the "naive Christ," treating the coming of Christ as a fact with exclusively religious meaning, "as if outside the historical-political framework of his era, and this framework is like a puppet drama planned by the Father so that in him redemption might be fulfilled." On the other hand is the "revolutionary Christ," a scheme in which "Christ was essentially a political revolutionary who rose against and collided with the established system. He confronted Roman

[21] Saúl Trinidad, "Cristología—conquista—colonización," in Míguez Bonino et al., *Jesús: Ni vencido*, 106.

imperialism and the dominating Jewish classes, and his death, that of a revolutionary martyr, was the result of this confrontation."[22] Galilea presents the following summary points.[23]

1. Given the incarnation and the historic nature of his mission, Jesus was part of Israelite society, its political tensions, and its conflicts over power. His own trial and his death are political realities.
2. On the other hand, Jesus did not present himself or act as a revolutionary or a political leader. His message did not contain a program or a strategy for political liberation. Jesus essentially announced the kingdom of God as a religious/pastoral message.
3. Nevertheless, in his pastoral-religious message Jesus generated energy, producing sociopolitical changes for his era and for all history to come.
4. The political consequences of Jesus' message in the society of his time resulted from his relativizing of Roman totalitarianism and calling the poor to the kingdom, a universal consciousness that he generated among his disciples and his proclamation of the values inherent in the Beatitudes.
5. In his conflicts with the established powers of his time, Jesus took on a prophetic-pastoral attitude. This led him to renounce all use of temporal power and all forms of violence.

Galilea comes to the pastoral conclusion that in Jesus there are certain attitudes he describes as "typically charismatic," "that is to say they are not normative for all Christians" in certain areas, such as renouncing violence or renouncing sociopolitical leadership, but whose value is recognized for the charisma that leads certain people to take the same stance as Jesus. These people are gifts necessary for the church.[24]

---

[22]Segundo Galilea, "La actitud de Jesús hacia la política," in Míguez Bonino et al., *Jesús: Ni vencido*, 148.

[23]Galilea, "La actitud de Jesús hacia la política,"; these texts are spread throughout 149-56.

[24]Galilea, "La actitud de Jesús hacia la política," 156-57.

A Self-Critique of Evangelical Preaching

Two evangelicals living in Costa Rica, Saúl Trinidad and Juan Stam, offer "El Cristo de la predicación evangélica en América Latina" (The Christ of evangelical preaching in Latin America), based on research undertaken in the Latin American Bible Seminary of San José. A team of professors and students studied numerous evangelistic sermons broadcast on the evangelical radio station Faro del Caribe (Lighthouse of the Caribbean); some INDEF surveys in Costa Rica and Chile; and two theses on the renewal movement and the effects of the Costa Rica Cruzada '72, an evangelistic crusade. This research led them to a self-critique exercise of great value from a theological and pastoral perspective. Trinidad and Stam affirm that "despite the christological deficiencies that should be identified in evangelical preaching, in Latin America this preaching has been 'the power of God that brings salvation to everyone who believes' (Rom 1:16). It has been so even in its weakness and madness." They recognize that "for the most part a Christ who is powerful enough to transform lives, especially where addictions and vices are concerned, has been proclaimed and lived." Further, they say, "For many people of Latin America our proclamation of Christ has restored their sense of life's meaning."[25]

However, the images of Christ that surface in numerous cases of preaching are deeply flawed. One of these is "the Christ of the good deal"—that is, a Lord who does not demand anything of his followers. Another is "the beggar Christ," whom people accept if it suits them: "Christ is offered using marketing techniques, as when salespeople try to wheedle the person into buying their product, even if only as a favor." Christ is also offered as "a magic pill" that resolves all problems or as "a passport to heaven." Another is the antisocial Christ, who leads his followers to break with family, social, cultural, and political relationships. "This 'dualist Christ' comes to draw a closed border, a kind of Maginot Line between two worlds: the religious and the profane. This dichotomy,

[25]Saúl Trinidad and Juan Stam, "El Cristo de la predicación evangélica en América Latina," in Míguez Bonino et al., *Jesús: Ni vencido*, 77, 78.

basically Neoplatonic in nature, has produced believers with a public and [completely separate] private life."[26] These and other faulty Christologies lead the authors to a severe conclusion:

> Evangelical preaching has for the most part been characterized by functional docetism in its Christology (also basically by deism in its doctrine of God, dualism in its concept of man, and legalism in its ethics). Although the "heavenly" and "spiritual" Christ has been real and personal for believers, Jesus of Nazareth in all his humanity and historicity has not been so for them.[27]

THE HERMENEUTICAL EXTREMES

Efforts to root the Christian life in following the historical Jesus led in some cases to the use of extreme hermeneutical methods that submit the biblical text to what Míguez Bonino calls "a hermeneutical circle of iron." In his introduction to the liberation theologies, this theologian spends significant time on the question of hermeneutics. Although he grants a need for mediating ideologies for the hermeneutical task, he cautions against the position in which "the text of Scripture and tradition is forced into the Procrustean bed of ideology, and the theologian who has fallen prey to this methodology cannot then hear anything but the echo of his own ideology. There is no redemption for this theology, because it has silenced the Word of God in its transcendence and liberty."[28]

Amid the revolutionary euphoria that began around 1968, it was popular to paint Jesus as a Zealot who was incarnated in contemporary times by certain revolutionaries. As noted in chapter nine, Peronist magazine *Cristianismo y Revolución* affirmed in 1971: "Camilo Torres and Ernesto Che Guevara are in our opinion the highest examples in Latin America today of a legitimately Christian attitude and of a true

[26]Trinidad and Stam, "El Cristo de la predicación evangélica en América Latina," 80, 82.
[27]Trinidad and Stam, "El Cristo de la predicación evangélica en América Latina," 84-85.
[28]José Míguez Bonino, *La fe en busca de eficacia* (Salamanca: Sígueme, 1977), 112.

realization of the new man in Our America."[29] Cuban theologian Sergio Arce Martínez arrived at a similar conclusion:

> Let us set aside biblical erudition; let's go to concrete reality. Jesus was not a Pharisee, he was not a Sadducee, he was not a publican, he was not an Essene, he was not a Herodian. What was he? Whom did he sympathize with? To whom (singular or plural) did he offer his help? What ideology did he sympathize with? What movement did he join? There is just one possibility: the only possibility that is opened by our own evangelical history. It is antibiblical and antievangelical to affirm that he was a Sadducee, a Pharisee, a publican, an Essene, a Herodian, etc. . . . The only possibility that accords with a biblical foundation is that he was a Zealot. . . . Said in another way, he was either a Zealot or at least pro-Zealot inasmuch as he was the Christ. Or he was Pharisee or at least pro-Pharisee and therefore he was not Christ of the Gospels, the Son of the living God. As far as we are concerned, either we believe in a Zealot or pro-Zealot Christ, or we are lying atheists from the point of view of the gospel.[30]

Behind this absolute choice, "Either he was this or he was the other," without any other possibility, we can see the same lack of tolerance evidenced in political life by those who say: "Either you are with the revolution [understood in Marxist terms] or you are fascist." The reading of the text had to confirm an already adopted political position.

Nicaraguan theologian Jorge Pixley, in his book *Reino de Dios* (Kingdom of God), also chooses a hermeneutical method rooted in a dialectical materialist analysis of reality. It is not a Messiah or Lord who emerges from his reading of the Gospels but a failed social leader. He summarizes Jesus' career in the following way:

> Jesus offered the multitudes of Palestine (the poor) the good news of the coming of the kingdom of God as a kingdom of justice and equality. . . . In his analysis of the situation of Palestine he sees the temple (correctly) as the center of exploitation and inequality. . . . His strategy failed due to the insecurity of the people regarding how Jesus would cast off the Roman yoke; the people preferred the strategy of confrontation with the Romans

[29]"Cuba: Los cristianos en la sociedad socialista," *Cristianismo y Revolución* (April 1971): 29.

[30]Sergio Arce Martínez et al., *Cristo vivo en Cuba: Reflexiones teológicas cubanas* (San José: DEI, 1978), 78-79.

> that the Zealots offered. . . . At such a remove, it is difficult to know now whether the people would have been better off if they had preferred Jesus' strategy. We do not know what Jesus intended to do about the problem of the empire. The texts don't record anything about his plans, and it's difficult to imagine how he planned to overthrow the imperial yoke.[31]

In reading these pages, one cannot avoid the sense that Pixley finds it unfortunate that Jesus was not familiar with the scientific Marxist analysis of reality, which would have permitted a correct analysis of the situation and a correct strategy toward Rome. But an incongruence in his use of content from the Gospels is also evident. Jesus' intentions regarding his death, and his "strategy," are clearly formulated both in the Synoptics and in John, but evidently Pixley does not accept them or believe them to be important.[32] His analysis reflects a weakness that critics have identified also in other theologians: a lack of attention to the theology of the cross, the deepest meaning of Christ's death as a work of redemption of human beings, which is so explicit in the New Testament texts.[33]

It is worth quoting from two comments by Argentinian Bible scholar Severino Croatto that are applicable to Arce Martínez's writing. First, Croatto critiques the tendency to interpret Christ as a Zealot, and he does so quite compellingly:

> Those who try to identify a Zealot-Christ do not realize that they do a disservice to the cause of liberation. The Zealots in effect were reactionary groups and of the "extreme right." If they pursued the expulsion of the Romans from Palestinian land, it wasn't in the first place to save man for a holistic, multidimensional human development but to reestablish the law and the lost political/religious institutions. The Zealots could not escape the "infernal circle of legalism." Christ could not fight or die in favor of the law; rather, he suffered the law's power as a structure of death. To yearn for a Zealot-Christ would be to follow a reactionary Christ, a religious nationalist, a "fascist."[34]

[31]Jorge Pixley, *Reino de Dios* (Buenos Aires: La Aurora, 1977), 82. Parenthetical material is Pixley's own.

[32]In Pixley's book Jesus' death appears to be entirely incidental.

[33]Jorge Mejía, *La cristología de Puebla* (Bogotá: CELAM, 1979), 11.

[34]Severino Croatto, "La dimensión política del Cristo libertador," in Míguez Bonino et al., *Jesús: Ni vencido*, 178-79.

In the same way Croatto refuses to accept a spiritualization of Christ that does not take into account the reality of the incarnation but instead aims to move from the universality of the person of Christ to the particularity of how to serve him today. While Pixley critiques the strategy of the people, Croatto has faith that the people know how to find the truth and will do so:

> In the trial against Jesus, it is the religious authorities, very clearly identified as such, who coordinate the greatest lie of human history. They are the accusers (see Luke 23:10). We Christians have been naive to sometimes blame the Jewish *people*, saying that "they had been turncoats," betraying Jesus after the triumphal entry into Jerusalem. The intrigue came from the religious authorities. Though indeed the people were present, we should delimit/note two things: One, we do not know what their numbers were (the people as such are not easily tricked due to their marvelous grasp of truth). Second, the collaborationist group had been "bought" (and could not therefore have comprised all the people) by the chief priests and the elders . . . (Matt 27:20).[35]

Two ecclesial events in 1979 became the framework within which important moments of christological reflection in Latin America took place at the close of the decade. In the Catholic context the CELAM conference took place in Puebla, Mexico in January 1979 with the presence of John Paul II, a new pope from Poland who was theologically traditional. In the Protestant context, CLADE II was held in Lima in October and November 1979. This was the culmination of the first—and quite intense—decade of reflection and dialogue of the Latin American Theological Fraternity (FTL). In both events Christology took a central place, and given their impact, lasting well into the following decade, the next chapter will focus on these events at some length.

Two Organic Christological Essays

Two works of this period are important to discuss because they are complete books of christological reflection with a pastoral and theological orientation. In 1974 *Jesucristo revolucionario* (The revolutionary Jesus

[35]Severino Croatto, introduction to *Liberación y libertad* (Buenos Aires: Mundo Nuevo, 1973).

Christ) by Anglican professor Andrés (J. Andrew) Kirk appeared in Buenos Aires, and in 1979 in Lima, *La práctica de Jesús* (The practice of Jesus) by Peruvian priest and professor Hugo Echegaray.[36] Both are characterized by a carefully worked exegetical base that pays special attention to the historical context of Jesus' life and ministry, and each takes into account the Latin American context in its exposition.

Kirk explains that his book will concentrate on one particular aspect, though not the only one, of the life and preaching of Jesus of Nazareth: "Revolution is the theme. The analysis centers on the revolutionary projections of the public ministry of the one who proclaimed himself to be Messiah: Jesus of Nazareth." Kirk defines revolution as "the irruption of a qualitatively new factor that radically changes the future of the historical process of a people that already has a long tradition." In the first chapter he affirms, "The first basic presupposition is that the documents that narrate the life, teaching, and mission of Jesus of Nazareth are historically correct. . . . This study rests on the historical value that is attributed to the four Gospels." Later he discusses the historic sources and gives a critical exposition of form criticism, its influence, and its severe limitations. For Kirk it is crucial that there is rigorous exegetical work: "It is essential that we not force the text to yield [our] preconceived ideas. Nor do we expect the text to answer all our questions. For this reason we should let the text speak for itself and perhaps critique the way in which the questions are asked."[37]

The twelve chapters of the book are written in a dense style and offer careful exegesis of numerous passages from the Gospels, paying attention to their relationship with the Old Testament. The kingdom of God is the topic of three chapters, which first explain the law of God's kingdom and later contrast it to the structures of power and certain forms of humanism. For Kirk, when Jesus' attitude toward the institutions and the ideas of his time is analyzed, "with a certain audacity it could be said that

---

[36]Andrés Kirk, *Jesucristo revolucionario* (Buenos Aires: La Aurora, 1974); Hugo Echegaray, *La práctica de Jesús* (Lima: CEP, 1979).

[37]Kirk, *Jesucristo revolucionario*, 12, 15, 16, 30.

all Jesus' teachings are revolutionary." Kirk considers, for example, whether it is possible to talk about Christ without religion. Examining various passages that demonstrate Jesus' attitude toward the religious institutions of his time, Kirk arrives at the conclusion that "in each case he says something radically new in terms of religion; something that returns religiosity to its principal cause, pointing toward the truth about God and man. In this sense, but only in this sense, one can speak meaningfully of an antireligious Christ."[38]

With care he takes up the subject of Jesus and violence, pointing out sayings and actions by Jesus that appear to be contradictory. He concludes that "Jesus never even insinuates that violence is justified: neither Roman violence nor that of its puppet rulers, neither that of his most bitter opponents." Kirk explains and evaluates Jesus' attitudes and sayings about violence, but, analyzing them in the light of a wider biblical theology, he concludes that for Jesus "only God has the right to final judgment, and he is the only one who will fold into his own purposes the inevitable violence perpetrated by human beings who have departed from his original path."[39]

The final chapter addresses "the revolutionary rules of Jesus' community," understanding their character from the point of view of the kingdom. For the kingdom of God, "the majority of revolutionary doctrines and their outworking are in reality counterrevolutionary actions." In the conclusion, with respect to how the Christian community should face the contemporary situation, Kirk says: "The best path, the path of the revolutionary of all times, Jesus of Nazareth, will have to be congruent, challenging, subversive, rigorously honest, indestructible, and pure, in the world [that is] loved by God but possessed by evil."[40]

Lucidity, clarity, and elegance mark the style of Hugo Echegaray in *La práctica de Jesús*. This work evidences an intense pastoral concern to place the work of theological and biblical erudition within the reach of

---

[38]Kirk, *Jesucristo revolucionario*, 33, 62.
[39]Kirk, *Jesucristo revolucionario*, 84.
[40]Kirk, *Jesucristo revolucionario*, 227, 240.

all readers. Translated into English and published in 1984, it reached a wide public.[41] A disciple and later colleague of Gustavo Gutiérrez, Echegaray began his reflection researching the attitude of Jesus toward poverty, and, as the title of his book says, he decided to examine the texts from the Gospels to understand *how Jesus experienced poverty.*

> How—according to the Gospels—did Jesus live poverty? What special emphases are to be found in his personal way of embracing a world of poverty that must have been marked by profound contradictions and filled with competing claims of every kind? Which traits—material, social, and spiritual—of this poverty have normative value for us simply because they were characteristic of the poverty of Christ?[42]

Echegaray sees his work as "a contribution to Christology on only a limited and particular point: the historical humanity of Jesus." He recognizes that there are other very important themes such as "the redemptive character of the death of Jesus, or the nature of his resurrection as a historical event and a faith event." In the pages of the book, as in other of his writings, he says, "My guiding light is my profession of faith in the incarnation of the Word and therefore in the divinity of Jesus that was fully manifested to his first disciples during the period when they had their overwhelming experience of the Easter Christ."[43] With a definition particular to liberation theologies, Echegaray reminds us that "the participation in faith of believers who allow themselves to be engaged in the current history of the poor gives a new opening to a current understanding of the person of Christ, Word made poor."[44]

He dedicates various pages to examining those known as Zealots in Jesus' time, summarizing a variety of existing research on the topic. He reminds us that "we would commit an error if we simply treated the Zealots as a political party in the modern sense of the word." For him,

---

[41]Hugo Echegaray, *The Practice of Jesus* (Maryknoll, NY: Orbis, 1984). South African theologian David Bosch, for example, quotes from it frequently in his *Transforming Mission* (Maryknoll, NY: Orbis, 1991).

[42]Echegaray, *Practice of Jesus*, 3.

[43]Echegaray, *Practice of Jesus*, 3.

[44]Echegaray, *Practice of Jesus*, 3.

"the Zealots in their time represented an unlimited thirst for freedom, which dwells on almost every page of the Old Testament."[45] While it's true that Jesus shared some of the Zealots' attitudes and visions, and some of them would have been attracted to him, he himself was not a Zealot: "Jesus awakens admiration and hope in terms that the people could grasp. Despite the fact that Jesus did not become a Zealot in the sense of Judas of Galilee, who later would be one of the leaders of this school of thought, this could not have occurred by accident. Jesus' project is different from and surpasses the Zealots' project in a number of key ways."[46]

For Echegaray, in the expulsion of the temple merchants, which some saw as a Zealot gesture, what Jesus is concerned about is the question of true worship, which is why he also clashes with the priests and expresses reservations about the purity laws. Furthermore, Jesus' stance is not nurtured by the narrow nationalism that characterized the Zealots:

> Jesus overcomes in this way the nationalist particularity that made the Zealots a group restricted only to Israel's horizon. Jesus' horizon was much wider. He is not imprisioned because of the particularity of the law, the nationalism of the temple, or the question of a legitimate priesthood. Jesus' backing is the Father and not only the God of the Jews. In his message the kingdom goes out to meet man, without restrictions that mark impassable national borders.[47]

Echegaray highlights what he calls a "rooted God-centeredness" in Jesus' consciousness, as the origin of this universal scope of his teaching and his practice that must guide, inspire, and be the model for the practice of Christians today:

> For believers, the inherent meaning in the practice of the Lord does not function, certainly, outside the dynamism established by his resurrection: there this practice has—for faith—its alpha and omega. The beginning and the end of humanity put in motion he who has unchained and freed

[45]Echegaray, *Practice of Jesus*.
[46]Echegaray, *Practice of Jesus*.
[47]Echegaray, *Practice of Jesus*.

our personal and collective existence, and in whom we can place our trust that the ordering and transforming force of the world will not let us down, nor finish being swallowed up by nothing. . . . The reference believing in Jesus Christ, true God and true man, permeates our praxis, placing in it the meaning of kingdom as the end value and Christ as the Son accepted by God as the optimal, unsurpassable of the human answer to his salvific gift.[48]

[48]Echegaray, *Practice of Jesus*.

13

JESUS CHRIST'S NEW TIME FOR REFLECTION AND DIALOGUE

On Reformation Day, October 31, 1979, Salvadoran theologian Emilio Antonio Núñez opened the Second Latin American Congress of Evangelization (CLADE II) in Lima with his message "Heirs of the Reformation," which centered on the four central ideas of the Reformation. This is what he said about Christ.

> But, which Christ? Definitely this is not about a Christ of dogmas, of purely human construction, nor the Christ of the ancient and modern imagination, nor the Christ of Latin American folklore, nor the superstar Christ of the opulent societies of the north Atlantic, nor the Christ of the socioeconomically powerful in our continent, nor the Christ of the latest ideologues. Rather, we seek the Christ revealed in the Scriptures, the Christ rediscovered by many pious souls in the darkest of medieval days and in the best times of the Protestant Reformation, the Christ who has found us, and whom, by the grace of God, thousands and millions of Latin Americans have found.
>
> *Divine Christ!* He is the eternal logos, member of the trinitarian council, eternally one with the Father and with the Spirit; creator and sustainer of heaven and earth; Lord of life and history; King, now and forever; Wonderful Counselor, Mighty God, Eternal Father, Prince of Peace, whose appearances are from the days of eternity; Alpha and Omega, beginning and end, he who is, who was, and who is to come, the all-powerful Lord.

Christ of history! Manifested in time and space, in the chosen date on God's calendar, in the current of human history, in the context of a specific geography, from a people, from a culture, from a society.

Human Christ! Begotten by the Spirit, conceived by the Virgin Mary, participant in flesh and blood, "made flesh," fully identifying with humanity. Christ, fully man and man for all others, who lives among human beings "full of grace and truth" (John 1:14).

Impoverished Christ! Born in a stable, resident of a village, known as "the carpenter," the son of a carpenter. The proletariat Christ, the one with callused hands from rough work, the one with the sweating forehead in his daily work. He was born, lived and died in deep poverty, like the poor of his people. However, he did not use the social resentment of his contemporaries to deepen the chasm between persons, between classes, or between peoples. He did not call his people to raise a flag of hate and revenge. Instead, he spoke of forgiveness and brotherhood. But he gave himself in bloody sacrifice to undo enmities on the cross and break down any wall that separates a human being from other human beings. Furthermore, his presence is an inevitable sign of contradiction to those who oppress the poor and live with their backs turned to human misery.

Prophet Christ! Herald of God the Father, interpreter of Deity, revealer of the divine will for his people and for all of humanity. His word lit on fire from heaven is consolation and hope for those of humble hearts, and an unavoidable warning of judgment for evildoers.

Christ the *Lamb of God!* He who takes away the sin of the world; he who gives all on Calvary for our redemption; he with the precious blood that cleanses us from every evil.

Living Christ! Through death he destroyed the one who ruled the empire of death, and he triumphed over the grave on the glorious day of his resurrection.

Christ our Priest! He who is seated at the right hand of Majesty in the heavenlies and who "is able to save completely those who come to God through him, because he always lives to intercede for them" (Heb 7:25).

Christ the coming King! Glorifier of his church, Judge of the living and the dead "in view of his appearing and his kingdom" (2 Tim 4:1). Messiah for whom we long in order that all peoples may be blessed, King of kings, Lord of lords, Christ of complete and utter renewal.[1]

[1]The compendium of the Congress is CLADE II, *América Latina y la evangelización en los años 80* (Mexico City: Fraternidad Teológica Latinoamericana, 1979).

These lines by Nuñez are a brief synthesis of the christological exploration that had been taking place in the Protestant context, and particularly in the Fraternidad Teológica Latinoamericana (FTL). Proclaiming the gospel, presenting the person of Jesus in the text of the Gospels to people groups and individuals who were not familiar with him, some lacking any knowledge whatsoever, had been the task of the first generations of evangelicals who traveled the continent in the first decades of the twentieth century. In the following generations, those I have characterized as precursors and founders brought poetic, journalistic, homiletic, and hymnological proclamation at both popular and academic levels. John Mackay was the precursor of an understanding of the Latin American social and religious situation from a theological perspective; he was followed by the new generations of Latin American evangelical thinkers in the second half of the twentieth century. A new contextual understanding of the person of Jesus Christ emerged in response to decades of social change and struggles for justice and against poverty. All this also had repercussions in Catholicism itself, which eventually, with the turmoil of Vatican II and its echoes in the Conference of Medellín, returned to the biblical sources of faith in Jesus Christ.

The CELAM Conference in Puebla

During the 1970s many priests, nuns, and bishops who took seriously the "preferential option for the poor" proposed by the CELAM conference in Medellín suffered at the hands of military and totalitarian regimes in countries such as Brazil, Chile, Argentina, Uruguay, Bolivia, El Salvador, and Guatemala. Mortimer Arias quotes a French magazine that compiled statistics regarding this persecution. It contains a list of almost fifteen hundred names: "They were arrested, interrogated, defamed, tortured, kidnapped, assassinated, or exiled in the decade from 1968 to 1978. Among them 71 were tortured, 69 were assassinated, and 279 were exiled (the majority of these being foreign missionary priests and members of religious orders)."[2] At the same time a contingent of conservative bishops

---

[2]Mortimer Arias, *El clamor de mi pueblo* (Mexico City: CUPSA; New York: Friendship, 1981), 119. Arias is quoting from the magazine *Diffusion de L'information sur L'Amerique Latine*.

who showed little enthusiasm for the preferential option for the poor under the terms of Medellín gradually took over the leadership of CELAM. Jesuit historian Jeffrey Klaiber says: "With the election of John Paul II, a conservative change was soon felt with respect to the policies of his predecessors. Particularly the episcopal appointments began to be given to men who were less progressive and in some cases had fundamentalist tendencies."[3] The tendency became evident in the second CELAM conference in Puebla, Mexico, which took place between January and February 1979.

The ferment of theological reflection unleashed in the Catholic Church is perceivable in the development of Christology in Puebla. In 1974 Pope Paul VI had published his encyclical *Evangelii Nuntiandi* with a strong emphasis in evangelization. In an echo of this, Puebla adopted as its motto "Evangelization in the present and in the future of Latin America." In its final document, after an articulation of a pastoral vision of the Latin American reality, there is a section on Jesus Christ as the central content of evangelization (actually the whole document has a christological thread): "We propose the proclamation of the central truths of evangelization: Christ, our hope, is among us, sent from the Father, encouraging the church with his Spirit and offering today's man his Word and his life to lead him to complete liberation."[4] The content of evangelization also includes the church, Mary ("Mary is . . . the guiding light of evangelization and the mother of the Latin American peoples"), and a Christian vision of human beings.[5]

Liberation theologians were prevented from participating in the CELAM Puebla conference, and it was evident that the most conservative bishops had taken over leadership of the event. In his opening speech John Paul II expressed the need for christological definitions, and these were

---

[3]Jeffrey Klaiber, SJ, *Iglesia, dictaduras y democracia en América Latina* (Lima: Pontificia Universidad Católica del Perú Fondo Editorial, 1997), 31.

[4]There are various editions of this final document authorized by CELAM, and it is divided into paragraphs that I will cite by number. I am using the edition published by the Secretariado Nacional del Episcopado Peruano: CELAM, *Puebla* (Lima: Paulinas, 1979), par. 166.

[5]CELAM, *Puebla*, pars. 167-69.

later gathered in the final document. The pope was concerned that a "solid" Christology be developed. He said to the bishops: "For you, pastors, the faithful of our countries wait, and demand more than anything a careful and watchful transmission of the truth about Jesus Christ. This is the center of evangelization and constitutes its essential content." Later the pope affirmed: "Today in many places—the phenomenon is not new—'rereadings' of the gospel are being propagated, the fruits of theoretical speculations instead of authentic meditation on the Word of God and a true evangelical commitment."[6] He goes to identify some specifically:

> In some cases either the divinity of Christ is silenced, or forms of interpretation in conflict with the faith of the church are undertaken. . . . In other cases some try to show Jesus as politically committed, as a fighter against the Roman domination and against the powers, even as involved in class warfare. This conception of Christ as a politician, a revolutionary, as the subversive of Nazareth, is not compatible with the catechesis of the church.[7]

It was evident that the pope was referring to the Christologies associated with liberation theologies, and his agenda regarding them was clear:

> In the face of such "rereadings" and the perhaps brilliant but fragile and inconsistent hypotheses derived from them, "the evangelization in the present and the future of Latin America" cannot cease to affirm the faith of the church: Jesus Christ, the Word and Son of God, became man to draw close to man and offer to him, by the compelling strength of his mystery, salvation, God's great gift.[8]

In a presentation about the Christology of Puebla, Argentinian Bible scholar and bishop Jorge Mejía, one of the expert consultants for CELAM in the conference, narrated the long process of writing the final document. First it was circulated as "a document in consultation" in 1977, and later it was studied by bishops throughout Latin America, who presented their proposals for modifications, adding or eliminating parts. Mejía's opinion is important and representative of an official

---

[6]CELAM, *Puebla*, pars. 9, 10.
[7]CELAM, *Puebla*, par. 10.
[8]CELAM, *Puebla*, par. 11.

voice, because he had been the secretary of the Department of Ecumenism for CELAM and later was made cardinal and went to work in Rome. Mejía says: "The idea of including a christological section in the final document from the conference of Puebla did not emerge at the conference itself. It has a long history, which is useful to know, at least in its general outline."[9]

Corrections to Liberation Theologies

Mejía remembers that in the final document from the Medellín Conference (1968) there were no christological definitions, and that in the following years "they began to appear here and there, by way of allusions arising in laying out a religious-political commitment, referring to reinterpretations of the figure and work of Christ with a strong political emphasis. The Lord had been the first 'revolutionary,' and so his life and his death (and his mission) should be read in this light."[10]

He points out that the debate was also taking place in Europe and goes on to review the work of Leonardo Boff, highlighting three critical points. First, "Boff begins without a clear reading of the Chalcedonian dogma, and therefore [he is unclear] in his formulation of the double nature of Christ, divine and human, joined in the unity of one person." Second, Boff's explanation of the relation between Christ and the church is also insufficient, and third, "Boff is quite negative regarding the sacrificial nature of the death of the Lord in its very intention. That would be 'one interpretation' . . . among many."[11]

Mejía warns in particular that in relation to Jesus, "Boff's tendency to detheologize his death is troubling, and (in my judgment) incompatible with a healthy exegesis of the New Testament. Coherent with this is his interpretation of Communion, reduced to a symbol of the eschatological banquet and devoid of all sacrificial dimension." In conclusion, for Mejía "it is easy to see that all this leads to a rereading of the person and mission

---

[9]Jorge Mejía, *La cristología de Puebla* (Bogotá: CELAM, 1979), 9.
[10]Mejía, *La cristología de Puebla*, 9.
[11]Mejía, *La cristología de Puebla*, 11.

of Christ more as a prophet, maybe a 'great prophet' (*passim* in the book), than as a redeemer in the biblical and traditional sense of this expression."[12]

Mejía's later criticism of Jon Sobrino's work touches on similar points to those about Boff, such as unsatisfactory interpretations of the Chalcedonian dogma, and he critiques the formulas with which Sobrino tries to explain the mystery of the divinity of Jesus and his relationship with the Father. He mentions some of these: "the divinity of Jesus consists in his concrete relationship with the Father"; "what Jesus reveals is the Son's path, the path to becoming the Son of God"; or "Christ is becoming man, and the man Jesus is becoming the son of God." Mejía writes: "In fact Sobrino critiques the soteriological conception of Jesus' death, which he considers 'distorted' when it is 'reduced to a noetic mystery,' and attempts are made to explain it from God's 'design' and from its 'salvific value.'"[13]

Thus responding to the christological debate that had blossomed in Latin America, the Puebla document begins by affirming "the truth about Jesus Christ, the Savior we announce." Mejía offers a short summary of the message from Puebla:

> Here these are accepted and declared, if always as elements not of a theological discussion but of the content of the evangelizing proclamation: the affirmation of Jesus' divinity with the Chalcedonian formula, properly repositioned in the New Testament context; the sacrificial nature of Jesus' death, with one paragraph synthesizing the different presentations of this death in the New Testament itself; the historical relationship of Jesus with the church; the transcendence of Jesus' message and mission, in opposition to "Enlightenment rationalism" but not neglecting to address the "inverse reaction."[14]

Under examination, the message from Puebla proves to contain well-articulated christological definitions with which an evangelical observer cannot but be in agreement. For example: "It is our task to clearly proclaim, without room for doubts or misunderstandings, the mystery of

[12]Mejía, *La cristología de Puebla*, 12. Mejía's own parenthesis.
[13]Mejía, *La cristología de Puebla*, 14.
[14]Mejía, *La cristología de Puebla*, 16.

the incarnation: equally the divinity of Jesus Christ as the church professes it and the reality and strength of his human and historical dimension." Reductionisms should be avoided: "We can not disfigure, partialize, or ideologize the person of Jesus Christ, whether by converting him into a politician, a leader, a revolutionary, or simply a prophet, or even reducing to the merely private sphere the one who is Lord of all history." In various parts a trinitarian framework is seen: "The church of Latin America wants to proclaim, therefore, the true face of Christ, because in it shines the glory and the goodness of the providing Father and the force of the Holy Spirit, who announces the true and complete liberation of each and every one of the men of our people."[15]

With respect to following Jesus there is also a clear statement:

> Thus Jesus, in a way that is original, incomparable, his own, demands a radical following that encompasses the whole man, all men, and envelops the whole world and the cosmos. This radicality means that conversion is a process that is never complete at either a personal or a social level. Because if the kingdom of God passes through historical expressions, it is never depleted, nor can it be identified with them.[16]

Following Jesus has a social impact on the world:

> For Latin America to become capable of converting its pain into growth toward a truly participative and fraternal society, it needs to educate men capable of shaping history according to Jesus' "praxis," understood as we have described it based on the biblical theology of history. The continent needs men conscious that God calls them to act in alliance with him.[17]

On the other hand, the message also contains some specifically "Roman" elements with which evangelical thought could never agree due to their lack of biblical foundation. The material on evangelization includes a large section about Mary. The affirmations in this section are categorical and eloquent: "The admirable fecundity of Mary has been revealed to us. She becomes Mother of God, of the historic Christ, in the

---

[15]CELAM, *Puebla*, pars. 175, 178, 189.
[16]CELAM, *Puebla*, par. 193.
[17]CELAM, *Puebla*, par. 279.

fiat of the annunciation, when the Holy Spirit covers her with his shadow. She is the mother of the church because she is mother of Christ, head of the mystical body."[18] Mary's exaltation goes even further as the message of Puebla quotes the encyclical *Evangelii nuntiandi* and the decree *Lumen Gentium*:

> With evangelization, the church conceives new children. This process, which consists of "transformating humanity from within," in "making it new" (EN 18), is a true rebirth. In this birth that takes place again and again, Mary is our mother. She, glorious in heaven, acts on earth. Participating in the Lordship of the risen Christ, "By her maternal charity, she cares for the brethren of her Son, who still journey on earth" (LG 62); her great care is that Christians might have abundant life and that they arrive at maturity in the fullness of Christ.[19]

Further, the exclusivity of the Roman church is affirmed: "Only in the Catholic Church is plenitude for the means of salvation (UR 36), a legacy given by Jesus to men through the apostles. For this reason we have the duty to proclaim the excellence of our vocation to the Catholic Church (LG 14), vocation which is at the same time an immense grace and a responsibility."[20] In the section of the Puebla message dedicated to dialogue for communion and participation, a picture is offered of the religious situation, which affirms that

> the Catholic Church constitutes the great majority, a fact that is not only sociological but also theological, which is very relevant. Together with the church there are Eastern churches and there are Western churches and communities. There are also what are known as "free religious movements" (popularly known as sects), among which some remain within the limits of the profession of a basically Christian faith; others, on the other hand, cannot be considered as such.[21]

Traditionally Catholics have used *sects* for all churches that evangelize and grow, while the term *church* is used for the few churches connected

[18]CELAM, *Puebla*, par. 287.
[19]CELAM, *Puebla*, par. 288.
[20]CELAM, *Puebla*, par. 225.
[21]CELAM, *Puebla*, pars. 1100-1102.

to the ecumenical movement that are willing to dialogue with Rome. With the newly adopted nomenclature also comes the derogatory judgment: "With regard to these groups, we cannot ignore their very marked proselytism, biblical fundamentalism, and strict literalism with respect to their own doctrines."[22]

Understanding Evangelization

It bears reflection that the theological production of both Protestants and Catholics at the end of the 1970s included a search for Jesus Christ with a kerygmatic and evangelizing focus. However, it is important to understand how evangelical theologians understand evangelization in contrast to Catholic bishops' understanding. On both sides we can see an effort to give evangelization a basic christological content, in which there are notable convergences and elements that coincide. But it is in the concept of evangelization that the differences are found. According to the evangelical vision, there is in Latin America an absence of Christ, to which the response should be the proclamation of his name and his gospel, calling all human beings to put their faith in Christ. In the Catholic vision, Latin America is already Christian, and evangelization is seen to be mostly the reactivation of an already existent faith.

Historic reasons are put forward for this: "Evangelization is in the origins of this New World that is Latin America. The church is present in the roots and the contemporary context of the continent." In the same way, "the founding evangelization is one of the relevant chapters of church history. . . . Our radical Catholic substratum with its vital and current forms of religiosity was established and energized by a vast missionary legion of bishops, religious workers, and laypeople."[23] A note of self-critique does not weaken the assertion that there is a rooted Christian faith:

> It is true that the church in its evangelizing task has had to bear the weight of discouragement, alliances with earthly powers, an incomplete pastoral

[22]CELAM, *Puebla*, par. 1109. I have focused on this theme more extensively in my book *Tiempo de misión* (Guatemala City: CLARA-Semilla, 1999), chap. 7.

[23]CELAM, *Puebla*, pars. 4, 6-7.

> vision, and the destructive force of sin. It should also be recognized that the evangelization that constitutes Latin America as "the continent of hope" has been much more powerful than the shadows that have unfortunately accompanied it within its historic context.[24]

Chapter eight pointed out self-critiquing work from various sectors of Latin American Catholicism, motivated by a deep pastoral concern, regarding the lack of knowledge of the Christ of the Bible and of faith, that had preceded the CELAM conference in Medellín. In contrast with the self-critiquing tone that characterized the Medellín document, the message from Puebla emphatically affirms in paragraph 171 that "the Latin American people, still deeply religious even before being evangelized, in their majority believe in Jesus Christ, true God and true man." The following paragraph is offered as proof of this, a long list of diverse aspects of the religious life of the people, especially of popular religiosity:

> Expressions of this, among others, are the multiple qualities of power, health, or consolation that are attributed to him; titles of Judge and King that are given; the dedications of sites that connect him to places and regions; the devotion to the patient Christ, his birth in the manger and his death on the cross; devotion to the risen Christ; and even more, the devotion to the Sacred Heart of Jesus and to his real presence in the Eucharist, demonstrated in First Communions, evening worship, the procession of Corpus Christi, and the eucharistic congresses.[25]

For this, in terms of evangelizing methodology, the starting point is a revaluing of popular religiosity, which for the bishops would be an expression and a measure of faith in Christ that serves as a starting point:

> Popular religiosity, despite its digressions and ambiguities, expresses the religious identity of a people and, in purifying it from possible deformations, offers a privileged place to evangelization. The great devotion and popular celebrations have been a distinctive characteristic of Latin American Catholicism, maintaining evangelical values, and they are a sign of belonging to the church.[26]

---

[24]CELAM, *Puebla*, par. 10.
[25]CELAM, *Puebla*, par. 172.
[26]CELAM, *Puebla*, par. 109.

The question is to what point popular religiosity had been fed by images and concepts contrary to the biblical witness, as evidenced in many of the practices evaluated and criticized by Catholic missionaries themselves during the 1960s. Was the Catholic Church represented in Puebla willing to take up the task of true and deep correction through its evangelization program? My introduction to the compendium of CLADE II pointed out that the CELAM conference in Medellín "had demonstrated signs of self-criticism within Catholicism in a direction that to evangelicals seemed promising: biblical renovation, corrections to the syncretism of popular religiosity, the creative application of reforms suggested by Vatican II." The course of events changed things:

> But in the months prior to CLADE II, the Episcopal Assembly of Puebla (January–February 1979) and the tendencies defined by Pope John Paul II demonstrated that by the end of the decade the gap between evangelicals and Catholics had widened. A clear change in direction returning to Mariology, a revalorization of popular religiosity, and the clear anti-evangelical declarations of the final document constituted sufficient elements that an alert evangelical would perceive a marked regression in religious terms.[27]

CLADE II: That Latin America May Hear the Voice of God

A deep-seated evangelizing vocation characterized the growing Latin American Protestantism, and theological reflection in the heart of the Latin American Theological Fraternity (FTL) during its first decade continued to be marked by this missionary direction. In preparing the program for the Second Latin American Congress of Evangelization (CLADE II), the FTL incorporated the evangelizing dimension of the Lausanne movement's covenant. The motto of the congress was "That Latin America might hear God's voice," and the program included study

[27]Samuel Escobar, "Espíritu y mensaje del CLADE II," in CLADE II, *América Latina y la evangelización en los años 80*, xii.

of the missionary needs of the continent, reports from some salient evangelizing efforts, and guidelines for a deep and effective communication of the gospel in the Latin American context.

The theological presentations constituted an effort to explore the biblical foundations of evangelization by pairing doctrinal concepts inherent in the basic Christian message: "Spirit and Word in the task of evangelization," presented by Baptist Rolando Guriérrez from Mexico and Pentecostal Norberto Saracco from Argentina; "Christ and the antichrist in proclamation," by René Padilla of Argentina and Lutheran Valdir Steuernagel from Brazil; "Sin and salvation in Latin America," by Baptists Russell Shed from Brazil and Orlando Costas from Costa Rica; and "Hope and despair in the continental crisis" by me and Methodist Mortimer Arias from Bolivia and Uruguay. Each pair involved two presentations by people from different denominations, countries, and generations, a cross-fertilization that significantly enriched this contextual effort. While just two of these presentations centered particularly on the person and work of Jesus Christ, all of them had a clear christological focus.

Here we will take a closer look at the presentation of Padilla and Steuernagel. The christological work of René Padilla, highlighted in previous chapters, calls attention to the eschatological focus of Jesus' message about the kingdom of God. This focus was deepened in "Christ and antichrist in the proclamation of the gospel" with Steuernagel. Working with the central truths of the gospel as their framework, they related these truths contextually to the historic moment of the continent. Padilla and Steuernagel insisted that the proclamation of Christ as Savior and Lord will always encounter opposition in a fallen world. Both authors undertook careful exegetical work. In his summary, Padilla reminded conferencegoers that the central pretension of the antichrist is to occupy the place that belongs to Christ and to receive the worship that only God deserves. The antichrist is active in the world and building his kingdom, based on error, deception, and lies, and his intention is to destroy the church. Therefore those who evangelize should remember:

> The time between the resurrection and the second coming is characterized by the opposition to the good news, opposition in which the final manifestation of the antichrist is foreseen. But opposition does not always appear in the form of persecution; it can also come in the form of seduction. Hence the importance of the warning presented in the Lausanne Covenant: "We need both watchfulness and discernment to safeguard the biblical gospel. We acknowledge that we ourselves are not immune to worldliness of thought and action, that is, to a surrender to secularism" (par. 12). The spirit of the antichrist is present today in opposition to every effort the church makes to fulfill its mission, using for this end the rules of the game and the values of the society that surrounds it.[28]

The consciousness of living in the eschatological tension between the "already" and the "not yet," and the very real opposition to the lordship of Jesus Christ, leads the church and the believer to a clear relativization of the political, economic, and social powers under which they must live. Using the categories given by Padilla, we can say that this relativization is important in terms of both the powers' persecution of the church and their attempts to seduce the church. Two aspects of the Christian mission are absolutely necessary: announcing the Lord and denouncing evil. As the Lausanne Covenant says: "The message of salvation implies also a message of judgment upon every form of alienation, oppression and discrimination, and we must not be afraid to denounce evil and injustice wherever they exist" (par. 5).

In Jesus' ministry, acts of service to meet human needs accompanied the proclamation of the gospel of salvation and the denunciation of sin, including prophetic warnings of the judgment of God. For this reason the proclamation of the gospel brought both acceptance and rejection. Steuernagel reminds us that it would be naive of us to preach the gospel with the assumption that everyone will accept it:

> The obvious conflict in the ministry of Jesus between his sovereign and powerful action and the demonic offensive against him also characterizes our action. The kingdom of the prince of darkness, although provisional,

---

[28]CLADE II, *América Latina y la evangelización en los años 80*, 228.

> is real—and seeks to keep all men under its dominion. Always when the gospel is preached, the circle of evil is broken and the authority of Satan is defeated. All proclamation of the gospel breaks the circle of darkness and provokes open conflict, over which we can be confident that we already have victory in the name of Jesus.[29]

In the Latin American context at this time, after the serious exegetical work came the duty of applying biblical teaching to the posture and mission of the church. Here the theological work took a form that we can call social critique of the powers. Padilla, for example, condemned "contemporary materialism, which with its one-dimensional vision of reality imposes its values and offers a salvation that is a negation of salvation in Christ, an antisalvation."[30] The theological criticism is not limited to protesting only against the obvious abuses and the violations of human rights by the powerful, but also critiques the underlying concepts that give form to certain government programs and the organization of society. It is critical of modernity imposed by economic empires at the cost of great sacrifices on the part of the multitudes who are victims rather than beneficiaries, which is fruit of the spirit of the antichrist. This means the church in Latin America must undertake a prophetic task:

> If in Latin America the kingdom of the antichrist takes the form of a society that absolutizes material possessions, with governments that are willing to pay high social costs to reach their economic development goals, the proclamation of the gospel must include the announcement of the good news of salvation in Jesus Christ and at the same time the denouncement of all in society that threatens the fullness of human life. The demand of the hour is not to criticize governments in religious language, but to confront the values and attitudes that make it possible for our peoples to be domesticated by propaganda; it is not to oppose the official myths with other secular myths, but to point out the judgment of God with respect to all attempts to build the kingdom of God.[31]

---

[29]CLADE II, *América Latina y la evangelización en los años 80*, 237.
[30]CLADE II, *América Latina y la evangelización en los años 80*, 228.
[31]CLADE II, *América Latina y la evangelización en los años 80*, 230.

On the other hand, during these decades Latin America was shaken by the rise of political military regimes that deified the state and steamrolled over the most elemental human rights, making use of torture, political assassination, disappearance of citizens, and concentration camps. Padilla comments,

> At times it seemed like scenes from *1984*, as if the novel by George Orwell had ceased being fiction and had become reality, especially in his description of the totalitarian character of society. The antichrist is also visible here, especially in the role played by the state, with its overwhelming concentration of political and economic power in almost all countries in Latin America.[32]

An Evangelical Assessment of Liberation Theologies

While it is true that evangelicals had taken the initiative to proclaim Christ and spread his message in societies where Christ was unknown or ignored, following Vatican II and Medellín the changes in the Catholic Church returned the person of Christ to its heart in both pastoral context and theological reflection, particularly among the liberation theologians. During the 1980s evangelical writings evaluating and analyzing liberation theologies appeared. Each of them includes a significant section focused on Christology, with particular attention to an understanding and evaluation of hermeneutics. From the evangelical context three organic works appeared: by Emilio Antonio Núñez there was *Teología de la liberación: Una perspectiva evangélica* (*Liberation Theology: An Evangelical Perspective*), and by me, *La fe evangélica y las teologías de la liberación* (Evangelical faith and liberation theologies).[33] These had been preceded by a work by J. Andrew Kirk that was not translated from its original English: *Liberation Theology: An Evangelical View from the Third World* (London: Marshall, Morgan & Scott, 1979), although it was written during his time

[32]CLADE II, *América Latina y la evangelización en los años 80*, 230.

[33]Emilio Antonio Núñez, *Teología de la liberación: Una perspectiva evangélica* (Miami: Editorial Caribe, 1986; English trans., *Liberation Theology: An Evangelical Perspective* [Chicago: Moody Press, 1985]); Samuel Escobar, *La fe evangélica y las teologías de la liberación* (El Paso, TX: Casa Bautista de Publicaciones, 1987).

in Argentina. These three works recognize the challenge of liberation theologies; they are based on exhaustive studies of liberationist texts and, as would be expected of evangelicals, are focused especially in the field of hermenuetics. The three placed the emergence of these theologies in the Latin American historical-social context. In their chapters on Christology they particularly evaluate the works of Boff and Sobrino, with their emphasis on the historical Jesus, but are not limited to them.

For Kirk, the Christology of the liberation theologians presents a certain typology in the use of the symbolic status of the historical Jesus. "This typology has at least a threefold dimension: the concept of grace in Jesus' teaching and attitudes; Jesus' attitude to the political reality of his time; and the Christology inherent in the 'parable' of the Last Judgment (Matt. 25.31–46)."[34] The question of grace is examined particularly in the work of Juan Luis Segundo, as a way of life in which the follower of Jesus should behave differently, in a way that does not seek retribution for evil, nor revenge, but the opposite, forgiveness and mercy. Later Kirk examines Jesus' attitudes toward the Zealot movement and toward other political groups of his time, the Herodians, Sadducees, and Pharisees, which eventually led to his death.[35] A careful exegete, Kirk examines the parable of the final judgment and the complete identification of Jesus with the poor and needy, the least of his brothers,[36] a favorite passage of theologians such as Gutiérrez, who wrote: "Our encounter with the Lord occurs in our encounter with others, especially in the encounter with those whose human features have been disfigured by oppression, despoliation, and alienation and who have 'no beauty, no majesty' but are the things 'from which men turn away their eyes' (Isa. 53:23)."[37]

Núñez's focus begins with evangelical systematic theology, and in his chapter about Christology, he examines the works of Boff and Sobrino and their theological method with care. Núñez places the origin of the

---

[34]J. Andrew Kirk, *Liberation Theology: An Evangelical View from the Third World* (London: Marshall, Morgan & Scott, 1979), 123-24.
[35]Kirk, *Liberation Theology*, 124-30.
[36]Kirk, *Liberation Theology*, 132-35.
[37]Gustavo Gutiérrez, *A Theology of Liberation* (Maryknoll, NY: Orbis, 1988), 116.

Christology of these two authors in christological reflections begun prior to Vatican II among European Catholic theologians such as Karl Rahner, Karl Adam, and Walter Kasper. However, he reminds us that "the Latin American liberation theologians critically evaluate the christological currents of the past and present, assimilating what they consider to be positive, and rejecting without a doubt all intents to reduce Christology to something purely metaphysical or dogmatic." With reference to the methodology of these theologians he says: "What about a biblical Christology? The liberation theologians are extremely interested in looking for the historical Jesus in the pages of the Gospels, but they seem to accept without reservations the criteria of modern textual criticism, including of course form, tradition, and redaction analysis."[38]

After studying Boff and Sobrino thoroughly, Núñez arrives at this conclusion from his conservative evangelical perspective:

> The liberation theology studied here does not question only the way in which the postapostolic church formulated its christological creed. It puts in doubt the authenticity of various portions of the New Testament and prefers to interpret biblical Christology in terms of a theological evolution. This means that New Testament Christology is for the most part the product of the first Christians' reflection following the resurrection of their Teacher. It is a Christology of human creation rather than of divine revelation. The inspiration and divine authority of the Scriptures is not given its due importance.[39]

Núñez does not limit himself to critiquing the liberation theologies but undertakes his own self-critique as a Latin American evangelical: "In some ways this new emphasis on the humanity of Christ is a reaction to the lack of equilibrium in a Christology that magnifies the deity of the the Word incarnated at the expense of his humanity." Núñez explains how Latin American evangelicals received an Anglo-Saxon Christology that was a result of the debates between fundamentalism and modernism in North America:

[38]Núñez, *Teología de la liberación*, 196, 198.
[39]Núñez, *Teología de la liberación*, 220.

> Necessarily in conservative evangelical Christology, the deity of the Word was emphasized without denying his humanity. A divine-human Christ was presented to us in theological formulas; but in practice he was found distant from the scenes of this world, without interfering in our social problems. . . . The Christ who was announced to many of us evangelical Christians gave the impression of being confined to the heavenly realm, from where he related with each one of us as individuals, preparing us for our transfer to glory and promising us that he will return to the world to give a solution to all humanity's problems.[40]

Núñez insists that we cannot evade the challenge of liberation theologies and cannot "give ourselves the luxury of despising it." There is a new theological agenda that Núñez welcomes:

> We already have signs of a christological awakening in the Latin American evangelical community. Everything seems to indicate that after liberation theology our Christology will not be the same in its emphasis, and it was to a certain point a product of an evangelical reaction to the Protestant liberalism of the nineteenth century. Without becoming isolated from our vital context, we must continue to diligently study the sacred Scriptures because they provide the essential and authentic testimony to the person and work of the Son of God.[41]

In my own study of liberation theologies, I also offer an evaluation of their Christology, especially in relation to the hermeneutical task. On the one hand, it can be recognized that Latin American theologians have returned to the theme of Christ: "We cannot but be joyful regarding the intense theological and cultural activity that in recent years has again put the figure of Jesus Christ in the center even of public debates."[42] On the other hand, studying various examples leads to this conclusion:

> Evidently it cannot be said that there is only *one* christological approach in liberation theology; rather, there has been an intense search that many times followed the paths of political preferences and the national context from which each theologian speaks. Ideally, in returning to the Word they

---

[40]Núñez, *Teología de la liberación*, 223.
[41]Núñez, *Teología de la liberación*, 223.
[42]Escobar, *La fe evangélica y las teologías de la liberación*, 150.

> would overcome the radical divergences and begin to see certain common principles. But if ideologies are stronger that the Word, instead of making things clearer, hermenuetics can obscure them.[43]

The chapter dedicated to the renewal of biblical theology argues that it rests on a revitalization of biblical hermeneutics:

> The hermenuetics of the church begins with a confession of the divine initiative both in the great events of salvation and in its revelation, which in addition to recording the events explains them and gives them meaning. Furthermore, hermeneutics culminates in obedience and through obedience is clarified and better articulated. In the confession of God's people the revelatory character of the biblical text is recognized, as well as its authority, the unity of its message, and the salvific intention of its Author.[44]

In the four elements that have been outlined, the content of the reflection is christological, and it is based fundamentally on a reflection from Peter's First Epistle: God has spoken, God has spoken in Christ, God has spoken in Christ to save us: "To confess in this way the divine initiative through revelation is only possible within the framework of the Christian community."

> In affirming the divine initiative, we are confessing our condition as creatures, our "creaturehood." Through Jesus Christ and from Jesus Christ we have learned that God is our Father. The Father that Jesus Christ reveals is not a name that theologians give to the forces of history in a Hegelian sense. Neither is it a name we can assign to the human impulse in a type of Promethean gesture.[45]

In 1 Peter 1:10-12 we arrive with Peter to the specific hermeneutical reference point: "The center is christological, and around him the prophetic announcement and apostolic preaching are integrated." For this reason I argue that an evangelical hermeneutics

> *refuses to establish polarities* between Old and New Testaments, between the Gospels and the Epistles, between Jesus and Paul, between the

[43]Escobar, *La fe evangélica y las teologías de la liberación*, 151-52.
[44]Escobar, *La fe evangélica y las teologías de la liberación*, 159.
[45]Escobar, *La fe evangélica y las teologías de la liberación*, 161.

> prophets of the left and the kings of the right. The key to the unity of the text is christological. Polarities often come from ideologies or philosophies external to the text and to the world of the Bible: opposite in content and intention to God's salvific purpose. This does not mean refusing to acknowledge a plurality of emphases and our own perspectives on the human and historical dimensions of revelation. However, just as there are ways of reading the text that end up eliminating a God who has taken the initiative, there are polarities imposed on the text that end up destroying even its christological center.[46]

From this conviction comes my principal evaluation of the liberation theologies: although they have gotten us to pay attention to the abundant biblical material about the liberating God and his demand for justice, and to Jesus' lifestyle of service, his proclamation, and his denunciations, they have failed to heed the totality of biblical revelation. I conclude, then: "We believe that in rejecting in any way the christological center that throughout the Bible points to cleansing from sin, expiatory sacrifice, and the call to worship the true God, [these theologies are] not doing justice to the biblical unity."[47]

A massive effort of Uruguayan Jesuit Juan Luis Segundo to write a work about Jesus that especially addressed people outside the church and the Christian faith merits mention as well. *El hombre de hoy ante Jesús de Nazaret* (The man of today before Jesus of Nazareth) is a work of three volumes and fourteen hundred pages. The first tome is *Fe e ideología* (Faith and ideology), and the second and third constitute two parts: *Historia y actualidad: Sinópticos y Pablo* (History and today's reality: Synoptics and Paul) and *Historia y actualidad: Las cristologías en la espiritualidad* (History and today's reality: Christologies in spirituality).[48] Those of us who have read his previous works *De la sociedad a la teología* (From society to theology) and *Liberación de la teología* (The liberation of

[46]Escobar, *La fe evangélica y las teologías de la liberación*, 162-63.

[47]Escobar, *La fe evangélica y las teologías de la liberación*, 164-65.

[48]Jean Luis Segundo, *El hombre de hoy ante Jesús de Nazaret*, vol. 1, *Fe e ideología*; vol. 2, *Historia y actualidad: Sinópticos y Pablo*; vol. 3, *Historia y actualidad: Las cristologías en la espiritualidad* (Madrid: Cristiandad, 1982).

theology) already knew of Segundo's pastoral sensitivity, his familiarity with the great figures of European thought, and his effort to make the subtleties of theological reflection understandable for laypeople.[49] These qualities also appear in the three volumes of *El hombre de hoy*, but the intention to be exhaustive in themes of faith, religion and ideology, theological method, and an anthropological understanding of the mentality of the contemporary human being challenge us with a text that is not simple to read. As a Lutheran commentator notes: "Surely the danger exists that such a dense and extensive book as this might be admired or condemned without being read. It would be a pity, because JN deserves to be read, studied, and discussed by those who are concerned about the meaning of Jesus for today."[50]

Christology and Christian Praxis

Other evangelical works evaluating liberation theologies and the development of an evangelical Christology began to appear during this decade. In 1981 the FTL relaunched the *Boletín Teológico* magazine, which had previously been published sporadically. The editor was Nicaraguan pastor Roland Gutiérrez, and it was published in Mexico, where he lived. In 1982, meanwhile, René Padilla founded the magazine *Misión*, which was published in Buenos Aires. Various Latin American evangelical theologians contributed to these two publications, and they serve as records of the course that evangelical theological reflection was taking.

The first issues of *Misión* featured two works by Padilla acknowledging the importance of liberation theologies and considering the challenges they represent for evangelicals. Given the negative reactions among diverse sectors of evangelicals, often we have not done justice to liberation theologians or honestly sought to understand their proposals. Padilla states the intention of his own work of analysis and evaluation: "My

---

[49]Juan Luis Segundo, *De la sociedad a la teología* (Buenos Aires: Carlos Lohlé, 1970); Segundo, *Liberación de la teología* (Buenos Aires: Carlos Lohlé, 1975).

[50]Juan R. Stumme, "Juan Luis Segundo sobre el ser humano y Jesús: Comentario (Parte I)," *Cuadernos de Teología* 7, no. 3 (1986): 199.

question is not 'How do I respond to liberation theology in such a way as to demonstrate its faults and incongruencies?' Rather, it is 'How can I articulate my faith in the same context of poverty, repression, and injustice from which liberation theology has emerged?'"[51] With his starting point established, Padilla values these new theologies' emphasis on Christian praxis. He affirms, "Let us spend time considering what could be considered the distinctive mark of all liberation theologies, that is, an understanding of theology as a reflection on what *is done* more than on what *is believed*."[52]

As a Bible scholar Padilla looks positively on the presupposition that "the true knowledge of God is equated to the practice of his will." He quotes José Míguez Bonino, who sustains that two blocks of biblical material confirm this understanding: the Old Testament prophetic literature and the writings of John in the New Testament. For both, the knowledge of God is not abstract or theoretical but entails active obedience to real demands made by God: "We do not meet God in the abstract and later deduce from his essence some consequences. We know God in the synthetic act of responding to his demands."[53] From a perspective such as this, historical praxis always precedes theological reflection. Padilla adds a christological focus: "From the biblical perspective, the *logos* of God (the Word) has been made flesh (an historical person), and therefore the knowledge of this *logos* is not a mere knowledge of ideas but a commitment, communion, participation in a new way of life."[54]

At the same time, however, Padilla shows that to define what the praxis should be, liberation theologians resort to the social sciences, in particular to a Marxist analysis of society, which they consider to be scientific and therefore true. For them this analysis provides the way of solidarizing with the poor and oppressed in the present situation. Padilla

---

[51]C. René Padilla, "La teología de la liberación: Una evaluación crítica," *Misión* 1, no. 2 (July–September 1982): 17.

[52]C. René Padilla, "Una nueva manera de hacer teología," *Misión* 1, no. 1 (March–June 1982): 21.

[53]Padilla, "Una nueva manera de hacer teología," quoting José Míguez Bonino, *La fe en busca de eficacia* (Salamanca: Sígueme, 1977), 114ff.

[54]Padilla, "La teología de la liberación," 17.

summarizes Juan Luis Segundo's argument in this way, suggesting a hermeneutical circle and a new way of producing theology. In this system the telos of social sciences is the starting point and determines the praxis adopted. Later he presents a direct critique: "When liberation theology finds in Marxism the strategy with which the kingdom of God is built by men 'in history beginning now,' clearly it has become prisoner to a humanist illusion that is in agreement with neither human experience in history nor biblical revelation. We are left a sociological captivity of theology, a sociologism."[55]

This is the point at which Padilla presents his critical questions, because the emphasis on praxis leads to a type of pragmatism wherein the truth is reduced to "what works." And he warns, "If there is no possibility of evaluating praxis based on a guideline that is over and above it, the way is open to justify any praxis as long as it works, with the end justifying the means." Once again, his argument is christological: "The *logos* of God is an incarnated *logos*, but it also is a *logos* that has spoken, and his words (his *rhemata*) are Spirit and life. No one can understand Jesus' teaching unless they are willing to do God's will. . . . To do the truth is not the same as *elaborating* the truth through praxis; instead it is *practicing* the truth that has been revealed."[56]

> The alternative is not a theology isolated from the social reality, incapable of perceiving the hardships and suffering of the poor and oppressed. Rather, it is a theology in dialogue with the Scripture and the concrete historical situation concerned for the *manifestation* of the kingdom of God through specific signs that point toward the kingdom that has already come in Jesus Christ, and to the kingdom that is still to come.[57]

[55]Padilla, "La teología de la liberación," 20. The phrase in quotes is from Segundo.
[56]Padilla, "La teología de la liberación," 17, 18.
[57]Padilla, "La teología de la liberación," 20.

14

JESUS AND THE LIFESTYLE AND MISSION OF THE KINGDOM

The images of Jesus Christ imported from the West have on the whole been found wanting—too conditioned by Constantinian Christianity with all its ideological distortions and cultural accretions, and terribly inadequate as a basis for the life and mission of the church in situations of dire poverty and injustice. This has led to the search for a Christology which will have as its focus the historical Jesus and provide a basis for Christian action in contemporary society.

René Padilla, "Christology and Mission in the Two Thirds World," in *Sharing Jesus in the Two Thirds World*

As we have seen up to this point, due to the situation of Christianity in Ibero-America, both Catholics and Protestants considering their faith and examining their identity were obliged to begin a christological exploration. José Míguez Bonino describes the steps that the reflection had taken: first "identify the Christologies historically present in Latin America," and then "offer a psychosocial and theological interpretation

Much of this chapter is adapted from Samuel Escobar, "Evangelical Theology in Latin America: The Development of a Missiological Christology," *Missiology* 19, no. 3 (July 1991): 315-32.

of them."[1] It could be said that the path being followed was the one laid out by Mackay, summarized in chapter two.

In the case of evangelical theology, the distinctive mark of this search was its evangelizing intention, the sense of mission. This emphasis determined that evangelical theological production would be different from that emerging from churches that had abandoned a vital concern for evangelization and tended to focus instead on correction of abuses. Evangelical theology also differed from the Catholic focus in that the Roman Catholic Church in Latin America, because of its sacramental theology, took it as a given that the population was already Christian. With this presupposition, evangelization was understood more as a call to commitment and discipleship than as a call to conversion. What we find in authors such as Padilla, Costas, Núñez, and Steuernagel is that their theology always points in the direction of mission, with the evangelizing capacity and intention of churches as a specific governing presupposition and a prerequisite for theological speech.

Milestones in a Christological Search

The 1980s brought the publication of some books expressing the christological search that was developing in Ibero-America. Each has a different emphasis due to the special circumstances or vocation of its author, but they have a common framework: the conception of the kingdom of God taken up in the 1972 FTL consultation in Lima. Earliest among these was the book *Venga tu reino* (Your kingdom come) by Mortimer Arias, at that time Methodist bishop of Bolivia, who, as was seen in the previous chapter, had participated in the global theological dialogue in the ecumenical context and beyond. Arias begins his book announcing: "We live in one of those moments of sudden recovery of the 'subversive memory of Jesus' in our own Latin American Christianity, and the topic of the kingdom is gaining an unexpected vigor."[2]

---

[1]José Míguez Bonino et al., *Jesús: Ni vencido ni monarca celestial* (Buenos Aires: Tierra Nueva, 1977), 9-10.
[2]Mortimer Arias, *Venga tu reino: La memoria subversiva de Jesús* (Mexico City: CUPSA, 1980), 7.

Chapter six above, discussing some earlier christological reflections, pointed out that Jesus' humanity has always been difficult to wrestle with. Even those expressing their adherence to this central teaching from primitive Christianity have found it hard to interpret the sober and clear Gospel texts with their challenges to radical discipleship. Arias explores what he calls "the eclipse" of teaching about the kingdom and some of the reductionist approaches on the topic within different evangelical traditions. Later he presents his own reading of the biblical material, highlighting the "already" dimension of the kingdom and its future dimension, the nature of Christian discipleship in the light of the kingdom, and the illuminating hope of the kingdom in the face of Latin America's desperate condition. In this way the memory of Jesus, through its rediscovery, is transformed into a subversive memory.

In 1983 Argentinian educator Daniel Schipani, at that time a professor at the Seminario Evangélico de Puerto Rico, published *El reino de Dios y el ministerio educativo de la iglesia* (The kingdom of God and the educative ministry of the church), an effort to reformulate the foundations and principles of Christian education.[3] After exploring the educational foundations, in particular the ideas of development and creativity in the human sciences, in laying out his biblical-theological basis he takes as key "the gospel of the kingdom of God." As a Mennonite thinker, he favors the categories outlined by John Howard Yoder in his contribution to the 1972 FTL consultation, but he also draws on intuitions and proposals from liberation theologians such as Boff and Sobrino. Schipani calls for "taking ownership of the kingdom":

> The purpose of Christian education is to facilitate people's taking ownership of the gospel of the kingdom of God, responding to the call of conversion and discipleship as part of the community of Jesus Christ, which promotes social transformation to increase human liberty, to make the knowledge and love of God accessible, and to stimulate human fulfillment and personal development.[4]

---

[3]Daniel S. Schipani, *El reino de Dios y el ministerio educativo de la iglesia* (Miami: Editorial Caribe, 1983).
[4]Schipani, *El reino de Dios*, 18.

In defining the distinctives of this community of disciples, Schipani expounds Jesus' example and practice as well as the nature of the messianic community in light of the kingdom. One of the authors whose work he incorporates is Brazilian educator Paulo Freire, who influenced some liberation theologians and in whose thought Schipani had become a specialist.

In 1986 Orlando Costas published *Evangelización contextual: Fundamentos teológicos y pastorales* (Contextual evangelization: Theological and pastoral foundations), based on expositions that Costas had presented in the Strachan Chair at the Seminario Bíblico Latinoamericano in Costa Rica the year before.[5] At that time Costas was teaching at Eastern Baptist Theological Seminary (now called Palmer Theological Seminary) and worked closely with Hispanic communities across the United States. This was intended as the first volume of a trilogy laying out a theology of evangelization, but the other volumes were not completed due to his early death at age forty-five. It is a mature work in which Costas lays out a biblical and theological foundation for evangelization, understood in integral and holistic terms, that had been developing in Latin America. Chapter four focuses on Jesus as evangelist "from the periphery," considering Mark's Gospel in particular with its emphasis on the Galilean identity of Jesus and some of his best-known followers. Costas connects his reflection to the condition of the US Hispanic minority, who live on what can be called the periphery of North American society, and explores the meaning of Galilee in the work of Jesus.

The year 1986 also saw the publication of *Misión integral: Ensayos sobre el reino y la iglesia* (Holistic mission: Essays about the kingdom of God and the church), a key work by René Padilla, who in nine chapters outlines his missiological journey.[6] The first three chapters are adapted

[5]Orlando E. Costas, *Evangelización contextual: Fundamentos teológicos y pastorales* (San José, Costa Rica: SEBILA, 1986); English, *Liberating News: A Theology of Contextual Evangelization* (Grand Rapids: Eerdmans, 1989).

[6]C. René Padilla, *Misión integral: Ensayos sobre el reino y la iglesia* (Buenos Aires: Nueva Creación; Grand Rapids: Eerdmans, 1986). The latest English version is *Mission Between the Times: Essays on the Kingdom* (Carlisle, UK: Langham Monographs, 2010).

from his previous book *El evangelio hoy* (The gospel today). In some ways this work reviews a global theological development that had been taking place within the Lausanne movement. Each chapter was originally an exposition Padilla presented in the missiological consultations that followed the 1974 Lausanne Congress. For example, he had written "Spiritual Conflict" for a symposium by fifteen authors from different parts of the world, which he later compiled and edited as *The New Face of Evangelicalism*, an exposition of the Lausanne Covenant.[7] "La unidad de la iglesia y el principio de unidades homogéneas" (The unity of the church and the principle of homogeneous units) was his presentation in a consultation on the notion of homogeneous units for church growth (Pasadena, California, June 1977). "La contextualización del evangelio" (The contextualization of the gospel) was his presentation in the Gospel and Culture consultation (Willowbank, Barbados, 1978). "La misión de la iglesia a la luz del reino de Dios" (The mission of the church in the light of the kingdom of God) was his exposition in a consultation about the relationship between evangelization and social responsibility (Grand Rapids, June 1982).

Notably, an important part of each of these essays consists of exegesis and interpretation of key biblical passages, drawing insights from them on controversial missiological questions of the moment. With a vigorous and unflinching voice, Padilla reminds us that

> The God who has always spoken to men from within the historic situation has assigned the church as an instrument for the manifestation of Jesus Christ in the midst of all men. . . . However, for the church to reveal Jesus Christ in the blueprint of history, it must first experience the death of Christ with reference to human culture. . . . In practical terms this means that the totality of life (including models of thinking and conduct, values, habits and roles) should be submitted to the judgment of the Word of God, in a way that only what is worthy of Christ will endure and reach its fullness.[8]

---

[7]C. René Padilla, *The New Face of Evangelicalism: An International Symposium on the Lausanne Covenant* (Downers Grove, IL: InterVarsity Press, 1976).

[8]Padilla, *New Face of Evangelicalism*, 103-4.

In the era of transitions of all types that began around 1980, the search for a missiological Christology emerged in part due to the crisis of traditional models of mission that could not survive the end of colonialism, the emergence of new nations, the valorization of autochthonous cultures, and the consciousness of oppression. A group of FTL theologians participated in the consultation Teólogos Evangélicos de la Misión en el Mundo de los Dos Tercios (Evangelical Theologians in Mission in the Two-Thirds World). "Two-Thirds World" had become a way of referring to what had in previous decades been known as the Third World: Asia, Africa, Latin America, and ethnic minorities in Europe and North America. In its first gathering in Bangkok, Thailand (March 1982), the theme was Christology, by consensus of its organizers. At this event René Padilla included in his presentation the paragraph I have used as this chapter's epigraph:

> The images of Jesus Christ imported from the West have on the whole been found wanting—too conditioned by Constantinian Christianity with all its ideological distortions and cultural accretions, and terribly inadequate as a basis for the life and mission of the church in situations of dire poverty and injustice. This has led to the search for a Christology which will have as its focus the historical Jesus and provide a basis for Christian action in contemporary society.[9]

The term "historical Jesus" here does not reference the expression generally associated with twentieth-century liberal theology in which "historical" means "product of the historical-critical method."[10] Evangelicals in Latin America share, in general, a premise that Padilla considers to be fundamental for his Christology: "that the Gospels are essentially reliable historical records and that the portrait of Jesus that emerges from them provides an adequate basis for the life and mission of the church today."[11]

---

[9]C. René Padilla, "Christology and Mission in the Two Thirds World," in *Sharing Jesus in the Two Thirds World: Evangelical Christologies from the Contexts of Poverty, Powerlessness and Religious Pluralism: The Papers of the First Conference of Evangelical Mission Theologians from the Two Thirds World, Bangkok, Thailand, March 22-25, 1982*, ed. Vinay Samuel and Chris Sugden (Grand Rapids: Eerdmans, 1984), 13.

[10]Walter A. Elwell, ed., *Evangelical Dictionary of Theology* (Grand Rapids: Baker, 1984), 584.

[11]C. René Padilla and Mark Lau Branson, eds., *Conflict and Context: Hermeneutics in the Americas* (Grand Rapids: Eerdmans, 1986), 83.

The Latin American context forced the suggestion of a rediscovery of Jesus' concrete actions just as they were recorded by the Evangelists, captured, contemplated, and understood as the model that could give form to contemporary discipleship. This theological task goes well beyond the systematization offered by the creeds, in which "the Christian message was cast into philosophical categories, and historical dimension of revelation was completely overshadowed by dogma."[12] To the degree that the missionary movement and the teaching of churches limit themselves to transmitting Christology as a propositional truth defined in the Nicene or Chalcedonian formula, they transmit images of Christ that could be "useful for personal piety or civil religion, but . . . neither faithful to the witness of Scripture concerning Jesus Christ nor historically relevant."[13]

The creedal formulations that define the humanity and the deity of Jesus became obstacles that did not capture the dimensions of Jesus' humanity that were very important for modeling life and mission today. Remember that in his study of liberation theologies, Emilio Antonio Núñez recognized that "this new focus on the humanity of Christ is a reaction to the lack of balance in a Christology that magnifies the deity of the incarnated Word at the expense of his humanity."[14] In this sense some Latin American evangelicals had inherited an Anglo-Saxon Christology arising from the North American debates between fundamentalism and modernism. The biblical clarification that Latin American theologians have taken on does not discard traditional creeds as invalid or useless, but they are treated as what they really are, forms of Christian tradition that should always be open to confrontation with Scripture.[15] The confrontation of the creeds with Scripture, both understood within their own historical context, helps us to appreciate the validity of the

---

[12]Padilla and Branson, *Conflict and Context*, 83.
[13]Padilla and Branson, *Conflict and Context*, 83.
[14]Emilio A. Núñez, *Teología de la liberación*, 2nd ed. (Miami: Caribe, 1987), 221.
[15]Regarding this point, there is a fascinating debate about Padilla's proposal in the 1984 consultation Hermenéutica en las Américas: Conflicto y Contexto (Hermeneutics in the Americas: Conflict and context). See Padilla and Branson, *Conflict and Context*, 92-113.

creeds and at the same time to recover depths of meaning in Scripture that could have remained in the shadows due to the historical relativity of creedal definitions.[16]

Three Key Questions

When we examine Scripture with a fresh perspective, one of the first questions that arises is "Who then was Jesus of Nazareth?" Padilla joins together material from the Gospels to form an image of Jesus and his work that "could not but puzzle people in general, provoke suspicion in many and infuriate those who held positions of privilege in the religious-political establishment."[17] The image obtained is eloquent and challenging: Jesus spoke with authority despite his lack of theological study, he affirmed that he had a relationship with God of a unique and singular nature, he was the friend of tax collectors and sinners, he affirmed that the kingdom of God had been made present in history and was demonstrated in the healing of the sick. He concentrated his ministry on ignorant, poorly educated people and people of ill repute; he attacked religious oppression and rejected empty religious ceremonies; he condemned wealth and called ambition idolatry; he defined power in terms of sacrificial service and affirmed nonviolent resistance, then called his followers to social nonconformity following his own example. For Padilla the consequence is clear: "If the Christ of faith is the Jesus of history, then it is possible to speak of a social ethic for Christian disciples who seek to fashion their lives in God's purpose of love and justice concretely revealed. If the risen and exalted Lord is Jesus of Nazareth, then it is possible to speak of a community that seeks to manifest the kingdom of God in history."[18]

A second important group of questions has to do with the way in which Jesus fulfilled his mission. Again, biblical exposition within the

---

[16]A more recent exploration of this topic can be seen in Justo L. González, *Teología liberadora: Enfoque desde la opresión en tierra extraña* (Buenos Aires: Kairós, 2006).

[17]Padilla and Branson, *Conflict and Context*, 87.

[18]Padilla and Branson, *Conflict and Context*, 89.

framework of missiological reflection was Padilla's approach to exploring the marks of Jesus' ministry. His basic presupposition is that "to be a disciple of Jesus Christ is to be called by him both to know him and to participate in his mission. He himself is God's missionary par excellence, and he involves his followers in his mission."[19] "I will make you fishers of men," Jesus said to his disciples. Jesus' mission involves "fishing for the kingdom"—in other words, when we proclaim the kingdom we always call for repentance and conversion to Jesus Christ as the way, the truth, and the life. This conversion to him continues to be the foundation for the formation of Christian community.

Christ's mission also involves *compassion*, resulting from an immersion among the multitudes. This does not mean a sentimental explosion of emotions, nor an academic option for the poor, but rather specific intentional acts of service with the aim of "feeding the multitudes" with *bread for life* and also with *the Bread of Life*. The mission includes *confrontation* of the powers of death with the power of the Suffering Servant, and thus *suffering* becomes the mark of Jesus' messianic mission, a fruit of battling injustice and the powers and principalities. Through a creatively contextual obedience, Jesus' mission not only becomes a fertile source of inspiration but also has the seeds for new missionary models that today are explored through practice and reflection. They are models characterized by a simple lifestyle, holistic mission, a quest for unity for the sake of mission, the kingdom of God as a missiological paradigm, and spiritual conflict that presupposes mission.

A third area of research is centered around the question "What is the gospel?" The most enthusiastic calls to missionary activism emerge from certain sectors of the evangelical world for whom this question appears irrelevant. Referring to one of these sectors, the "church growth" missiological school, Yoder said, "It is assumed that we have an adequate theology which we have received from the past. . . . But we do not really

[19]René Padilla, "Bible Studies," *Missiology* 10, no. 3 (1982): 319-38. This is a series of biblical expositions that Padilla was invited to present in the annual meeting of the American Society of Missiology.

need any *more* theological clarification. What we need now is efficiency."[20] Padilla believes that as a result of this assumption among many evangelicals, "the effectiveness of evangelization is measured in terms of [numerical] results, without any reference (or very little reference) to faithfulness to the gospel."[21] This concern is not limited to Latin America. Missiologists exploring what it means to evangelize and to be a missionary in North America also consider this a basic question. George Hunsberger says the following:

> The central question of theology—What is the Gospel?—must be asked in more culturally particular ways. And the more particular the question, the more will be our sense that the answer will emerge in unexpected ways. It will come more out of Christian communities that increasingly learn the habit of "indwelling" the gospel story so deeply that it shapes their life of common discipleship.[22]

What the gospel *is*, the *what* of the gospel, determines *how* the new life resulting from the impact of the gospel is lived. For this reason questions about the content of the gospel are so important. Understanding the richness of the gospel's meaning in biblical revelation and the demands of obedience to faith allows us to avoid proclaiming a message that is actually "culture Christianity," as are many forms exported from the United States, especially through mass communication. Padilla underlines the eschatological and soteriological dimensions of the Christian message centered on the person of Jesus Christ. He is the center of the message found in the Old and New Testaments, which are complementary in the process of promise and fulfillment.[23] Padilla had worked on a clear presentation of the gospel based in his core Christology, from which he extracts the conclusion that "the apostolic

---

[20]John H. Yoder, "Church Growth Issues in Theological Perspective," in *The Challenge of Church Growth*, ed. Wilbert Shenk (Elkhart, IN: Institute of Mennonite Studies, 1973), 27.

[21]Padilla, *Misión integral*, 60.

[22]George R. Hunsberger, "The Newbigin Gauntlet: Developing a Domestic Missiology for North America," *Missiology* 19, no. 4 (1991): 406.

[23]Mexican biblical scholar Edesio Sánchez Cetina united various works on the way the Old and New Testaments are related in the exegetical task in *Fe bíblica: Antiguo Testamento y América Latina* (Mexico City: Publicaciones El Faro, 1986).

mission is derived from Jesus Christ. He is the content, the model, and the goal of gospel proclamation."[24] For this reason Christian preaching must be molded by the Word of God and not simply grasp at relevance: "Preachers for whom relevance is the most basic consideration in preaching are frequently mistaken—they fail to see the link between relevance in preaching and faithfulness to the gospel. There is nothing more irrelevant than a message that simply mirrors man's myths and ideologies!"[25]

A Critical Missiology Beginning with Christology

The consequence of deepening the content of the gospel is critical in two directions. First is to reject the unilateral emphasis on the humanity of Jesus that reduces Christian action to mere human effort. It is necessary to critique the Christology of some liberation theologians, such as Jon Sobrino, who seem to not take the whole gospel seriously: "It is no mere coincidence that Sobrino should see the Kingdom of God as a utopia to be fashioned by men rather than as a gift to be received by faith."[26] Equally unacceptable are the liberationist Christologies that focus on the political dimension of Jesus' death at the expense of its soteriological meaning. Padilla, for example, accepts the truth that Jesus' death was a historical consequence of the type of life he lived, and he does so because of this truth's rootedness in the text of the Gospels. Jesus suffered for the cause of justice, and he calls us to follow his example. However, this theologian finds it necessary to issue a warning: "Unless the death of Christ is also seen as God's gracious provision of an atonement for sin, the basis for forgiveness is removed and sinners are left without hope of justification. . . . Salvation is by grace though faith. . . . Nothing should detract from the generosity of God's mercy and love as the basis of joyful obedience to the Lord Jesus Christ."[27]

[24]Padilla, *Misión integral*, 72.
[25]C. René Padilla, "God's Word and Man's Myths," *Themelios* 3, no. 1 (1977): 3.
[26]Padilla, "Christology and Mission in the Two Thirds World," 28.
[27]Padilla, "Christology and Mission in the Two Thirds World," 28.

Second, Padilla critiques the managerial forms of missiology within the evangelical world because these, with their focus on methodology, give insufficient weight to questions relating to the content of the gospel.[28] Other evangelical critiques have pointed out the biblical and theological deficiencies of theories such as "church growth" that are based on "a narrowed-down version of the evangelical hermeneutic and theology."[29] From a christological perspective Padilla questions the rigidity of the structural-functional framework of cultural anthropology used by church growth. The principle of homogeneous groups in this form of managerial missiology shortcuts the message of unity in Christ that is central to the gospel and to the biblical vision of the church. Thus it can be said of church growth that "it has become a missiology customized to churches and institutions whose main function in society is to support the status quo."[30]

Part of the error of this theology is having remained with an extremely individualistic version of salvation that is limited to reconciliation with God, without deepening to the recovery of true humanity to which this reconciliation leads in the fullness of the divine purpose. Here we are at the crux of Pauline Christology in Ephesians and Colossians. The holistic gospel allows us to understand the richness of New Testament teaching regarding the nature of being human that comes precisely within a missiological framework. Christology is key for anthropology because to begin with, as Sidney Rooy points out, "The human relationship with God is defined in Christian anthropology by the relationship of each individual with Jesus Christ."[31] This is why it is important to have safeguards against the hermeneutical traps into which "church growth" falls, as its method seems to be an effort to locate within the biblical text the values of North American social sciences. Rooy explains this point further:

[28]I have described the management current of missiology and other alternatives in my book *Tiempo de misión* (Guatemala: Semilla,1999), 28-31. See also my article "Managerial Missiology," in *Dictionary of Mission Theology: Evangelical Foundations*, ed. John Corrie (Downers Grove, IL: IVP Academic, 2007).

[29]Charles Taber, in *Exploring Church Growth*, ed. Wilbert Shenk (Grand Rapids: Eerdmans, 1983), 119. This work by various missiologists is a critical description founded on the theory of church growth.

[30]Padilla, *Misión integral*, 162.

[31]Sidney H. Rooy, "Una teología de lo humano," *Boletín Teológico*, no. 54 (June 1994): 141.

> The historic meaning of the incarnation extends into the future and back into the past. The life, death, and resurrection of Christ mark a critical point in human history. We can call it "the mountain pass" through which the course of creation must go. The same path both extends far back from the top until it arrives at the beginnings of creation and continues meandering forward until it arrives at humanity's destiny. . . . The basic affirmations [of the Old Testament] remain valid regarding human identity as the only being created in God's image and responsible for the care and development of the natural world. These affirmations are reconstructed and renewed in the reconciling work of Christ, the new person.[32]

Church growth proposed that churches be "homogeneous units" according to race and social class because, as the theory's creator, Donald McGavran, said, "people like to become Christians without crossing racial, linguistic or class barriers."[33] In questioning this proposal, Rooy and Padilla have insisted on the community dimensions of New Testament teaching regarding the new self, the new human being. Beginning with the epistle to the Ephesians, they develop an ecclesiology derived from the work of Jesus Christ, because the new humanity is humanity *in Jesus Christ*: "The only new people here are evidently the new humanity, the church made up of what previously was two, that is, Jews and Gentiles."[34] Carrying out a cautious exegesis, Padilla demonstrates that the apostle's missionary practice involved forming churches to be living expressions of this new humanity in Christ.[35] The "new thing" that Paul announces is integrally connected with his own missionary work as a Jew who undertook mission among the Gentiles. And precisely what he was doing was founding churches, communities of a new people that must express this newness brought by the gospel, although it occasioned many pastoral problems, addressed in the epistles, as Jews and Gentiles began to coexist. Padilla concludes: "It's impossible to exaggerate the impact that the primitive church produced among non-Christians due to the Christian fraternity that overcame natural barriers."[36]

---

[32]Rooy, "Una teología de lo humano," 142.

[33]Quoted in Padilla, *Misión integral*, 136.

[34]Rooy, "Una teología de lo humano," 142. There is an indirect quote of Eph 2:15.

[35]The chapter "La unidad de la iglesia," in *Misión integral*, had been originally presented in a consultation on homogeneous units at Fuller Seminary, Pasadena, California (1977).

[36]Padilla, *Misión integral*, 158.

The Ethics of José Míguez Bonino

Possibly the Latin American theologian who has most consistently explored and displayed the ethics of the kingdom of God is José Míguez Bonino. In 1972 he published *Ama y haz lo que quieras: Una ética para el hombre nuevo* (Love and do as you please: An ethic for the new man), a book conceived as an introduction to ethics, a subject he had taught for years at Instituto Superior Evangélico de Estudios Teológicos (ISEDET), one of the four ecumenical seminaries in Latin America.[37] The utopian movement in Latin American culture at this time had brought into public discourse "the new man," a phrase that Che Guevara had used in one of his popular writings. Some evangelicals tried to use the expression to present the gospel. In a program together with the United Bible Society, evangelical university groups distributed half a million copies of the booklet *Jesús: Modelo del hombre nuevo* (Jesus: Model of the new man), a selection of texts from the Gospels, and it was very well received on campuses. It presented the texts without commentary, ordered chronologically, following a biographical sequence illustrated with contemporary photos from Latin America. Hundreds of students throughout the continent also began study courses based on this book. At the end of the decade, pastor and psychologist Jorge A. León, resident in Argentina, published an introduction to the Christian faith in dialogue with psychology and contemporary sociology with the title *¿Es posible el hombre nuevo?* (Is a new man possible?).[38]

Míguez Bonino's ethics is openly Christocentric and replete with the figures and themes of the history of salvation. He is convinced that "the ethical contribution of the gospel in face of the moral crisis—that of the first century and of ours—does not consist primarily or fundamentally of new principles, institutions or laws, but in *a new man*. What Jesus Christ brings into this world is a new humanity, a new way of being man."[39] What we find in the New Testament are some paradigms, through which we are told: "This is love—now go and live it out."

[37]José Míguez Bonino, *Ama y haz lo que quieras: Una ética para el hombre nuevo* (Buenos Aires: América, 2000), 1970.
[38]Jorge A. León, *¿Es posible el hombre nuevo?* (Buenos Aires: Certeza, 1979).
[39]Míguez Bonino, *Ama y haz lo que quieras*, 26.

> The first and fundamental paradigm is Jesus Christ himself. In him love itself—the creating and redeeming love of God—was made a concrete and visible reality. To walk in love and to follow Jesus Christ are therefore the same thing. The Gospel and John's Epistles highlight this with particular emphasis. Jesus washes the disciples' feet, then explains: "I have given you an example so that you might do the same as I have done for you." The Lord made himself a servant with the purpose of cleansing and purifying the life of men.[40]

The same Christ-centered vision characterizes another book in which Míguez Bonino tried to explain for both believers and nonbelievers the meaning of the Christian faith: *Espacio para ser hombres* (Space to be men). It is an effort to articulate an anthropology that explains what biblical revelation says regarding human beings, particularly in relation to Jesus Christ. Míguez Bonino says that human beings encounter Jesus Christ via one of two paths, challenge or comfort:

> Those who accept Jesus' challenge, however, will soon discover that he himself will press much deeper that what was initially expected. The call to change the world is immediately turned back onto those who heed it: "You who desire to transform the world, are you transformed? . . . Are you really pursuing the kingdom of God, serving your neighbor, or are you searching only for a new means of satisfaction and self-promotion?"[41]

Míguez's political ethics is summarized masterfully in a book that sadly is not available in Spanish, *Toward a Christian Political Ethics*; it is based on presentations given in various theological seminaries in the United States.[42] It is a mature work that systematically addresses some of the answers that emerged as Latin American churches had to take positions within a context full of conflict and tensions.[43]

---

[40]Míguez Bonino, *Ama y haz lo que quieras*, 63.

[41]José Míguez Bonino, *Espacio para ser hombres* (Buenos Aires: Tierra Nueva, 1975), 77-78.

[42]José Míguez Bonino, *Toward a Christian Political Ethics* (Philadelphia: Fortress, 1983).

[43]Among the many works that study the thought of Míguez, the most recent and complete is Paul J. Davies, "Faith Seeking Effectiveness: The Missionary Theology of José Míguez Bonino" (PhD diss., University of Utrecht, 2006).

The Kingdom of God and Ethical Dilemmas

In the heart of the FTL and likeminded movements, the ferment of previous decades led some to participate in political activity and others to undertake service-oriented actions and projects, nurtured by a desire for holistic mission, following Jesus' example. Two continental consultations became landmarks in this reflection process, and the resulting books are indications of the focus and themes. The growing participation of Latin Americans in political arenas of their countries brought a new agenda to theological reflection regarding the kingdom of God. In May 1983 a consultation was organized about "theology and practice of power" in Jarabacoa, Dominican Republic.[44] This theme was given its focus in a presentation by René Padilla, "El estado desde una perspectiva bíblica" (The state from a biblical perspective), followed by expositions on models of the church-state relationship in the Calvinist and Baptist traditions by Sidney Rooy and Pablo Deiros, respectively. My own presentation was "El poder y las ideologías en América Latina" (Power and ideologies in Latin America), and it was followed by four case studies of the "structure of power" in Brazil, the Dominican Republic, Nicaragua, and Venezuela. The ideological currents in Latin America were presented by Pablo Deiros, and finally three models of political action with an evangelical presence: Venezuela, Argentina, and Nicaragua.

The participants in the consultation formulated the Jarabacoa Declaration, which summarized on the one hand the exercise of deepening the biblical sources, and on the other hand the variety of experiences of Christian practice that were present. This document had strong pastoral influence in some critical situations that arose in Nicaragua, Peru, and Brazil in the following years. Justice was categorized in the declaration among the principles for political action, alongside the value of the person, truth, and liberty:

> Under a well-functioning rule of law, justice is the application of the law with the goal that all persons enjoy their rights and fulfill the their social

---

[44]Pablo Alberto Deiros, *Los evangélicos y el poder político en América Latina* (Buenos Aires: Nueva Creación; Grand Rapids: Eerdmans, 1986).

> duties. For this goal to be reached, the administration of justice must be impartial, equitable, accessible, independent, rapid and effective. Justice will be present when all human beings find in the judicial order a resource of protection from abuse and a defense against any violation of their rights. A just political action is one that seeks justice for everyone, especially the poor and marginalized of society.[45]

Note that both in Padilla's biblical survey and in the declaration, which incorporates convictions originating in the practice of evangelicals, there is a notion that is functionally parallel or equivalent to the "preferential option for the poor." In all societies and systems there are beneficiaries and victims; God's justice pays special attention to those who are victims and prophetically confronts those who exploit them.

The time of reflection and teaching in which the Latin American contribution to the Lausanne Covenant had been shaped prior to 1974, and later the reverberations of the covenant itself in the following years, led to the creation of numerous projects of holistic mission, efforts to serve basic human needs. There was a growing conviction that Christian compassion should not be limited to tending the victims of unjust systems but also had to include efforts to transform society. In December 1987, ninety people from seventeen countries gathered for the consultation Hacia una Transformación Integral (Toward Holistic Transformation), organized by the FTL. More than thirty social service organizations were represented. A summary of the biblical-theological reflection, the report, and the deliberations were compiled by Ecuadorian theologian Washington Padilla and given the same title, *Hacia una transformación integral*. One chapter summarizes the biblical-theological bases of the concept and path followed, and again a christological focus is predominant. "Our action of service and love is not based on any humanist theory or desire to be 'in fashion,' but on the beautiful example of our Lord."[46] Padilla reviews the distinctive stages of Jesus' mission: incarnation, ministry, death, and resurrection.

---

[45]Deiros, *Los evangélicos y el poder político*, 350.

[46]Washington Padilla, *Hacia una transformación integral* (Buenos Aires: FTL, 1989), 12. The author clarifies that this is not an official report from the event but his own personal summary, but the editors thought that it transmitted well the spirit of the event and summarizes the materials utilized.

The consequence of taking Jesus' incarnation seriously is that "we are called to enter into the situation of our people, to accompany them in their pressing needs, in their frustrations, in their problems, in their hopes. It is not possible to fulfill the mission Jesus entrusted to his church if we remain distant from the real life of our people." After Jesus' ministry of proclamation is considered, we are reminded that the good news of the kingdom of God was directed especially to "the poor" (Lk 4:18-19; Mt 11:4-6). "The gospel, then, is the message of God's free forgiveness to bad people, those who are not worthy, those who know that they do not deserve to be received by God, but who accept his kingdom of justice, peace, and joy with the simplicity and naivete of a small child."[47] Then Jesus' passion and death point to the cost of following the Teacher:

> Jesus' call to his church is to serve sacrificially, and this many times means literally "lay[ing] down our lives for our brothers and sisters" (1 Jn 3:16). There are many Christians in recent years who have suffered in serving their brothers and sisters. It is enough to remember two: Martin Luther King, assassinated in 1968 for his nonviolent struggle in favor of the black population in the United States, and Bishop Oscar Romero, assassinated in El Salvador in 1980 for his work in service to the poor of his country. Neither of the two sought a violent revolution; but they were faithful imitators of Christ, as they opposed injustice and exploitation of the poor in their respective societies, and ended up giving their lives in favor of the weak and needy. To follow Christ in the way of service leads to Calvary; but this is the only way to find true life. Beyond the cross is resurrection life.[48]

The consultation assembled a list of the characteristics of a just society: the goals toward which evangelicals' transforming action should work. Padilla's notes reflect theological contributions and also the input of the experiences and use of social sciences. Various theories of social development are critically examined, with a view toward their significance for the work of the church:

---

[47]Padilla, *Hacia una transformación integral*, 12, 13.
[48]Padilla, *Hacia una transformación integral*, 17.

> Now then, in discussing holistic transformation in relation to the diverse theories of development, we do not want to say that this is a *better theory* than these others. Instead we want to highlight the unique contribution that the church of Jesus Christ can make toward changing the conditions of life for the great majority of our continent's inhabitants. It is not about another "development model" but rather about the indispensable conditions that any model of development and any effort for change should fulfill to be true from the Christian perspective.[49]

The Kingdom of God and Social Ethics

To commemorate the first twenty years of the FTL, the consultation Teología y Vida en Latinoamérica (Theology and Life in Latin America) was organized as a celebration in Quito, Ecuador (December 4-12, 1990), and the reflection was based on four central themes: "Violence and nonviolence," "Poverty and stewardship," "Oppression and justice," and "Authoritarianism and power." It was obvious that the rediscovery of Jesus' humanity and the centrality of the kingdom of God in his teaching had led to a theological agenda with crucial ethical questions for those who considered themselves disciples of Jesus, and for their churches, in the agitated Latin American context. Teología y Vida had been preceded by regional consultations on themes relevant to the country and region where each one took place. Numbers 37 to 40 of the *Boletín Teológico*, published throughout 1990, testify to theological production that reflects not only the academic interest of pastors, theological educators, and professionals who participated in the consultations, but also their participation in the political life of their countries and the creation of holistic service projects responding to human needs.

Thus Latin American evangelical theology throughout the 1980s was enriched with reflection on social and political practices among a growing number of evangelicals and their churches. Each consultation featured a description of the context, a fresh exploration of the biblical teaching, and a declaration outlining the direction of obedience to the

---

[49]Padilla, *Hacia una transformación integral*, 33.

biblical imperative. In the following paragraphs I will highlight just a few points from the consultations that are related to our christological theme. The cycle opens in number 37 of the *Boletín Teológico* with a work by Mexican economist Jesús Camargo about economic dependence in Latin America, and another by Ecuadorian economist Franklin Canelos about international financial institutions and the right to development. Later comes a creative and rigorous biblical exploration of the significance of repentance: "Metanoia y misión" (Metanoia and mission), by Venezuelan biblical scholar Aquiles Ernesto Martínez. Martínez begins by identifying the shades of meaning that the terms *repentance* and *conversion* have acquired in evangelical discourse and practice, such as "magical transformation of being" and "a mystical or spiritual change affecting just one's personal relationship with God," which are quite distant from John the Baptist's and Jesus' uses of these words.

Martínez reminds us that "the calling to *metanoia* was an essential part of the proclamation of the good news in the missional journey of Jesus and the primitive church as is recorded in the pages of the New Testament (Mt 4:17; Lk 15:7, 24; Acts 2:38; 5:31)."[50] He pays special attention to the content of the term in the preaching of John the Baptist and concludes that

> from a linguistic perspective, in the ministry of John the Baptist *metanoia* means "*change of ethical behavior or moral conduct*." In the narratives found in the Synoptics that discuss the work of this prophet (Mt 3:1-12; Mk 1:1-8; Lk 3:1-20) *metanoia* appears as a type of ethical-religious experience that human beings are called to through the proclamation of the kingdom of God.[51]

In the prophetic biblical teaching from which John the Baptist's and Jesus' preaching emerged, *conversion* and *repentance* imply a change in attitude in two dimensions: vertically, from the person toward God, and horizontally, from the person toward their neighbor. For Martínez, we face a challenge:

---

[50]Aquiles Ernesto Martínez, "Metanoia y misión," *Boletín Teológico*, no. 37 (March 1990): 59.
[51]Martínez, "Metanoia y misión," 62.

> As a community of faith we urgently need to establish an equilibrium in our praxis of proclamation of the gospel, taking up the horizontal or social dimension of *metanoia*. . . . As evangelicals we should recover, orchestrate, and spread the concept of *metanoia* as a "conversion toward the marginalized," that is to say, as a change of attitude and behavior toward the poor that translates into their social well-being, and not leave the liberationists with all the weight of reflection and responsibility.[52]

The consultation that took place in Buenos Aires in April 1980 touched on a controversial theme in the Southern Cone region: totalitarianism. Experience of military governments in Argentina, Chile, and Brazil had left societies profoundly affected. It was necessary to try to understand this phenomenon theologically. Chilean sociologist and lawyer Humberto Lagos presented an exposition titled "Los cristianos frente al totalitarismo politico" (Christians facing political totalitarianism) and began by affirming:

> We have been witnesses and contributing subjects in the historic structural changes that have shaken Chile, in which we have shown it is possible to politically break a totalitarian regime using means that are compatible with the life and dignity of the people, and that don't retake the sinister path of violence. There are many of us evangelical Christians who chose, with a persistent ethical stance, to confront General Pinochet and his henchmen, inspired by Jesus' negation of "divinity" to Caesar, and in the certainty that the perverse arguments of death wielded by a deified power do not correspond to the authority "loved by God."[53]

For Lagos, on the occasion of Jesus' famous saying regarding giving to God what is God's and to Caesar what is Caesar's, Jesus the Christ rises against the proposal of a deified political power: "Jesus' questioning of Caesar is the challenge Christianity sets before all human power that is deified, and particularly political power." Here Jesus denies "the absolute claim for himself for the temporality of the human because 'we must obey God rather than men.'"[54]

---

[52]Martínez, "Metanoia y misión," 67.

[53]Humberto Lagos, "Los cristianos frente al totalitarismo político," *Boletín Teológico*, no. 38 (June 1990): 81.

[54]Lagos, "Los cristianos frente al totalitarismo político," 94.

The Final Document of this consultation summarized the different sociological, philosophical, and theological contributions made and offered theological positions and pastoral suggestions. It affirms: "The Christian message is related to the totality of human existence, as it presents an omniscient God, omnipresent and all-powerful, and Jesus Christ as the Lord of the universe." But a clarification immediately follows: "However, God is not totalitarian, for this Lord is the Suffering Servant. His lordship is service; he is the crucified King. The omnipotent God is the God of love."[55] The following appeared among the final recommendations: "To proclaim Jesus Christ as Lord of the world and of history. This proclamation puts into evidence the futility of any intent to claim an absolute character for any sphere of reality. On the other hand, it highlights the necessity of holistic discipleship that understands Christian liberty in terms of obedience to Jesus Christ in all areas of life."[56]

In August 1980 the FTL organized a theological consultation in Santiago de Chile, dedicated to the theme "Los cristianos frente a la dependencia económica y la deuda externa en América Latina" (Christians facing economic dependence and external debt in Latin America). Chilean economist Renato Espoz presented the central exposition with a strong tone to denounce the historic situation of colonialism that underlies crushing external debt in Latin American countries. He pointed out the lack of ethical basis in the economic policies of creditor countries, and the necessity of an impartial tribunal that could mediate in the conflicts that economic relationships produce. The presentation was later analyzed and evaluated from a theological and pastoral perspective. The Final Declaration reflects the conviction that "conditions for commerce and international trade do not permit Third-World nations to satisfy the basic necessities of their populations nor develop their lives with the minimum liberty to support the dignity of the person."[57]

---

[55]Documento Final, *Boletín Teológico*, no. 38 (June 1990): 129.

[56]Documento Final, 130.

[57]"Los cristianos frente a la dependencia económica y la deuda externa: Documento final," *Boletín Teológico*, no. 39 (September 1990): 245.

In September 1980, in a Peru afflicted with the guerrilla violence of Shining Path and military and political repression that took many innocent victims, the FTL organized a theological consultation called Christians Facing Violence. Reports were presented about "the culture of death" in Colombia and violence and human rights in Chile, Ecuador, and Peru. Two biblical expositions guided the reflection: Estuardo McIntosh focused on violence in the Old Testament, and René Padilla explored violence in the New Testament. Padilla's work examined institutionalized violence, revolutionary violence, the path of Jesus, and the dilemma of Christians facing violence. He concluded by suggesting what the ethics of Jesus might mean for the messianic community:

> The church is called to be a nonviolent alternative in the midst of a violent society. It is the hermenuetics of the gospel of peace. It is the community of the kingdom of "shalom." "A heroic individual might gain our admiration, but only a human community dedicated to practicing and proclaiming a system of radically different values can change the world." This ethic is for everyone, but presupposes conversion to Jesus Christ. It cannot be expected of those who do not recognize Jesus as their Messiah and Lord. For the disciples, however, it is not optional: it is the only possible ethics.[58]

The FTL also organized two regional consultations on poverty, held in Brazil in May and September 1980. Poverty in the urban context was the topic presented by Raquel Prance, while Marcos Adoniram Monteiro focused on missiological and pastoral care in response to poverty. The biblical presentations were "Pobreza, shalom y reino de Dios" (Poverty, shalom, and the kingdom of God), by Marcos Feitosa, and "La materialidad del discipulado bíblico" (The materiality of biblical discipleship), by Paul Freston. Feitosa's exposition culminated in a christological moment:

> And if Jesus of Nazareth is the Anointed One of God, then the promised new age has been inaugurated and the kingdom has been made present: the poor of this world, the oppressed, those who are nothing, can be joyful

[58]René Padilla, "La violencia en el Nuevo Testamento," *Boletín Teológico*, no. 39 (September 1990): 207. The quoted sentence is from Juan Driver, "La misión no violenta de Jesús y la nuestra," *Misión*, no. 21 (1987): 15.

> because shalom is now possible. Justice, harmony, reconciliation, love, true worship of God, liberty, fullness of life in every sense, are now not just an intellectual exercise, a dream, or a utopia. Immanuel made this dream possible; the yeast is leavening the dough, and now it is a question of time until the kingdom is fully established.[59]

Freston's sociological and theological presentation dealt carefully with the biblical material and was at the same time courageous and creative in its application to Brazilian realities. By 1990 Brazil already had a significant number of politicians coming from evangelical churches, from both historical Protestant churches and Pentecostal churches, including charismatic megachurches that had emerged from the 1960s onwards. Freston, who had undertaken extensive sociological studies on evangelical politicians, pointed out that in their political practice Brazilian evangelicals, lacking informed biblical criteria, had easily fallen "into the clutches of public projects for popularity, favors for candidates, and 'physiologism' (negotiating certain parliamentary votes in exchange for benefits for themselves and their churches)."[60] Freston taught from two passages in James (James 1:9-11; 5:1-11) and three from Luke (Lk 12:13-34; 16:1-31; 18:18-30), all of them very challenging, indeed radical, regarding wealth and possessions, and all pointing toward a "materiality" of discipleship that Jesus expects from his followers.

Commenting on Jesus' saying "Where your treasure is, there your heart will be also" (Lk 12:34), Freston reminds us that "The heart, the vital center of decisions, lies under our possessions, and also the (visible) localization of our possessions reflects the (invisible) localization of our heart. There is a dialectical relationship here, but it does not allow us to escape the 'materialism' of Christ." He draws out a radical conclusion: "Hence the absurdity of the saying that the last part of a man to be converted is his wallet. If the wallet is not converted, there was no conversion! If my treasure is the work of the kingdom of God (or God's

[59]Marcos Feitosa, "Pobreza, shalom y reino de Dios: Una perspectiva bíblico-teológica," *Boletín Teológico*, no. 40 (December 1990): 298.

[60]Paul Freston, "La materialidad del discipulado bíblico: Las posesiones en Santiago y Lucas," *Boletín Teológico*, no. 40 (December 1990): 316.

projects in the history of the world), my intimate decisions will be there too." Freston argues that evangelicals, who are often from the middle class, tend not to take seriously Jesus' teachings to the rich and the poor. As we do not consider ourselves one or the other, we assume we are not being spoken to. He reminds us that "for responsible members of (relatively) democratic societies, it is necessary that this change of values [brought by conversion] also translates into a change in political behavior, with a view to bringing society closer to God's original plan for possessions."[61]

◆ ◆ ◆

Thus when celebrating the first twenty years of the FTL in the consultation Teología y Vida in Latin America, participants considered the organization's history in light of a comprehensive understanding of the person and teaching of Jesus and what they mean for his disciples today. But this celebratory consultation was not limited to a review of the previous two decades; it also acknowledged the gaps that still existed in the process of theological practice and production. René Padilla remembers: "In effect, one the principal objectives of the gathering in Quito was to define the theological agenda for the remaining years of the twentieth century, with the hope of filling these empty spaces. It is to be hoped that the new generation, who were widely represented in the gathering, take up the cause with dedication and enthusiasm."[62]

---

[61]Freston, "La materialidad del discipulado bíblico," 314, 319.

[62]René Padilla, "Presentación," *Boletín Teológico*, nos. 42-43 (September 1991): 77, dedicated to the consultation Teología y Vida.

15

WITH JESUS IN GLOBAL MISSION

Those who are familiar with Jesus' teachings know that the missionary mandate is prominent among them—that is to say, Jesus hoped that his message, his words, and the witness of his life, passion, and death would be taken by his disciples "to the ends of the earth" (Acts 1:8). And if twenty centuries later Jesus' message has reached people from thousands of cultures and has been translated into hundreds of languages, this is because some of those disciples were willing to cross seas and all types of boundaries in obedience to his mandate. The form that this obedience takes has varied over the centuries. Christian testimony came out of the Jewish world and went from Jerusalem to the Gentile and Greco-Roman world, carried by a group of disciples who were persecuted by Jewish authorities. As they escaped, these anonymous disciples went along founding communities of Jesus followers; among them was the church of Antioch, which became a center for missionary action. Today there are Korean, African, and Latin American Christians who go to other countries as missionaries, carriers of the gospel, using modern means of communication and technology. Like those of the first century, they give themselves to the same task of crossing boundaries with the message of God's kingdom: to serve the poor in Bangladesh or Algeria, to serve newborn Christian communities in Japan or New York City, to minister to immigrants enthusiastic in their faith in Germany or Spain.[1]

[1]A historical-theological study that takes into account various models of missionary action is Valdir Steuernagel, *Obediencia misionera y práctica histórica* (Buenos Aires: Nueva Creación,

In Search of the Poor of Jesus Christ

The five-hundredth anniversary of Columbus's arrival to the Americas in 1992 prompted theologians, historians, and thoughtful Christians to embark on retrospective reflections on the mission that took place in the name of Jesus Christ in the sixteenth century and the lessons it holds for Christian mission in the twenty-first century. That year Gustavo Gutiérrez, possibly the best-known Latin American Catholic theologian in the world, published his book *En busca de los pobres de Jesucristo: El pensamiento de Bartolomé de Las Casas* (*Las Casas: In Search of the Poor of Jesus Christ*).[2] This monumental work of seven hundred pages, which took him twenty years to write, was published in English and Spanish at almost the same time. Gutiérrez dedicated his book thus: "To Vicente Hondarza, to Ignacio Ellacuría and his companions, and in them to all who, born in Spain, have come to live and die in the Indies, in search of the poor of Jesus Christ." This dedication demonstrates that there is still strong Catholic missionary activity from Spain to Latin America, and that in recent years many Spanish missionaries have worked among the poor; some, such as Hondarza and Ellacuría, suffered persecution and died for identifying with them.

Gutiérrez undertook exhaustive research on Bartolomé de las Casas (1584–1566), the Dominican missionary from Seville who directly criticized the way his fellow Spaniards undertook conquest and mission in the sixteenth century. In offering a masterful picture of Las Casas, his work, his thought, and his fight for justice in the Indies, Gutiérrez also offers a detailed history of how a theology of mission that denied the gospel emerged. Facing this theology, the Dominican rose up, and Gutiérrez tells us: "The Sevillian lives and thinks amid the cruel death of the Indians, their death 'before their time.' Thus, the question of justice is posed with urgency. It was not only a preliminary question. It framed his whole existence. In the Indians dying prematurely and

1996). A complete, panoramic history is Justo González and Carlos Cardoza Orlandi, *Historia general de las misiones* (Barcelona: CLIE, 2008).

[2]Gustavo Gutiérrez, *Las Casas: In Search of the Poor of Jesus Christ* (Eugene, OR: Wipf & Stock, 2003).

unjustly he sees Christ. There is a christological focus, then, at the root of his reflection."[3] Making reference to the title of his book, Gutiérrez says, "Here was the life of Bartolomé de Las Casas as well. For these poor he fought, and from them out of their midst he announced the gospel in a society being established on a foundation of plunder and injustice. This is why his proclamation of the Christian message is invested with characteristics of prophetic denunciation that maintain all their validity today."[4]

LATIN AMERICA IN GLOBAL EVANGELICAL MISSION

In the evangelical context, 1992 was also a year of study, reflection, and critique of missionary work from Spain following the arrival of Columbus. However, here the focus was on the missionary responsibility of Latin American evangelicals, through an authentically Christian presence and proclamation of the Christ of the Gospels in Latin America itself and in the rest of the world. In 1992 the FTL organized CLADE III in Quito, Ecuador: All the Gospel for All Peoples from Latin America. In 1976 evangelical university students in Brazil had organized the first Latin American Missionary Congress, in the spirit of Lausanne '74, and some of those participants had later embarked on global mission in Africa, Europe, and other Latin American countries. Eleven years later, in 1987, various Latin American missionary agencies that sent missionaries to other parts of the world held a conference in which Cooperación Misionera Iberoamericana (COMIBAM), a network of missionary action from Latin America, was formed.

CLADE III became a platform for those wanting to reflect on what it meant to follow Christ in global mission entering into the twenty-first century. The response to this call was surprising: 1,080 people from twenty-four countries participated. And the issues considered at CLADE III have continued to resonate: mission from the margins has been a prominent theme in the early twenty-first century.

---

[3]Gutiérrez, *Las Casas*, 13.
[4]Gutiérrez, *Las Casas*, 11.

Mission from the Margins

Two significant developments in these first decades of the twenty-first century are having a profound influence on the development of new models of mission and are increasingly being addressed by theologians. The influence of Constantinian-style Christianity united to the power of the state (Catholic or Protestant) has rapidly declined in Europe and North America. John Howard Yoder describes a concurrent theological shift as follows: "It is one of the widely remarked developments of our century that now one dimension, now another, of the ecclesiastical experience and the ecclesiological vision once called 'sectarian' are now beginning to be espoused by some within majority communions."[5] It is likely that as Christians and churches look for more authentic forms of obedience to Jesus Christ in our century, they will increasingly encounter the experience of being outside the established order. Like those called sectarians in the past, they are discovering that even in their own country they have to learn to live as, in the phrase used in Peter's first epistle, "resident aliens."[6]

On the other hand, we observe today what missiologist Andrew Walls has called "a massive southward shift of the center of gravity in the Christian world, so that the representative Christian lands now appear to be in Latin American, Sub-Saharan Africa, and other parts of the southern continents."[7] Given this shift, the existence of flourishing churches in what was called the Third World confronts old European and North American churches with a new set of theological questions and new ways of approaching the Bible. What Walls deduces from this situation may seem like an exaggeration, but it is based in his own missionary experience and notable familiarity with the history of missions and missiological reflection:

---

[5]John H. Yoder, *The Priestly Kingdom: Social Ethics as Gospel* (Notre Dame, IN: University of Notre Dame Press, 1984), 5.

[6]See the commentary on the first epistle of Peter by John H. Elliott, *A Home for the Homeless: A Sociological Exegesis of 1 Peter, Its Situation and Strategy* (Philadelphia: Fortress, 1981).

[7]Andrew Walls, *The Missionary Movement in Christian History* (Maryknoll, NY: Orbis, 1996), 9.

> This means that Third World theology is now likely to be the representative Christian theology. On present trends (and I recognize that these may not be permanent) the theology of European Christians, while important for them and their continued existence, may become a matter of specialist interest to historians. . . . The future general reader of Church history is more likely to be concerned with Latin American and African, and perhaps some Asian, theology.[8]

Despite their self-proclaimed Latin Americanism, liberation theologies in general were actually part of a Western discourse to the melody of Marx and Engels, of Moltmann and the European theologians from Vatican II. Although located in borderline situations between wealth and misery, liberation theologians move within the categories of the Enlightenment and modernity. If we are going to take seriously the emergence of the new churches as part of a "a massive southward shift of the center of gravity in the Christian world," we should prepare ourselves for something different. The new pastoral situations and theological questions emerge from churches that move on the boundary between Christianity and Islam, from churches surrounded by cultures molded by the animism of the great ethnic religions, from ethnic churches in poverty-stricken neighborhoods of secularized Western cities, from Pentecostal churches in Latin America, and from old churches reborn in a post-Marxist Eastern Europe. These are the missionary churches of today and tomorrow, and theologians will have to tune their ears to hear their message, their songs, their groans, and at the same time be attentive to the Word of God.

The idea of a missiology that comes from the periphery of the modern world is relevant when we explore the future.[9] During a christological consultation in Asia, Argentinian Pentecostal theologian Norberto Saracco explored the meaning of the Galilean origin of Jesus' ministry. This was no contrived effort to find parallels between Jesus' world and our own in order to detect a type of magical relationship

[8]Walls, *Missionary Movement in Christian History*, 10.

[9]Part of this section is adapted from Samuel Escobar, "Evangelical Theology in Latin America: The Development of a Missiological Christology," *Missiology* 19, no. 3 (July 1991): 315-32.

that would take neither the text nor our content seriously. Instead Saracco explored the meaning of the options Jesus chose for his own ministry "that were both relevant to the context and in accordance with his redemptive project."[10]

Orlando Costas built on this reflection systematically, developing it as a creative summary of a new dimension for a missiological Christology. Concentrating on the Gospel of Mark, he explored a model for evangelization rooted in Jesus' ministry. It can be characterized as an evangelizing legacy, "a contextual model of evangelization from the periphery." Costas considers it especially significant that Jesus chose Galilee, a racial and cultural crossroads, as a base for mission. He also explores the meaning of Jesus' identity as a Galilean, and the universal implications of Galilee as a landmark and starting point for mission to the nations. Costas's understanding of his own contemporary context highlights the "peripheral" nature of some of the points and places where Christianity has blossomed and has great energy today. His missiological proposal is that "the global scope of contextual evangelization should correspond to the Galilean principle. This means concretely that evangelization should be geared, first and foremost, to the nations' peripheries, where the multitudes are found and where the Christian faith has always had the best opportunity to build a strong base."[11]

During CLADE III, Valdir Steuernagel examined the missionary challenge represented by the universality of Jesus Christ in a world of religious plurality. He reminded us of the FTL's long path in search of a missiological Christology. He concluded that the principle of incarnation must guide ecclesial and missionary practice from Latin America: "Incarnation theology protects us from the temptation of becoming followers of a theology of glory that does not perceive, respect, or suffer with the suffering experienced by the majority of our people."[12]

---

[10]Norberto Saracco, "The Liberating Options of Jesus," in *Sharing Jesus in the Two Thirds World*, ed. Vinay Samuel and Chris Sugden (Grand Rapids: Eerdmans, 1984), 50.

[11]Orlando Costas, *Liberating News: A Theology of Contextual Evangelization* (Grand Rapids: Eerdmans, 1989), 67.

[12]Valdir R. Steuernagel, "La universalidad de la misión," in *CLADE III: Tercer Congreso Latinoamericano de Evangelización Quito 1992* (Buenos Aires: Fraternidad Teológica Latinoamericana, 1993), 347.

When the affirmation of Christ's universality was connected to missionary outreach "from above," from the centers of power, and sometimes came intertwined with the European or North American colonializing enterprise, it was impossible to avoid a certain mark of triumphalism and imposition. The affirmation of Christ's universality from the periphery avoids this tendency. Steuernagel said:

> The mark of Jesus' ministry was service. The mark of the Christendom model is to be served, sometimes at a very high cost. It is essential to return to Jesus' model. The hypothesis of [Christ's] universality must not produce arrogance, nor clothe itself in a cloak of superiority. The universal Christ was the servant *par excellence*. This is the model we are invited to follow, whether in the church, in the neighborhood, or in faraway lands.[13]

Today's Latin American missionaries do not carry the baggage of their country's technological, military, or political superiority; they are learning to do mission in the name of Jesus Christ "from below." On the other hand, historian and theologian Justo González, who identifies with the Hispanic minority of the United States and has struggled to help Hispanic churches find their own theological and pastoral voice, has titled his introduction to theology *Mañana: Christian Theology from a Hispanic Perspective*.[14]

The Incarnation of Jesus Christ and Christian Mission[15]

One of the manifestations of the apostle Paul's practice of holistic mission was the offering organized among Gentile churches to help the church members in Jerusalem who were suffering an economic crisis.[16] Writing to the Corinthians about their financial participation in the mission to help those impoverished believers (2 Cor 8:1-8), Paul grounds

---

[13]Steuernagel, "La universalidad de la misión," 347.

[14]Justo L. González, *Mañana: Christian Theology from a Hispanic Perspective* (Nashville: Abingdon, 1990).

[15]In this section I revisit my contribution to Pedro Arana, Samuel Escobar, and C. René Padilla, *El trino Dios y la misión integral* (Buenos Aires: Kairós, 2003).

[16]I have focused on the importance and meaning of this collection in "Pablo y la misión a los gentiles," in *Bases bíblicas de la misión: Perspectivas latinoamericanas*, ed. C. René Padilla (Buenos Aires: Nueva Creación, 1998), 346-49.

his arguments in the example of the believers in the region of Achaia, of whom he says, "In the midst of a very severe trial, their overflowing joy and their extreme poverty welled up in rich generosity" (2 Cor 8:2). He then rounds out his argument with what we could call a fundamental note of missionary Christology: "You knew the grace of our Lord Jesus Christ, that though he was rich, yet for your sake he became poor, so that you through his poverty might become rich" (2 Cor 8:9). Again the incarnation of Jesus Christ provides a model for life and participation in mission. This christological note is rooted in Paul's Christology, as presented in Philippians 2:1-5 and in his other epistles, especially 1 and 2 Corinthians.

There is a sense in which the life and death of Jesus has a unique character and cannot be imitated: it was a life without sin and a death for others. But there is another sense in which Jesus' life and his death on the cross are models for the presence and mission of Christ's disciples in the world. John's account of the sending of the apostles into the world clearly contains a double meaning: "As the Father has sent me, I am sending you" (Jn 20:21). On the one hand there is an imperative dimension, as it is an order given by the Lord: "I am sending you." On the other hand, its normative dimension makes reference to a model: "as the Father has sent me." John Stott, who contributed significantly to the rediscovery of this version of the Great Commission in the evangelical context, rightly said that "although these words represent the simplest form of the Great Commission, it is at the same time its most profound form, its most challenging and therefore its most neglected."[17]

The rediscovery of John's emphasis on the incarnation has been useful for critiquing colonialist missionary models and also for suggesting a model for incarnational mission. Mission that takes place from a position of economic, political, or technological power almost forces missionaries to act from a distance and from a position of privilege, to proclaim a Jesus who descended from heaven to save but whose messengers

[17]John Stott, "The Great Commission, Part 1," speech at World Congress on Evangelism, October 27, 1966, Berlin.

do not "descend" socially or culturally. Missionaries' immersion in the real life of the receptors of their action requires sacrifice, a downward mobility, and a renouncing of paternalism. Likewise the church resulting from this missionary work should have an incarnational presence in its own social situation if it is to be capable of proclaiming the gospel in a relevant and transforming way. Here Jesus' real incarnation, insisted on by biblical testimony, as opposed to a merely apparent (docetic) one, provides a model and a source of inspiration.

Jesus' Missionary Style and Christian Mission

That Jesus' incarnation is real and not just apparent (docetic) takes us back to Jesus' way of doing mission. Let us examine some keys from the biblical witness. A first key in Jesus' mission is his identity as "*the one sent by the Father*." With respect to John's Gospel, Pedro Arana has emphasized that the notion of being sent is fundamental and that this takes us back to understanding Jesus' incarnation as a fulfillment of God's will, as a divine initiative in mission. The origin of Christian mission is the saving will of God, who loves the world he created and who becomes human to fully reveal himself to human beings and to fulfill his purpose.

Exploring Jesus' style of missionary action throughout the Gospel of John, Arana highlights distinctive principles that together comprise a kind of outline for holistic mission. There is *worship*, introduced in the prologue and saturating Jesus' prayers; *brotherly love*, which is the distinctive mark of the disciple; *salvation*, the culmination of the work for which Jesus was sent; *service*, dramatized and explained in the foot-washing of the disciples; the *priestly prayer* in the Upper Room; and the emphasis on the disciples' *unity* as a reflection of the unity of God himself. Arana says:

> Five missionary movements are evident in the Gospel. John the Baptist is sent by God, the One who sends, to give testimony of Jesus (Jn 1:6-8; 3:28). Jesus is sent by the Father to give testimony to the truth and to do the work (Jn 18:37; 4:34). The Spirit is sent by the Father and by the Son to give witness to Jesus (Jn 14:26; 15:26). The disciples are sent by Jesus to follow

his incarnational, liturgical, koinoniac, soteriological, diaconal, priestly, ecumenical, and prophetic model.[18]

A second key is the *contextual* and the *universal* in the presence and the work of Jesus. Luke the Evangelist highlights this in presenting Jesus as a man of his environment and of his time who proclaims a gospel for the whole human race. There is a premonitory vision of this in the words of Simeon, the elderly man who takes the baby Jesus in his arms in the temple:

For my eyes have seen your salvation,
  which you have prepared in the sight of all nations:
a light for revelation to the Gentiles,
  and the glory of your people Israel. (Lk 2:30-32)

Jesus was a son of Israel, trained in the customs and spirituality of the best of this people, and his message reflects the vocabulary and the particular ideas of the Jewish context at that moment in history. His vision of himself is expressed in the vocabulary and the figures of speech particular to a community shaped by the written revelation it treasured. In this sense Jesus is "the glory of [God's] people Israel," the highest culmination of their historic expectation. But this message, this life, this language are destined to be carriers of God's Word for *all* human beings, a "light for revelation to the Gentiles" beyond narrow provincial and nationalistic differences.

A third key is Jesus' preference for the marginalized, the small, the poor. Peruvian theologian Darío López, pastor of a Pentecostal church on the southern periphery of Lima, offers a review of various modern exegetical works that insist on this principle, especially in the Gospel of Luke. "Luke also points out that God has a special love for the poor and the marginalized, including the fragile, those on the periphery, the needy and the destitute, the ragged of the world and the 'nobodies' that predominant society has condemned to social ostracism and the basement of history."[19] López reminds us that opposition to Jesus from

[18]Pedro Arana, "La misión en el Evangelio de Juan," in Padilla, *Bases bíblicas de la misión*, 306.
[19]Darío López, *The Liberating Mission of Jesus: The Message of the Gospel of Luke* (Eugene, OR: Pickwick, 2012), 2.

the powerful religious, political, financial, and military elites was a reaction of those who were displeased and saw themselves threatened by Jesus' preference for the poor. Today it is easy to forget that, for twenty centuries of Christian history, renewal movements and missionary advances have arisen precisely among the poor and insignificant, those who are rich in devotion and conscious of their own need.

The "Galilean option" referred to earlier can be placed here as well. Orlando Costas reminds us that Galilee was at that time a symbol of the cultural, social, political, and theological periphery, a place despised by those who held the religious-political power in Israel. "For Mark," Costas says, "the fact that Jesus came from Galilee and not Jerusalem seems to be charged with profound theological significance. Mark sees in Jesus the eternal Son of God who became 'a nobody' in order to make women and men 'somebody' and bring into being a new creation."[20] This reference has special importance now that the missionary impulse comes more from churches that are on the periphery of the world than from those in the centers of commercial, financial, and military power.

A fourth key, related to the previous one, is what can be called the *dignifying compassion* of Jesus' missionary action. In Matthew's Gospel we find a significant passage for missionary sending. On the one hand, Jesus' multiple activities can be described as holistic, as he responds with the Word and power to people's different needs: "Jesus went through all the towns and villages, teaching in their synagogues, proclaiming the good news of the kingdom and healing every disease and sickness" (Mt 9:35). On the other hand the passage describes the sense of urgency that seizes the Lord: "When he saw the crowds, he had compassion on them, because they were harassed and helpless, like sheep without a shepherd" (Mt 9:36). Jesus' mission is fueled by compassion, which is the result of an immersion among the multitudes. Jesus walks among the people with a sense of urgency. The text insists on the breadth and geographical totality of the space he occupies—"*all* the towns and villages"—and

[20]Costas, *Liberating News*, 56.

similarly on the variety of his compassionate actions: "teaching . . . proclaiming . . . healing." It is not a sentimental outpouring nor an academic option for the poor, but defined and intentional acts of service with the goal of responding to all the needs of the people.

Neither is it about a proselytizing impulse that sees human beings as possible followers and not as people. Jesus always treated people as those created by God who have their own dignity. Jesus did not convert people into passive objects of his action but took them as conversation partners in the reconciling act of his Father, which leads them to fullness of life. He expresses this in a controversial statement when he at one point defines his mission in the Gospel of John: "The thief comes only to steal and kill and destroy; I have come that they may have life, and have it to the full" (Jn 10:10).

A fifth key is the *transforming effect* of Jesus' presence and ministry. In the Gospels human beings from the most diverse social classes and conditions are transformed by the touch of the Teacher. Sick people are cured, rich people share their possessions with the poor, fishermen are transformed into preachers, women see their social and moral condition dramatically changed. Interpreting this in the light of his own experience as a persecutor of Christians, later converted into a persecuted Christian, the apostle Paul affirms: "If anyone is in Christ, the new creation has come: The old has gone, the new is here!" (2 Cor 5:17).

In other works I have explored the biblical foundation of mission as transforming service, highlighting the impact of the presence and action of Jesus on the totality of people's lives, including their vertical relationship with God and their horizontal relationship with others.[21] Those who have closely observed the social effect of the gospel in Latin America can prove that Jesus Christ continues to holistically transform people today in a wide variety of contexts.[22] Due to its massive growth, the

---

[21]See chap. 9 of my book *The New Global Mission* (Downers Grove, IL: InterVarsity Press, 2003), 142-54.

[22]See, for example, the works collected in C. René Padilla, ed., *Servir con los pobres en América Latina* (Buenos Aires: Kairós, 1997).

Latin American Pentecostal movement was the first to catch the attention of sociologists interested in social change related to religious experience. Beginning with studies undertaken by Emilio Willems on Pentecostalism in Chile and Brazil, and later Christian Lalive D'Epinay in Chile, scholars have researched the social impact of the conversion experience among the masses.[23] In a now-classic 1990 book, British sociologist David Martin critically summarized hundreds of such research papers from previous decades.[24] Relating Pentecostal growth to internal migrations in Latin America and calling it a parallel migration of the Spirit, Martin says, "In undertaking the migration people become 'independent' not at all by building up modest securities but by the reverse: by the loss of all the ties that bind, whether these be familial, communal or ecclesial."[25] He then summarizes: "Above all it renews the innermost cell of the family and protects the woman from the ravages of male desertion and violence. A new faith is able to implant new disciplines, re-order priorities, counter corruption and destructive machismo, and reverse the indifferent and injurious hierarchies of the outside world."[26]

The Crucifixion of Christ and Christian mission

What has been said with respect to Jesus' missional works is sufficient evidence of the incarnation in time and space, described by the Evangelists and interpreted by the authors of the Epistles. However, John the Evangelist insists on highlighting one of Jesus' works in particular. It is something unique and definitive, to which Jesus himself makes frequent reference, something that no one but he can do. In his work on the Gospel of John, Pedro Arana points out two themes related to the person of Jesus that particularly mark the final chapters of the Fourth Gospel. First is the sense of time, encapsulated in the expression "my hour," which

[23]Emilio Willems, *Followers of the New Faith: Culture Change and the Rise of Protestantism in Brazil and Chile* (Nashville: Vanderbilt University Press, 1967); Christian Lalive D'Epinay, *El refugio de las masas* (Santiago: Editorial del Pacífico, 1968).

[24]David Martin, *Tongues of Fire* (Oxford: Basil Blackwell, 1990).

[25]Martin, *Tongues of Fire*, 284.

[26]Martin, *Tongues of Fire*, 284.

Jesus uses many times as the culminating hour of his death on the cross comes closer. Second is the distinction between "the works," such as his miracles, and "the work" of which Jesus speaks in what is called his priestly prayer in John 17, taken to be the totality of his life, which culminates in the cross. In this missionary prayer par excellence Jesus says to the Father, "I have brought you glory on earth by finishing the work you gave me to do" (Jn 17:4). Arana sees a relationship between glory and cross, a classic insight of Reformed theology:

> How does Jesus glorify the Father on the cross? In the only way possible: obeying him. The temptations that are narrated in the Synoptic Gospels and that appear in John 6, when the multitudes want to crown Jesus as earthly king, were intended to prevent him from arriving at the cross. Jesus glorified the Father on the cross, offering him perfect obedience in perfect love.[27]

John the Evangelist expresses with brilliant clarity the truth that the cross of Christ manifests God's unlimited love for his creation and his creatures. John tells us this in the celebrated passage that Luther called "the miniature gospel": "For God so loved the world that he gave his one and only Son, that whoever believes in him shall not perish but have eternal life. For God did not send his Son into the world to condemn the world, but to save the world through him" (Jn 3:16-17). Jesus' obedience as the Son of God reveals at the same time God's deep love. As biblical scholar Stan Slade says:

> Jesus' death is not glorious because God is a sadomasochist. John does not want to exalt suffering in itself. God's glory is manifested in Jesus' death precisely because it was the instrument to give life to human beings. The clearest manifestation of God's nature appeared in the action that demonstrated his unbreakable will to bless his beloved creatures by accepting the destruction and death that our rebellion had set loose. The cross demonstrated the glory of God precisely because it revealed its essence: love (John 3:16; 1 John 4:8, 16).[28]

---

[27]Arana, "La misión en el Evangelio de Juan," 292.

[28]Stan Slade, *Evangelio de Juan* (Buenos Aires: Kairós, 1998), 306.

Also in the Synoptic Gospels we find defining moments for Jesus' mission, in which his death on the cross is shown to have a redemptive purpose. For example, the apostle Peter's confession of faith facing Jesus' question about his identity constitutes a crucial moment in the gospel story (Mt 16:13-24; Mk 8:27-29; Lk 9:18-20). Jesus asks, "But what about you? Who do you say I am?" "You are the Messiah, the Son of the living God," affirms Simon Peter (Mt 16:15-16). The authors of the three Synoptic Gospels affirm that, from this moment on (e.g., Mt 16:12), Jesus began to teach about his afflictions and death, a teaching not easily accepted by his disciples. Peter himself tries to divert his Teacher from the way of suffering—an effort that Jesus calls satanic: "Get behind me, Satan! You are a stumbling block to me; you do not have in mind the concerns of God, but merely human concerns" (Mt 16:23). From this moment on, Jesus is portrayed as consciously and intentionally going toward the cross. His teaching presents the act of following him, of being a disciple, as a lifestyle marked by the cross. "Whoever wants to be my disciple must deny themselves and take up their cross and follow me" (Mt 16:24).

In Matthew 20, when calling his disciples to a spirit of service that should be distinctive of them, Jesus' teaching culminates in the affirmation, "The Son of Man did not come to be served, but to serve, and give his life as a ransom for many" (Mt 20:28). These lines communicate forcefully a vision of life as faithfulness to a vocation of service, service that culminates in the death that Jesus takes on voluntarily as a way of rescuing human beings.

Uncountable legions of Jesus' followers through the centuries have been inspired by his teaching and example to give their own lives in service to others, many times to their death. However, they have never attributed redemptive value to their sacrifices in the unique sense that only Jesus himself offered. Nancy Bedford says:

> In addition to responding to others' suffering, Jesus takes human suffering on himself in a process that culminates in the cross. Jesus' compassion (*Mit-leid*) means precisely to suffer *with and for* others. Faith in Jesus Christ, then, is faith in a suffering Messiah. In all the New Testament this

> faith and the resultant following of Jesus Christ imply the willingness of the believer to share the cross and the suffering of their Lord.[29]

A Christology for holistic mission recognizes these two dimensions of Jesus' crucifixion. On the one hand, there is the unique and singular character of Christ's death, the redemptive and expiatory meaning of his death within the framework of Old Testament concepts and language adopted and adapted in the New Testament. Jesus' death and resurrection constitute an integral part of the gospel itself. The announcement of Christ's coming and his work for the sake of humanity is the nucleus of the message that the church has for all humanity. The apostle Paul says it with singular force: "Jews demand signs and Greeks look for wisdom, but we preach Christ crucified" (1 Cor 1:22-23). The apostle also has a strong sense of obligation with respect to the proclamation of the message of Jesus Christ: "Woe to me if I do not preach the gospel!" (1 Cor 9:16). Proclamation of the word of the cross is indispensable for a holistic Christian mission.

On the other hand, Jesus' crucifixion is also the mark of a lifestyle to which the followers of Jesus are called and which also characterizes the Christian missionary style. Here we have a biblical key to missionary spirituality that the apostle Paul expresses with singular conviction in the midst of contrasting his previous Judaism and his experience with Christ: "I have been crucified with Christ and I no longer live, but Christ lives in me. The life I now live in the body, I live by faith in the Son of God, who loved me and gave himself for me" (Gal 2:20). If we are followers of the Christ who died on the cross, we will undertake missionary work in a way that is consonant with Jesus' own missionary style. This is a style devoid of triumphalism, of manipulative intentions, of reliance on military, economic, technological, or social power. It is a style that draws on all the resources and gifts that God provides and that knows how to read the signs of the times, but that most of all is marked by the spirit of service that characterized Jesus himself.

---

[29]Nancy Elizabeth Bedford, "La misión en el sufrimiento y ante el sufrimiento," in Padilla, *Bases bíblicas de la misión*, 393.

This orients us to understand how holistic missionary action can follow the model suggested by the image in one of Jesus' teachings regarding discipleship and mission: "Very truly I tell you, unless a kernel of wheat falls to the ground and dies, it remains only a single seed. But if it dies, it produces many seeds" (Jn 12:24). The incarnation of a missionary in the world to which he or she is sent often supposes attitudes and actions of renunciation and self-denial, which are required for movement across cultures. Some do fulfill their mission in the context of their own culture, but others come from another culture and practice "inculturation," that is to say, an immersion in the world of the other. A transforming immersion, to be sure, but certainly an immersion. Holistic mission is not congruent with a bureaucratic style of welfare in which the employees of an organization occasionally visit the place where their poor clients live. Rather, holistic mission, which involves coming near to the other for the transmission of Christ's message and service in his name, requires inculturation. Only in this way will fruit be produced: communities rooted in their own reality and propelled by the Spirit to form a transforming movement.

Mission in the Power of the Resurrection

According to New Testament accounts, Timothy was a young missionary chosen by Paul as his colleague and disciple. In the second epistle that Paul writes to him, Paul's clear purpose is to encourage, affirm, and motivate him in faithfulness. The letter writer is in prison for the cause of the gospel, but he does not seem to be inhibited or defeated by this. On the contrary, he looks at the present and the future with gratitude to God. His apostolic exhortation says: "Remember Jesus Christ, raised from the dead, descended from David. This is my gospel, for which I am suffering even to the point of being chained like a criminal. But God's Word is not chained" (2 Tim 2:8-9). The disciple must remember the human Jesus, Son of David, but also the one who was exalted after being raised from the dead. The call to *remember*, to bring to mind, take into account, was so important for the identity of the people of God in the Old Testament that it is taken up again in the New. As Thorwald Lorenzen writes, "Between the past remembered and the future anticipated, the present is lifted to remember, in which the past event is actualized and in this way effectively influences the configuration of the future."[30]

In New Testament teaching, just as real and important as the incarnation and Jesus' death on the cross is the resurrection of the crucified Lord. Writing to the church in Corinth, the apostle Paul affirms categorically: "And if Christ has not been raised, our preaching is useless and so is your faith" (1 Cor 15:14). The four Gospels end with the story of the shock of the disciples, both women and men, before the empty tomb, and the experience of encounter with the risen Jesus. This experience is the frame within which the disciples receive the mandate to launch themselves into the world with a sense of mission. Uruguayan theologian Mortimer Arias says in his masterful study on the Great Commission:

> The historic, verifiable fact of the Easter experience is the emergence of a new community, the Church, possessed by a sense of universal mission. It emerges from the ashes, like the phoenix, in the midst of a small, marginal group, overwhelmed by distress over Jesus' sentencing and crucifixion, dispersed and disheartened, that suddenly rises to testify to the presence and power of Christ working in and through them.[31]

Jesus' resurrection is the triumph of life over death; it is the vindication of the victim, the confirmation that with the arrival of Jesus a new reality, that which Jesus called the kingdom of God, has irrupted in human history. The forces that felt threatened by Jesus' presence and style presented opposition from the beginning of his public ministry. This growing opposition, recounted in the Gospels, meant ongoing conflict in reaction to Jesus' work. Because his teaching was popular, it attracted the ridicule and jealousy of the Pharisees and scribes, the official religious teachers. His miracles and the novelty of his message were perceived as threats by the Sadducees, administrators of the temple, symbolizing the dominant religious institutions, and its functionaries, the

---

[30]Thorwald Lorenzen, *Resurrección y discipulado* (Santander: Sal Terrae, 1999), 271.
[31]Mortimer Arias, *La gran comisión* (Quito: CLAI, 1994), 13-14.

priests. Those responsible for imposing imperial Roman order, governors such as Pontius Pilate or petty kings such as Herod, saw him as a threat to the strict order brutally imposed by the empire's force. They all coincided on a plot to get rid of Jesus promptly and without the least intent of seeking justice. Anyone familiar with the history of empires from the pharaohs to our day knows that the story of Jesus' passion is plausible because it is repeated again and again.

However, the distinctive of Jesus' story is the meaning that he himself attributes to his death and the fact that the tomb could not hold him, nor death keep him silent forever. He who on the cross cried out "My God, my God why have you forsaken me?" (Mk 15:34) was lifted up from among the dead by the power of God. This progression is at the heart of New Testament Christology, which is masterfully summarized by the apostle Paul in the hymn quoted in his letter to the Philippians:

> In your relationships with one another, have the same mindset as Christ Jesus:
> Who, being in very nature God,
> did not consider equality with God something to be used to his
> own advantage;
> rather, he made himself nothing
> by taking the very nature of a servant,
> being made in human likeness.
> And being found in appearance as a man,
> he humbled himself
> by becoming obedient to death—
> even death on a cross!
> Therefore God exalted him to the highest place
> and gave him the name that is above every name,
> that at the name of Jesus every knee should bow,
> in heaven and on earth and under the earth,
> and every tongue acknowledge that Jesus Christ is Lord,
> to the glory of God the Father. (Phil 2:5-11)

Faith in the resurrected Christ was motivation for mission, but this fact in itself does not explain the advance of the church from a remote corner of the Roman Empire to the global reality of our times. The Father and

Son as the resurrected Lord send the Holy Spirit as the companion and the powerful force that opens the way for missionaries in the world and will sustain them in the midst of all kinds of conflicts and suffering. According to Jesus' teaching, the Holy Spirit will be present with the apostles (sent ones) as counselor and comforter (Jn 14:16), leading them into an understanding of the person of Christ himself (Jn 15:25-26), who will be glorified (Jn 16:13-15) and will act in the world with his own power, proving "the world to be in the wrong about sin and righteousness and judgment" (Jn 16:8). Jesus' promise of his presence with his messengers until the end of the world (Mt 28:20) or where two or three gather in his name (Mt 18:20) becomes real by the presence and ministry of the Holy Spirit.

In a christological reflection on the relationship between Jesus' resurrection and the Holy Spirit's presence, Jürgen Moltmann reminds us that there was one step from the perception of Christ's presence when he appeared following the resurrection to the experience of Christ's presence in the Spirit. For this reason he affirms: "The early Christian faith in the resurrection was not based solely on Christ's appearances; it was at least equally strongly moved by the experience of God's Spirit. Paul therefore calls this divine Spirit 'the life-giving Spirit' or 'the power of the resurrection.' Believing in the risen Christ means being seized by the Spirit of the resurrection."[32] This correlation leads us to an important consequence for the personal life and the task of those who respond in obedience to Jesus' missionary call. Paul affirms it in one of the most beautiful sections of his epistle to the Romans: "And if the Spirit of him who raised Jesus from the dead is living in you, he who raised Christ from the dead will also give life to your mortal bodies because of his Spirit who lives in you" (Rom 8:11). Spiritual vitality and missionary hope are guaranteed by the action of the same Spirit that resurrected Jesus. All the limitations and weaknesses of the missionary's human condition, often tried by personal difficulties or those in the place where they work, can

[32]Jürgen Moltmann, *Jesus Christ for Today's World*, trans. Margaret Kohl (Minneapolis: Fortress, 1994), 74-75.

be transformed by the Spirit of God. And in itself, as pointed out in the section about the incarnation, our presence and missionary proclamation among fellow human beings have a transforming character.

Faith in the resurrection of Jesus Christ also gives our mission a firm sense of hope despite the precariousness of the historical situation in which it takes place. Jesus warned his disciples that he sent them "like sheep among wolves" to a hostile world that would not welcome them (Mt 10:16). His pragmatic training speech, which John the Evangelist places prior to the priestly prayer and his passion, culminates in an affirmation that is realistic and hopeful at the same time: "I have told you these things, so that in me you may have peace. In this world you will have trouble. But take heart! I have overcome the world" (Jn 16:33). A classic passage of Paul's explaining the resurrection and its meaning closes in a similar way: "Therefore, my dear brothers and sisters, stand firm. Let nothing move you. Always give yourselves fully to the work of the Lord, because you know that your labor in the Lord is not in vain" (1 Cor 15:58).

Holistic mission leads the missionary into direct contact with pain, injustice, the dead end of endemic poverty, the abyss of corruption. The sense of futility can end up having a contagious effect, affecting the Christian with lack of hope and pessimism particular to the postmodern era in which many human utopias have died. As never before it is important to hold on to Christian hope. Mission requires a dose of realism regarding human nature and its fallen condition, such as that which characterized Jesus' ministry. But it also requires the certainty that the kingdom of God has already been manifested, and the giving of the Holy Spirit's power, which raised Jesus Christ from the dead, lifts us above sociological fatalism or cynicism. In Romans 8 Paul sets forth this tension within which the Christian lives. "I consider that our present sufferings are not worth comparing with the glory that will be revealed in us" (Rom 8:18): a powerful affirmation that the apostle also makes in Romans 3:28; 6:11. Suffering and glory always go together in the Christian life. It is a conviction regarding the glorious hope of the believer that mitigates suffering in the present and shrinks it to insignificance in the light of future glory. In these lines Paul contrasts two eras: the present era, with its weight of contradictions that will end, and the future, which began with the triumph of Christ in the cross and whose fullness will be seen only when Christ is finally revealed.

The apostle then, in Romans 8:19, describes humanity's condition in this present era. Some versions have "the creation" as subject of this prayer, giving an understanding that includes the animate and inanimate totality of the cosmos. Others think that the vocabulary used refers instead to humanity, more specifically nonbelieving humanity, contrasting with those who are already God's children. The Nueva Biblia Española's rendering can be translated like this: "In fact, humanity watches from above, impatiently waiting for what it means to be children of God to be revealed" (Rom 8:19). In any case, the apostle observes an encompassing vastness and tells us that it is filled with expectation, as if on tiptoe, "looking down," that is to say, watching anxiously in the hope that God's children will be revealed. Out there, beyond the walls of church buildings or the confines of Christian communities, there is an immense world filled with expectation. We need to recover this sense, this vision, attentive to the necessity and the expectation of humanity, of all creation. Care of the earth should not be something strange, let alone unimportant, for the Christian who takes this Pauline vision seriously.

The apostolic sensibility is made up in the first place of realism regarding the fallen, suffering, needy condition of humanity and the sin that has affected all created things with wasting and deterioration. There are no illusions to be cherished, no romantic humanism to embrace. At the same time, however, the apostolic sensibility sees this condition as a challenge, as a call to mission, because there is a note of expectation, of contrast, of a revelation of the redeemed condition of God's children to be revealed. The Bible's missional language is charged with a tone of hope, of looking to the future for liberation in the fullest sense of this word: the hope "that the creation itself will be liberated from its bondage to decay and brought into the glorious freedom and glory of the children of God"

(Rom 8:21). It is worth recovering this vision today, to become conscious of the immensity of humanity, of the complexity of the global situation, even of the ecological realities of God's creation.

Christian hope speaks to all of this, and the following statement holds a unique relevance for our time: "We know that all creation has been groaning as in the pains of childbirth right up to the present time" (Rom 8:22). Here the apostle does not resemble those apocalyptic preachers who announce a final catastrophe, in the light of which there is no need to be concerned for anything more than rescuing converts from the world like embers from a fire. The verb *groaning* expresses well the agonizing situation about which the apostle speaks. This groan of suffering and pain does not become a shout because there is not even the strength for that. It is a groan that announces labor pains, the convulsions that come with giving birth, a promise. This image of the pains of childbirth belongs to Hebrew literature. It is not a death rattle, nor the creaking of a building that is collapsing irremediably. The children of God know this, those who know the Spirit's power, the reality of his promises.

At this point comes Paul's deep sense of mission that is not at all indifferent to the groans of humanity and creation: "Not only so, but we ourselves, who have the firstfruits of the Spirit, groan inwardly as we wait eagerly for our adoption to sonship, the redemption of our bodies" (Rom 8:23). Christians carry within them the marks of the transforming power of the resurrection and already live in the new era inaugurated by Christ´s triumph. They share the tensions of the present era, but with the power of hope. Hope allows them to see the way out of the darkness of the tunnel. This hope sustains them in their own spiritual battle. Colombian theologian Harold Segura expresses this well: "Theology tells us that our faith is utopic in the sense of being founded on hope, in being fed by the promise and of projecting forward with the desire to find the surprise of another world: the world promised by God. The Christian faith betrays its meaning when it anchors itself in the past and stops dreaming of God's future."[33]

---

[33]Harold Segura, *Más allá de la utopía* (Buenos Aires: Kairós, 2006), 24.

Human beings cannot know this by simple observation of nature or history. The pessimism and cynicism of today's postmodern culture is due precisely to the realistic observation that humanist utopias—whether of liberalism or of Marxism—have no foundation. If there is going to be hope, there must be a word that comes neither from nature nor simply from human history. The Word of God in Christ, by the power of the Spirit, is the word of hope. The resurrection of Christ, whose power we already see in action in ourselves, is the guarantee of the final liberation of all creation.

Paul affirms that salvation itself is the source of hope; the salvation that Christ offers is for hope. In Romans 8:24-25 Paul returns to the tension between the "already" and the "not yet" of the Christian life, between what can be seen and what is hoped for but cannot yet be seen. In Romans 8:23 this is described as our own groan, in the framework of the whole creation's groans. In Romans 8:25 he describes it as a resolute hope for the glory that has not yet been revealed. They are two dimensions of the same reality.

Now Paul returns to consider the way in which the Holy Spirit acts in us. We are not perfect beings, nor always triumphant. Paul has no problem with speaking clearly of the vulnerability of the Christian and writes in first-person plural, including himself in the description: "our weakness. We do not know what we ought to pray for" (Rom 8:26). But this mention of our weakness is to affirm the goodness and grace of God, who by his Spirit helps us. Paul writes of the divine compassion (*com-pathos*, which puts itself alongside us in our suffering) with the same language of groaning (Rom 8:22-23) for the way the Spirit intercedes for us: "through wordless groans" (Rom 8:26).

If this is truth, we cannot be communities that transmit a general pessimism, churches with apocalyptic messages that wait anxiously for the end of the world, or who isolate themselves in a convent of the mind with a sectarian attitude. We cannot be communities that fear change and tremble in the face of the future. If the Spirit of God lives in us and transforms us and fills us, we are to be light in the darkness. We live in a difficult time, but we know that God has the final word. We confess that sometimes uncertainty invades us; then we bend our knee and even between groans ask the Spirit to intercede for us. Only the Word of God in the power of his Spirit gives us a renewed sense of identity and mission as believers in Jesus Christ, incarnate Lord, crucified and resurrected; he gives us discernment to distinguish true Christian practice and doctrine in this era of confusion, and this gives us hope to be able to live in the tension of a spirituality open to the future that Christ has opened for us.

This book opened with a quote from Rubén Darío written in 1892. The famous Nicaraguan poet, whose life oscillated between moments of Catholic religiosity and an exaggerated enjoyment of pagan pleasures, wrote his "Canto de esperanza" (circa 1904; "Song of hope") with a tone of eschatological impatience:

> A great flock of ravens stains the blue sky.
> A millenary breeze carries the whiff of plagues.
> Men are assassinated in the Far East. . . .
> The earth is pregnant with such deep pain
> That the dreamer, the pensive imperial,
> Suffers with anguish of heart for the world. . . .
> O Lord Jesus! Why do you take so long, why do you wait
> To offer your hand of light over the beasts
> And make your divine flags shine in the sun?

During CLADE III in 1992, Argentinian Methodist Bishop Federico Pagura lifted as a prayer a supplication that he had written some years previously in Guatemala:

> O Christ of a continent
> whose entrails are red
> from so much spilt blood
> From diseased ambition,
> so many fratricidal swords,
> so much greed that kills.
> Rise up soon and pronounce
> your sovereign word
> that halts the arrogance

that gallops through these lands
and usher in for the poor
of this American land
a dawning of justice
a dawning of hope
and bury forever
the night that has been so long. . . .
Doesn't it seem, my Christ,
my Lord of hope,
that the hour draws nigh,
that it is already the third morning,
and my America sighs
to contemplate you at daybreak?[34]

Pagura wrote from his own church practice over a major part of the twentieth century, courageous and committed to serving the poor, the defense of human rights, the preaching of the gospel, the composition of hymns that thousands of people sing throughout America, evangelical militancy in following Jesus.

[34]Federico Pagura, "La evangelización desde la perspectiva del Consejo Latinoamericano de Iglesias (CLAI)," in *CLADE III*, 793-94.

Appendix

PRESENT DIRECTIONS OF EVANGELICAL THEOLOGICAL REFLECTION

The rediscovery of Jesus in Latin America that we have been exploring began with the arrival and presence of evangelical Protestantism at the end of the nineteenth century. Changes were brought to the heart of Latin American Catholicism in the mid-twentieth century and led both Catholics and Protestants into a theological blossoming beginning in the 1960s and continuing to this day. This book has particularly examined christological development in the Protestant context, and more specifically what took place in the Fraternidad Teológica Latinoamericana (FTL) during its fifth decade of life and thought. This appendix will briefly outline some of the currents of reflection that have emerged in the second decade of the twenty-first century.

The Trinity as a Hermeneutical Criterion

Due to their continuity with the previous decades, I will first mention four theologians whose work has extended to this moment: José Míguez Bonino, Justo L. González, René Padilla, and Juan Stam, who have continued to contribute works of long-term value. Míguez Bonino's *Rostros del protestantismo latinoamericano* (*Faces of Latin American Protestantism*) offers a masterful interpretive proposal that culminates in a theological proposal. For Míguez Bonino, the "theological weakness" of

Latin American Protestantism is not that it lacks theology or at times digresses but rather its "reductionisms." According to his analysis, the legacy of the Anglo-American "awakenings" or "revivals," whose value should not be lost, has led to a particular form of reductionism:

> Thus, theology is practically swallowed up in Christology, and this in soteriology, and, even more, in a salvation which is characterized as an individual and subjective experience. It is true that, slowly, we have attempted to go beyond these narrow views. Once again, nevertheless, these efforts have moved almost exclusively in a "christological key," without succeeding in placing Christianity within the total framework of revelation.[1]

In light of this, Míguez Bonino makes a proposal that is clear and transparent: "I want to plead for a trinitarian perspective that will broaden, enrich, and deepen the Christological, soteriological and pneumatological understanding which is at the very root of our Latin American Protestant tradition."[2]

Míguez Bonino proposes a theology in which the Trinity is the hermeneutical criterion. That is, our theology must overcome the situation he describes in the following way: "Few Latin American Protestants would deny the Trinity, but I do not think it is unjust to say that this affirmation has remained a generic doctrine which does not profoundly inform the theology, and what is worse, the piety and the life of our churches."[3] I believe it is fair to say that the christological development I have described up to this point does move in the direction Míguez Bonino calls for, as some of the theologians presented and discussed here have related their christological exploration to the totality of biblical revelation. Still, I resonate with Míguez's diagnosis as I reflect on my own experience and in the history of my generation within the FTL. The Cochabamba Declaration with which this evangelical organism made its appearance does not make any reference to the Trinity, although it includes brief affirmations regarding the work of God, of Christ, and of the

[1]José Míguez Bonino, *Faces of Latin American Protestantism* (Grand Rapids: Eerdmans, 1995), 112.
[2]Míguez Bonino, *Faces of Latin American Protestantism*, 112.
[3]Míguez Bonino, *Faces of Latin American Protestantism*, 113.

Holy Spirit. With respect to the Holy Spirit it says only that the Spirit inspired the Bible and helps us in understanding and interpreting the Word. A consciousness that we needed to move forward in this sense led us in 1979 to include expositions on "the Spirit and the Word in the evangelizing task" in CLADE II. Later, in CLADE III (1992), we asked two Pentecostal theologians to present theological expositions on "the gospel of power." The theme for CLADE IV (2000) was explicitly "The Evangelical Witness Toward the Third Millennium: Word, Spirit, and Mission."

Three recent works by Justo L. González could be considered as steps in the direction Míguez suggests, although González did not necessarily follow the suggestion explicitly or intentionally. On the foundation of his monumental work *A History of Christian Thought*, which is well-known both in English and in Spanish, González offers a rereading of the history of theological reflection with keys specific to the twenty-first century: *Christian Thought Revisited: Three Types of Theology*.[4] In identifying three types of theology—moral, metaphysical, and pastoral—and showing how they have developed and coexisted throughout human history, González helps us to avoid the exclusivist tendency that is sometimes associated with the effort to write theology. He labels the three types A, B, and C and suggests that the third is the most pertinent for our time, but he also helps us to see the validity of the other two types and the contribution they have made to universal theology. On the other hand, his *Mañana: Christian Theology from a Hispanic Perspective* was published in Spanish sixteen years later as *Teología liberadora: Enfoque desde la opresión en una tierra extraña* (Liberating theology: A perspective from oppression in a strange land). It is an introduction to theology that offers a contextual and carefully articulated trinitarian framework responding to the concerns and questions of this time, from the perspective of the Spanish-speaking minority in the United States.[5] A hermeneutical

---

[4]Justo L. González, *A History of Christian Thought* (Nashville: Abingdon, 1975); González, *Christian Thought Revisited: Three Types of Theology* (1989; rev. ed., Nashville: Abingdon, 1999; Spanish translation, *Retorno a la historia del pensamiento cristiano: Tres tipos de teología* [Buenos Aires: Kairós, 2004]).

[5]Justo L. González, *Teología liberadora: Enfoque desde la opresión en una tierra extraña* (Buenos Aires: Kairós, 2006).

trinitarian focus also guides González's commentary on the Acts of the Apostles in the Comentario Bíblico Iberoamericano series.[6]

A Theology of Mission Rooted in the Salvation Story

The thinkers we are considering are notable for making an effort to base their theology on careful biblical exegesis. Together with their typically Protestant convictions, this exegetical work requires adequate tools such as a good translation and up-to-date commentaries. In the final decades of the twentieth century, a group of esteemed Bible scholars and Latin American evangelical theologians participated in projects to provide these tools. In 1999 the Nueva Versión Internacional was completed based on translation from the Greek and Hebrew biblical sources. Coordinated by Colombian biblical scholar Luciano Jaramillo, René Padilla led the New Testament translation team and Esteban Voth the Old Testament team. The rich work with the original texts and the translation led logically to the following step: production of Bible commentaries that respond to the specific needs of Latin American evangelical readers. Having worked together on the translation, teams of scholars reconvened to cooperate in the theological task toward Christian education and pastoral care, based in the whole Bible and the history of salvation.

Valdir Steuernagel drew together twenty-six works by Latin American theologians that constituted a valuable compendium: *La misión de la iglesia: Una visión panorámica* (The mission of the church: A panoramic vision).[7] This book opens with a chapter by Juan Stam titled "La historia de la salvación y la misión integral de la iglesia" (The history of salvation and the holistic mission of the church). Two books edited by René Padilla seek to establish a biblical base for the development of a Latin American evangelical missiology; surveying the totality of the biblical revelation, they make progress in the trinitarian direction called for by Míguez Bonino. In 1998 Padilla edited *Bases bíblicas de la misión: Perspectivas latinoamericanas* (Biblical foundations for mission: Latin

[6]Editorial Kairós in Buenos Aires publishes this ongoing series.

[7]Valdir Steuernagel, *La misión de la iglesia: Una visión panorámica* (San José, Costa Rica: Visión Mundial, 1992).

American perspectives) with the work of fifteen Latin American theologians, almost all members of the FTL, among them Nancy Elizabeth Bedford and Catalina de Padilla, who contributed chapters on suffering and laypeople, respectively.[8] Then in 2006 René Padilla and Harold Segura edited *Ser, Hacer y Decir: Bases Bíblicas de la misión integral*, with the cooperation of ten Bible scholars and theologians.[9]

The work of Nancy Bedford in the first collection merits special attention. Addressing the theme of suffering, she explores *dolorismo*, the glorification of pain in piety and particularly in Catholic imagery, following the line Mackay took (see chapter two above). She writes of "the glorification of suffering for its own sake, beginning with the example of the suffering Christ often represented as a passive and blood-stained victim," and warns that "evangelicals too can fall into the temptation of identifying suffering as a virtue in itself." She contrasts *dolorismo* with the triumphalism of some contemporary charismatic evangelical hymns, which present a glorified Jesus Christ, not crucified, which "can lead to an individualist evasion of suffering whose concrete results, paradoxically, are similar to the passive resignation produced by the Catholic Jesus Christ of pain."[10] How can these distortions be avoided?

> They can be overcome only if the theology and theopraxis of churches in their mission base themselves on a solid Christology and *Christopraxis* with deeply biblical roots. Only by being immersed in the life, death, and resurrection of Jesus Christ will we discover the equilibrium that we need in order to confront the reality of suffering. These experiences take us to the heart of the trinitarian God himself, who acted through his Son and who lives in us through his Spirit.[11]

This trinitarian vision and this central concern for the basic and ineluctable nature of the New Testament *kerygma* also guide Bedford's

---

[8]C. René Padilla, *Bases bíblicas de la misión: Perspectivas latinoamericanas* (Buenos Aires: Nueva Creación; Grand Rapids: Eerdmans, 1998).

[9]C. René Padilla and Harold Segura, Eds. *Ser, hacer y decir: Bases bíblicas de la misión integral* (Buenos Aires: Kairós, 2006).

[10]Nancy Elizabeth Bedford, "La misión en el sufrimiento y ante el sufrimiento," in *Bases bíblicas de la misión*, 385, 386.

[11]Bedford, "La misión en el sufrimiento y ante el sufrimiento," 387.

courageous and at times unsettling exploration of the challenges of feminist theologians in her recent book *La porfía de la resurrección: Ensayos desde el feminismo teológico latinoamericano* (The tenacity of the resurrection: Essays from Latin American feminist theology).[12]

There are efforts to synthesize, such as the brief reflections of Arana, myself, and Padilla in our book *El trino Dios y la misión integral* (The triune God and holistic mission).[13] There are also new efforts at deepening biblical content, such as the already-mentioned book edited by René Padilla and Colombian theologian Harold Segura in 2006, *Ser, hacer y decir: Bases bíblicas de la misión integral* (To be, to do to say: Biblical bases for holistic mission).[14] They worked on this project with experienced theologians such as Justo. L González and Mortimer Arías and younger Bible scholars such as Ecuadorian Juan Carlos Cevallos and Peruvian Juan José Barreda. René Padilla also edited other missiological works combining efforts to articulate a theological understanding of some aspects of Christian mission and case studies from different Latin American countries that describe current missionary practice and lead to reflection on it. In 2003, together with Tetsunao Yamamori, Padilla edited *La iglesia local como agente de transformación* (The local church as an agent of transformation), which seeks to articulate an ecclesiology for holistic mission and includes work from Nancy Bedford exploring the feminist perspective.[15] The same editors later published *El proyecto de Dios y las necesidades humanas* (God's project and human needs), with two chapters about holistic mission and seven case studies from Paraguay, Argentina, Chile, Peru, Bolivia, El Salvador, and Guatemala.[16]

---

[12]Nancy Elizabeth Bedford, *La porfía de la resurrección: Ensayos desde el feminismo teológico latinoamericano* (Buenos Aires: Editorial Kairós, 2008).

[13]Pedro Arana, Samuel Escobar, and René Padilla, *El trino Dios y la misión integral* (Buenos Aires: Kairós, 2003).

[14]René Padilla and Harold Segura, eds., *Ser, hacer y decir: Bases bíblicas de la misión integral* (Buenos Aires: Kairós, 2006).

[15]Tetsunao Yamamori and René Padilla, eds., *La iglesia local como agente de transformación* (Buenos Aires: Kairós, 2003).

[16]Tetsunao Yamamori and René Padilla, eds., *El proyecto de Dios y las necesidades humanas* (Buenos Aires: Kairós, 2006).

In CLADE III in 1992 a concerted effort was made to touch on key gospel themes with a perspective that took into account the history of salvation. The theological expositions addressed themes such as forgiveness, reconciliation, the community of faith, culture, power, justice, and the new creation. Juan Stam presented "El evangelio de la nueva creación" (The gospel of the new creation), which the participants had received prior to the event. Later during the same event Stam followed up with a talk incorporating the observations received in the process of preparing and going deeper on various points. These presentations and the following reflections were integrated into his book *Las buenas nuevas de la creación* (The good news of creation). Stam is convinced that "a theology of creation should play a decisive role in our vision of the gospel, of mission, of the church and our discipleship and the beginnings, here and now, of the new creation."[17]

As the year 2000 approached, the quest to do theology from the perspective of the history of salvation, in response to growing interest in eschatology in many evangelical churches, led Stam to explore the prophetic literature in his next book: *Apocalipsis y profecía: Las señales de los tiempos y el tercer milenio* (Revelation and prophecy: The signs of the times and the third millennium). In an initial commentary about Dietrich Bonhoeffer as a theologian responding to a critical moment, Stam expresses his conviction that "the theologian, more than a knowledgeable guru in the sacred and inscrutable mysteries of the faith, should be understood as an adviser or one who orients the community of faith in their missionary tasks. The theologian should be a specialist in interpreting the Word of God and the signs of the times."[18] The pastoral and teaching spirit of Stam's biblical work can be seen in his four-volume commentary on Revelation.[19] Around the same time, Argentinian Alberto Fernando

[17]Juan Stam, *Las buenas nuevas de la creación* (Buenos Aires: Nueva Creación; Grand Rapids: Eerdmans, 1995), 10-11.

[18]Juan Stam, *Apocalipsis y profecía: Las señales de los tiempos y el tercer milenio* (Buenos Aires: Kairós, 1998), 9-10.

[19]Juan Stam, *Apocalipsis*, vol. 1, *Capítulos 1 al 5*, 2nd ed. (Buenos Aires: Kairós, 2006); vol. 2, *Capítulos 6 al 11* (Buenos Aires: Kairós, 2003); vol. 3, *Capítulos 12 al 16* (Buenos Aires: Kairós, 2009); vol. 4, *Capítulos 17-22* (Buenos Aires: Kairós, 2012).

Roldán produced a systematic work, *Escatología: Una visión integral desde América Latina* (Eschatology: A broad perspective from Latin America), in which he places the theme of eschatology within contemporary European theology and in relation with the tendencies of Latin American culture.[20] He then focuses carefully and critically on the predominant eschatological currents in the Latin American evangelical context, including a creative exploration of hymnody.

Theology and the Holy Spirit

As could be expected from the growth in the contribution of Pentecostal thinkers to theological reflection, the Holy Spirit has been the center of much recent theology. For this reason at CLADE III two Pentecostal theologians, Norberto Saracco from Argentina and Ricardo Gondim from Brazil, were asked to give expositions on "el evangelio de poder" (the gospel of power). Both not only spoke on the theology of the Holy Spirit in Pentecostal practice but also demonstrated how theological exploration could support a critique of abuses in the exercise of spiritual power, both in the pastoral sphere and in Pentecostal political participation. I have offered an analytic summary of these works from a missiological perspective in chapter eleven of my book *Changing Tides: Latin America and World Mission Today*. As was noted previously, for CLADE IV in Quito in 2000, the theme chosen was "El testimonio evangélico hacia el tercer milenio: Palabra, Espíritu y misión" (Evangelical witness toward the third millennium: Word, Spirit, and mission). One fruit of this gathering was a book edited by René Padilla, *La fuerza del Espíritu en la evangelización: Hechos de los apóstoles en América Latina* (The force of the Spirit in evangelization: Acts of the Apostles in Latin America).[21] It contains explorations of social, cultural, and ecclesiastical realities in Latin America and also a series of biblical expositions on passages chosen

[20]Argentinian Alberto Fernando Roldán, *Escatología: Una visión integral desde América Latina* (Buenos Aires: Kairós, 2002).

[21]René Padilla, ed., *La fuerza del Espíritu en la evangelización: Hechos de los apóstoles en América Latina* (Buenos Aires: Kairós, 2006).

from Acts of the Apostles. The exegetical and contextual work of three young Latin American female theologians in this book should be highlighted: Angelit Guzmán from Peru wrote "¿Vino nuevo en odres viejos?" (New wine in old wineskins?); Rebeca Montemayor from Mexico wrote "La comunidad del Espíritu como nueva humanidad" (The Spirit-filled community as a new humanity); and Rachel M. B. Perobelli from Brazil contributed "Testigos en el poder del Espíritu hasta lo último de la tierra" (Witnesses in the power of the Spirit to the ends of the earth). Another of the biblical expositors was Eldin Villafañe, a Hispanic Pentecostal theologian from the United States whose talk was called "Espiritualidad cristiana y espiritualidades contemporáneas" (Christian spirituality and contemporary spiritualties). Villafañe had published *El Espíritu liberador* in Spanish in 1996 (published earlier in English as *The Liberating Spirit*), with the subtitle *Hacia una ética social pentecostal latinoamericana* (*Toward an Hispano American Pentecostal Social Ethic*).[22] In this work Villafañe interprets Hispanic Pentecostalism in the United States using a pneumatological paradigm that he later employs to articulate a social spirituality and a Pentecostal social ethic.

Special attention should be given to the work of multifaceted Peruvian Pentecostal theologian Darío López. He is the pastor of a church on the southern periphery of Lima and a respected leader in the National Evangelical Council of Peru (CONEP). Lopez's biblical work can be appreciated in his first book, *La misión liberadora de Jesús* (The liberating mission of Jesus), a missiological reading of Luke's Gospel.[23] He defended his doctoral thesis, titled "Evangelicals and Human Rights," in England at the Oxford Center for Mission Studies. It is an interpretive and documented narrative of CONEP's social experiences during 1980–1982.[24] During this time terrorist guerrilla group Shining Path was confronted

[22]Eldin Villafañe, *El Espíritu liberador: Hacia una ética social pentecostal hispanoamericana* (Buenos Aires: Nueva Creación; Grand Rapids: Eerdmans, 1996); Eldin Villafañe, *The Liberating Spirit: Toward an Hispano American Pentecostal Social Ethic*, 2nd ed. (Grand Rapids: Eerdmans, 1993).

[23]Darío López R., *La misión liberadora de Jesús* (Lima: Puma, 1997); English, *The Liberating Mission of Jesus* (Eugene, OR: Pickwick, 2012).

[24]A Spanish edition was published as *Los evangélicos y los derechos humanos* (Lima: Centro Evangélico de Misiología Andino-Amazónica, 1997).

with indiscriminate repression from the country's armed forces, which resulted in thousands of victims, rural farmers dead or displaced by the violence. The answer offered by the evangelical community and CONEP went beyond expectations, demonstrating the capacity of civil society to respond and to provide solutions in an unprecedented social crisis. As Professor Alan Angell from St. Anthony College in Oxford points out on the back cover of the book, López "writes with the perspective of a member of the community, but also with academic objectivity."

The same combination of academic rigor and rootedness in his church characterizes Lopez's books in which he analyzes the Pentecostal movement. In 2000 he released *Pentecostalismo y transformación social* (Pentecostalism and social transformation), in which he brings together works that aim to confront the stereotypes of Pentecostalism in theological and academic circles with the reality of provable facts in Pentecostal churches.[25] Two years later he published another book: *El nuevo rostro del pentecostalismo latinoamericano* (The new face of Latin American Pentecostalism), a sociotheological interpretation of new developments in the Pentecostal movement.[26] The insertion of Peruvian evangelicals in public life, motivated by their defense of human rights during the 1980s, was followed by open political activity during the 1990s. López offers a well-documented narrative along with an ethical evaluation that takes a prophetic tone in his book *La seducción del poder* (The seduction of power).[27]

Paul Freston, a Brazilian researcher who has studied both sociology and theology, has accumulated a wealth of research on Pentecostalism and Protestantism in general, specializing in the political participation of religious minorities. The data reaped from sociological observation allows him to offer precise analysis as he seeks to understand the political conduct of evangelical candidates, for whose benefit he marshaled a

---

[25]Darío López, *Pentecostalismo y transformación social* (Buenos Aires: Kairós, 2000).

[26]Darío López, *El nuevo rostro del pentecostalismo latinoamericano* (Lima: Puma, 2002).

[27]Darío López, *La seducción del poder: Los evangélicos y la política en el Perú de los noventa* (Lima: Nueva Humanidad, 2004).

biblical scholarship that has been corrective, pastoral, and prophetic. This is the case with his book *Evangélicos na política brasileira: Historia ambígua e desafío ético* (Evangelicals in Brazilian politics: An ambiguous history and ethical challenge).[28] Earlier he had contributed an important chapter to a key book edited by René Padilla: *De la marginación al compromiso: Los evangélicos y la política en América Latina* (From marginalization to engagement: Evangelicals and politics in Latin America).[29] A university professor in the United States, Canada, Brazil, and Portugal, in recent years Freston has published important works in English on Latin Americans and politics.[30]

The History of the Church: Human History

The combination of active commitment and academic rigor in describing and analyzing the history of Protestant churches can be seen as one consequence of theology's renewed acknowledgment of the full humanity of Jesus. This acknowledgment precedes the acknowledgment of the church as a human institution, which allows the work of historians and sociologists, although they are often hostile and do not understand some aspects. In more recent years a new generation of evangelical historians has been working on critical histories that avoid hagiography (accounts of saints' lives intended for praise, offering no sociological analysis of the context in which the churches grow and the evolution taking place). Chapter eleven stated that liberation theologies brought with them a new vision of biblical history, human history, and Christian praxis. In the final three decades of the twentieth century, the history of Christians in Latin America began to be researched and newly presented from a critical perspective both internally and externally. Catholic historian Enrique

[28]Paul Freston, "Brasil: En busca de un proyecto evangélico corporativo," in *Evangélicos na política brasileira: Historia ambígua e desafío ético* (Curitiba: Encontrão, 1994).

[29]Paul Freston, in *De la marginación al compromiso: Los evangélicos y la política en América Latina*, ed. René Padilla (Buenos Aires: FTL, 1991).

[30]Paul Freston, ed., *Evangelicals and Politics in Asia, Africa and Latin America* (Cambridge: Cambridge University Press, 2001); Freston, *Protestant Political Parties: A Global Survey* (Farnham, UK: Ashgate, 2004); Freston, *Evangelical Christianity and Democracy in Latin America* (New York: Oxford University Press, 2008).

Dussel was a pioneer in this, doing work that flourished in the commission of historical studies of the Church in Latin America (CEHILA) body, in which there is currently both Protestant and Catholic presence.

Within the FTL, Sidney Rooy has been a pioneer is historical studies. Rooy is a historian from the United States who spent a number of decades as professor and researcher in Argentina and Costa Rica, and who wrote *Misión y encuentro de culturas* (Mission and cultural encounter) about the pioneers of Protestantism in Latin America.[31] In a number of collective volumes on themes such as political power or theological education, Rooy's works are models of academic rigor and pastoral sensitivity. In recent years new efforts to tell the story of the Protestant presence have flourished, among which we can appreciate the work of a new generation of historians such as Mexicans Carlos Mondragón, Carlos Martinez, Rubén Ruiz Guerra, and Lourdes de Ita; Lindy (Luis) Scott from the United States; Peruvians Juan Fonseca Ariza and Tomàs Gutierrez; and Colombian Pablo Moreno.

With no pretense of being exhaustive, here are some examples to illustrate this fertile work. Ruiz Guerra focuses on the role of Methodist educative work in the modernization of Mexico in *Hombres nuevos: Metodismo y modernización en México (1873–1930)* (New men: Methodism and modernization in Mexico [1873–1930]).[32] Modernization is also a theme in Fonseca Ariza's *Misioneros y civilizadores: Protestantismo y modernización en el Perú (1915–1930)* (Missionaries and civilizers: Protestantism and modernization in Peru [1915–1930]), which in addition to notable work based on primary sources offers a valuable reflection on Protestantism as a topic of study.[33] This book was published by the Catholic University of Lima. Another historical work published by a Catholic university is by Pablo Moreno Palacios, *Por momentos hacia atrás . . . por momentos hacia adelante* (Sometimes backward . . .

---

[31] Sidney Rooy, *Misión y encuentro de culturas* (Buenos Aires: Kairós, 2001).

[32] Rubén Ruiz Guerra, *Hombres nuevos: Metodismo y modernización en México (1873-1930)* (Mexico City: CUPSA, 1992).

[33] Juan Fonseca Ariza, *Misioneros y civilizadores: Protestantismo y modernización en el Perú (1915–1930)* (Lima: Pontificia Universidad Católica del Perú, 2002).

sometimes forward), a history of Protestantism in Colombia from 1825–1945.[34] In the prologue Jean Pierre Bastian says that Moreno has applied an innovative methodology, framing the Protestant presence within the transformations wrought in Latin America by religious secularization and modernization.

A similar approach is taken in Carlos Mondragon's master's thesis in Latin American studies, which was adapted as a book under the title *Leudar la masa* (To leaven the dough).[35] Taking the historical approach of ideas or mentalities, it helps us to understand the evolution of Latin American Protestant thought during 1920–1950 and its interaction with Catholicism and liberalism. In 1994 Lindy (Luis) Scott published *Salt of the Earth: A Socio-political History of Mexico City Evangelical Protestants (1964–1991)*, a careful work in its use of primary sources adapted from his doctoral thesis from Northwestern University in Evanston, Illinois.[36] Carlos Martínez García used newspaper articles as primary material for his *Intolerancia clerical y minorías religiosas en México* (Clergy intolerance and religious minorities in Mexico), examining works published in the daily newspaper *Uno Más Uno* with the attentive eyes of a sociologist and historian.[37] His book examines an ongoing battle for information in a country where full religious liberty continues to be lacking.

Spanish-speaking Protestantism in the United States is the topic of a book edited by Juan Francisco Martínez Guerra, professor at Fuller Theological Seminary, and Lindy (Luis) Scott, professor at Whitworth University's Costa Rica campus: *Iglesias peregrinas en busca de identidad*.[38] Martínez makes it clear that the first six chapters of this book, which

---

[34]Pablo Moreno Palacios, *Por momentos hacia atrás . . . por momentos hacia adelante* (Cali, Colombia: Universidad de San Buenaventura, 2010).

[35]Carlos Mondragón, *Leudar la masa* (Buenos Aires: Kairós, 2005).

[36]Lindy "Luis" Scott, *Salt of the Earth: A Socio-political History of Mexico City Evangelical Protestants (1945–1991)* (Mexico City: Kyrios, 1991); Luis Scott, *La sal de la tierra: Una historia socio-política de los evangélicos en la Ciudad de México (1964–1991)* (Mexico City: Kyrios, 1994).

[37]Carlos Martínez García, *Intolerancia clerical y minorías religiosas en México* (Mexico City: CUPSA, 1993)

[38]Juan Francisco Martínez Guerra and Lindy (Luis) Scott, *Iglesias peregrinas en busca de identidad* (Buenos Aires: Kairós, 2004); English trans., *Los evangélicos: Portraits of Latino Protestantism in the United States* (Eugene, OR: Wipf & Stock, 2009).

focus on different denominations, do not constitute history as such but rather a narrative that is the first step in that direction. The other six chapters of the book explore aspects of what we could call Hispanic evangelical culture in the United States. From this comes the subtitle of this work, *Cuadros del protestantismo latino en los Estados Unidos* (Portraits of Latino Protestantism in the United States).

Finally, in this section it is worth mentioning a trilogy originating from the productive pen of Justo L. González, a historian who has worked intensively to raise academic quality and promote new vocations for research and theological production among Hispanics in the United States. In these three works González reflects theologically on his own need and the action of those who work in the field of the history of Christianity. In *Mapas para la historia futura de la iglesia* (Maps for the future history of the church) González lays out the importance of geography for understanding and for historical studies, and shows how contemporary maps reflect the incredible transformations that have taken place, such as the emergence of what he calls "the polycentric character of Christianity today."[39] His reflection takes as its key Psalm 46:1-3 as "an invitation to march toward the future, in the midst of the new maps that are emerging, always guided by the compass of God's Word."[40] I consider chapter five of this work to be of fundamental importance; here González considers the catholicity of the church and offers a proposal that could be of particular help to Protestant thinkers in responding to the exclusivist Roman Catholic concept of catholicity.

Second, in *La historia también tiene su historia* (History also has its history) González reflects on how the history of the church has been written and on recent changes that have contributed to the development of the perspective we have today.[41] Third, *La historia como ventana al futuro* (History as a window to the future) collects didactic and pastoral works that were presented in various theological institutions in Chile,

---

[39]Justo L. González, *Mapas para la historia futura de la iglesia* (Buenos Aires: Kairós, 2001).
[40]González, *Mapas para la historia futura de la iglesia*, 7.
[41]Justo L. González, *La historia también tiene su historia* (Buenos Aires: Kairós, 2001).

Paraguay, and Argentina. The author says that the connecting thread of these works is "the need to relate the history of the church with the life of the church"; "what interests me is to demonstrate that the history of the church is not only the study of past times and people who are now dead, but a study that begins in the present while looking toward the future, and thus is closely related to the life and mission of the church."[42]

Together with these works by González, an exploration of the philosophy of history was written by a person who taught this subject for twenty years in the University of Tucumán, Argentina: Elsie Romanenghi Powell, author of *Interrogantes sobre el sentido de la historia y otros ensayos* (Questions about the meaning of history and other essays).[43] In a meditative and lyrical style, Powell offers a Christian reflection in dialogue with contemporary thinkers who have considered the topic.

Christian Mission and Social Responsibility

One of the most ambitious efforts to systematize recent decades of work in the field of evangelical social responsibility is the three-volume work by Humberto Fernando Bullón, a Peruvian scholar with extensive experience in service organizations in various countries, together with advanced degrees in agronomy, economics and theology: *Misión cristiana y responsabilidad social* (Christian mission and social responsibility).[44] In the first volume, *Ética cristiana y responsabilidad social* (Christian ethics and social responsibility), he develops an ethical paradigm; in volume two, *Historia de la iglesia y responsabilidad social* (History of the church and social responsibility), he examines a variety of historic models; and in the third, *Transformación de América Latina y responsabilidad social* (Transformation in Latin America and social responsibility), he presents various case studies of projects developed recently in Latin America.

---

[42]Justo L. González, *La historia como ventana al futuro* (Buenos Aires: Kairós, 2002), 9.

[43]Elsie Romanenghi Powell, *Interrogantes sobre el sentido de la historia y otros ensayos* (Buenos Aires: Kairós, 2006).

[44]Humberto Fernando Bullón, *Misión cristiana y responsabilidad social* (Buenos Aires: Kairós, 2008).

Related to this theme is the missionary work that has been undertaken among indigenous communities. From decades of experience in northern Argentina comes a book that describes a missionary work that is outside the box in its intention, methodology, and attitude: *Misión sin conquista: Acompañamiento de comunidades indígenas autóctonas como práctica misionera alternativa* (*Mission Without Conquest: An Alternative Missionary Practice*) is by Willis Horst, Ute Mueller-Eckhardt, and Frank Paul, a Mennonite team who have worked in the Chaco region of Argentina.[45] The work aims to establish a contrast between traditional missionary methods, which have not been able to abandon the ideas of conquest, and a method that reads the biblical material "from below," from the perspective of service in the style of Jesus. The book allows us to hear the voices of indigenous people themselves and not only those of the missionaries.

A work that examines the historic roots of evangelical social ethics is by Federico A. Meléndez, dean of the faculty of theology in the Universidad Mariano Gálvez in Guatemala City: *Ética y economía: El legado de Juan Wesley a la iglesia en América Latina* (Ethics and economy: The legacy of John Wesley to the church in Latin America).[46] It is a contemporary reading of the Wesleyan heritage of Methodism from a Latin American perspective. Interestingly, Meléndez, who is from the Nazarene Church, represents a third Latin American approach to the Wesleyan inheritance. The first was that of Gonzalo Báez-Camargo in 1962, and the second that of José Míguez Bonino from a perspective sympathetic to liberation theologies in 1983.[47]

---

[45]Willis Horst, Ute Mueller-Eckhardt, and Frank Paul, *Misión sin conquista: Acompañamiento de comunidades indígenas autóctonas como práctica misionera alternativa* (Buenos Aires: Kairós, 2009); English trans., Willis Horst, Ute Paul, and Frank Paul, *Mission Without Conquest: An Alternative Missionary Practice* (Carlisle, UK: Langham Global Library, 2015).

[46]Federico A. Meléndez, *Ética y economía: El legado de Juan Wesley a la iglesia en América Latina* (Buenos Aires: Kairós, 2006).

[47]Gonzalo Báez-Camargo, *Genio y espíritu del metodismo wesleyano* (Mexico City: CUPSA, 1962). The second work consists of five chapters by José Míguez Bonino in *La tradición protestante en la teología latinoamericana: Primer intento: lectura de la tradición metodista*, ed. José Duque (San José, Costa Rica: DEI, 1983).

Generational Continuity

I am of the opinion that the leadership style practiced in the Latin American Theological Fraternity (FTL) and its functional, scholarly, and nonhierarchical structure have allowed a measure of generational continuity in its theological work, without significant confrontations or ruptures. The appearance of various festschrifts in recent decades could be taken as evidence of this. We begin with one dedicated to Salvadoran theologian Emilio Antonio Núñez, whose ministry took place mainly in Guatemala but who is known throughout the Spanish-speaking world. It was edited by Oscar Campos as *Teología evangélica para el contexto latinoamericano* (Evangelical theology for the Latin American context) and included contributions from twelve colleagues and former students of Núñez.[48] Four chapters focus on theological education, an area of need where he was distinguished.

In Argentina Peruvian theologian Juan José Barreda edited *Diálogos de vida* (Dialogues for life), a collection of theological and pastoral works dedicated to Methodist pastor and theologian Jorge A. León, Cuban but resident in Argentina since 1967.[49] Active in the FLT, León is also known in the Spanish-speaking context for his consistent and systematic work in the field of pastoral psychology.

The book *Comunidad y misión desde la periferia* (Community and mission from the periphery), edited by Milka Ridzinski and Juan Francisco Martínez, is a somewhat different case.[50] Some of its contributors are members of the FTL, and it celebrates the life and ministry of Juan Driver, a Mennonite theologian who served as a missionary in Puerto Rico, Uruguay, and Spain and whose works are known throughout the Spanish-speaking world. He participated in the FTL and contributed to the diffusion of Anabaptist theological perspectives in Latin America. I consider especially valuable his books about Anabaptist ecclesiology,

---

[48]Oscar Campos, ed., *Teología evangélica para el contexto latinoamericano* (Buenos Aires: Kairós, 2004).

[49]Juan José Barreda, ed., *Diálogos de vida* (Buenos Aires: Kairós, 2006).

[50]Milka Ridinski and Juan Francisco Martínez, *Comunidad y misión desde la periferia* (Buenos Aires: Kairós, 2006).

among which are *Pueblo a imagen de Dios . . . hacia una visión bíblica* (People in the image of God. . . . toward a biblical vision) and *Contracorriente: Ensayos sobre eclesiología radical* (Against the current: Essays on radical ecclesiology).[51] To the degree the situation of Christendom continues to decline in Latin America and Spain, the ecclesial search that Protestant theologians must undertake will benefit from the radical ecclesiology of the Anabaptists.

Speaking of the Anabaptist heritage, a Mennonite theologian from Paraguay has published a valuable introduction to theology of almost five hundred pages: *Vivir desde el futuro de Dios* (To live from God's future) by Alfred Neufeld.[52] Neufeld was born in Paraguay and educated in Europe and North America. He has worked as a pastor and theological educator in Asunción and as the dean of the faculty of theology at the Universidad Evangélica de Paraguay. He writes from an eschatological perspective in the best sense of the word. Neufeld shows his familiarity with the history of theology and the evangelical theological canon, beginning with questions from his own context that have also been part of the FTL's theological search. Each of the seven chapters in this work offers a historical reference, exegetical work on some biblical passages, and an effort to relate the reflection to problems facing Christians in Latin America. It is clear that the work is rooted in Neufeld's pastoral and teaching practice, but neither in style nor in content is it an exclusively Mennonite work.

Another festschrift I find valuable was edited by Mexican biblical scholar Edesio Sánchez Cetina in honor of theologian Plutarco Bonilla Acosta, who, as was pointed out in chapter seven, did pioneering exegetical work involving christological reflection. *Enseñaba por parábolas* (He taught in parables) surveys the genre of parables in both Old and New Testaments.[53] Its sixteen chapters come from various Latin American

[51] Juan Driver, *Pueblo a imagen de Dios . . . hacia una visión bíblica* (Bogotá: Clara-Semilla, 1991); Driver, *Contracorriente: Ensayos sobre eclesiología radical* (Bogotá: Semilla, 1998).

[52] Alfred Neufeld, *Vivir desde el futuro de Dios* (Buenos Aires: Kairós, 2006).

[53] The book does not have publishing details, nor date, but it can be deduced from the contents that it appeared in approximately 2003, possibly in Costa Rica.

and North American biblical scholars, plus one from Curaçao, almost all of them with ties to the United Bible Society and some members of the FTL. This book is a prime example of the importance of high-quality biblical work as a foundation for theological reflection. It offers fresh ways of interpreting parables in light of advances in literary studies and the questions resulting from contemporary theologies.

Toward an Evangelical Spirituality

It is now common, especially in North America, to say that when Protestants explore the theme of spirituality they tend to go to Catholic sources. Possibly this is because the word *spirituality* as such has not been part of the traditional Protestant or evangelical vocabulary, but it should be clear that there is a Protestant spirituality and different traditions that cultivate the spiritual life associated with movements such as Puritanism, Pietism, and Methodism. In chapter five I pointed out that members of the founding generation of Latin American Protestantism, such as Báez-Camargo and Estrello, wrote works that fall into the category of spirituality. For example, Báez-Camargo's interpretation of Methodism highlights the relationship between spirituality and social militancy in the Wesleyan inheritance, using intriguing phrases such as "a rational enthusiasm" and "an illustrated piety."[54] In 1993 Mexican biblical scholar Mariano Ávila and Brazilian theologian Manfred Grellert compiled the first volume of a series of publications about spirituality and mission with sixteen works by members of the FTL, grouped into three sections: "Conversion and Discipleship," "The Holy Spirit," and "Spirituality and Mission."[55]

In the first decade of the twenty-first century evangelical theologians have published various works to clarify what spirituality is, each with the aim of presenting a specific proposal. Colombian theologian Harold Segura, of Baptist origins, published *Hacia una espiritualidad evangélica*

---

[54]Gonzalo Báez-Camargo, *Genio y espíritu del metodismo wesleyano* (Mexico City: CUP, 1962).

[55]Mariano Ávila and Manfred Grellert, eds., *Conversión y discipulado* (San José, Puerto Rico: Vision Mundial, 1993).

(Toward an evangelical spirituality), concerned by "the divorce between piety in the church and life in the world; between individual religiosity and social behavior; between Puritan morals and Christian life." He describes the situation clearly from a practical point of view:

> We are known for our practices of fasting, prayers, Bible reading, for our emotive church services, for our fervency in evangelizing, and because we do not smoke or drink alcohol, but also because we have not been able to articulate this evangelical spirituality in the particular spaces of daily life, such as the family, business, school, public life, and society. Something, then, is wrong, and we should worry about it.[56]

In dialogue with thinkers from the FTL, Protestant and Catholic theologians from Europe, and contemporary Latin American intellectuals, Segura bases his proposal for an evangelical spirituality on the centrality of the kingdom of God: "The fundamental idea of our spirituality should be the cause of Christ, that is, the kingdom of God. Followers of Jesus Christ should cling to the Teacher's model instead of the expectations of the institutionalized church, or the anxieties of our legalistic religiosity, or the desires of human self-realization."[57] The essays collected in this book explore the incarnation as mystery and model, the call to be church for the other, the prophetic role of the Christian in society, and a theology of human rights.

In *Más allá de la utopía* (Beyond utopia), Segura focuses specifically on servant leadership and Christian spirituality.[58] Our era is characterized by the resurgence of spiritualties on the one hand, and on the other the imposition of a managerial culture in all areas of life. From his own experience as a pastor, an educator, and an executive in evangelical institutions, Segura knows that, in the field of spiritualities and managerial functions, questions arise that in the end lead to the question of the meaning of the human being. If we respond simply by following current trends, we risk

---

[56]Harold Segura Carmona, *Hacia una espiritualidad evangélica comprometida* (Buenos Aires: Kairós, 2002), 9.

[57]Segura Carmona, *Hacia una espiritualidad evangélica comprometida*, 20.

[58]Harold Segura, *Más allá de la utopía: Liderazgo de servicio y espiritualidad cristiana* (Buenos Aires: Kairós, 2006).

falling into attitudes, concepts, and practices counter to the model for life that we should imitate: Jesus. "In this thirst for spirituality and this hunger for efficiency there are seeds of mission and foundations for transformation. We should respond, not just react or assimilate. Critical lucidity and sensitive dialogue will be the most useful tools for finding the answer."[59] Putting into practice these virtues, Segura explores the book of Ecclesiastes, Jesus' practice and teaching, the inheritance of the desert fathers, the Way of St. Benedict, spirituality as a praxis of liberty from a Lutheran inheritance, and the spirituality of liberation theologians. Organized for group discussion or individual learning, the book includes questions for reflection and selected readings for each of the chosen topics.

For his part, Juan Driver in *Convivencia radical* (Radical coexistence) seeks first to clarify the concept of spirituality, critiquing a notion of spirituality that is "interior and spiritualizing . . . fundamentally individualistic and privatizing." He sustains that in contrast

> the spirituality of Jesus' first disciples involved all aspects of life. To understand spirituality in the light of the Bible it would be necessary to overcome the false dichotomies that divide in two segments: the interior spiritual part, disconnected from this world, and the exterior, material part that is worldly. Christian spirituality does not consist in a life of contemplation instead of action, nor of retreat instead of a full participation in society. Rather, it is about all dimensions of life being oriented to and given life by the Spirit of Jesus himself.[60]

Driver dedicates two chapters to Christian spirituality in the first century and then two chapters to Anabaptist spirituality during the sixteenth century. This second part is of particular interest because this important aspect of radical reform movements tends to be overlooked. The particular Anabaptist style of life and mission has endured to our day, for example among the Mennonites and Brethren in Christ. Driver reminds us that the Anabaptist movement is only one among many other radical

---

[59]Segura, *Más allá de la utopía*, 14.

[60]Juan Driver, *Convivencia radical: Espiritualidad para el siglo 21* (Buenos Aires: Kairós, 2007), 14.

reform movements that emerged throughout Christian history: with their roots in Jesus and the first-century Christian community, these movements have recovered in a notable way—in their life experiences and their historic contexts—spiritualities quite similar to those that characterized Christian communities in the first century.[61] The final chapter, "Espiritualidades del siglo 21" (Spiritualities for the twenty-first century), reflects on the possibilities for ecumenical dialogue among diverse spiritualties present in our time.[62]

A Brazilian pastor and theologian with a Presbyterian background offers a different approach to spirituality: Ricardo Barbosa de Souza in *Por sobre todo cuida tu corazón: Ensayos sobre espiritualidad cristiana* (Above all guard your heart: Essays on Christian spirituality). Barbosa explores the knowledge and experience of God beginning from what he observes as a weak area: "We know a lot about God, theology, mission, ethics, morality, worship, but our personal and affective experience with our God is excessively poor."[63] In the essays compiled here Barbosa presents biblical material enriched with contemporary and historical theological quotations, and contemporary illustrations drawing on diverse experiences. The themes he explores are Job as a paradigm for Christian spirituality; Trinity and spirituality; the place of the desert in the conversion of the heart; rediscovering the Father; the centrality of the Father in the spirituality of Jesus; and communion through confession. The style of this book reveals a pastoral heart and a sensitivity toward the experiences of the common Christian.

Narrative Theology

In our day we have seen a return to the narrative as a form of theological communication. In my twenty years of experiences with Afro-American

[61]Driver, *Convivencia radical*, 15.

[62]I have explored the Anabaptist heritage in relation to the missionary movement from Latin America in "Notas anabautistas para una misiología latinoamericana," in *Comunidad y misión desde la periferia*, ed. Milka Ridzinski and Juan Francisco Martínez (Buenos Aires: Kairós, 2006), 147-64.

[63]Ricardo Barbosa de Souza, *Por sobre todo cuida tu corazón: Ensayos sobre espiritualidad cristiana* (Buenos Aires: Kairós, 2005), 13-14.

communities in the United States and with Pentecostal communities in Latin America, I have learned to appreciate the power of narrative as a means of communication. After all, it was the form of communication most commonly used by the Teacher of teachers. The Word of God comes to us in the form of narrative cycles such as those in the book of Genesis or the historical books, and without a doubt it is the main communicative form in the Gospels and Acts. The narrative can especially be appreciated when it reaffirms the expressive force of the biblical narrator, not with the idea of entertaining an audience but of transmitting the truth of God's Word through this medium, with all its power to confront, comfort, be with, challenge, and exhort.

Although I may be mistaken, I believe two books from our circle of authors could be placed in the category of narrative theology. First is a refreshing work from Costa Rican Plutarco Bonilla, mentioned above, whose title is in itself challenging: *Jesús, ¡ese exagerado!* (Jesus, so over the top!).[64] The book collects twelve pieces written over the years, presented to a variety of audiences, and published in magazines and journals in different countries. As some of the titles illustrate—particularly "Y Jesús se equivocó" (And Jesus made a mistake)—Bonilla has found some surprising and almost shocking angles. Pausing over some scenes and sayings of Jesus, he calls our attention to details that are easily overlooked. He reminds of "the important role played by exaggeration (or hyperbole, in literary lingo) in the teaching work of the Nazarene. The Galilean master was a consummate maestro in the narrative arts, and especially in wielding this literary instrument."[65] As a Bible scholar, Bonilla works the texts thoroughly.

Next we have Brazilian Valdir Steuernagel in *Hacer teología junto a María* (Doing theology with Mary).[66] As if with the brushstrokes of an expert painter, the author takes eight texts relating to Mary in the Gospels of Mark, Luke, and John and in Acts and produces a surprising

---

[64]Plutarco Bonilla, *Jesús,¡ese exagerado!* (Quito: CLAI, 2000).
[65]Bonilla, *Jesús, ¡ese exagerado!*, xi.
[66]Valdir Steuernagel, *Hacer teología junto a María* (Buenos Aires: Kairós, 2006).

and eloquent portrait. Reading this contextual re-creation of the passages, nuanced at times by Mary's soliloquies, we are surprised by the force and the beauty of the text. With this Steuernagel wants us to discover something like a code of requirements for creating theology. Just as Mary listened to the angel's voice, he says, the texts should be listened to and examined, and "the theology comes later; it belongs to the second moment."[67] Later he says, "The only one who understands the theology is the one who offers her womb. . . . The theologian Mary shows the pregnant womb to help us understand that theology matures in the process of active waiting for the fulfillment of God's action."[68] The Magnificat is a matter of "making poetry with the historic action of God. Theology is done by people who join past, present, and future . . . who know themselves to be in service to the germination of God's tomorrow."[69] Further, "theology needs to be born in the stable. . . . Theology needs to learn again to be amazed, to find the shepherds, and with them walk to the stable."[70]

In his introduction Steuernagel tells us, "My intention is not to remove academic rigor from the theological task. Rather, what I desire is to go beyond this rigor—that is, to put theological rigor to the service of mission and return theology to the heart of the believing community."[71] Similarly, Plutarco Bonilla clarifies in the introduction to his book discussed above,

> In these articles we have not tried to create speculative or philosophical Christology. Our only intention has been to understand the biblical texts better. In the end, according to our humble knowledge and understanding, this should be the task of the Christian theologian. . . . Nothing that follows was written for the professional theologian. They already have abundant bibliographical resources with which to exercise their vocation.[72]

---

[67]Valdir Steuernagel, *Hacer teología junto a María* (Buenos Aires: Kairós, 2006), 21-32.
[68]Steuernagel, *Hacer teología junto a María*, 37.
[69]Steuernagel, *Hacer teología junto a María*, 45.
[70]Steuernagel, *Hacer teología junto a María*, 49.
[71]Steuernagel, *Hacer teología junto a María*, 12.
[72]Bonilla, *Jesús, ¡ese exagerado!*, xiv.

In these two books, then, we have excellent examples of Latin American creativity put to the service of shedding light on the biblical text and spreading it among the people.

Regarding the FTL

The theological work that has been done in the context of the FTL has caught the attention of scholars in different parts of the world. By the time we celebrated the first twenty-five years of the organization, we could count three doctoral theses and another four master's degrees that had been written about the FTL in Europe and the United States.[73] Since then three more in-depth studies about the FTL have appeared, two of which were doctoral dissertations. I will survey them just briefly here.

In Brazil, Luiz Longuini Neto, pastor from the periphery of Rio de Janeiro and professor in various Methodist and Baptist theological institutions, undertook a comparative study of the ecumenical and evangelical movements in Latin American Protestantism during the twentieth century. More than a detailed analysis of these movements, his work examines pastoral leadership and mission in the thought of those who have participated in these movements. This study was adapted into a book: *O novo rosto da missão* (The new face of mission).[74] Beginning with the Panama Congress of 1916, Longuini Neto covers movements and concepts up to the time of CLADE IV in Quito in 2000 and traces the evolution of the basic concepts of pastoral leadership and mission—that is to say, the new face of mission.

Sharon E. Heaney is an Irish scholar, currently teaching at Oxford, who spent various years preparing her doctoral thesis on the FTL at Queens University in Belfast. She worked in libraries in the United Kingdom, then late in 2003 researched in Buenos Aires both in ISEDET and in the Kairós Center, and in 2004 worked briefly in Spain. The fruit of this work is a book, *Contextual Theology for Latin America: Liberation*

[73]Samuel Escobar, "La fundación de la FTL: Breve ensayo histórico," *Boletín Teológico*, nos. 59-60 (July–December 1995): 7-25.

[74]Luiz Longuini Neto, *O novo rosto da missão* (Viçosa, Brazil: Ultimato, 2002).

Themes in Evangelical Perspective.[75] Emphasizing contextual aspects of the theological work of the FTL, Heaney describes the Latin American context and the evangelical presence within. She presents and compares the theological methods and contextual hermeneutics in the FTL and the liberation theologies. Having identified six themes in Latin American contextual theology, she concludes by describing the search for a contextual theology in three areas: Christology, ecclesiology, and missiology, with a chapter devoted to each. To date this book is the most complete and systematic study of four decades of the FTL's work.

Colombian scholar Daniel Salinas earned his PhD at Trinity International University and has been a missionary and teacher at universities in Uruguay, Bolivia, and Paraguay. His doctoral thesis concentrated on the foundation and first decade of the FTL, between CLADE I in 1969 and CLADE II in 1979. It too has been published as a book: *Latin American Evangelical Theology in the 1970s: The Golden Decade*.[76] Salinas researched the behind-the-scenes personal and institutional interrelations of missionaries, evangelical leaders, and members of the FTL in those early years, when the debates that were generated had international repercussions. Unfortunately the dialogue of that time between theologians of English-speaking America and Spanish- and Portuguese-speaking America often fell on deaf ears. Salinas's book offers an ordered panorama that reveals how these behind-the-scenes relationships sometimes conditioned the course of the reflection and the articulation of concepts.

Those of us who have participated in the process I have attempted to describe are grateful for these books that review what has been a great intellectual adventure. Even more, they have been an effort to go deep into what it means to follow Jesus Christ here and now in Ibero-America.

---

[75]Sharon E. Heaney, *Contextual Theology for Latin America: Liberation Themes in Evangelical Perspective* (Milton Keynes, UK: Paternoster, 2008).

[76]Daniel Salinas, *Latin American Evangelical Theology in the 1970s: The Golden Decade* (Leiden: Brill, 2009).

NAME INDEX

SCRIPTURE INDEX